GÜNTHER BORNKAMM
GERHARD BARTH
HEINZ JOACHIM HELD

TRADITION AND INTERPRETATION
IN MATTHEW

THE NEW TESTAMENT LIBRARY

Advisory Editors

ALAN RICHARDSON Dean of York

C. F. D. MOULE Lady Margaret Professor in Divinity in the University of Cambridge

FLOYD V. FILSON Professor of New Testament Literature and History
at the McCormick Theological Seminary Chicago

GÜNTHER BORNKAMM
GERHARD BARTH
HEINZ JOACHIM HELD

TRADITION AND INTERPRETATION IN MATTHEW

The Westminster Press
PHILADELPHIA

Published by The Westminster Press

Philadelphia, Pennsylvania

PRINTED IN THE UNITED STATES OF AMERICA

CONTENTS

HEINZ JOACHIM HELD

MATTHEW AS INTERPRETER OF THE MIRACLE STORIES

PREFACE

THE INVESTIGATIONS combined in this volume are contributions on the theology and unique form of Matthew's Gospel. On the question at issue, the methods and aim of our enquiries, their relationship to the form-critical research into the Synoptic Gospels, and to the recent investigations into the theology of the historical work of Luke, and the Gospel of Mark, the introduction will provide more detail. The first of these studies to be undertaken, that on the stilling of the storm in Matthew, will serve as one example to indicate the independent treatment of the tradition in his Gospel. It has already appeared in *Wort und Dienst*, Jahrbuch der Theologischen Schule Bethel (1948), pp. 49–54. The most important results of my work on 'End-expectation and Church in Matthew's Gospel' were the subject of a brief survey given at the meeting of German theologians, in 1954 (cf. *TLZ* 79 [1954], pp. 341–6). The essay itself, worked out and more carefully documented, first appeared in German in *The Background of the New Testament and its Eschatology* (Studies in Honour of C. H. Dodd), 1956, pp. 222–69. At some points I have worked over it again and expanded it. How fruitful and rewarding a careful investigation of Matthew's way of working and his theology can be was first confirmed and made fully clear to me by the two studies of my pupils, Gerhard Barth and Heinz Joachim Held, who, working on the same lines independently, looked more deeply into the question. Both studies were accepted by the Theological Faculty of Heidelberg as Dissertations (1955 and 1957). The unity in method of approach and thesis led us to the decision to submit our complementary studies together in this volume. It was unavoidable that particular texts and themes are treated over again in each contribution. We hope, however, that our conclusions will on that account be found the more convincing.

GÜNTHER BORNKAMM

INTRODUCTION

I T BELONGS TO the established conclusions of Synoptic research
that the first three evangelists were, in the first place, collectors and
editors of traditions handed on to them. The stereotyped expressions
with which Mark frames and connects sayings and individual pericopes, utterly barren as far as questions of historical practice are
concerned, and the corresponding editorial methods used by
Matthew and Luke (especially in the treatment and grouping of their
sources), leave no room for doubt about the correctness of this judgment. This is true in spite of the fact that the first three Gospels are
documents expressing a definite, though in each case very different
theology, which gives to each of them, without detriment to what
they have in common, a more or less consistently and systematically
developed theme, which makes it possible to recognise as their
background, different communities with their particular problems
and views.

The particular theology and theme of the first three Gospels goes
deeper into the substance of them than is generally recognised, and
modifies their message not insignificantly, even though over large
areas their traditions are the same. The means used by the Synoptic
writers to present their theology are obviously modest, as a comparison with John's Gospel particularly shows, and allow each of them
only limited scope. This is the reason for the often recognisable
tensions between their handling of the tradition and the theological
views it is made to serve. At the same time the Synoptic writers show
—all three and each in his own special way—by their editing and
construction, by their selection, inclusion and omission, and not least
by what at first sight appears an insignificant, but on closer examina-
tion is seen to be a characteristic treatment of the traditional material,
that they are by no means mere collectors and handers-on of the
tradition, but are also interpreters of it.

The work begun above all in connexion with form-critical
research must therefore be continued in a new direction. However
irrevocably right their distinction between tradition and redaction in
the Synoptic Gospels, and however important their pioneer work in
the systematic analysis of the oral tradition which preceded the

writing of the Gospels,[1] nevertheless the process of development in
redaction and arrangement must be studied more exactly. Undoubtedly J. Schniewind was right when he characterised the
Gospels as 'Kerygma of a definite situation and task'.[2] Yet this
widely acknowledged insight must be made fruitful to a degree
hitherto unattained, and its significance for the understanding of the
Gospels must be worked out in particular and in general. In the case
of Luke's Gospel H. Conzelmann has carried out these enquiries in
a penetrating and fruitful way,[3] and W. Marxsen has analysed
Mark's Gospel on similar lines.[4] The important investigations of the
source of the sayings, in the work of H. E. Toedt, should also be
mentioned in this connexion.[5] The following studies are designed to
show the significance of the findings mentioned above for Matthew's
Gospel, especially in relation to some important particular problems
and texts.[6]

[1] Cf. esp. the works of M. Dibelius, *Die Formgeschichte des Evangeliums* (Tübingen
1959[3]; ET *From Tradition to Gospel* of the 2nd ed.) and R. Bultmann, *Die Geschichte
der synoptischen Tradition* (Göttingen 1957[3]; ET *History of the Synoptic Tradition* 1963).
On further study and discussion cf. G. Iber, *TR* N.F. 25 (1958), pp. 283 ff.

[2] Zur Synoptikerexegese, *TR* N.F. 2 (1930), p. 153; cf. p. 152: 'our Synoptic
Gospels in their completed form are still a pattern of the primitive Christian
kerygma'. B. W. Bacon, *Studies in Matthew* (1930), p. xiii, also finds in the
Gospels 'later adaptions which adjusted the story to the needs and beliefs of a post-
Apostolic age'. Likewise C. H. Dodd, *The Apostolic Preaching and its Developments*
(London, 1944[2]), p. 47, calls Mark's Gospel 'a form of Kerygma' (cf. pp. 46 ff.).
On Matthew's Gospel cf. G. D. Kilpatrick, *The Origins of the Gospel according to St
Matthew* (Oxford, 1946), p. 2: 'The context or "Sitz im Leben" of a new gospel was
as important a feature in its production as it was in the shaping and carrying on of
unwritten tradition. While we may not say that the gospel was created by a
community, yet it was created in a community and called forth to meet the needs
of a community.'

[3] H. Conzelmann, *Die Mitte der Zeit. Studien zur Theologie des Lukas* (Tübingen
1960[3]). Cf. p. 6: 'Luke addresses himself to the situation into which the Church
has been placed through the delay in the parousia and the development of her
history within the world. He attempts to master it by the fact of his historical
writing.' ET: *The Theology of St Luke* (London and New York, 1960).

[4] W. Marxsen, *Der Evangelist Markus* (Göttingen, 1956). I will not conceal the
fact, however, that in spite of so many fruitful insights which the book contains, I
cannot agree with some of his major theses. A further important contribution to
the theology of Mark's Gospel is J. M. Robinson's *The Problem of History in Mark*
(London, 1957). In both books, it must be said, the fundamental results of
W. Wrede's work, *Das Messiasgeheimnis in den Evangelien* (Göttingen, 1901) are not
taken sufficiently into consideration.

[5] H. E. Toedt, *Der Menschensohn in der synoptischen Überlieferung*, 1959, pp. 210–
47.

[6] Those who are familiar with recent Old Testament research, particularly the
works of G. von Rad, will easily realise how questions raised in the study of the
Old and New Testaments have drawn close together.

ABBREVIATIONS

For commentaries on the Gospels, a fuller reference is given in contexts where the author's name would not be a sufficient guide.

W. C. Allen	*A Critical and Exegetical Commentary on the Gospel according to St Matthew* (ICC), Edinburgh, 1912[3].
ATD	Das Alte Testament Deutsch, ed. V. Herntrich and A. Weiser, Göttingen, 1949 ff.
Billerbeck	H. L. Strack and P. Billerbeck, *Kommentar zum NT aus Talmud und Midrasch* I–IV, 1922 ff.
BKW	Bible Key Words (translations of articles from *TWNT*), London, 1949 ff.
EvTh	*Evangelische Theologie.*
ExpT	*The Expository Times.*
JBL	*Journal of Biblical Literature.*
E. Klostermann	*Das Markusevangelium* (Handbuch z. NT), Tübingen, 1950[4].
	Das Matthäusevangelium (Handbuch z. NT), Tübingen, 1938[3].
	Das Lukasevangelium (Handbuch z. NT), Tübingen, 1929[2].
E. Lohmeyer	*Das Evangelium des Markus*, Göttingen, 1951.
	Das Evangelium des Matthäus, ed. W. Schmauch, Göttingen, 1956.
A. Loisy	*Les Evangiles Synoptiques* I–II, 1907 f.
A. Merx	*Das Evangelium Matthäus*, Berlin, 1902.
J. Schniewind	*Das Evangelium nach Markus*, Göttingen, 1949[5].
	Das Evangelium nach Matthäus, Göttingen, 1950[4].
SynT	R. Bultmann, *The History of the Synoptic Tradition*, Oxford, 1963 (translation by John Marsh of *Geschichte d. syn. Tradition*, Göttingen, 1957[3]).
TB	*Theologische Blätter.*
TLZ	*Theologische Literaturzeitung.*
TR	*Theologische Rundschau.*

TSK	*Theologische Studien und Kritiken.*
TWNT	*Theologisches Wörterbuch zum NT.*
T. Zahn	*Das Evangelium des Matthäus*, Leipzig, 1922[4].
ZAW	*Zeitschrift für alttest. Wissenschaft.*
ZNW	*Zeitschrift für neutest. Wissenschaft.*
ZTK	*Zeitschrift für Theologie und Kirche.*

END-EXPECTATION AND CHURCH IN MATTHEW*

Günther Bornkamm

I. THE UNION OF ESCHATOLOGY AND ECCLESIOLOGY IN THE CONSTRUCTION OF THE DISCOURSES

W E BEGIN WITH the construction of Matthew's various discourses. These are recognised to be especially significant for the literary and theological character of the evangelist. They show throughout a union of end-expectation and conception of the Church peculiar to him. This is already clear in the *discourse of the Baptist* (3.1–12). Matthew differs not insignificantly in this section from the other Synoptic writers. Mark does not devote a whole section to John alone but simply, in a few sentences, draws together his importance for salvation-history, his baptism and message of repentance, his activity and appearance and—in the first logion—the announcement of the expected Messiah, and then he immediately begins in 1.9 ff. with the baptism, temptation and public appearance of Jesus. Luke is different: he sketches the public appearance of the Baptist in a historically fixed section (3.1 ff.) which is complete in itself (cf. esp. 19 f.), and thereby assigns his figure to a particular historical and 'salvation-historical' epoch which he expressly indicates in 16.16.[1] Matthew, on the other hand, unites the Baptist and his message in the closest manner with the message of Jesus. The preaching of the Baptist and the preaching of Jesus are combined in the same saying by Matthew alone: μετανοεῖτε· ἤγγικεν γὰρ ἡ βασιλεία τῶν οὐρανῶν (3.2 and 4.17). Thus the Baptist becomes also a preacher of the Christian congregation. His function for salvation-history is differentiated by Matthew from that of Jesus.[2] Hence the

* See Preface. Translated by permission of Cambridge University Press.
[1] Cf. H. Conzelmann, *op. cit.*, 13 ff.
[2] Matthew also ascribes no power to forgive sins to John's baptism; it is εἰς μετάνοιαν (3.11), not εἰς ἄφεσιν ἁμαρτιῶν (Mark 1.4).

first passage (3.3) is linked with the prophecy of the one who prepares the way (Isa. 40.3); the second, on the other hand, with an
Old Testament passage which pronounces the fulfilment of the
prophecy (4.15 f.).[1] The announcement of the coming βασιλεία, and
with it of the approaching judgment, and the call to repentance
which is based on it, however, are the same in both passages as the
later repetition in the Sermon on the Mount (7.19) of the threat
about the tree which fails to bring forth fruit, is cut down and cast
into the fire (3.10) shows. The place of the Pharisees and Sadducees
(3.7) is, of course, taken in 7.15 ff. by the false prophets in the Christian congregation. Both instances represent a conception of the
Church which Matthew strongly rejected, in that the former appeal
in presumptuous security to the fact that they are Abraham's children, and the latter to the fact that they are disciples of Jesus and
have wrought charismatic miracles in his name, and are not willing
to admit that membership of the Messianic community of the coming
judge of the world is decided according to one and the same standard,
namely, whether they have brought forth the 'fruits of repentance'
and whether they have done the will of their heavenly Father. In that
way, in the preaching of the Baptist already, the simple basic
thoughts of Matthew's understanding of the Church, fashioned in
expectation of the coming judgment, are expressed. They run
through his whole Gospel.

End-expectation and conception of the Church also determine the
structure of the *Sermon on the Mount*. H. Windisch has rightly designated it as 'proclamation through the mouth of Jesus of the conditions of entrance ordained by God'.[2] Matthew arranges the Beatitudes already as a list of requirements for admission[3] and in the
sayings that follow, by the double use of ὑμεῖς ἐστε, gives to the word
about salt and light (linked with the saying about the city set upon
the hill), and to the figure of the lamp set upon a stand which is
interpreted quite differently by Mark and Luke, and to the admonition: 'Let your light so shine . . .' a clear interpretation of discipleship, which should prove itself before the world to be such by its
'good works'. To the same realm also belongs the programmatic
word about the 'better righteousness' (5.20) without which no one

---

[1] Notice how the tenses differ from those of the LXX in the quotation from Isa.
9.1 φῶς εἶδεν μέγα as against ἴδετε and φῶς ἀνέτειλεν αὐτοῖς as against λάμψει.

[2] H. Windisch, *Der Sinn der Bergpredigt* (Leipzig, 1937[2]), p. 9.

[3] M. Dibelius, 'Die Bergpredigt', *Botschaft und Geschichte* I (Tübingen, 1953),
pp. 92 f.

can enter the βασιλεία, and the interpretation of this word in the antitheses (5.21–48), the rules for devout living (6.1 ff.) and all the other commands down to the golden rule (7.12). The eschatological alignment of the whole discourse which is visible from the first Beatitudes (5.3 ff.), through 5.20, the sayings about rewards (6.1 ff.), about seeking the βασιλεία and its righteousness (6.33) and the saying about judging, is finally brought out with great forcefulness by the emphatic words about the narrow gate,[1] marking as they do a new section—the warning (7.15 ff.) about false prophets (whose appearing, as 24.4 ff., 23 ff. shows, belongs to the signs of the end), the description of the judgment of the world (7.21 ff.) and the concluding parables.

In this arrangement of motives Matthew was able to follow, to a considerable degree, the order of the sayings already provided in the source from which they came; he considerably expands them, however, and adds detail and gives to the whole something of the character of a catechism. This becomes immediately clear when the parallelism between the structure of the Sermon on the Mount and the outline of the *Didache* is considered. Beatitudes, sayings about disciples, and antitheses have parallels in the teaching of the Two Ways in *Did.* 1–6 (both concluding with the call to perfection, Matt. 5.48 and *Did.* 6.2). Further, the rules for the congregation which immediately follow, about fasting and prayer (Matt. 6.; *Did.* 8 —here also the Lord's Prayer) are similar in both cases, though in the *Didache*, of course, they are expanded by directions about baptism and the eucharist (making use of Matt. 7.6). Finally the warnings about the false prophets (Matt. 7.15 ff.; *Did.* 11–13) and the eschatological conclusion of the whole are similar and occur at the same place in the whole structure. The same outline is so unmistakable in the two writings that one may draw the conclusion that a settled 'catechism pattern' provided the basis for their composition and in the *Didache* this actually acquires the character of an ecclesiastical discipline. In the one as in the other, hortatory sayings are placed at the beginning as the law of admission, directions are given for the conduct of worship and for the behaviour of the congregation and in the conclusion attention is directed towards the end.

Matthew's *Missionary Discourse* also has a peculiarly eschatological slant and character and here again conception of the Church and end-expectation are strictly related to each other. We direct our

---

[1] εἰσέλθετε διὰ τῆς στενῆς πύλης (7.13).

attention here again to the construction of Matthew and its theological motives. The evangelist opens the discourse with the summary, which embraces the Sermon on the Mount and the deeds of Jesus (9.35 = 4.23), and by linking the saying from Mark 6.34 (there in connexion with the story of the feeding!) with it places the whole mission under the motive of the compassion of Jesus for the languishing and leaderless people.[1] Then the sending forth does not follow immediately, but the exhortation to the disciples to pray to the Lord of the harvest for labourers. This saying already stood in a missionary discourse in the source, as Luke 10.2 shows; it is instructive because the familiar picture of the harvest in connexion with the judgment of the world is already applied here to the mission. Indeed, one may argue that the saying as it appeared in Q already presupposes the mission to the heathen for the eschatological picture of the harvest always refers to the judgment of the nations (Isa. 24.13; Joel 3.10 ff.; Rev. 14.15 f.); hence Luke has good reason for putting the saying at the beginning of the sending forth of the seventy (10.1 ff.; in contrast to the sending forth of the twelve, ch. 9), as John 4.35 has for echoing the saying about the harvest in the context of the mission to the Samaritans. Matthew, however, as the unfolding of the discourse shows, quite markedly does not apply the saying to the mission to the heathen, but restricts the missionary task of the disciples to Israel (10.5 f.). The saying in Matthew is also instructive because it brings to expression the fact that the disciples are not as such missionaries, but rather their sending forth is reserved for the free decision of God, implored in the prayers of the congregation (cf. Acts. 13.1 ff.).

The content of the missionary task of the disciples is to announce the nearness of the kingdom of God and to carry out the signs of it by healing the sick, raising the dead, and casting out demons (10.7 f.). They journey in the light of the imminent coming of the Son of man (10.23) and of the judgment of the world and the miseries that precede it. In view of the approaching end the disciples have to answer persecution with confession and separation with decision (10.17–39). This last part of the missionary discourse is no longer missionary instruction in the proper sense, but it gives directions to the Church as a whole and indicates what the disciples of Jesus as a whole must expect and endure. Here again the nature and the way of disciple-

---

[1] Is there a connexion with the fact that in the missionary orders in 10.7 f., which otherwise refer back to 4.17, the call to repentance is missing?

ship are wholly set in an eschatological light. For this reason the evangelist incorporates in the last part of this discourse already a not insignificant number of sayings from the collection in Mark 13 and from the Source.[1]

The construction of the seven *kingdom-of-God-parables* (ch. 13) also shows the combination of eschatological and ecclesiastical motives. Matthew's interest in the Church can be seen in his more firmly fashioned section, in comparison with Mark, on the aim of the parables of Jesus: the disciples are the ones to whom it is given to know 'the mysteries of the kingdom of heaven' (13.11)[2] and as such they are the witnesses whose eyes and ears are pronounced blessed (note the similar insertion in 13.16, 18 as in 5.13), in contrast to the hardened and now, for its guilt,[3] condemned 'people' (13.15).[4] Thus there is here the same contrast between discipleship and Israel which is characteristic of the whole of Matthew's Gospel. But the no less characteristic thought for Matthew that the 'Church' is not a collection of the elect and eternally secure, but a mixed body which has to face the separation between the good and evil[5] at the final judgment, is most clearly expressed in the parables of the tares among the wheat (13.24–30, 36–43) and the drag-net. The meaning of the coming judgment precisely for the Church is the aim of the whole construction.[6]

When we pass on to the *discourse to the congregation* (ch. 18) we must be careful to note, in order to understand its position in the whole work, that it is preceded by Peter's confession and the saying about the founding of the Church (16.13–23), with the pericopes that follow, already pertinently grouped together by Mark (prophecy of suffering and of the sufferings of the disciples in following Christ) down to the second announcement of the passion. But the pericope about the Temple tax (17.24–27), inserted immediately before the discourse to

---

[1] Cf. with Matt. 10.17–22: Mark 13.9 ff.; Luke 21.12 ff.; 12.11 f.; and with Matt. 10.34 ff.: Luke 12.51 ff.

[2] τὰ μυστήρια τῆς βασιλείας τῶν οὐρανῶν in contrast to τὸ μυστήριον τ. βασ. τ. θεοῦ (Mark) obviously refer to the teaching of Jesus.

[3] Matt. 13.13 ὅτι instead of Mark 4.12 ἵνα!

[4] The saying in 13.12 inserted here by Matthew supports this contrast.

[5] Note the same motive and figure here as in the discourse of the Baptist: 3.12.

[6] It is clear that the double parable of the treasure and the pearl, inserted by Matthew between the parables of the tares and the drag-net, is intended to illustrate the behaviour of those who hereafter as 'the righteous ones' (13.43) 'will shine like the sun in the kingdom of their Father', the behaviour of utter dedication, of radical obedience.

the congregation, also unmistakably supports Matthew's under-standing of the Church. It shows that the congregation which Matthew represents is still attached to Judaism and that it in no sense claims for itself exemption from the taxation of the diaspora-congregations, but accepts it, though clearly conscious of its own special position: the disciples of Jesus pay the Temple tax as free sons, merely in order not to give offence.

A further indication that the discourse presents the conception of the Church completely in the light of the coming βασιλεία is immedi-ately shown by the formulation Matthew gives to the dispute about rank from Mark 9.34: τίς ἄρα μείζων ἐστὶν ἐν τῇ βασιλείᾳ τῶν οὐρανῶν; (18.1), and his use of the saying about turning and becoming like children, which first occurs in Mark in connexion with the blessing of the children (Mark 10.15), by means of the words οὐ μὴ εἰσέλθητε εἰς τὴν βασιλείαν τῶν οὐρανῶν (18.3) and the saying in 18.4 (οὗτός ἐστιν ὁ μείζων ἐν τῇ βασιλείᾳ τῶν οὐρανῶν) which refers back to the opening question, is admirably suited to the context. The motive of the final judgment already occurs in the context of sayings in Mark, which Matthew continues to follow for a time, and he simply took it over.[1] His own construction first begins at 18.10. In this connexion the setting of the sayings about the exercise of congregational disci-pline (18.15–18) is obviously very deliberate and significant. These very instructions about congregational discipline are set in a frame-work by Matthew in which he puts the parable of the lost sheep (18.12–14) before them, and follows them with the words about readiness to forgive without limit and the parable of the unmerciful steward (18.21 ff.), which he alone reports. This parable also, and thereby the whole discourse, ends with a reference to the judgment which will inexorably fall on those members of the congregation who are unwilling to forgive (18.35).

The characteristically Matthaean thought that the coming judg-ment applies even to the disciples (see above on Matthew 13) is also expressed in *the parables of the vineyard and the marriage feast*. Though the former is in the first place directed against priests and Pharisees yet by the sentence formulated by him alone, and reasserted with emphasis at the end, that the vineyard (21.41)—the βασιλεία τοῦ θεοῦ (21.43)—will be taken away from the wicked vine-dressers (Israel) and given to those 'who bring forth good fruits' Matthew asserts the norm of the coming judgment, in which, as the whole Gospel says,

[1] But note the apocalyptic threat which he still inserts in 18.7.

all and particularly those presumed to belong to the people of God, will be measured. The same, with express reference to the congregation, is also stated by the closing scene of the parable of the marriage feast, which Matthew adds (22.11–13),[1] but so does the expression πονηρούς τε καὶ ἀγαθούς already, which occurs in 22.10, and which, like the closing parables of ch. 13, points towards the final separation, and finally so does the concluding sentence in 22.14, which is so characteristic of Matthew: 'Many are called but few are chosen.'

There is no need to emphasise that the *discourse concerning the Pharisees*, with its sevenfold 'Woes', is shot through with the thought of the final judgment (23.13, 33 ff.). The lamentation over Jerusalem, with the announcement of the coming of Jesus to judge the world at the end of it (23.37–39) and the placing of the discourse concerning the Pharisees immediately before the eschatological discourse, confirm the aim already set out in ch. 23. In its opening verses the discourse clearly shows that the congregation does not yet regard itself as freed from union with Judaism (23.1–3), but at the same time, in the contrast with the hypocrisy of the Pharisees and scribes, shows the nature of the Christian community. It is expressly addressed, in conjunction with the words about the human vanity of the Jewish leaders, in the command 23.8–12 (ὑμεῖς δέ) not to use the terms rabbi, father and master in the congregation of Jesus.

Finally, a firm outline of Matthew's conception of the Church and the way in which it is governed by the thought of the end is shown by the construction of his last great discourse, the *apocalyptic discourse* of ch. 24, with the eschatological parables in ch. 25. Matthew differs from Mark (13.1–4) in that the discourse is not introduced as esoteric instruction for the first four disciples but as instruction for disciples in general (note the stereotyped formula προσῆλθον οἱ μαθηταί as in 5.1; 13.10, 36; 18.1) and is more clearly than in Mark made to serve the theme: τί τὸ σημεῖον τῆς σῆς παρουσίας καὶ συντελείας τοῦ αἰῶνος; (24.1–3). Then follows, as in Mark 13.5–8, the 'beginning of the woes' (24.4–8) and next, not as in Mark the announcement of the persecution which the congregation will undergo at the hands of Jewish courts (this passage in the discourse has already been anticipated in 10.17 ff.) but the summary announcement of the suffering (τότε παραδώσουσιν ὑμᾶς εἰς θλῖψιν καὶ ἀποκτενοῦσιν ὑμᾶς) by which

---

[1] Perhaps this was originally the motive of a separate parable. Cf. J. Jeremias, *Die Gleichnisse Jesu*, Göttingen, 1958⁵, pp. 39 and 155, [cf. forthcoming revised ET *The Parables of Jesus*] with reference to Bab. *Shabbath* 153a.

—and this is characteristic of Matthew—the disciples undergo the fate of the 'Jews' among the Gentiles (καὶ ἔσεσθε μισούμενοι ὑπὸ πάντων τῶν ἐθνῶν διὰ τὸ ὄνομά μου 24.9);[1] then the announcement of the signs of the approaching end 'inside' the congregation: apostasy, betrayal, hatred, seduction by false prophets, multiplication of wickedness, love grown cold. And finally the promise of the proclamation of 'this' (represented by Matthew) Gospel of the kingdom in the whole world as the prelude to the end.

That here the picture of the Jewish-Christian congregation arises, which holds fast to the law and has not yet broken away from union with Judaism but rather stands in sharp contrast to a doctrine and mission set free from the law (which Matthew would regard as lawless) is crystal clear.[2] This Jewish-Christian congregation shares the fate of the Jewish nation, the desecration of the Temple and the horrors of flight. The warning that follows about 'false Messiahs' and 'false prophets' and the announcement of the parousia of the Son of man suddenly and openly before the whole world (24.23–28) is also more richly developed in Matthew than in Mark, and so is the description of the parousia so soon to take place, at which in the midst of cosmic catastrophes the 'sign of the Son of man' in heaven appears (cf. 24–30), all 'the tribes of the earth' mourn as they see the Son of man in power and great glory and his angels 'with a loud trumpet call' will gather the elect from the four winds of the whole world. The Markan apocalypse needs to be strengthened by Matthew only in a few details. The resulting picture, which is completely Jewish, brings out more clearly than the Markan text that the parousia results in putting the nations of the world to shame and in saving the elect from all the world.

The eschatological parables which Matthew subjoins here under the heading οὕτως ἡ παρουσία τοῦ υἱοῦ τοῦ ἀνθρώπου (24.37, 39)

---

[1] Correctly noticed by G. Harder, 'Das eschatologische Geschichtsbild der sogenannten kleinen Apokalypse Markus 13', *Theologia Viatorum*, 1952, pp. 80 f.

[2] In his outstanding book *The Origins of the Gospel according to St Matthew* G. D. Kilpatrick discusses in detail on pages 101–23 the question of 'The Gospel and Judaism' and shows convincingly that the Jewish opposition in Matthew's Gospel cannot simply be identified with the Judaism of the time of Jesus, but belongs to the time between 70 and 135 when the Jewish sects along with the Christians are accused of heresy and excommunicated. The first Gospel clearly mirrors the as yet unfinished process. The controversy with the Judaism led by the Pharisees is in full course (sharp controversies, persecution), but the union is not yet torn apart and is tenaciously defended by the congregation itself, which regards itself as the true Judaism.

describe, in terms of the catastrophe of the flood, the sudden destruction which will break upon the thoughtless and careless (as does the parable of the thief in the night 24.43). Matthew, however, immediately uses the latter as a call to the disciples to watch and be prepared (24.42, 44; 25.13)[1] and sets before them, by the parables of the faithful and the wicked servant (24.45–51), the wise and foolish virgins (25.1–13) and the talents (25.14–30) what faithfulness, readiness and zeal for the good work (ἐργάζεσθαι 25.16) mean. It is at the same time instructive to notice how the experience of the delay in the parousia clearly leaves its mark on the parables and how the understanding of 'wisdom' alters: in 24.48 the words χρονίζει ὁ κύριος μου are characterised as an illusion of the wicked servant, whereas in 25.1–3 the delay of the bridegroom is the real test whereby the wisdom of the virgins who had prepared for a long time of waiting is established, while the foolish ones have not taken with them sufficient oil for their lamps.[2] Their illusion is thus precisely that they counted on his nearness. The parable of the talents also, as 25.19 shows, counted on a long absence of their master (μετὰ δὲ πολὺν χρόνον). In these parables the thought of judgment is solely directed to the Church. The threat of judgment concludes 24.51 f., 25.12, 30 and the counterpart of judgment is not missing at least from the parables of the virgins and the talents (entrance into the marriage feast, commendation of those with the five and the two talents).

It would be difficult to maintain that the description of the judgment of the world, with which—no longer in parabolic form—the whole construction of the discourse concludes, refers only to the judgment that is to come upon the Gentiles in distinction from the members of the community of Jesus.[3] Rather it is typical for the end-expectation of Matthew that by means of a great picture[4] already current among the Jews the judgment of the world is announced as applying to 'all nations', but now in such a way that no distinction is made between Jews and Gentiles, nor even between believers and unbelievers. All are gathered before the tribunal of the judge of the world and are judged by the 'one' standard, namely that of the love

---

[1] The translation of the parables of Jesus into the situation of the congregation has most recently been carefully and comprehensively investigated by J. Jeremias, *The Parables of Jesus.*

[2] Cf. G. Bornkamm, 'Die Verzögerung der Parusie', *In memoriam E. Lohmeyer* (Stuttgart, 1951), pp. 119 ff.

[3] Thus most recently J. Jeremias, *op. cit.*, p. 175.

[4] Cf. Billerbeck IV, pp. 1199 ff.; R. Bultmann, *SynT*, pp. 123 f.

they have shown towards, or withheld from, the humblest. That decides who belong to the righteous, who enter into eternal life, and who have to go into eternal punishment. Here yet again it is clear that discipleship of Jesus is not confined to the company of the chosen but includes at first the company of those who are 'called', and the final destiny is determined by the doing of God's will.

This short analysis of Matthew's Gospel has shown us the close linking of conception of the Church and end-expectation there, but it has also repeatedly revealed wherein the link between the two consists, namely in the understanding of the law and thereby of the new righteousness, which distinguishes the disciples of Jesus from the Pharisees and scribes and is at the same time the standard by which the members of the Church themselves are to be judged by the coming judge.[1] The question of the understanding of the law in Matthew's Gospel must now be more closely considered.

2. THE BETTER RIGHTEOUSNESS

The law is binding down to the jot and tittle. Matthew gives to the words in 5.17–19, which obviously stem from the Jewish-Christian congregation and are directed against a tendency to abandon the law, a representative place and a programmatic meaning. Along with the unabridged validity of the Torah the interpretation of the scribes is also axiomatically binding for him. This is seen in the antitheses that follow, where, above all, there is no question of setting Torah and scribal interpretation over against each other, but what was said 'to them of old time' is at times quoted in the form which was self-evident to the Jew, namely that which tradition gave to the word of Scripture.[2] In fact, Matt. 23.2 grants to the scribes and Pharisees that they sit on the κάθεδρα of Moses; their teaching is not attacked but declared to be binding (23.3). What is attacked is the discrepancy between what they teach and what they do, their hypocrisy (23.4 ff.; 6.1 ff.).[3] To be sure this criticism is radicalised in 15.3 ff. to the accusation that the opponents also misuse their παράδοσις to make the law of God void and to put precepts of men in the place that belongs to the will of God (15.6.9); hence they are called blind leaders of the

---

[1] Cf. A. Schlatter, *Die Kirche des Matthäus* (Gütersloh, 1929), pp. 29 f.

[2] To the prohibition of the Decalogue (Ex. 20.15; Deut. 5.18) is added the designation of punishment (5.21), to the command to love the neighbour the command to hate the enemy (5.43).

[3] Cf. E. Haenchen, 'Matthäus 23', *ZTK* 48, 1951, pp. 38 ff.

blind (15.14), and the disciples are warned against the 'leaven', that is, the teaching of the Pharisees and Sadducees (16.6, 11).

The question at issue between Jesus and his disciples on the one hand and their Jewish opponents on the other is thus the question about the right interpretation of the law. There must also be scribal interpretation in the Christian congregation, hence the title γραμματεύς is also used for the disciples (23.34); only the disciple is a γραμματεύς μαθητευθεὶς τῇ βασιλείᾳ τῶν οὐρανῶν (13.52). But what is the right interpretation?

The answer to this question is given in the series of antitheses in the Sermon on the Mount (5.21–48). Its motive from beginning to end is to break through a law which has been perverted into formal legal statements under cover of which the disobedient heart fondly imagines that all is well, and at the same time to urge the original radical will of God with its call to 'perfection'. This is expressed in the line of thought which runs right through the antitheses: 'not . . . alone—but . . . already', anger already, the lustful look already, the 'legal' putting away of the wife already, even love of the neighbour which leaves room for hatred of the enemy, are contrary to the will of God.

Matthew obviously understands this radicalising of the divine demand, which, in fact, only means a sharpening of the law in the first, second and fourth antitheses, but in the third, fifth and sixth its abolition, as a confirmation of the validity of the law down to the jot and tittle, without being aware of the inconsistency between these antitheses and the binding force of the 'letter' as stated in the Judaistic Jewish-Christian formulation of vv. 18 f., which was firmly held down to the jot and tittle. His allegiance to Jesus' own words and to the understanding of the law in the Judaistic Jewish-Christian tradition stand here in unmistakable tension with each other.

The answer to the question concerning the right interpretation of the law is also a major concern in the discussion about divorce (19.1–12). Its setting in Matthew is in several respects instructive in comparison with Mark's. It is not only that he 'magnificently corrects'[1] the awkward construction of Mark and adds the saying in 19.12, he inserts the decision of Jesus into the question in dispute between the Rabbis about the adequate ground for divorce (κατὰ πᾶσαν αἰτίαν; 19.3) and by the obviously subordinate clause about adultery (19.9, cf. 5.32) in effect makes Jesus represent the strict standpoint of the

[1] Bultmann, SynT, pp. 26 f.

school of Shammai. The radical prohibition by Jesus, to which the whole line of argument, even in Matthew, in vv. 4 ff. (Mark 10.6 ff.), is aimed, is thereby undoubtedly robbed of its stringency. For all that, the norm by which, according to the words of Jesus here, even the Torah of Moses (not only its interpretation) should be judged, is still recognisable in Matthew and the original will of the Creator is pronounced as the principle of interpretation in contrast to the Mosaic concession to human σκληροκαρδία. The will of God manifest in creation is a familiar argument in the demand of Jesus (5.45; 6.26 ff.), particularly in sayings reported by Matthew. The evangelist himself—to what extent he is here ruled by actual sayings of Jesus may remain open—is wont to regard the question about the right principle of interpretation as the question about the epitome of 'law and prophets', or alternatively, what is weighty in the law. This is shown by the formulation of the golden rule by Matthew (7.12), by the formulation of the twofold commandment (22.40, again only in Matthew), and of the 'weightier matters of the law' (23.23), which scribes and Pharisees leave undone (κρίσις, ἔλεος, πίστις). The twice-quoted saying from Hos. 6.6: 'I desire mercy and not sacrifice' (9.13; 12.7), also belongs here.

Among the different expressions in which Matthew summarises the essentials of the law, the trio 'judgment, mercy and faith' (Matt. 23.23) occasions special interest. Without doubt it links on to Old Testament and Jewish expressions, such as 'justice and mercy' (Micah 6.8) or 'mercy and truth' (Prov. 14.22), although, as far as I am aware, it is not to be found literally in this formulation either in the Old Testament or in Judaism. Its three members are for Matthew's Gospel of differing importance. The first requirement, to provide justice for the poor, appropriate in the address to the Pharisees and scribes as the administrators of ruling authority, and frequently found in the Old Testament, plays no part in the Gospel otherwise. This is not surprising in a congregation which still recognises the general Jewish ruling authority and has still not developed any administration of justice of its own. By so much the more, however, does the command of mercy, under which the disciples of Jesus stand, run through the whole Gospel (5.7; 18.33; 9.13; 12.7 and—according to its content—25.31 ff.). Matthew emphatically recalls it to the memory of the congregation, as we saw, at the very point where the first rules for the exercise of congregational discipline are given. Finally, as far as the third notion of the trio (πίστις) is concerned, it cannot, in combination with the other two, be understood simply as 'faith', but rather as 'faithfulness', but scarcely as faithfulness to other men (this use would be unique in the whole Gospel), but in the comprehensive sense of behaviour directed towards God, i.e. as faithfulness to his will as revealed in the law and the prophets. Only in this way does the notion add a new element to the other two and the trio becomes an exhaustive formula for the essentials of the law. Most important of all, however, it is only from this comprehensive meaning directed towards God that a bridge can be built to the use of πίστις and πιστεύειν elsewhere in the Gospel.

When one surveys the linguistic usage of these concepts in Matthew, it is evident that the evangelist speaks in numerous places of faith in the sense used in the Christian tradition with which he was familiar. Faith here means trust directed to the ἐξουσία of Jesus (8.10; 9.2) and experiencing his miraculous power (8.13; 9.22.28 f.). The disciples are called to this faith in the saving, miraculous power of Jesus (contrast the doubt in 21.21). Jesus himself lays it under the promise that nothing will be impossible to it, even if it is no bigger than a grain of mustard seed (17.20; 21.21). Sharply to be differentiated from this faith is 'little faith' (a favourite expression of Matthew), which fails precisely when it is most needed—in the storm and the waves (8.26; 14.31), in the face of anxiety (6.30; 16.8)—and is not adequate to meet the assault of demonic powers (17.20). Matthew uses and illustrates this point as no other evangelist does.[1] For all that, he is speaking here in the usual language of primitive Christian exhortation and comfort. The development of the dogmatic language of primitive Christianity is also discernible in Matthew. He clarifies the bare πιστεύειν (Mark 9.42; 15.32) by πιστεύειν εἰς ἐμέ (Matt. 18.6), and πιστεύειν ἐπ' αὐτόν (27.42). This specifically Christian concept, relating to the person of Jesus, is not used by him, it is worth noting, before the confession of Peter.

In none of these passages, however, are πίστις and πιστεύειν connected with law and end-expectation. That first occurs in two passages in which another specifically Matthaean construction and interpretation can be discerned. The first passage is 21.32, an originally independent saying modified by Matthew (cf. Luke 7.29 f.) and placed by him at the end of the parable of the two dissimilar sons. He thereby gives to the behaviour of the one who says

[1] The expression is found elsewhere only in Luke 12.28.

'No' and the one who says 'Yes' a very definite interpretation: the former was fulfilled in the 'faith' of the publicans and harlots in the presence of John the Baptist who came with 'the way of righteousness', the latter in the refusal of repentance and faith on the part of the Pharisees and scribes, who for that reason cannot enter the βασιλεία.[1] It is instructive in this interpretation that it (1) pronounces a completed event in terms of salvation-history and no-salvation-history, that it (2) regards the two opposed decisions as taken in the presence of the Baptist and thereby affirms the validity of his demand for righteousness in its complete range, and (3) that it describes the obedience demanded by John as 'repentance' and 'faith' and makes it a condition of entrance into the future βασιλεία.

The second passage is the pericope about the centurion of Capernaum (8.5 ff.). Again the construction is the means of interpretation. First Matthew inserts into the framework of the narrative the originally independent saying of 8.11 f. (in Luke it occurs in a wholly different context, 13.28) and thereby gives to the narrative a meaning so stretched in the direction of eschatology that the faith which Jesus has found in the centurion, but has sought in vain in Israel, is manifest as the attitude which decides about membership of the true people of God and entrance into the coming kingdom of God. Both passages show how Matthew understands the concept of faith and unites it with his understanding of righteousness and the kingdom of God. He actually takes it from the primitive Christian tradition, which did not develop it in connexion with the law, but he anchors it in these very passages, where we see him at work as an interpreter of the tradition, where he is fusing his doctrine of law and end-expectation.

In this connexion the use of πίστις in the formula of 23.23 is important. Without losing its Old Testament and Jewish meaning it

[1] That Matt. 21.32 is a secondary interpretation of the parable has been rightly shown by J. Jeremias, op. cit., pp. 62 f. I do not believe, however, that the evangelist received the parable with this interpretation (as Jeremias does), but himself inserts it in the form of v. 32 to elucidate the illustrative meaning which the parable also has in the context of the preceding pericope about authority (esp. for 21.25). The expression ἐν ὁδῷ δικαιοσύνης unquestionably refers to the teaching of John, the demand for righteousness. Thus agreeing with Billerbeck I, pp. 866 f.; G. Schrenk, TWNT II, p. 201 [BKW Righteousness, p. 36], E. Klostermann ad loc. (in Handbuch zum NT, Tübingen), et al., against O. Michel, TWNT V, pp. 90 f. Besides, the recently-discovered commentary on Habakkuk (VIII. 2 f.) now presents an instructive, factual and linguistic parallel to 21.32: 'God will save them from the house of judgment because of their travail and their faithfulness to the teacher of righteousness.'

becomes a parenthesis between the conduct demanded by the law and the faith of the disciples, which is directed to the authority and person of Jesus. The evangelist is able to make plain from both sides at the same time, the essence of the better righteousness by which discipleship of Jesus can be recognised: from the angle of its allegiance to the law, which Jesus fulfils, i.e. authoritatively interprets, and also from the angle of its allegiance to the person and way of the Messiah. Fulfilment of the commandments and perfection can no more be realised anywhere except in 'following' Jesus. This is seen most clearly in the pericope of the rich young man (19.16–30). It was provided for Matthew from the tradition, but he alters and underlines certain elements, as when he alters the reply of Jesus in Mark 10.18 τί με λέγεις ἀγαθόν; to the question τί με ἐρωτᾷς περὶ τοῦ ἀγαθοῦ; (19.17) and thereby ascribes to Jesus the very predicate which he had refused in Mark 10.18, and when he immediately afterwards inserts the imperative εἰ δὲ θέλεις εἰς τὴν ζωὴν εἰσελθεῖν, τήρει τὰς ἐντολάς and in v. 21 inserts the expression εἰ θέλεις τέλειος εἶναι (cf. 5.48), which is characteristic of his understanding of the law. In following Jesus the perfection demanded by the law is thus fulfilled. The promise holds for his disciples, who have left all and followed him, that in the 'regeneration', when the Son of man appears for the judgment, they will sit upon twelve thrones and judge the twelve tribes of Israel. By means of the context and the saying in 19.28, again inserted at this point by Matthew only, discipleship is firmly linked with the concept of the law and the promise that holds for the true people of God.

Yet a further not unimportant departure from the tradition discernible in the Markan text is significant in this pericope. Matthew says nothing of a reward awaiting the disciples already in this aeon (as does Mark 10.30), but promises it only for the coming aeon (19.29), and then to the disciples of Jesus only, in express contrast to Israel. It is in this sense that he understands the parable of the labourers in the vineyard which is added to the pericope, as is shown by the concluding sentence in Matt. 20.16, which repeats verbatim 19.30.[1] Thus both pericopes are made by him to support his own conception of salvation-history.[2] The most important factor, however, is the radically eschatological understanding of the promise given to the disciples. In this aeon there awaits the disciples nothing

[1] Cf. J. Jeremias *op. cit.*, pp. 24 f.
[2] Cf. especially 12.33 ff.; 22.1 ff.

but the suffering destiny of the prophets (5.12; 23.32 ff.). Hence Matthew has altered the account of the Stilling of the Storm (8.23–26) and made it an illustrative picture of what following Jesus means, and given it a symbolic meaning.[1] This is made clear by the fact that, in a context otherwise exclusively devoted to stories of miracles, he precedes the account of the Stilling of the Storm with the well-known sayings about discipleship from Luke 9.57 ff., and links the two with the catchword ἀκολουθεῖν (8.19, 22, 23). Further, the not inconsiderable modifications of the story—the erasing of novelistic details, the formulating of the cry of the disciples as a prayer (κύριε, σῶσον, ἀπολλύμεθα), the prefixing of the accusing words of Jesus to the disciples before the miracle itself (with the use of his beloved word ὀλιγόπιστοι), and finally the designating of the emergency on the sea as a σεισμός, an expression which otherwise belongs to the description of the eschatological distress—these things all clearly show that he is giving to the scene a typically figurative meaning for the discipleship and following of Jesus. Readiness to suffer (10.17 ff.; 16.24 ff.), poverty (19.23 ff.; 6.19 ff.), lowliness (18.1 ff.), love (25.31 ff. and often), renunciation of worldly honour (23.7 ff.) and service (20.20 ff.), these are the marks of discipleship. It is only to disciples, who stand the test and show themselves approved in these matters, as none of the passages fails to say, that reward in the kingdom of God is promised.

How firmly and consistently Matthew, in spite of all the specifically Christian motives which he employs, orientates everything he has to say about the essence of discipleship, around the law and righteousness, is shown, finally, by the concepts δίκαιος and δικαιοσύνη, which in his writings alone occupy a predominant place. Jesus himself is righteous (27.19), he fulfils 'all righteousness' (3.15), he is true and teaches the way of God in truth (22.16), the persecution of the disciples for his sake is equivalent to persecution for righteousness' sake (5.10 f.); righteousness is the all-embracing notion for the piety of the disciples as a whole (6.1). Never, however, are the disciples altogether and, as such, already righteous. Rather, they are summoned to the better righteousness (5.20; 6.33); not until the coming judgment will the righteous shine as the sun (13.43), when the angels will separate the wicked from the midst of the righteous (13.49). The Beatitude in 5.6 applies to those who hunger

[1] Cf. G. Bornkamm, 'The Stilling of the Storm in Matthew's Gospel'; below pp. 52–7.

the first place he is satisfied with the evidence that they are all based on Scripture. Nevertheless, traces of such reflection are not lacking, even though when he makes them Matthew largely remains within his own tradition. At this point the debate about the relationship between the title son of David and the title Lord (Matt. 22.41 ff.), which cannot be understood in the sense of an either-or,[1] at least by the evangelist, who elsewhere brings Jesus' sonship of David into considerable prominence, calls for mention. The question εἰ οὖν Δαυὶδ καλεῖ αὐτὸν κύριον, πῶς υἱὸς αὐτοῦ ἐστιν; (22.45) can only be intended to point to the paradoxical combination of the two titles which both belong to Jesus, and to indicate that in his earthly lowliness he is David's son, but as the Exalted One he is Lord, as David himself called him in Ps. 110.1.

Reflection on the connexion between the dignity of Jesus as Christ and Son of God, and as the Son of man who will judge the world, is also disclosed by the question of the high priest at the trial and the reply of Jesus (26.63 f.), in which he already lays claim to the former and proclaims his coming as the Son of man in the words of Dan. 7.13. It is significant that Matthew (similarly to Luke) heightens the Markan text by the emphatic words ἀπ' ἄρτι ὄψεσθε (26.64). Matthew as theologian and interpreter is seen more plainly at work in his account of the triumphal entry (21.1 ff.), in so far as he alone expressly quotes Zech. 9.9 (linked with Isa. 62.11) and thus designates Jesus as the 'lowly king'. As in Mark, the cry Hosanna also resounds in Matthew from the mouth of the multitude accompanying Jesus (v. 9), but he deletes the second half of the cry (εὐλογημένη ἡ ἐρχομένη βασιλεία τοῦ πατρὸς ἡμῶν Δαυιδ—Mark 11.10) and immediately replaces the multitude by the band of children, in whom, as frequently in his Gospel, the discipleship of Jesus, which is sharply rejected by the high priests and scribes, is prefigured and mirrored.

---

[1] It is scarcely possible that Mark, who also made use of the title Son of David elsewhere in his Gospel (10.47 f., cf. 11.9), intended in this sense, the question in 12.37, though the original meaning of the pericope may well have been to deny that the Messiah was the Son of David (Wrede, Bousset, Klostermann, Bultmann with a reference to *Barn.* 12.10 f.); for the question would have had to be asked, if the point of departure had been the Davidic sonship of the Messiah and it had been considered within the pattern of lowliness/exaltation: If the Messiah is David's son, how can he be his Lord? The unquestioned use of the title Son of David elsewhere in the Gospels, however, compels the conclusion, as the Christological formulae in Rom. 1.3; II Tim. 2.8; Ignatius, *Smyr.* 1.1; *Trall.* 9, etc., show, that they use it in reference to his earthly-human figure, in distinction from his exaltation. It is thus Christian reflection, no longer Jewish, which is presupposed.

He thus obviously avoids equating the kingdom of God, consistently understood eschatologically by him, with 'the kingly rule of David'. It is the king of lowliness who is present here and now; the kingdom of God, in which he is the world-judge of all nations (Matt. 25.31), is in the future.

Even where Matthew actually—once only—speaks of the βασιλεία τοῦ θεοῦ as having come, with a saying derived from Q ('But if I by the Spirit of God cast out devils, then is the kingdom of God come upon you', 12.28), the present is still characterised by the context as the time of decision (12.30), the future nature of the judgment is retained (12.27, 36 f.), and the distinction between this (still continuing) and the future aeon is not abandoned (12.32). In fact, from the saying inserted here by Matthew—which is taken from Mark but expanded and interpreted in a Christian way by means of the Q-version—about the unforgivableness of the blasphemy against the Spirit in distinction from the forgivableness of utterances directed against the Son of man (12.31 f.), one may infer a still more exact differentiation between the 'epochs' of salvation-history. As Mark 3.28 f. shows, the original meaning of the saying of Jesus is: all sins and blasphemies can be forgiven except the blasphemy against the Holy Spirit as he is manifest in the victory of Jesus over the demons. Matthew (or alternatively Q already, Matt. 12.32; Luke 12.10) differentiates between the Son of man and the Spirit and the blasphemy against them both, and thus discriminates between a time in which Jesus, still before the Spirit is present, is encountered as 'Son of man' (i.e. here clearly in the state of a still ambiguous lowliness), and a time in which, through the Holy Spirit (hence after his exaltation) the attitude to him (and his Church) takes on the character of a clear either-or. Now, for the first time, blasphemy can be an unforgivable sin, for in the Spirit the self-revealing exalted Lord is speaking. Both times belong to this aeon. They must still be differentiated from the coming aeon, which will bring the final judgment. In the sense of this division of salvation-history into epochs, in which the appearance of Jesus as the Son of man is associated with the period before his exaltation and the Spirit, on the other hand, with the period of his clear and binding revelation, hence the time of the Church of the Exalted One, the final judgment forming the still awaited consummation, the saying is intelligible.[1]

[1] Cf. also for the understanding of this difficult passage C. K. Barrett, *The Holy Spirit and the Gospel Tradition* (London, 1947), pp. 103 ff.

All these passages, in which Matthew (to some degree also his sources) interprets theologically the received tradition, aim at the distinction between the earthly lowliness of Jesus and his future appearance in glory for the judgment.

However, the earthly function of Jesus as Messiah—apart from his miracles, to which Matthew, of course, allows considerable space, although they take second place to his teaching (4.23; 9.35, etc.)—is above all *interpretation of the law*. Here the Matthaean Christology can first be readily perceived. It has often been rightly observed that Jesus appears in Matthew as a second Moses,[1] that the typology of Moses dominates the pre-historical stories, that the mountain of the Sermon on the Mount may possibly be intended as an analogy to Sinai, and that the whole history and teaching of Jesus are presented under the motive of the fulfilling of the law (5.17), 'of all righteousness' (3.15).

The relationship of Jesus to Moses is thereby not intended in the sense of an antithesis, as it is, for example in John's Gospel (1.17; 6.32 ff.), but in the sense of correspondence. In spite of the authoritative 'But I say unto you' the teaching of Jesus is constantly proved from the law and his authority not simply asserted. His words ἐγὼ δὲ λέγω ὑμῖν (5.22, 28, etc.) do not express any claim that he renounces proof; it is no word of revelation in the sense of the Johannine ἐγώ εἰμι-sayings. As the Scripture validates him in his Messianic rank and dignity, so the law validates his teaching, and particularly his Messianic ἐξουσία, as a teacher in opposition to the Pharisees and scribes.[2]

[1] So above all B. W. Bacon, *Studies in Matthew*; F. W. Green, *The Gospel according to Matthew* (Oxford, 1949⁴); cf. also G. D. Kilpatrick, *op. cit.*, pp. 107 f.—Bacon's thesis that Matthew has divided his Gospel into five sections in imitation of the Pentateuch has found wide approval. I do not find it convincing.

[2] The relationship of Jesus to the law does not seem to me to be quite adequately characterised when Kilpatrick declares, 'The central position that Judaism gave to the Law, the Gospel gives to Jesus' (*op. cit.*, p. 108) and maintains that the law has in Matthew 'an important, though subordinate place in the Christian scheme' (p. 109). The saying in Matt. 18.20 can, in fact, say of Jesus what the Rabbis correspondingly said of the Torah (*Pirke Aboth* 3.2, 'when two sit (together) and there are words of the Torah between them, there the Shekina sojourns between them'), and Matthew also puts sayings from the Wisdom literature into the mouth of Jesus. This does not mean that Jesus is put *in the place* of the law (or Wisdom), but rather, in the sense of 5.17 ff., is the confirmation of the law. It should be noted that in Matthew's Gospel there is no concept of a *nova lex* (Bacon, Kilpatrick, etc.) and could not be. Matt. 12.6 says: 'A greater than the *temple* is here', not: than the *law*; the law is summoned as a witness by Matthew precisely to 12.6 (12.3–7); it validates the Son of man as Lord also of the Sabbath (12.8). On the positive meaning of the statement ὅτι τοῦ ἱεροῦ μεῖζόν ἐστιν ὧδε cf., the apt comments of A. Schlatter in *Die Kirche des Matthäus*, pp. 31 ff.

If the question is asked concerning the relation of the statements in which the dignity of Jesus as Χριστός, as son of David, as king of Israel, as Son of God, etc., is spoken of, to those which describe him as a teacher of the law, we see that Matthew does not leave the two unconnected, but that he links them firmly together.

Instructive in this connexion already is the conversation which he constructed and which, for that matter, he alone reports, between John the Baptist and Jesus, with which he—and this is generally overlooked in the exegesis—not only introduces the account of the baptism, but at the same time links it with the immediately preceding announcement of the Messiah and *his* baptism. (The use of τότε, so frequent in Matthew, already supports this connexion.) There is nothing to justify the interpretation of this conversation exclusively in terms of the sinlessness of Jesus, as the Gospel of the Hebrews already does, for this makes the meaning of his baptism a problem and its adoption a humble concession to the pious practice of the people. The Baptist's question also means more than simply a respectful recognition of the superiority of Jesus. The conversation is, in fact, yet another expression of a theological reflection on salvation-history. It poses the question of the relation of the Messianic baptism just announced by John (with the Spirit and with fire) and the baptism of Jesus by the Baptist just taking place, and of the function of the Messiah who has now come, appearing surprisingly not as the one who baptises, but as the one to be baptised, without the fan in his hand. The words of the Baptist: 'I have need to be baptised of thee, and comest thou to me?' therefore mean: My time and my baptism are past, and the hour of thy (Messianic) baptism has arrived. The reply of Jesus is programmatical: 'Suffer it now; for thus it becometh us to fulfil all righteousness' (3.15).

The proclamation and fulfilment of the δικαιοσύνη demanded by God is thus the function incumbent upon the Messiah here on earth. As the one who undertakes it he is proclaimed as 'Son of God'. He himself fulfils it in his obedience to the law and proves himself at once, in warding off the temptations of the devil, as the Son of God (again the characteristic τότε 4.1), obedient 'in the sense of the piety of the Anawim',[1] or in the words of Matthew, as the one who is πραΰς and ταπεινὸς τῇ καρδίᾳ (11.29).[2] If, then, here in the temptation

---

[1] W. Sattler, 'Die Anawim im Zeitalter Jesu Christi', *Festgabe für Adolf Jülicher*, Tübingen, 1927, p. 10.

[2] A. Schlatter, *Der Evangelist Matthäus* (Stuttgart, 1957⁴), pp. 95 ff., and

story 'Jesus is differentiated from a magician and the Christian performance of miracles from magic',[1] and thereby the understanding of his Sonship of God from the Hellenistic υἱὸς τοῦ θεοῦ, who proves himself by miraculous deeds, the question inevitably arises how this Hellenistic picture of the υἱὸς τοῦ θεοῦ, which is undoubtedly present in Mark's Gospel and was certainly taken over by Matthew, fits in with it. The discussion of this question did not first occur in Matthew's Gospel; it is already visible in the source, as the temptation story shows, but Matthew takes it further when he places Jesus' teaching and healing in Galilee in the summaries which he makes in 4.12 ff. and 4.23 ff., which enclose the call of the first disciples, under the word of salvation to those who dwell in the land and shadow of death (Isa. 9.1 f.; Matt. 4.15 f.), and when in 9.36 he describes him as the shepherd who is moved with compassion for the scattered flock, and when he sees in the saving deeds of Jesus the fulfilment of the prophecy of God's Servant (Isa. 53.4; 42.1 ff.; Matt. 8.17; 12.18 ff.). Thus the miracles here are no longer the manifestation of the θεῖος ἀνήρ, but of his mercy and lowliness. The fundamental rejection of the Hellenistic picture of the miracle-worker is thus declared, admittedly without Matthew withholding himself entirely from its attraction.

The πραΰτης of the Messiah and his mercy towards the unprivileged, both understood as the fulfilment of all righteousness, runs through the whole Gospel of Matthew, right down to the description of the judgment of the world (25.31 ff.), in which the Son of man calls the unprivileged his brethren. Further, corresponding absolutely with this, as we have already seen, there is also the interpretation which he gives to the law of God ('I desire mercy and not sacrifice', 9.13; 12.7), the summons to love, to become as little ones, to humility, to readiness to suffer and so on. These all describe the 'better righteousness', the fruits which will be asked about in the judgment, the perfection of which the end of the antitheses of the Sermon on the Mount speaks.

The consistent and radical acceptance of the law (in its actual intention) thus stands for Matthew in the closest connexion with his Christology. Till heaven and earth pass away all that the law says

---

R. Bultmann (*Syn T*, pp. 254 ff.) have rightly disputed the Messianic character of the temptations and worked out the meaning of the pericope for the understanding of the law in general.

[1] R. Bultmann, *Syn T*, p. 255.

must be fulfilled; till then the promise of greatness in the kingdom of heaven belongs to those who teach and do the new righteousness without diminution (5.18 ff.), are ready, as νήπιοι (11.25) to take upon themselves the yoke of meekness and lowliness of heart (11.29) and thereby to become μαθηταί of him who himself is meek and lowly in heart, until he comes in glory as judge and will separate the good and evil according to their works and will exalt the lowly.[1]

4. ECCLESIOLOGY AND CHRISTOLOGY

No other Gospel is so shaped by the thought of the Church as Matthew's, so constructed for use by the Church; for this reason it has exercised, as no other, a normative influence in the later Church. Statements in which the eschatological self-consciousness of primitive Christianity is expressed run through the whole Gospel: here alone the congregation is called the ἐκκλησία (Matt. 16.18) (i.e. the qᵉhal Yahweh of Old Testament-Jewish expectation), the βασιλεία of the Son of man (13.41); the disciples of Jesus are the free sons of

[1] The linking of teaching of the law and message of the kingdom, so characteristic of Matthew, is already expressed in the connecting of διδάσκειν and κηρύσσειν, which occurs in his Gospel only (4.23; 9.35; 11.1). That this is a specifically Matthaean linguistic usage is noticed by neither K. H. Rengstorf (διδάσκω, TWNT II, pp. 138 ff., esp. pp. 141 ff.) nor G. Friedrich (κηρύσσω, TWNT III, pp. 695 ff., esp. p. 713). Mark uses διδάσκειν without any distinction, the same for Jesus' teaching on the Sabbath in the synagogue or in the Temple (1.21 f.; 6.2; 12.35) as for any other teaching by Jesus, in the introduction to the parables (4.1), for example, or to the cleansing of the Temple, but most notably in connexion with the instructing of the disciples about the suffering and resurrection of the Son of man (8.31; 9.31). The content of the concept 'teaching' is thus not fixed. With Matthew it is different. The parallels to the Markan passages which have been mentioned show that διδάσκειν is used only where Jesus is clearly designated Rabbi (teacher of the law), thus in Matt. 7.29 (= Mark 1.22); 13.54 (= Mark 6.2); 22.16 (= Mark 12.14); 26.55 (= Mark 14.49; notice in Matthew the addition of the word ἐκαθεζόμην!). In such passages Matthew can even go beyond Mark in speaking of Jesus' 'teaching' (4.23; 9.35; 11.1; 21.23, and above all in the introduction to the Sermon on the Mount, 5.2). On the other hand, he consistently avoids the word in passages where the subject is not specifically Jesus' teaching on the law, for example in the introduction to the parables on the kingdom of heaven (cf. Matt. 13.3 and Mark 4.2), similarly in connexion with the instructing of the disciples about the destiny of the Son of man (cf. Matt. 16.21 and Mark 8.31; Matt. 17.22 and Mark 9.31); the expression is also lacking in 21.13 (cf. Mark 11.17) and 22.41 (cf. Mark 12.35). Likewise the parallels to Mark 2.13; 10.1, are wanting in Matthew. In the light of this peculiarity in Matthew's linguistic usage the combination of διδάσκειν and κηρύσσειν (4.23, etc.) is intelligible. Close as the two are together, they are by no means equivalent. Formally the usage covers the field of tension of the whole Matthaean theology: law and kingdom of God.

God (17.26); they are entrusted with the mysteries of the kingdom of heaven (13.11), eye- and ear-witnesses of the fulfilment of that which prophets and righteous men desired in vain to see and hear (13.16 ff.); they are the salt of the earth and the light of the world, the city set upon the hill (5.13). And yet it must be agreed from the beginning that in spite of all these passages only the most meagre beginnings of a real ecclesiology, centred in the Church as an independent, empirically circumscribed entity, are to be found in Matthew's Gospel. There is no similar number of ecclesiological concepts and words corresponding to the wealth of Christological titles and statements. One never reads: you are 'the true Israel', the 'saints', the 'elect', the 'church of the new covenant'. There are no self-designations in Matthew's Gospel, such as are to be found in the Damascus Document and the recently discovered texts from the Dead Sea, but also in primitive Christianity. Also lacking are all signs of special offices, as they are to be found, for example, in an exactly graded hierarchical structure in the 'rules for the sect'.[1] One would not specifically look for such statements in a work belonging to the class of the Gospels, and yet, at least where directions are given for the exercise of discipline in the congregation, one might expect them (ch. 18). They are wanting, however, even here, and the command not to use the title 'Rabbi', 'father', 'master', of individuals in the community of Jesus, is expressly stated (23.8 ff.). Matthew's Gospel confirms throughout that the congregation which he represented had not yet separated from Judaism. The Messiahship of Jesus and the validity of his teaching are therefore, as we have already seen, presented and defended throughout in the framework of Judaism, and in the saying in 23.34, in which significantly a Wisdom-saying is put into the mouth of Jesus (cf. Luke 9.49), the disciples are characterised only by Old Testament-Jewish expressions, as the prophets, wise men and scribes sent out by Jesus. The struggle with Israel is still a struggle within its own walls.

Thus Matthew's conception of the Church remains imprisoned in the Jewish tradition, yet it is peculiarly opened in the direction of the Gentile world. In this respect it corresponds to the Christology of the

---

[1] Nevertheless one may draw the conclusion, from the polemic against false teachers (5.18 f.) and false prophets (7.15 ff., etc.), from the mention of προφῆται, σοφοί and γραμματεῖς (23.34), from the striking prominence given to the twelve Apostles (10.1 f.) and Peter (16.17 ff.) and from the prohibition in 23.8 ff., that the congregation was not devoid of order and particular functionaries. For more detail see Kilpatrick, *op. cit.*, pp. 124 ff.

Gospel: Jesus is the Messianic king of Israel, sent to the lost sheep of the house of Israel (15.24), but as the One raised from the dead entrusted with ἐξουσία over heaven and earth, who now through his disciples summons all nations to discipleship (28.19), and as the Son of Man who is to come, will judge them (25.31 ff.).

The most frequent designation of the disciples in Matthew's Gospel, as in the other Gospels, is μαθηταί, the correlative concept to διδάσκαλος.[1] The evangelist takes these concepts from the Christian tradition that lay before him. Their derivation from Judaism is well known; they contain, as such, nothing specifically Christian, but link on directly to the school terminology evolved by the Rabbinate. Admittedly both concepts had taken on a new content long before Matthew. Discipleship of Jesus does not arise on the basis of a free attachment to a teacher, but on the basis of a call to follow him which issues from Jesus. Jesus does not exercise authority over his disciples on account of his knowledge of the Torah, nor is he a means to the end of gaining a similar wisdom in the law. Further, the position of a μαθητής is not a preliminary stage, with the intention that the disciple himself shall become a διδάσκαλος (23.8 ff.), but signifies a lasting relationship to Jesus. Hence Jesus nowhere enters into discussion with his disciples; those who take part with him in debates about the law are always his opponents. Further, his disciples are not bearers of a teaching which he has left behind, which can be detached from his Person, but—though this expression is not yet found in Matthew—they are his witnesses.

All these traits in the concept of the μαθητής, characteristic also for the other Gospels, are also to be found in Matthew's Gospel. It is not the teaching of Jesus, as contained in the Sermon on the Mount, that is the motive for the disciples following him. The call precedes it rather, and the separating of the disciples from the multitude surrounding Jesus occurs at the beginning. Hence the commission of the disciples in the missionary discourse is, in the first place, nothing other than to proclaim the nearness of the kingdom of God (κηρύσσειν 10.7), announced by Jesus with authority, not to hand on his interpretation of the law; they are also entrusted by him with ἐξουσία over unclean spirits. Even at the point where they are actually charged with the teaching, 'to observe all things whatsoever I commanded you' (28.20), it is preceded by the call μαθητεύσατε

---

[1] On what follows cf. the articles διδάσκαλος and μαθητής by K. H. Rengstorf, *TWNT* II, pp. 154 ff. and IV, pp. 444 ff.

πάντα τὰ ἔθνη, based on the resurrection of Jesus and his power over heaven and earth, hence on his dignity as Lord. And the teaching of his commandments is not bound up with the appeal to him as was usual with a Rabbi of the past, but takes place under the promise of the Risen One: 'I am with you alway, even unto the end of the world' (28.20, cf. 18.20).[1]

Further peculiarities of Matthew's Gospel correspond very consistently with this understanding of discipleship and its relationship to Jesus. One such instance is when Matthew alone (10.25) continues the general statement 'A disciple is not above his master' with the parallel statement: 'and a servant is not above his lord', and shows by 25b that this is not to be understood as a general truth but with reference to Jesus as Κύριος and οἰκοδεσπότης. Jesus thereby ceases to be a διδάσκαλος in the Jewish sense.

With this in mind it is very significant that though Matthew frequently uses the title διδάσκαλος or alternatively ῥαββί, he never uses it as a mode of address in the mouth of the disciples, with one exception—Judas Iscariot.[2] The Pharisees and strangers call him διδάσκαλε. His disciples call him κύριε.[3] This observation is the more weighty since the received tradition, as Mark shows, very frequently and ingenuously places the term of address διδάσκαλε or ῥαββί in the mouth of the disciples (Mark 4.38; 9.5; 9.38; 10.35; 13.1; Luke also uses it, e.g., in 21.7, when he does not choose the term ἐπιστάτης, which was more intelligible for Greek ears, Luke 5.5; 8.24, 45; 9.33, 49; 17.13). Matthew, on the other hand, quite consistently changes to κύριε (cf. 8.25 and Mark 4.38; Matt. 17.4 and Mark 9.5; Matt. 20.33 and Mark 10.51; ῥαββί in Mark 11.21 is omitted by Matthew). Those who do not belong to the disciples say to the disciples 'your master' (9.2; 17.24); likewise, over against the Jews he is designated by the disciples as 'the Master' (26.18), but among the disciples themselves this title is not adequate for him, but only the Lord-title will do.

It is, of course, disputed whether the κύριε form of address as used by the disciples may be understood without further ado as a term of

[1] The sayings of the Lord can therefore never be reckoned as a kind of 'Pirke Aboth'.
[2] Cf. 26.49 and 26.25; note how the distinction is made here between the address κύριε on the part of the disciples (26.22) and ῥαββί by Judas. Mark and Luke provide no parallels.
[3] Overlooked by K. H. Rengstorf, TWNT II, p. 156; rightly observed, on the other hand, by W. Foerster, TWNT III, p. 1092 [BKW Lord, p. 106].

Majesty, or whether it does not simply bear the meaning of a term of respect addressed to a man. Certainly, as Bousset already emphasises,[1] a distinction has to be made between the quite isolated usage ὁ κύριος, which occurs in Matt. 21.3 (= Mark 11.3) alone with reference to Jesus, and the term κύριε, which 'has a very much wider compass' and is used in the New Testament not only with reference to God, Christ and heavenly beings, but as passages of even Matthew's Gospel show (13.27; 25.11, 20, 22, 24; 21.30), is also used between servant and lord, and son and father. Hence Bousset concludes that the linguistic usage of Matthew is on the whole the same as that of Mark, but the term κύριε (not in the titular sense) has intruded in a number of passages. In actual fact 10.24, for example, does show that the relationship of the servant to his lord and of the pupil to his teacher in a general sense essentially remains for the attitude of the disciples. Yet in Matthew's Gospel κύριε is by no means simply an expression of human respect, but is intended as a term of Majesty. It is the form of address to Jesus as the miracle-working *Saviour* (8.2, 6, 8; 9.28; 15.22, 25; 17.15; 20.30, 33), whether from the mouth of the sufferer who implores him for mercy,[2] or from the disciples who cry to him to save them (8.25; 14.30) or in other circumstances declare his Majesty with this term of address (16.22; 17.4; 18.21; 26.22). Above all, however, it is applied to Jesus as the coming *judge of the world* (7.21 f.; 25.11, 37, 44). Even where ὁ κύριος is used in a parable and where, in the first place, it denotes an earthly lord, the concept immediately passes over from the parabolic half into the actual, and becomes the title of the Son of man. This is clear, for example, in Matt. 24.42: 'Watch, for ye know not on what day *your Lord* cometh', which (cf. 25.44) is placed at the beginning of the parable of the thief at night (where the reference is to the master of the house in the earthly, figurative sense).[3]

From the evidence presented it follows: the title and address of Jesus as κύριος in Matthew have throughout the character of a

---

[1] W. Bousset, *Kyrios Christos* (Göttingen, 1921²), pp. 79 f.

[2] ἐλέησον (9.27; 15.22; 17.15; 20.30) repeated in combination with the title son of David (9.27; 15.22; 20.30).

[3] The experience of the delay in the parousia of the κύριος is written, with unmistakable allegorising, into the parables of the wicked servant (24.48) and the talents (25.19) as into the parable of the ten virgins. To the process of allegorisation, which begins already in the parables, there corresponds at the end the threat of eternal judgment, which bursts open the framework of the parable (24.51; 25.30).

divine Name of Majesty. The legitimation of this from Scripture is found in Ps. 110.1 (22.41 ff.).

In spite of the clearly recognisable withdrawal from the title διδάσκαλος, and its supplanting by the κύριος-title in every place where Matthew expresses the relationship of the disciples to Jesus not from without but from within, οἱ μαθηταί nevertheless remains *the* distinctive designation of the disciples down to the missionary command of the Risen One. This should not be regarded merely as a clinging to an accepted tradition which expresses the relationship of Jesus and his disciples in Jewish categories; rather the concept of disciple remains for Matthew, since the Christian tradition had filled it with new contents (imitation, readiness to suffer, etc.), valid and exhaustive as an ecclesiastical term because in an exemplary way it retains and expresses along with the abiding allegiance to Jesus and his teaching—the constant 'learning of him' (11.29)—the point of the future nature of the βασιλεία and of the judgment. οἱ μαθηταί is the designation of the disciples here and now, they are disciples of the *one* Master and 'brothers' one of another (23.8), called by him to discipleship and summoned to the new righteousness. In the statements about the future, on the other hand, they are no longer referred to as 'disciples'; it is not 'the disciples' but 'the righteous' who will shine as the sun in the kingdom of their Father (13.43), and who will stand on the right hand of the Son of man in the judgment (25.31 ff., 37). And not 'the disciples', but 'the elect' will be gathered by the angels on the day of the Son of man (24.31). 'The elect', however, are not the members of the Church simply, but the υἱοὶ τῆς βασιλείας, who as the good seed have been sown in the field of the world and are alongside the tares which the devil has sown in the same field (13.36 ff.).[1] We have constantly drawn attention to the way in which this theme of the separation only in the future dominates the whole Gospel. This is expressed, as we have already pointed out, with all the clarity that could be desired in the Matthaean conclusion of the parable of the wicked husbandmen. This parable in Mark 12.1 ff. obviously refers to the rejection of Israel *which has already taken place* and to the *subsequent* handing over of the vineyard to others; in Matthew, on the other hand, it is translated into the future so that the disciples themselves are now drawn into the judgment and the question is thus put before them whether they are the nation bringing forth the fruits of the kingdom (21.43). The

[1] Cf. especially 22.14 (20.16: variant reading).

conclusion added by Matthew in 22.11 is no different: here, too, at the end, the decision about the marriage feast, which in the parable has already been presented and made, is surprisingly reopened in the direction of the judgment still to come in the future. The remarkable alteration made in this way in the Matthaean pericope, in comparison with Luke 14.15–24, is well known.

The existing Church is thus according to Matthew, as 13.36 ff. says, the βασιλεία of the Son of man, but it is not identical with the company who enter into the kingdom of God. The terminology of this clearly secondary allegorical interpretation of the parable of the tares[1] is in many respects noteworthy, and is certainly, as Jeremias has shown with minute references,[2] Matthew's own work. It presupposes, what is self-evident for him especially, the equating of the earthly Jesus with the Son of man (the Sower = the Son of man), it speaks of the Church as his earthly βασιλεία (13.41)[3]—an expression which terminologically even clashes with Matthew's own language,[4] even though it coincides in content with his outlook—and in 13.41 employs the title υἱὸς τοῦ ἀνθρώπου in a different way from that in 13.37 (but just as self-evidently) for the coming judge of the world, thus here again clearly distinguishing between his earthly and future form and function and at the same time combining them. To this Christological view there corresponds the differentiating and at the same time co-ordinating of the Church and the coming βασιλεία, in other words: the calling of the many which has already taken place and the future selection of the few righteous.

To the context of these especially characteristic Matthaean views about Church and end-expectation, stated in 13.36–43, there also belongs his famous ἐκκλησία-saying (16.17–19). The numerous exegetical problems and problems of the history of the tradition in connexion with this passage cannot be debated here. The vast diver-

---

[1] The point of this in the interpretation is the lost patience.

[2] *Op. cit.*, p. 70.

[3] Thus correctly E. Klostermann *ad loc.*, C. H. Dodd, *The Parables of the Kingdom* (1935), 1952, p. 183, J. Jeremias, p. 65. R. Bultmann, for some reason which is not understandable, disputes this equation with the Church and understands ἐκ. τ. βασιλ. αὐτοῦ as meaning: out of the kingdom *then* appearing (*SynT*, p. 187 note 3). To the kingdom *then* appearing, however, belong the υἱοὶ τῆς βασιλείας (13.38) *only*; it is the kingdom of their Father, not the kingdom of the Son of man. Cf. also *ad loc.* C. H. Dodd, 'Matthew and Paul', *ExpT*, 1947, p. 294 (also in *New Testament Studies*, London, 1953).

[4] In 16.28 (cf. also 22.21) the reference is to the coming Son of man, who will appear with his (future) rule.

gence in present-day research's judgment about the genuineness of the ἐκκλησία-saying is shown by two statements from the most recent publications on the question. While Oscar Cullmann in his recent book on Peter repeats and defends[1] the thesis that he had developed earlier, that the impugning of the genuineness of Matt. 16.17 ff. cannot be 'scientifically justified',[2] H. von Campenhausen gives it as his judgment:[3] 'that the founding of the Church on Peter is unthinkable in the mouth of Jesus, and in spite of recent efforts to preserve the saying this judgment should not be called in question'. I also hold that the saying belongs to the period after Easter, for many reasons which have been given often and adequately, despite the linguistic and historical indications which support its great age. Against the arguments recently put forward, by Oepke[4] and Cullmann especially, for the genuineness of the saying, there weighs, in my opinion, the fact that the ἐκκλησία of Matt. 16.18 cannot be comprised within the traditional thought of the Jewish people of God, but bears throughout an institutional character, characterised by the authority in doctrine and discipline of a particular apostle. Although it is an eschatological entity, it is associated with a time which, from the point of view of the scene itself, is in the future (the thrice-repeated future tense in 16.18 f. οἰκοδομήσω, οὐ κατισχύσουσιν, δώσω —and yet it is an earthly future, to be distinguished from the future of the coming βασιλεία and of the future judgment; the first reference to this future (of the new aeon) is to be found in the twofold ἔσται δεδεμένον/λελυμένον ἐν τοῖς οὐρανοῖς (16.19). Peter, as the rock of the Church, thus receives the office of the keys for the time after the resurrection, but before the parousia. This is the time of the Church, which Jesus calls 'my Church' and to which he gives the promise that it will stand against the powers of death.[5] Thus the Church is earthly not heavenly, to be differentiated from the βασιλεία τῶν οὐρανῶν, but associated most closely with it, because its decisions about doctrine

[1] *Petrus* (Zürich, 1952), p. 214 (cf. rev. ET, London, 1962, p. 217); R. Bultmann, 'Die Frage nach der Echtheit von Matth. 16.17–19' (*TB*, 1941, pp. 265 ff.) takes it as the starting-point for his investigation which leads to the opposite conclusion. In his case as in that of Cullmann and A. Oepke, 'Der Herrnspruch über die Kirche Matth. 16.17–19 in der neuesten Forschung' (*Studia Theologica*, 1948/50, pp. 110 ff.), there is a careful résumé of recent discussion.

[2] *Königsherrschaft Christi und Kirche* (1946²), p. 22.

[3] *Kirchliches Amt und geistliche Vollmacht* (1953), pp. 140 f.

[4] See n. 1.

[5] The assault of the powers of death is here unquestionably to be understood as that which precedes the appearance of the Son of man and his rule (16.28; 24.8, 29 ff.).

and discipline, its binding and loosing, will be confirmed in the coming βασιλεία, will be 'ratified'.[1]

Matthew again interprets this text by the simple means of construction. The first questions to be asked in order to reach an understanding of his interpretation are concerned with the context into which Matthew fits the ἐκκλησία-saying. Unquestionably the first section to be counted as belonging to the context is that in Matt. 16.13–23 (the confession of Peter and the first prophecy of suffering), already provided by Mark 8.27–33, but no less the section that follows, about the sufferings that await the disciples as they follow Christ (Mark 8.34–9.1; Matt. 16.24–28). Of course, it is possible with some justification to regard 16.20 as the conclusion of the Peter-pericope and the emphasised ἀπὸ τότε ἤρξατο . . . of 16.21 as beginning a new section.[2] This narrower limitation of the pericope, however, must not disguise the fact that 16.21–23 already, and 16.24–28 no less, stand in close and essential connexion with the Petrine saying. The function of the prominent insertion in 16.21 is to separate 'text' and 'interpretation' from each other so to speak; of course, as scarcely needs to be said, the idea of the interpretation should be taken with a pinch of salt, since it actually consists of the addition of another piece of the tradition, which has its own theme and point. We must now establish more precisely the meaning we have attached to the context of 16.13–28.

Mark had already excellently prepared the ground here for Matthew; for he presents in 8.27–9.1 a context which is quite factually determined and theologically thought through: *1.* (8.27–33): Peter's confession and the command of silence; in the place of that the open announcement of the suffering and resurrection of the Son of man; rebuke of Peter (note the enclosing of 8.27–33 by the catchwords οἱ ἄνθρωποι 8.27 and τὰ τῶν ανθρώπων 8.33). *2.* (8.34–9.1): the sayings about the disciples' suffering imitation[3] of Christ, closing with the announcement of the coming of the Son of man in glory and the imminent coming of the βασιλεία.[4]

[1] Thus Church and kingdom of God must not be understood at all in the sense of kingdoms standing alongside each other simultaneously; they are detached from each other in terms of time. The Church looks forward to the coming kingdom and judgment.

[2] Cf. H. Lehmann, 'Du bist Petrus . . .', *EvTh*, 1953, pp. 47 ff.

[3] Note the linking expression ὀπίσω μου, 8.33, 34; J. Sundwall, *Die Zusammensetzung des Markusevangeliums* (Åbo, 1934), p. 56.

[4] The combination of the announcement of suffering and imitation in lowliness is repeated in 9.31 ff., 33 ff.; 10.32 ff., 35 ff.

Matthew does not alter this construction, but tightens and strengthens the context, in that he binds 16.13–23 and 24–28 more closely together by the use of his beloved copula τότε,[1] avoids the circumstantial new insertion of Mark 8.34 by omitting the multitude, and at the end twice makes the announcement of the parousia of the Son of man in glory—to judge every man according to his deeds (16.27!).

If one looks first of all at the narrower context (Matt. 16.13–23; Mark 8.27–33), it is immediately clear that Matthew gives to Peter's confession a completely different meaning, and attributes to it a different valuation from Mark. In the strict sense only the Matthaean pericope should be designated a 'Peter-confession', whereas the Markan should have some such superscription as 'Rejection of Peter's confession'.[2] The aim in Mark, the theologian of the Messianic secret, is this: Jesus is now the Son of man moving towards suffering and the resurrection, the confession of him as Messiah cannot and must not occur till after Easter.[3] For Matthew, on the other hand, the idea of the Messianic secret no longer has the same overruling force, although the subject is not simply abandoned. Peter's confession is therefore at first endorsed and is the ground for making him the rock of the Church.

The pronouncing of the Apostle blessed, the promise to found the Church upon him as the rock, and the sharp rebuke of Peter immediately afterwards, stand in a relation of extreme tension to each other in Matthew, which threatens to tear apart the factual connexion between the first and second Petrine sayings. Yet it may not be said that after the Ecclesia-saying to Peter, Matthew only outwardly follows the line of the Markan context which lay before him. He adopts it quite deliberately; in fact, he not only does not omit it as Luke does, but portrays the scene in even sharper outline than Mark does, as is shown by the indignant reply of Peter to this announcement of suffering and still more by the answer of Jesus: ὕπαγε ὀπίσω μου, σατανᾶ· σκάνδαλον εἶ ἐμοῦ ('You would lead me astray').[4]

---

[1] τότε for the linking together of a series of pericopes is well known to be frequent and beloved in Matthew. Cf., e.g., 3.13 and 4.1, where it is clear that the evangelist is concerned with a factual connexion, as in the first passage the linking word βαπτίζειν (3.11, 13 ff.) shows, and in the second the linking expression υἱὸς τοῦ θεοῦ (3.17; 4.3, 6).

[2] Cf. on this H. Lehmann, op. cit., pp. 44 ff.

[3] Cf. W. Wrede, Das Messiasgeheimnis, pp. 115 ff.

[4] σκάνδαλον, σκανδαλίζεσθαι are again terms most frequently used by Matthew, used repeatedly for seduction and apostasy in the congregation as phenomena associated with the end (thus 13.21, 41; 17.7; 24.10).

The question concerning the inner connexion of the whole pericope is thus clearly posed; we must not be satisfied with the conclusion that there is here an external linking up of disparate pieces of tradition. The conclusion then follows: the dialectic already clear in the Markan text between the dignity of Jesus as Christ and his suffering as Son of man is in no way abolished, or simply toned down by Matthew; it is for him, however, no longer an apologetic theologoumenon, but is of the highest importance for the Church itself. The position now is—and in this it differs from Mark—he who *is* already Christ and Son of God, is so as the suffering Son of man here on earth. As such he places his disciples on the way of suffering imitation (16.24 ff.; in Matthew addressed purely to the disciples). This very suffering Son of God and Son of man, however, is the Son of man-'judge of the world' who is soon to come, who will 'render unto every man according to his deeds' (16.27 f.).

If it is now asked what this whole context yields for the interpretation of the ἐκκλησία-saying in particular, the answer will have to be: it is obviously not simply a matter of the history of the tradition, but something in the mind of the evangelist of theological importance that Matthew anchors a saying that points to a time after Easter and possibly goes back to an Easter story, in the pre-Easter story of Jesus, and particularly in the framework of the context provided by Mark. The Church after Easter with its life and the office of the keys sanctioned by Jesus, is thus subjected to the law of the life and suffering of the earthly Jesus. If the decisions made by the Church are to be valid in the coming judgment it is clear that the forgiving and retaining of sins is thereby placed under the same standard as that of which 16.24–27 (κατὰ τὴν πρᾶξιν αὐτοῦ) speaks: imitation in suffering and life-devotion.[1]

This interpretation is confirmed by the context into which Matthew, in his discourse to the congregation in ch. 18, puts the saying about the office of the keys (there the whole congregation is entrusted with it): here clearly, with the demand expressed in ch. 18

[1] On Matt. 16.19 H. von Campenhausen (*op. cit.*, p. 137) altogether pertinently remarks: 'The saying is not based, for example, on a decision already fixed in heaven, by which the Church, for her part, has to be guided; it sets out rather, on the contrary, from the authoritative reality of the Church's judgment and decision, and promises that at the last day God will assent to it, recognise it as valid, and "ratify" it.' Yet this does not preclude in any way that Matthew, interpreting by means of construction, sets the saying, which has been handed on, in relation to the future judgment and the standard that will obtain there.

for turning and lowliness, for avoiding giving occasions of stumbling, there is given unmistakably the norm for the command of radical obedience and unlimited readiness for reconciliation, under which the whole life of the disciples, and at the same time also the exercise of the office of the keys which is entrusted to them in 18.18 stands.

Matt. 16.17–19 must therefore not be isolated, but must be understood in the whole context of 16.13–28. Now only can it be seen that the saying about Peter's (or the Church's) office of the keys not only expresses the fixing of the formal authority of the Church's decisions, which will in actual fact be adopted in the judgment of the world, but that it also contains the institution of the office of the keys by the Messiah-'Son of man' with the attention fixed on the judgment soon to be executed by him according to clear, unmistakable standards. The conception of the Church expressed in 16.17–19 finds its counterpart and basis in the Christology of the context of 16.13–28. From this suffering and rising Christ who in this aeon calls his disciples to an imitation of him which involves suffering, the Church is derived, is entrusted in the person of Peter with the keys of the kingdom of heaven, and, as the Church, is armed against the powers of death but in all her members still awaits the future judgment according to deeds.

Our investigation set out to examine the theological peculiarities and theme of Matthew's Gospel. It has attempted to show to what a high degree the first evangelist is an interpreter of the tradition which he collected and arranged. It should have become clear in the process that tradition and theological conception stand in a mutual relation to each other. Just as theology is placed at the service of tradition, the opposite is also true.

Matthew appears in his Gospel certainly, first of all, as the representative of a congregation. It is not adequate, however, to look upon his Gospel as simply the outcome of a congregational theology. The carefulness, and the planned nature of his work, point emphatically to an individual figure of primitive Christian literary history, even though the hunt for names and biographical traces is renounced. If one wishes to characterise him it can best be done by calling him, in the words of his own Gospel, a scribe 'who has been made a disciple to the kingdom of heaven and who is like unto a householder, which bringeth forth out of his treasure things new and old' (13.52).[1]

With the expression 'things new and old' a wealth of questions is

[1] The dative τῇ βασ. τ. οὐρ. can surely only be a dative of accommodation.

posed for research, the solution of which has long occupied scholars and will continue to do: about the literary sources which the Gospel uses, and the kind and aim of the oral tradition which preceded them; then the question of the relation of the Gospel to the figure, message and history of the historical Jesus. None of these questions can be divorced from the further questions: about the dependence of Matthew on Palestinian, and also—and this must not be under-estimated—diaspora Judaism,[1] similarly about its attitude to the Palestinian and Hellenistic primitive Church and its place in the history of the coming Great-church; and of ecclesiastical and hereti-cal Jewish-Christianity.[2] With these there is closely connected the difficult question of the ecclesiastical area from which Matthew derives.[3]

All these are questions which can by no means be disposed of wholesale as hopeless and theologically of no consequence, and in a cheap sort of way be sacrificed in the interests of the 'kerygma' or the 'doctrinal concept' of the Gospel.[4] If we have largely excluded these questions it is only because the investigation of our problem, which could not be carried through without a deliberate concentration, is also an indispensable presupposition for the answering of those questions.[5]

[1] Also its relation to the Jewish sects, the investigation of which has recently entered on a new stage, will also have to be examined afresh.

[2] J. Weiss, Das Urchristentum (Göttingen, 1917), p. 584 [ET History of Primitive Christianity, London, 1937, p. 736], and H. J. Schoeps, Theologie und Geschichte des Judenchristentums (Tübingen, 1949), pp. 64 f., 343 ff., correctly place Matthew's Gospel close to the Epistle of James; both are correctly separated by Schoeps from heretical Ebionitism. On Matthew and Paul cf. C. H. Dodd, 'Matthew and Paul', ExpT, 1947, pp. 293 ff.

[3] Obviously the only kind of area possible is one where the connexion of the Christians with Judaism remains and where the continuation of Palestinian traditions (Jewish and Christian) and also a strong diaspora-Jewish and Hellen-istic-Christian influence are operative. Against Jerusalem and Judaea there is the archaic (and in the Jerusalem Church soon no longer possible) Peter-tradition which Matthew has preserved. Hence there is much in favour of Syria (in a broad sense), yet amazement grows at what found room in this area, from Paul via Luke (and John?) to Ignatius. G. D. Kilpatrick argues, with considerable grounds, for a coastal town of Phoenicia, op. cit., pp. 124 ff.

[4] This observation is directed against a 'frame of mind' current in Germany, and is also intended to obviate a misunderstanding of the intentions of my own thesis.

[5] The manuscript of this essay was already written in the autumn of 1953. I can therefore only refer here to the instructive investigations of K. Stendahl, The School of St Matthew (Uppsala, 1954), and H. Ljungman, Das Gesetz Erfüllen (Lund, 1954), which appeared later. Yet I may remark that the latter has not proved me wrong in the view that Matt. 5.17 refers to Jesus' teaching and 3.15 to his obedi-ence. K. Stendahl's thesis that behind Matthew's Gospel there is a Christian

school of scribes I find completely convincing. Yet, at the same time, the treatment of the Christian tradition in Matthew's Gospel reveals a high degree of distinctive theological work, which Stendahl, in my opinion, considerably underestimates. I also regard as incorrect Stendahl's thesis that Matthew's Gospel should not really be called a Gospel (in the sense that Mark's is) but a manual of doctrine and administration in the Church (p. 35). W. Marxsen, admittedly (*op. cit.*, pp. 77–101), has convincingly proved that the concept εὐαγγέλιον is specifically Markan and is used differently by Matthew, and is not used by Luke at all. Yet this does not mean such a far-reaching difference as literature and historical species. Cf. my article 'Evangelien; synoptische' in *RGG*, esp. pp. 760–3.

I can also only enter briefly on the not very rewarding book by P. Nepper-Christensen, *Das Matthäusevangelium—ein judenchristliches Evangelium?* (Aarhus, 1958). The writer seeks to show that the view held in the ancient Church and down to the modern investigation, that Matthew's Gospel was written for Jews or Jewish Christians, is untenable and cannot be proved either by its linguistic character, or the 'thought of fulfilment' (quotations referring back to the Old Testament), or by the typology which is ostensibly characteristic of Matthew, or by a supposed particularistic bias in the matter of mission. In spite of some observations and arguments which are correct in themselves, I cannot regard the book as furthering the study. The way of posing the question about the circle of readers of Matthew's Gospel is already too narrow and at the same time too indefinitely taken up. The concept 'Jewish Christians', against which the author inveighs (that it does not mean what the early Christian history of the sects took it to mean has long been recognised), is not adequately clarified, nor does the book bring out the real theological problem and theme of Matthew, which actually unmistakably arose out of its tense and differentiated relation to Judaism (in dependence and struggle). Only by examining this question will an answer be found as to the congregation from which Matthew stems and for which it was written.

THE STILLING OF THE STORM IN MATTHEW

Günther Bornkamm

IT HAS INCREASINGLY become an accepted result of New Testament enquiry and a principle of all Synoptic exegesis that the Gospels must be understood and interpreted in terms of *kerygma* and not as biographies of Jesus of Nazareth, that they do not fall into any category of the history of ancient literature, but that in content and form as a whole and in matters of detail they are determined and shaped on the basis of faith in Jesus Christ. We owe the methodical establishing of this knowledge above all to form-critical research into the Gospels. This work put an end to the fiction which had for so long ruled critical investigation, that it would eventually be possible to distil from the Gospels a so-called life of Jesus, free from and untouched by any kind of 'over-painting' through the faith of the Church. Faith in Jesus Christ, the Crucified and Resurrected, is by no means a later stratum of the tradition, but its very foundation, and the place from which it sprang and grew and from which alone it is intelligible. From this faith in Jesus, the Crucified and Exalted, both characteristics of the primitive Christian tradition can be understood—the obvious pains taken to preserve the tradition about Jesus conscientiously and faithfully but at the same time the peculiar freedom with which this tradition is presented in detail.[1] The evangelists do not hark back to some kind of church archives when they pass on the words and deeds of Jesus, but they draw them from the kerygma of the Church and serve this kerygma. Because Jesus is not a figure of the past and thus is no museum piece, there can be no 'archives' for the primitive Christian tradition about him, in which he is kept. This insight into the nature of the tradition about

[1] Cf. J. Schniewind, 'Zur Synoptikerexegese', *TR* N.F. 2 (1930), pp. 161 ff. On the question of faith and history in the Gospels cf. G. Bornkamm, *Jesus of Nazareth* [ET, London, 1960], pp. 13–26.

Jesus is confirmed in detail again and again. The pericope which is here to serve as an example for making clear the evangelist's method of working is the story of the stilling of the storm.

The story is found in the first three Gospels: Mark 4.35–41; Matt. 8.23–27; Luke 8.22–25. It is reported by Mark and Luke in the same context and to all intents and purposes in the same form.[1] Mark begins with it a series of miracle stories which are geographically grouped around the sea of Galilee.[2] Mark had already prepared the scene around the boat in 4.1 (Luke—8.22—presents Jesus as now first entering the boat); the discourse on parables in chapter 4, which is only partly paralleled in Luke, has already taken place. Luke significantly concludes the discourse immediately after the interpretation of the parable of the sower and the sayings about the meaning of the parables as a whole (8.16 ff.) with the saying of Jesus about his true relations (those who hear the word of God and do it), which in Mark and Matthew occurs in another context (Mark 3.31 ff.; Matt. 12.46 ff.—Luke 8.19 ff.). Matthew links the miracle stories which are found in Mark 1 and 2, 4 and 5, with the Sermon on the Mount and arranges his material according to a principle which is indicated by the fact that the same sentences are used as introduction (4.23) and conclusion (9.35). Thus the nature miracle of the stilling of the storm is taken out of a biographical context and placed in a series which consists predominantly, though not exclusively, of healing miracles which set forth the 'Messiah of deed' after the presentation of the 'Messiah of the word' has already occurred in chapters 5–7 (Schniewind).

This characterisation of the story of the stilling of the storm as a 'nature miracle' does not, however, exhaust its meaning for Matthew. By inserting it into a definite context and by his own presentation of it, he gives it a new meaning which it does not yet have with the other evangelists. In Mark it bears more strongly than in Matthew the character of a straightforward miracle story. The storm and the peril at sea and the sleep of Jesus on a cushion in the stern of the boat are described with clarity and at length. The disciples' question, with which they wake him, has no kind of pious sound; it runs quite profanely: 'Master, carest thou not that we perish?' There then follow the word of Jesus with which he commands the wind to be silent, and

---

[1] The non-essential differences between Mark and Luke need not be considered here.

[2] J. Sundwall, *Die Zusammensetzung des Markusevangeliums*, pp. 29 f.

its miraculous effect; the question of Jesus which puts the disciples to shame: 'Why are you afraid? Have you[1] no faith?'; the awe of the disciples and their amazement: 'Who then is this, that even wind and sea obey him?' M. Dibelius has classified the narrative on account of these matters of style in a group which he calls 'tales', i.e. a literary group of narratives characterised by a special vividness and realism in presentation.[2] Pious motives are pushed into the background here. Jesus is to be seen as the great miracle worker. Jesus' word of command to the raging elements (καὶ διεγερθεὶς ἐπετίμησεν τῷ ἀνέμῳ καὶ εἶπεν τῇ θαλάσσῃ· σιώπα, πεφίμησο) is not only externally but in the inner structure of the narrative the centre of the whole. Everything here turns on the reality of the occurrence. The words καὶ ἐγένετο γαλήνη μεγάλη, which are in striking contrast to the description of the weather (4.37), and the words of confirmation from the astonished disciples similarly demonstrate it.

It must be admitted that in Matthew this characteristic of the story is not completely abandoned. In his case, too, though some of the novelistic details are omitted, the striking contrast between beginning and end (σεισμὸς μέγας—γαλήνη μεγάλη) occurs, and yet the story is made to serve a new motive and is modified in its course in a characteristic way. The evangelist brings out this new motive by the context in which he places the pericope. He puts before it the two sayings of Jesus about discipleship (Matt. 8.19–22), the first introduced by the offer of a scribe who wants to follow him, the second by the request of a disciple who first asks for leave to go and bury his father.[3] Both cases are concerned, however, with ἀκολουθεῖν, in the one case in the warning against an unconsidered decision and in the other in the summons to a radical decisiveness.[4] Matthew alone inserts the sayings in this context. And he alone introduces the story of the stilling of the storm with the words καὶ ἐμβάντι αὐτῷ εἰς τὸ πλοῖον ἠκολούθησαν αὐτῷ οἱ μαθηταὶ αὐτοῦ. Here, in distinction from the account in Mark, Jesus goes ahead[5] and the disciples follow him. The word ἀκολουθεῖν is the catchword which links the pericope with what has preceded. But this conclusion is obviously inadequate; the

---

[1] τί δειλοί ἐστε; οὔπω ἔχετε πίστιν; this should be the reading according to the best evidence. Cf. E. Klostermann and E. Lohmeyer *ad loc.*

[2] *Die Formgeschichte des Evangeliums*, 1959³, pp. 66 ff. [ET², pp. 70 ff.].

[3] On the form of the instances cf. R. Bultmann, *SynT*, pp. 55 ff.

[4] The third instance of discipleship in Luke 9.61 f. is not recorded in Matthew.

[5] Mark's statement can be explained on editorial grounds (linking up with 1); in Matthew and Luke the pericope has its original independence.

preceding sayings about discipleship rather serve to illustrate the meaning of what takes place in the stilling of the storm. Of course, there is no question of disputing that ἀκολουθεῖν in 8.23 bears in the first place the simple meaning of follow after, but at the same time it is given by the preceding sayings (8.19 f. and 21 f.) a deeper and figurative meaning. It would certainly be wrong to assume that the pregnant meaning which the word ἀκολουθεῖν already had had now suddenly in 8.23 lost its significance.

If this observation is correct it means: Matthew is not only a hander-on of the narrative, but also its oldest exegete, and in fact the first to interpret the journey of the disciples with Jesus in the storm and the stilling of the storm with reference to discipleship, and that means with reference to the little ship of the Church.[1] Certain details of the pericope which are only appropriate in Matthew agree with this interpretation. Only in his case is the disciples' cry for help an ejaculatory prayer: κύριε, σῶσον, ἀπολλύμεθα. The term of address thus designates him not only, as in Mark (διδάσκαλε) and Luke (ἐπιστάτα), with a human title of respect, but with a divine predicate of majesty. This is obviously the meaning of κύριε. It occurs in each separate pericope from 8.1 ff. (8.2, 6, 21), partly on the lips of those crying for help who know of the δύναμις (8.2) and ἐξουσία (8.8 f.) of Jesus,[2] and partly from the lips of the disciples (8.21).[3] This title of majesty occurs already in Matthew in 7.21 f. (in conjunction with τῷ σῷ ὀνόματι and as a term of address of the judge of the world), later on the lips of a disciple in 14.28, 30 (κύριε, σῶσόν με), 16.22; 17.4; 18.21; 26.22, and then ὁ κύριος in 24.42, etc.; and the term of address κύριε in 25.37, 44, denotes the coming judge of the world. The cry of the disciples in 8.25 is thus a prayer; κύριε contains a confession of discipleship.

A further peculiarity of Matthew's construction of the pericope with which we are concerned consists of the transposition of the accusing remark directed against the disciples and the miracle itself.

---

[1] Cf. on this usual and altogether legitimate exegesis from the time of the early Church (Tertullian de Baptismo 12; for further information see K. Goldammer, 'Navis ecclesiae', ZNW 40 [1941], pp. 76 ff.) the lovely remark of J. A. Bengel on the word πλοῖον: Jesus habebat scholam ambulantem et in ea schola multo solidius instituti sunt discipuli, quam si sub tecto unius collegii sine ulla sollicitudine atque tentatione vixissent. [Jesus had a travelling school and in that school the disciples were far more substantially provided for than if they had lived under the roof of one college without any anxiety and strain.]

[2] Cf. also 9.28; 15.27; 17.15; 20.30, 31, 33.

[3] The γραμματεύς in 8.19 calls him διδάσκαλε.

In Mark and Luke the miracle occurs first, in Matthew it follows after. Before the elements are brought to silence, thus in the midst a mortal threat, the word of Jesus goes forth to the disciples and puts them to shame for their little faith. The expression ὀλιγοπιστία (or ὀλιγόπιστος) is a favourite word of Matthew's; apart from Luke 12.28 he is the only evangelist to use it (6.30; 8.26; 14.31; 16.8; 17.20) and it always denotes a faith that is too weak, that is paralysed in the storm (8.26; 14.31) and in anxiety (6.30; 16.8), and thus is exposed as an appearance of faith (17.20) which is not sufficiently mature to withstand the pressure of demonic powers. Further, by the choice of this expression the special situation of the disciples, which in Mark is denoted by the question οὔπω ἔχετε πίστιν; becomes a typical situation of discipleship as a whole.

Hence it is not likely to be by chance that already in the introduction of the pericope Matthew reports the description of the stormy weather (Mark: λαῖλαψ μεγάλη ἀνέμου, cf. also Luke) with the expression καὶ ἰδοὺ σεισμὸς μέγας ἐγένετο ἐν τῇ θαλάσσῃ which is extremely unusual for a storm at sea, but often occurs as a designation of apocalyptic horrors (Mark 13.8; Matt. 24.7; Luke 21.11; Matt. 27.54, 28.2; Rev. 6.12; 8.5; 11.13, 19; 16.18). As the need of the disciples on the sea becomes a symbol of the distresses involved in discipleship of Jesus as a whole, so also in the same connexion the great peace which his word evokes takes on the meaning of the Johannine saying: ἐν τῷ κόσμῳ θλῖψιν ἔχετε, ἀλλὰ θαρσεῖτε, ἐγὼ νενίκηκα τὸν κόσμον (John 16.33).

Finally, it should be noted in our context that in Matthew it is not the disciples but the men who, by their astonished question in 8.27, confirm what has happened. Such 'choral endings' are a feature of the style especially of paradigmatic narratives in the Gospels.[1] The ἄνθρωποι in our passage, however, are obviously intended to represent the men who are encountered by the story through preaching. Their question corresponds, for example, to the acclamation with which the ἰδιῶται and ἄπιστοι reply to the preaching in the service of worship, according to I Cor. 14.25: ὄντως ὁ θεὸς ἐν ὑμῖν ἐστιν. The setting of the pericope is thus extended, its horizon is widened and from being a description of discipleship in which the disciples of Jesus experience trial and rescue, storm and security, it becomes a call to imitation and discipleship.

In more recent Synoptic investigation we have learned to look

---

[1] Dibelius, op. cit., pp. 54 f. [ET², pp. 57 f.].

upon the single pericope, the single saying and the single deed of Jesus as the primary data of tradition and to regard context and framework of the single pericopes on the other hand as secondary. We do not propose to attack these conclusions. It will be necessary to be more careful, however, than has generally been the case up to the present, to enquire also about the motives in the composition of the individual Gospels, as should be clear from the example of the stilling of the storm. Such efforts will only be fruitful in individual cases and care will have to be taken to guard against reading out of the text or into it more than is warranted. Unquestionably the evangelists worked to a large extent simply as collectors and often arranged the individual portions of the tradition according to relatively superficial points of view (geographical data, catchwords and the like). This makes all the more significant the proof of definite theological intentions such as the evangelist Matthew shows in the passage under consideration by the surprising combination of sayings about discipleship, the localisation of which in the context of the miracle stories has no other possible motive.

With all due reserve we are justified in drawing out these connecting links which are only hinted at by Matthew, and seeing in the story of the stilling of the storm a description of the dangers against which Jesus warns anyone who over-thoughtlessly presses to become a disciple: here is, in fact, the Son of Man who has not where to lay his head. At the same time, however, the story shows him as the one who subdues the demonic powers[1] and brings the βασιλεία of God[2] and who therefore can also demand and is able to reward the sacrifice of abandoning earthly ties such as stand in the way of the second follower. In this sense the story becomes a kerygmatic paradigm of the danger and glory of discipleship.

[1] ἐπιτιμᾶν is the regular expression for rebuking the threats of demonic powers, 17.18; Mark 9.25; Luke 9.42; Mark 1.25; Luke 4.35.

[2] The subduing of the flood by Jahweh and rescuing from the raging waves of the sea is already in the OT an illustration of the experience of the community. Cf. Pss. 29.3; 65.8; 89.10; 93.4; 107.25 ff.; 124.4 f. On this see J. Schniewind on Mark 4.35 ff.; E. Hoskyns, F. N. Davey, *The Riddle of the New Testament*, London, 1931, new edition 1952, pp. 91 ff.

MATTHEW'S UNDERSTANDING OF THE LAW

Gerhard Barth

IT HAS OFTEN BEEN rightly acknowledged and emphasised that the question of the law plays a special part in Matthew's Gospel; sufficient differentiation has not been made, however, between what belongs to tradition and what to editorial interpretation. It is the task of this investigation to demonstrate not only the evangelist's interpretation of particular sayings connected with the law, but his understanding of the law as a whole.

I. EXPECTATION OF THE JUDGMENT AND EXHORTATION TO DO THE WILL OF GOD

If the question is asked concerning the place of the law in Matthew's Gospel as a whole, the first thought that arises is the marked emphasis on the expectation of the judgment, and the exhortation to do the will of God. In none of the other Gospels is the expectation of judgment and the exhortation to the doing of God's will so prominent as in Matthew. Since this has often been observed and demonstrated[1] a short summary is all that is necessary here:

The statistics of Matthew's vocabulary already show among his favourite words and expressions a number that belong to the warning of judgment: κρίσις,[2] ἡμέρα κρίσεως,[3] μισθός,[4] εἰς τὸ σκότος τό ἐξώτερον,[5] ἐκεῖ ἔσται ὁ κλαυθμὸς καὶ ὁ βρυγμὸς τῶν ὀδόντων;[6] corresponding to these are others which emphasise obedience, the doing

---

[1] Cf. above all G. Bornkamm, above; also E. Haenchen, *ZTK* 48, pp. 38 ff., G. D. Kilpatrick, *Origins*, pp. 108 ff., Bacon, *Matthew*, pp. 412 ff.

[2] Matt. 12 times; Mark—; Luke 4 times.

[3] Matt. 4 times; Mark—; Luke—.

[4] Matt. 10 times; Mark once; Luke 3 times.

[5] Matt. 8.12; 22.13; 25.30.

[6] Matt. 8.12 (= Luke 13.28); 13.42, 50; 22.13; 24.51; 25.30.

of God's will: ποιεῖν τὸ θέλημα τοῦ πατρός,[1] δικαιοσύνη,[2] κελεύω,[3] τηρέω,[4] ἀνομία,[5] the ὑποκριτής[6] who is only outwardly devout is attacked; he who observes the commandments, on the other hand, is a φρόνιμος.[7]

Of the twelve duplicates in Matthew's Gospel, which cannot be derived from Mark and Q, six are relevant to our context: 5.29 f. = 18.8 f.; 7.16 ff. = 12.33 ff.; 10.15 = 11.24; 24.42 = 25.13; 3.10 = 7.19; 19.30 = 20.16. Their editorial character is, in most cases, obvious. Even if one is prepared to agree with Kilpatrick that they already occurred with special frequency in the liturgical usage of the congregation, this was nevertheless for theological reasons, and Matthew at least adopted them.

Among the Gospels only Matthew contains detailed descriptions of the final judgment: 25.31 ff.; 13.36 ff.; 7.21 ff. The interpretation of the parable of the tares among the wheat[8] furnished by Matthew is characteristic: the actual point of the parable, the exhortation to patience, is not touched in the interpretation. Instead, a description of the final judgment is given, which has a purely hortatory aim: membership of the Church means no security before the judgment, which will destroy the doers of lawlessness. The Church is a mixed body in which righteous and unrighteous are together. On the question of entrance into the kingdom, the Son of man-'judge of the world' decides according to one standard which is valid for all: whether God's will was done. Matthew repeats this thought at almost every opportunity: thus 22.11–14; good and evil are invited (22.10), but yet the unworthy is finally rejected.[9] In 16.27 Matthew

---

[1] Matt. 12.50 (= Mark 3.35); 7.21; 21.31; עשה רצון is a frequent expression in the Rabbinate (cf. Billerbeck I, p. 467).

[2] Matt. 7 times; Mark.—; Luke once.

[3] Matt. 7 times; Mark.—; Luke once.

[4] Matt. 6 times; Mark once; Luke—.

[5] Matt. 4 times; Mark—; Luke—.

[6] Matt. 13 times; Mark once; Luke 3 times.

[7] Matt. 7 times; Mark—; Luke 3 times.

[8] Cf. J. Jeremias, Gleichnisse, pp. 64 ff.

[9] 22.11–13 has obviously been added (cf. R. Bultmann, SynT, p. 189; J. Jeremias, op. cit., pp. 34 ff., 52 f.) by Matthew after the pattern of a Rabbinic parable (cf. Billerbeck I, p. 878); it corresponds entirely with the concern of 13.36 ff.; Matthaean peculiarities of language occur more frequently than elsewhere: εἰσελθών an introductory participial construction to link up with what has preceded is typical of Matthew; cf. E. Klostermann, Matthew, p. 10. θεάσασθαι: Matt. 4 times; Mark—; Luke 3 times. τότε: Matt. 90 times; Mark, 6 times; Luke 15 times, one of the most characteristic words. ἔνδυμα: Matt. 7 times; Mark—; Luke once. ἑταῖρε: in the NT in Matthew only, 3 times. δήσαντες

uses a brief suggestion of Mark (8.38) to underline independently the thought of judgment according to works. He has provided the parable of the drag-net with a similar interpretation to that of the wheat and tares (13.49 f.). The portions taken from Q and the special source serve the same concern: Matt. 3.7–10, 12; 7.13 f., 24 ff.; 8.11 f.; 10.15, 28; 11.20 ff.; 12.33 ff., 41 ff.; 12.36 f., and 21.28 ff. Everywhere the threat of judgment has a hortatory aim: to incite to the doing of God's will. The judgment threatens the disciples in particular. The hortatory direction of Matthew's interpretation is especially clear in his additions to the parable of the wicked husbandmen, in Matt. 21.41 and 43.[1]

Here, above all, the Sermon on the Mount calls for consideration, for by its place in Matthew's Gospel as a whole it gains a special importance. The Beatitudes in Matthew have already become a description of the 'virtues which the Christian should practise. They present a doctrine about the true heirs of the heavenly kingdom.'[2] From the saying about salt and light a hortatory admonition is drawn in 5.16.[3] 5.20 provides a heading for the interpretation of the commandments that follows, and at the same time, in a certain sense, the theme of the whole Sermon on the Mount: it concerns the 'better righteousness' as the condition of entrance into the kingdom of God.[4] Here the whole Sermon on the Mount should be written out, for in it Matthew returns again and again to this theme, and in the conclusion emphasises it with unsurpassable force in the sayings about the narrow gate in 7.13 f., about fruits in 7.16–20, in the description of the judgment in 7.21–23, and in the parable of the two builders in 7.24 ff.: what matters is the doing of God's will; this is all that is enquired about at the judgment; the commandments are the conditions of entrance into the kingdom of God, which the disciples are required to fulfil.[5]

ἐκβάλετε: when two actions belong jointly to an event, Matthew puts the aorist participle for the preparatory one and follows it with the aorist of the main verb: cf. A. Schlatter, *Der Evangelist Mt.*, p. 23. εἰς τὸ σκότος τὸ ἐξώτερον. ἐκεῖ ἔσται ὁ κλαυθμὸς καὶ ὁ βρυγμὸς τῶν ὀδόντων (cf. above).

[1] Note his alterations in the parable of the Sower. Mark refers to the fruit in an increasing series, showing the point to be the unexpected richness of the yield; Matthew reverses the series and thus interprets the parable in hortatory terms.

[2] M. Dibelius, 'Bergpredigt', *Botschaft und Geschichte*, p. 93.

[3] Construction of Matthew, cf. R. Bultmann, *SynT*, p. 92.

[4] Construction of Matthew, cf. R. Bultmann, *SynT*, p. 150; similarly 6.1.

[5] Reference here should be made to H. Windisch (*Sinn der Bergpredigt*), who

In the apocalyptic discourse of Matt. 24 and 25 this tendency is evident not only in the parables in 24.37 ff., 42 ff., 45 ff.; 25.1 ff., 14 ff. (the exhortations to watchfulness in 24.42; 25.13, are understood by Matthew as exhortations to the doing of God's will) and in the closing description of the judgment, but also in smaller modifications: ὑπομένειν εἰς τέλος in 24.13 here means being steadfast in ἀγάπη (24.12)! The mourning of the tribes of the earth in 24.30 strengthens the threat of judgment. The exhortations to watchfulness in Matt. 24.42 and 25.13 show particularly the displacement of the proclamation of Jesus. In this case the point was behaviour in face of the immediately imminent irruption of the rule of God. In Matthew this expectation recedes, exhortation comes to the fore.

The great debate with the Pharisees in Matt. 23 is determined by the same concern, that the will of God shall be done. E. Haenchen has demonstrated this in convincing fashion.[1] They are here accused not only because of their teaching, but because of their practice: they do not what they teach (23.3); there is a contradiction between their external pious appearance and what they actually are (23.5, 28); they leave the actual will of God undone (23.23 ff.). Haenchen establishes that the basic accusation against the Pharisees, under which Matthew embraces all the different elements, is that of hypocrisy.[2] This does not mean, as J. Schniewind thinks (p. 231), the objective self-contradiction, but, as 23.28 clearly shows, the contradiction between their outward appearance and their interior life. 'From this angle the essence of true piety as he [Matthew] understands it can be seen: men should not be at pains to gain the recognition of men, but of God.'[3] Admittedly Matt. 23 does not contain all that Matthew has to say against the Pharisees,[4] but it does become

---

strongly emphasises that the commands of the Sermon on the Mount are really regarded as demands to be fulfilled, 'conditions of entrance' into the kingdom of God. On the question whether they can be fulfilled cf. R. Bultmann's debate with Windisch in 'Die Bedeutung des gesch. Jesus für die Theol. d. Pls.', *TB* 8, 1929, pp. 137 ff.

[1] *ZTK* 48, pp. 38 ff.
[2] Matt. 23.13, 15, 23, 27, 28, 29, and 5a and 28 (construction of Matthew).
[3] E. Haenchen, *op. cit.*, p. 46.
[4] E. Haenchen really goes too far, when, on the basis of Matt. 23, he pronounces that the theologian Matthew has nothing of which to accuse the Pharisees, apart from their persecution of the Church, except their religious hypocrisy: 'The scribes and Pharisees are not the pious people that they claim to be' (p. 59). It should be noted that Matt. 23 is by no means the only debate the evangelist reports with Pharisaism. No less important alongside it is Matt. 12. There, in

clear here how deeply Matthew feels the concern that the will of God shall really be done. Matt. 23 also ends with the threat of judgment (23.33, 35 f.).

Thus in Matthew, more firmly than in the other Gospels, the warning of the judgment and the exhortation to the doing of God's will are emphasised. Hence the adoption by Matthew of sayings from the tradition has a theological meaning. At the same time it is clear that this marked emphasis must be grounded in the situation of the author, or alternatively, of his congregation. It is necessary to know this in order to understand his interpretation. Every false security which appeals to descent from Abraham (3.7–10) or to spiritual gifts (7.21 ff.) should be broken by the threats of judgment. The judgment stands inevitably ahead, and there everyone will be asked about his deeds (16.27). In this way the question of the soteriology of Matthew, and in this connexion, that of his understanding of the law, is posed.

II. THE ABIDING VALIDITY OF THE LAW

Matthew contains a number of sayings about the understanding of the law, which he found already in the Christian tradition.[1] We must start, however, from those statements which clearly demonstrate his own understanding, for even the sayings on the law which he adopts from the tradition may be understood somewhat differently by him. It is significant for his understanding of the law already that the

---

addition to the Messianic claim of Jesus, the understanding of the law is the point that drives the Pharisees to condemn Jesus to death. For this, see below. Besides, the accusation of hypocrisy should not be pressed theologically. In the first place it is the accusation 'which the Christian congregation of Matthew's time has taken over from the preceding generation' (Haenchen, p. 58); in the second, it derives from a time of embittered struggle, in which the Jews were only known as fanatical enemies. Thus Haenchen: 'Here all is at stake, and so arise those black and white colours, which can no longer see any good in the enemy' (p. 59). In such situations it is generally found that the enemy is accused of hypocrisy. Thus for *Did.* 8.1 the Jews are generally 'the hypocrites'. In Herm. *Sim.* 8.6.5; 9.18.3; 9.19.2 f. the heretics are called hypocrites. The same applies to the gnostic heretics in I Tim. 4.2, and Josephus denotes his enemies by the same term (*Bell.* 2.587). For Judaism Christians were generally styled as 'the hypocrites' (*Genesis Rabba* 48: כל חנופה שנאמר במקרא במינות הכתוב מדבר; cf. A. Schlatter, *Die Kirche Jerusalems vom Jahre 70–130*, 1898, p. 28). The accusation of hypocrisy must not on that account be disdained. Matthew is able to make so much more room for it here because it suits his major concern. It should also not be exaggerated.

[1] Matt. 5.18 f.; 23.2 ff., 23 f., 25 f.; 10.5b.

godlessness against which he fights is designated by a compound of νόμος: it is ἀνομία, lawlessness. Granted νόμος is also found in Luke, but there it is never—in contrast to Matthew—developed into a theological concept.[1] Matthew often inserts νόμος: thus 23.23 τὰ βαρύτερα τοῦ νόμου; 22.36 which commandment is the greatest ἐν τῷ νόμῳ; in 15.6 instead of λόγον (as Mark) he has put νόμον τοῦ θεοῦ.[2] The formula ὁ νόμος καὶ οἱ προφῆται is important; Matthew supplies it four times: 5.17; 7.12; 22.40; 11.13 (in the opposite sequence cf. Luke 16.16).

Matt. 11.13

In the present text of Matthew, 11.13 follows the saying about violence in 11.12. Both sayings obviously stood together in Q (Matt. 11.12 = Luke 16.16b, Matt. 11.13 = Luke 16.16a). The saying about violence is more originally preserved in Matthew's version: Luke 16.16b shows a refinement in comparison with Matt. and betrays a Lukan vocabulary.[3] The case of the saying about the law and the prophets, however, is different (Matt. 11.13); here the Lukan version is the more original, and Matthew has altered it[4]. The addition ἐπροφήτευσαν betrays a refinement in comparison with Luke 16.16a. On the other hand, it is unthinkable that the saying could have been handed on as a single saying in its Matthaean form (it does not belong to the saying about violence and is only loosely connected with it in Matthew), but it could in the form of Luke 16.16a. It is also impossible to explain why Luke should have altered the saying to the form in 16.16a. Thus, if one follows Conzelmann's interpretation of Luke 16.16 f., with reference to Luke's scheme of salvation-history, according to which until John there was 'only' the law and the prophets but from then on the preaching of the kingdom (op. cit., p. 14), 16.16a first acquires the meaning of this 'only' through the addition of 16.17. That means, however, that 16.16a must have been received by Luke in that form; otherwise he would have expressed his thought more clearly. However, if one rejects

[1] Cf. H. Conzelmann, Mitte der Zeit, p. 138.
[2] Although this reading is not so well attested (sin. C T^c 13, 124, 346, against B D a b ff^{1,2}e syr^cop arm eth Iren.; the Koine texts have τὴν ἐντολήν), it may be granted preference because of its agreement with Matthew's tendency. The reading λόγον is an assimilation to the Markan text.
[3] On the saying about violence cf. R. Bultmann, SynT, pp. 164 f., and recently W. G. Kümmel, Promise and Fulfilment, London 1957, pp. 121 ff.
[4] Thus W. G. Kümmel, 'Jesus und der jüdische Traditionsgedanke', ZNW 33 (1934), p. 129, note 89; E. Hirsch, Die Frühgeschichte des Evangeliums II (Tübingen, 1941), pp. 65 f.; E. Klostermann ad loc.

Conzelmann's interpretation one must agree with Hirsch[1] that Luke already received the group in 16.16–18 as a whole and inserted it here. But in that case, too, Luke has not altered 16.16a.

For what reasons, then, did Matthew alter it? Undoubtedly there is significance for him in his desire to incorporate the saying into the Baptist pericope. But the modifications within 11.13 cannot be explained by the context of 11.7–19. Matt. 11.7–11 had expressed the greatness and the limitations of the Baptist. From 11.12 it is no longer the Baptist who occupies the centre, but that which is new, the βασιλεία, which suffers violence. In 11.12 the Baptist simply marks a time boundary. 11.13 continues: 'for all the prophets . . . prophesied until John'; i.e. even this verse is not intended to call attention to the greatness of John as a prophet, but to bear witness to that new thing, which occupies the field since the days of the Baptist, and which all that is past only prophesied. Thus the point of 11.14 also is less to exalt the Baptist to the dignity of Elijah than much more to witness thereby to the irruption of the Messianic age. For this, however, the alteration of 11.13 was not necessary. In that case Matthew can only have recoiled from the saying itself; indeed, it maintains that the law and the prophets were only valid until John, and no longer after him![2] Such a statement is impossible for Matthew. If he is to accept the saying, he must alter it to avoid 'misunderstandings'. Hence the usual order of law and prophets is also reversed.

It is evident here already that the evangelist does not share the attitude of the Hellenistic churches to the law, but holds fast to the lasting validity of the law. Is the dispute about the law still alive in his Church? The adoption of a number of sayings which express a conservative attitude to the law is now seen to have more meaning for Matthew: these correspond—to some degree at least—to the evangelist's own view. The addition οὗτος γάρ ἐστιν ὁ νόμος καὶ οἱ προφῆται in 7.12 and ἐν ταύταις ταῖς δυσὶν ἐντολαῖς ὅλος ὁ νόμος κρέμαται καὶ οἱ προφῆται in 22.40 is now clear: it says that through these commandments the enduring validity of the law and the prophets is confirmed.

Matt. 5.17 ff.

The section was—at least to a considerable degree—already taken

[1] *Op. cit.*, II, p. 65.
[2] Cf. B. H. Streeter, *The Four Gospels* (London, 1924), p. 233; W. G. Kümmel, *ZNW* 33, pp. 129 f.

over by Matthew (on account of Luke 16.17 perhaps from Q). 5.18 obviously stems from the debate of the conservative (Palestinian) congregation with one not bound by the law (Hellenistic).[1] In the light of the understanding of the law in 5.18 one will have to agree with W. G. Kümmel: 'in this figurative saying the smallest letter of the Hebrew alphabet and the embellishments which were added to individual letters (תגין = little crown), are designated imperishable. With the same figure, however, the Rabbis described their faith that the Torah, with all the Rabbinic additions, was eternal: God spake —Solomon and a thousand like him will pass away but I will not permit the smallest stroke of thee to pass away (Exodus Rabba 6.2, §6.1). Since the saying in Matt. 5.18 not only reproduces the Jewish thought of the eternity of the law, but literally agrees with expressions of the Rabbis, it seems to me inadmissible to understand this verse in any but the Jewish sense' (ZNW 1934, p. 127).[2] To what extent did Matthew receive the contents of the saying from tradition?

On the analysis of 5.17 ff.: it is certain that Matthew found 5.18 already to hand, with the possible exception of the conclusion ἕως ἂν πάντα γένηται. For the ἕως ἂν πάντα γένηται of 5.18c there are the following possible interpretations: a. πάντα means the eschatological events, i.e. the clause says the same as 'until heaven and earth pass away', 5.18a; b. πάντα means the law or, alternatively, what the law demands.[3] On neither of these interpretations, however, could the clause have belonged to the original verse 18: according to the former, as a repetition of verse 18a which adds nothing, it is senseless, and further it blunts the edge of it, because ἕως ἂν παρέλθῃ ὁ οὐρανὸς καὶ ἡ γῆ in 5.18a simply means in the popular mind 'until the end of the world', which means never (E. Klostermann, ad loc.). The second interpretation also has a weakening effect, and that does not fit in with the original polemical intention of the saying. Even if

---

[1] Thus R. Bultmann, SynT, p. 138; B. H. Streeter, p. 256; W. G. Kümmel, art. cit., p. 127.

[2] H. Ljungman (Das Gesetz erfüllen, pp. 38 and 68 ff.) has indeed again recently denied this. The completeness with which the law should be kept is to be interpreted in the light of the righteousness of 5.20 as the uniting factor in the commandments. But may one interpret 5.18 in the light of 5.20? In 5.18 the 'completeness' of the law is determined by ἰῶτα ἓν ἢ μία κεραία, which Ljungman completely ignores.

[3] C. G. Montefiore's interpretation (The Synoptic Gospels, London, 1927², p. 52) with reference to the Messianic prophecies is ruled out because it is not called forth by anything in the context.

ἕως ἄν were not intended to denote a limit to the validity of the law but the goal until which the law must remain valid, yet that means a new thought beyond the polemical sentence of 5.18a plus b, and that is clearly only loosely connected with this one. 5.18c is therefore regarded by Klostermann and Montefiore as a later gloss; but this is only necessary if it cannot be understood as an addition by Matthew. The question then arises: Why did Matthew add it?

5.20 has been diagnosed by R. Bultmann as a construction of the evangelist.[1] In that case 5.19 and 5.18 were already found together by Matthew, for the leap between 5.19 and 5.20 is too great for both to have come from Matthew. Matt. 5.18 and 5.19 can well have stood together as a unit. Out of the sentence doubtless first constructed, a dogmatic one, entirely in keeping with the spirit of Judaism, a firm practical application is drawn in 5.19.[2] Did 5.17 belong to this original saying about the law? If 5.18 f. is shaped by the struggle between the conservative group in the congregation and that which had freed itself from the law, 5.17 could be understood in that light. Although the Christian teachers whom 5.18 has in mind obviously represented a doctrine like the one rejected in 5.17, that Christ has abolished the law, the point in dispute, that a part of the law has been declared invalid and treated as invalid, finds in 5.18 a more fitting echo: even the smallest part of the law will never perish. The prominence given to πληρῶσαι in 5.17 as outdoing οὐκ . . . καταλῦσαι takes the matter a step further.[3] In the actual question in dispute it no longer has any place. It follows, then, that 5.17 in its present form cannot have been conceived along with 5.18, but was

---

[1] *SynT*, p. 150; editorial heading for 5.21–48.

[2] To what does the demonstrative pronoun in μίαν τῶν ἐντολῶν τούτων τῶν ἐλαχίστων refer? Montefiore cannot see any commandments mentioned. Klostermann, Zahn, and Ljungman (p. 48) refer it to ἰῶτα and κεραία. Or should τούτων be explained in the light of the discussion, since the saying is a construction of the congregation? It is possible that behind τούτων there is a Semitism, as in the Rabbinate the demonstrative often stands for a general sense (cf. Matt. 18.6, 10, 14; 25.40, 45, and J. Jeremias, *Gleichnisse*, p. 25, n. 8); I owe the latter point to Prof. K. G. Kuhn.

[3] On the meaning of πληρῶσαι see below. πληρῶσαι does not mean here simply a οὐκ καταλῦσαι in the sense presupposed in the question in dispute in 5.18. According to Ljungman, p. 60, πληρῶσαι is meant to be an adequate and positive reply to καταλῦσαι, but he can only say that because καταλῦσαι does not have for him the meaning of the abolition of the law. He orientates καταλῦσαι rather to οἰκοδομεῖν, and it often appears as its opposite in the NT, it means then 'pull down'. Such circumlocutions, however, are unnecessary since the use of καταλύω as meaning 'destroy', 'annul',' render invalid', is adequately attested (cf. Bauer Arndt and Gingrech] *s.v.* καταλύω).

added later; between 17 and 18 there is a seam.[1] Further, 5.17 displays Matthew's linguistic usage in a striking way: μὴ νομίσητε ὅτι ἦλθον . . . οὐκ ἦλθον . . . ἀλλά[2]—τὸν νόμον ἢ τοὺς προφήτας—πληρῶσαι[3]—according to this, at any rate, 5.17 in its present form could well be a construction of Matthew's.[4] But at the same time 5.17 provides an interpretation by the evangelist of 5.18 which belonged to the tradition he received. This will be investigated in what follows.

The statement of Jesus in 5.17 is designed to meet a misunderstanding of the content of his mission.[5] Μὴ νομίσητε indicates that a conception exists which Jesus must reject. This conception is formulated to state that Jesus has come to abolish the law and the prophets. Matthew adopts thereby the concern of 5.18, the disavowal of antinomian tendencies.[6] At the same time he interprets: ἀλλὰ πληρῶσαι. The meaning of πληρῶσαι in 5.17 is hotly disputed. For a number of exegetes πληρῶσαι means set forth in its true meaning and in this sense 'complete'.[7] This interpretation has the advantage of combining 5.17 closely with 21–48, for it interprets πληρῶσαι basically in the light of 21–48. G. Dalman (*Jesus-Jeshua*, pp. 57 ff.) translates Matt. 5.17 back into the Aramaic mother-tongue of Jesus and thus explains πληρῶσαι in the light of קִיֵּם: to bring into effect, confirm, and because of 5.21–48, by teaching. P. Fiebig[8] similarly starts from קים and proceeds to classify πληρῶσαι with Rabbinic oath-terminology: Jesus declares that the law is binding, valid. A third group explains πληρῶσαι in

[1] νόμος in 5.18 also suits the question under discussion better than νόμος (καὶ) προφῆται. For this reason ἢ τοὺς προφήτας is deleted by C. G. Montefiore, W. C. Allen, G. Dalman (*Jesus-Jeshua* [ET, London, 1929], p. 62) and others. The seam between 5.17 and 5.18 is also observed by McNeile, *The Gospel according to St Matthew*, London, 1915, and G. D. Kilpatrick (*Origins*, p. 18).
[2] Cf. Matt. 10.34 ff., where the parallel in Luke 12.51–53 is more original. Matthew has refined the text and shortened it. Hence μὴ νομίσητε ὅτι ἦλθον also probably belongs to the linguistic peculiarities of Matthew.
[3] Matt. 16 times; Mark twice; Luke 9 times.
[4] B. W. Bacon also regards 5.17 as a construction of the editor (*Matthew*, p. 273).
[5] R. Bultmann (*SynT*, p. 138): the ἦλθον of 5.17 refers back to the activity of Jesus.
[6] Cf. A. Schlatter on Matt. 5.17: 'They had to conduct the same struggle in their own midst against those who in the name of freedom held the view: we may do anything.'
[7] Thus e.g. Wellhausen, Klostermann, Allen, Kümmel, M. Dibelius ('Bergpredigt', p. 125). In the reproduction of our word in Shabbat 116a it has the meaning: add, finish building (Hiphil of יסף); but πληρῶσαι does not have this meaning anywhere in the NT.
[8] P. Fiebig, *Jesu Bergpredigt* (Göttingen, 1924), p. 27.

the sense of 'doing', bringing into actuality by doing.[1] Since in the case of πληρῶσαι we are dealing with something that is specifically Matthaean, the deciding criterion with regard to all these interpretations can only be, in the first place, how far they agree with the context, and in the second how far they agree with the usual linguistic usage of πληρόω in Matthew and his environment. Hence E. Schweizer[2] rightly demands that πληρόω must be interpreted in the light of its use elsewhere by Matthew.

Matthew frequently uses the passive of πληρόω in connexion with quotations from the Old Testament, while in 5.17 and 3.15 he uses the active πληρῶσαι. According to the quotations the 'fulfilment' is achieved in the activity of Jesus. It concerns an eschatological Messianic event. But πληρωθῆναι τὸ ῥηθέν is achieved in an event, in something done; it denotes the realisation of what was uttered in the word. The use of πληρόω in the LXX means the same. With few exceptions πληρόω in the LXX reproduces מלא (nowhere קים).[3] Where πληρόω refers to a spoken or written word it means to bring this word to realisation by deed.[4] Hence the use in connexion with prophecies and promises: in I Kings 2.27 לְמַלֵּא אֶת־דְּבַר יהוה? = πληρωθῆναι τὸ ῥῆμα κυρίου, I Kings 8.15, 24; II Chron. 6.4, 15; 36.21, 22. According to H. Ljungman (pp. 27 and 36), πληρόω does not actually place the accent on carrying out or actualising, but on the state of the case, that *everything* will happen. One can agree with Ljungman that πληρόω includes the thought that everything will be fulfilled, but an accentuating of this kind, that πληρόω lays the emphasis on 'all' in contrast to emphasising the actualisation contradicts the passages quoted. When I Kings 8.15, 24; II Chron. 6.4, 15 sets what the Lord has spoken 'with his mouth' over against the 'fulfilment with his hands', the accent clearly lies upon the actualisation. The idea behind this is obviously that the actualisation necessarily belongs to the word, which without the actualisation remains 'void'. In the same way the use in connexion with the fulfilling of requests and

---

[1] Thus Zahn, Schniewind, Schlatter, *ad loc.*; the latter sees קים behind πληρῶσαι, with Dalman.

[2] 'Mt. 5.17–20, Anmerkungen zum Gesetzesverständnis des Matthäus', *TLZ*, 1952, pp. 479 ff.

[3] The reproduction of 'fulfil' and 'be fulfilled' by *malli* and *itmalli* in the Peshitta and Palestinian Evangeliarium agrees with this as G. Dalman (p. 53) shows.

[4] The only exception appears to be I Kings 1.14: πληρώσω τοὺς λόγους σου = confirm through the statement of another, empower. The idea here, however, is not that the word itself, but the two voices necessary for the testimony, must be fulfilled.

intentions in Ps. 19.5, 6 (LXX), is to be explained, and the carrying out of a saying or commission Jer. 51.25 (LXX), I Macc. 2.55. This agrees with the use in Philo: πληρῶσαι τοὺς λόγους ἔργοις ἐπαινητοῖς[1] and in the New Testament: Rom. 8.4; 13.8, 10; Gal. 5.14.[2] As the actualisation belongs to the prophecy, so it also belongs to request and command.

The interpretation of A. Schlatter and others, that πληρῶσαι = 'do', would agree well with this linguistic usage; but the context does not speak of Jesus' 'doing' of the law; in what follows it is rather the teaching of Jesus that is decisive. On the other hand, the interpretation represented by many exegetes, that πληρῶσαι means 'set forth the true meaning of the commandments', is also unsatisfying. In the way of this stands the common linguistic usage, according to which to 'fulfil' (πληρόω) a word does not mean to modify or clarify its contents, but to perform what the word says, bring it to actualisation. Hence the most acceptable way of understanding πληρῶσαι in 5.17 is: 'establish'[3] the law and the prophets. This complete establishing of the will of God, of the law by Jesus occurs here—corresponding with the context—by Jesus' teaching, as it is worked out in 5.20 ff. This interpretation is further supported by the following fact: the establishing of the will of God as *the* work of Christ plays an important part in the Christology of Matthew, as will be shown below. The use of πληρῶσαι in 3.15 corresponds to this,[4] for there it likewise means the complete establishing of the will of God.

---

[1] *De praemiis et poenis* 83; cf. *Or. Sib.* III. 246, Polyc. 3.3; Justin *Dial.* 12.3 πεπληρωκέναι τὸ θέλημα τοῦ θεοῦ; 93.2 ἐν δύσιν ἐντολαῖς πᾶσαν δικαιοσύνην καὶ εὐσέβειαν πληροῦσθαι; Preisigke, *Wörterbuch d. griech. Papyrusurkunden* (1925 ff.), II, 320.47 πλήρωσον τὸ κεκελευσμένον; different: Justin *Dial.* 45.1 πληροῦν τοὺς λόγους = (resume and) end words.

[2] Cf. Bauer, *s.v.*; Col. 1.25 also does not contradict this usage, cf. E. Lohmeyer *Kolosserbrief* (1953), *ad loc.* (pp. 80 f.). No more does Rom. 15.19, where πεπληρωκέναι does not refer to the word but to the activity of preaching. No more does Luke 7.1 concern us here, for the idea behind that passage is of a speech as a self-contained whole, which is fulfilled = completed. Notice that in the passages parallel to Luke 7.1 (Matt. 7.28; 11.1; 13.53; 19.1; 26.1) Matthew never uses πληρόω, but always τελέω. W. G. Kümmel builds his interpretation 'to bring to completion by teaching' (*ZNW* 33, p. 129) on Gal. 5.14, but passes by all other passages. But in Gal. 5.14 also πεπλήρωται = fulfil = do, as H. Schlier (*Galaterbrief*, 1949, p. 177) proves.

[3] More is meant by this than is contained in the rabbinic קים (= show laws to be valid by teaching); πληρόω has a more comprehensive meaning: the establishing of the law is by no means restricted to Jesus' teaching. It should also be said, with reference to E. Schweizer's thesis, that Matthew is thinking above all of the commandment of love.

[4] Cf. below, pp. 137 ff.

5.18c, ἕως ἂν πάντα γένηται, says the same. Here it is also confirmed that in both places Matthew's interpretation occurs. For of the two possible interpretations mentioned above the first (πάντα = the eschatological events of 5.18a) is unsatisfactory. Even if this interpretation accords without difficulties with the views of Matthew about the imperishableness of the law, and even if it seems from 24.34 linguistically the most obvious, it still remains difficult to explain why Matthew should have added this tautology. According to the second interpretation πάντα means that which the law demands. Linguistically, according to Zahn (p. 216) that is possible, and would better allow for the words to be understood as an addition. But what is it intended to say? That by his obedient activity Jesus did what the law demanded, in the sense that thereby the law was abolished (thus in the sense of Rom. 7.4; 8.4; 10.4) cannot be meant here. That the validity of the law was ended is precisely what Matthew contests.[1] The interpretation of B. Weiss, however, who understands it in terms of 6.10 does appear possible:[2] till God's will is wholly done. That means: ἕως does not express a limitation of the validity of the law, but the sentence is intended simply to express the goal, the aim of the whole event—the complete accomplishing of the will of God. Thereby a comprehensive goal is named, which the validity of the law serves.

It has now become clear that Matthew does not simply take over the sayings about the law (5.18 f.) and pass them on, but at the same time interprets them by incorporating them into the totality of his plan of salvation-history (5. 18c!) and linking them with his Christology. Jesus did not come to abolish the law but to establish it. This establishing of the will of God takes place here in 5.17 ff. through Jesus' teaching.[3] Jesus' teaching is thereby incorporated into a whole

[1] This renders unnecessary T. Zahn's interpretation, that the law was 'fulfilled' bit by bit by the historical development and became superfluous.

[2] The third petition of the Lord's Prayer may well be an addition by Matthew (thus B. W. Bacon, Matthew, p. 276; G. D. Kilpatrick, Origins, p. 21); the specifically Matthaean way of thinking would support this. On the linguistic question cf. Kilpatrick (p. 21): 'heaven and earth are associated twice in Mark (13.27, 31), once or twice in Q (Matt. 5.18; 11.25) and five times in Luke, in Matthew they are associated thirteen times (Matt. 5.34 f.; 6.10; 6.19; 16.19; 18.18 f.; 23.9; 24.35; 28.18)'. 'Thy will be done' not only expresses submission, but 'assent to the comprehensive execution of what God wills' (G. Schrenk, TWNT III, p. 55).

[3] Matt. 5.18 expressly declares that the letter is imperishable; Matthew, however, shows by the antitheses that follow and his whole interpretation of the law according to the love-commandment (see ch. III below) that he can only understand 5.18 figuratively, against its literal wording.

context about the establishing of the will of God, which runs through the whole Gospel, and in which the concern cannot then be simply the teaching of Jesus. By taking over 5.18 f., as well as by his own construction of 5.17, Matthew has made his own the concern of the conservative congregation in its struggle for the law. It must be concluded from this that for him, too, this struggle—with whatever shifts and modifications in the time after AD 70—is still acute. The extended interpretation itself which he associates with the saying shows how intense his interest in this question is. Thus the evangelist himself is also engaged in the struggle with those who wish to abolish the law, in opposition to whom he thinks he must emphasise its abiding validity.[1]

That the evangelist is engaged in discussion with those who wish to abolish part of the law the frequent use of πᾶς in contexts associated with the law will show:

23.3: πάντα οὖν ὅσα ἐὰν εἴπωσιν ὑμῖν ποιήσατε
3.15: πληρῶσαι πᾶσαν δικαιοσύνην
5.18: ἕως ἂν πάντα γένηται
28.20: τηρεῖν πάντα ὅσα ἐνετειλάμην ὑμῖν.[2]

23.3 was received by Matthew,[3] the other passages show to a considerable extent the hand of the evangelist.[4] The prominence given to 'All' is best explained in contrast to those who wished to abolish a part of the law. An interesting parallel to this is to be found in the Scrolls discovered in 1947 in a cave near Ain Feshcha in the neighbourhood of the Dead Sea.[5] Here there is a particularly

[1] H. J. Holtzmann also (*Lehrbuch der NT Theologie* I, 1911², p. 502) finds these battle-fronts in Matthew and goes on to the thesis that Matthew appropriated the slogans πληροῦν τὸν νόμον and καταλύειν τὸν νόμον from the language used by Paul in his teaching. The use of καταλύειν, however, with reference to laws and commandments is general (cf. Bauer, *s.* καταλύω). As far as I know the combination of πληροῦν with νόμος is not found anywhere else, but it is with ἐντολή, κεκελευσμένον, θέλημα θεοῦ, δικαιοσύνη. The question, whether the opponents of Matthew are a Pauline group, will have to engage us in the last chapter.

[2] Cf. further 7.12, where the πάντα may well also be due to Matthew; the Lukan version is more original than Matthew's.

[3] Cf. E. Haenchen, *ZTK* 48, p. 40. Matthew, no doubt, did not understand the verse literally (= Scripture and Tradition), but related the 'All' to the reproduction of the OT; cf. below, p. 85.

[4] On 3.15 and 28.20 cf. below, pp. 137 ff. and 131 ff.

[5] On this subject, recently, H. Braun, *Spätjüdisch-häretischer und frühchristlicher Radikalismus* I (Tübingen, 1957), p. 28. For the time of the origin of these writings the pre-Christian time has increasingly gained favour (cf. on this K. Elliger, *Studien zum Habakuk-Kom.*, Tübingen, 1953 and H. H. Rowley, *The Zadokite Fragments and the*

frequent use of כּוֹל in 1QS and 1QpHab. K. Elliger (*Studien zum Habakuk-Kom.*, p. 111) sees in this, with regard to 1QpHab., simply a sign of the passionateness of the expositor. This will also largely apply to 1QS, especially as there כּוֹל is often a purely customary addition, as, for example, in 4.3. This does not adequately explain, however, the special frequency, precisely in contexts concerning the law, in 1QS. The expressions run: everything, which he (God) has commanded or forbidden: 1.3, 4, 17; 5.1, 8; 9.25; everything evil: 1.4, 7; 2.3, 5; 5.1; 8.18; 9.21; everything good: 1.5; 2.2; every revelation: 1.8; 8.1, 15; 9.13, 19; every word of God: 1.13 f.; 3.11; (5.3; 9.25); all his (God's) ways: 2.2; 3.10; 4.2, 17; every law: 3.8; 5.7, 20, 22; 6.15; 8.1, 17; 9.3, 9; every deed of man: 3.25 f.; 4.1, 4, 15, 20 f., 23; 5.18 f.; 9.24; 11.16; all sins: 3.6, 7, 22; 11.14. This is best explained in terms of the contrast to an opponent who does not hold everything which according to the opinion of the sect belongs to the Torah. This is confirmed by the following: the chief mark of the sect is its special attitude to the Torah. Hence it is called the house of the Torah (בית התורה), *Dam.* 20.10, and consists of the men of truth, who keep the Torah (עשׂה) 1QpHab. 7.11; 8.1; 12.5; who are willing to do the חוקי אל 1QS 1.7, 15; 3.8; 5.20.[1] It looks upon itself in this matter as in opposition to official Judaism. This opposition can be understood—in the opinion of the sect—as nothing other than fundamental: the opponents hold a part of what for the sect belongs to the fulfilling of the law, as superfluous or as not commanded at all. When 1QS 1.14 forbids the altering of the times for meeting, there obviously lies behind it not only an irregularity but a settled general alteration of the times of the feasts.[2] We learn still more about this opposition to official Judaism in the Damascus Document, where the opposition to the introduction of alleviations is clear.[3] This sect also according to this document is engaged in a

---

Dead Sea Scrolls, Oxford, 1952). It has further been shown that the Damascus writing also belongs to the circle of these writings of heretical Judaism, even though its relationship to the Ain-Feshcha Scrolls still calls for much clarification in details (cf. K. Kahle, 'Die Gemeinde des neuen Bundes und die hebr. Handschriften aus der Höhle', *TLZ*, 1952, pp. 401 ff. and Rowley). In what follows the statements of the Damascus work are not simply equated with those of the Ain-Feshcha Scrolls, but are drawn on with them as far as possible to assist interpretation.

[1] Cf. further *Dam.* 6.4; 7.4 f.; 19.4; 1QS 6.6.
[2] Cf. K. Kahle, *TLZ*, 1952, p. 405, for references to calendar reform.
[3] Cf. *Dam.* 5.20 ff.; 4.17 ff.; 5.6 ff.; 20.25. Against alleviations in respect of marriage (4.21; 5.6 ff.) and Levitical purity (6.18; 7.3; 10.11–12.2; 12.12–18).

similar struggle against those who desire to abolish the law (in their opinion). Hence the emphasis on כול.

Matt. 7.12–27

Since 5.20 is constructed by Matthew as a heading for 5.21–48, 5.17–19 cannot also be a heading to 5.21–48. Rather 5.3–19 is seen to be one half of the framework into which the individual concrete directions of the Sermon on the Mount in 5.20–7.12 are fitted. The Golden Rule in 7.12 summarises with οὖν[1] all the preceding directions in the command of neighbourly love and continues: for this is the law and the prophets. In that way 5.17 ff. is taken up again: the directions between the brackets are the contents of the law and the prophets, and conversely they confirm their enduring validity.

The interpretation of the demand of God is thus concluded. From 7.13 onwards there follow concluding exhortations to the doing of the will of God as thus set forth. Among them 7.15 ff. and 21 ff. in particular call for special consideration. From 7.16 onwards Matthew again follows a context which lay before him in Q and which he expands by insertions. Before the figure of the tree and the fruit he puts in 7.15 a warning against false prophets, who are not simply announced here as to appear in the future (as in 24.11, 24), but are regarded as a present danger. The figure of the sheep's clothing says more than that they look harmless. The sheep are Christians[2] and the false prophets claim that they are real Christians, and outwardly can hardly be distinguished from them. Thus there is at the basis of this passage a similar understanding of the Church to that in Matt. 13.24 ff., 36 ff.[3] But who is meant by the false prophets?

As ritual purity is also especially emphasised in 1QS, this opposition is also seen there. In *Dam.* the emphasis on כול is displaced by the emphasis on the exact interpretation of the law (פרוש התורה 4.8; 6.14, 18, 20; 13.6; 14.17, 18). That does not mean any alteration in principle, however, but obviously only a further development of the question under the influence of apologetics. *Dam.* also fights against the same opponents, who wish to 'move the boundary' (1.16; 5.20; cf. 19.16 and 20.25); by the boundary the Sinai-law is meant according to 1.16.

[1] For this reason the meaning of οὖν is often not understood, E. Klostermann: 'in its present position . . . it has no deeper justification'! Cf. W. C. Allen; A. H. McNeile *ad loc.* is correct: 'οὖν is not in logical sequence with 7.11 but sums up the Sermon to this point.'

[2] 7.15 is surely a construction of Matthew (cf. R. Bultmann, *SynT*, p. 124); πρόβατον is a favourite word of Matthew's, used eight times as a figure for the faithful, or alternatively, the congregation.

[3] In contrast to 13.24 ff., 36 ff., in 7.16 ff. marks are named by which the 'wolves in sheep's clothing' can be recognised.

In the figure of the tree and the fruit, which Matthew uses again in 12.33 ff. in another context, only 7.16b and 18 are taken directly from Q. Matt. 7.17 is a pedantic positive new construction to offset the negative statement in 7.18.[1] In 7.19 Matthew has inserted a threat of judgment after the pattern of 3.10, and by 7.16a and 20 he links the section with the warning against the false prophets: he now offers the criterion by which they can be recognised: they yield no fruit, do no good works.

What follows from this with regard to the false prophets? That they yield no fruit, i.e., fail to do the will of God, is not intended here simply to discredit them ethically, but to strike a blow at their teaching. Of course, it is a common thing elsewhere simply to belabour heretics with moral accusations,[2] but the connexion with the following verses, in 7.21–23, shows that it is not simply a matter of formal, conventional accusations.

As the basis of Matt. 7.21 there is a saying from Q, which has been retained in a more original form by Luke (6.46) and has been completely altered by Matthew. Above all 7.21b shows his editorial hand: in the expression 'he that doeth the will of my Father which is in heaven' he again shows his central concern. With that is linked a further saying from Q (7.22 f. = Luke 13.26 f.), which again Matthew has considerably altered. He actualises the saying by relating it to the false prophets (ἐπροφητεύσαμεν), i.e. imports the situation of his congregation into the saying. The series of exhortations to do God's will, which begin in 7.13, is concluded in 7.24–27 by the parable of the two builders.

A. Schlatter (ad loc.) thinks the false prophets were Zealots. His chief reason is historical: during the Jewish revolt there are repeated reports of Zelotic prophecy (for this reason the Pharisees withdraw). But this contradicts the Matthaean text, where the false prophets confess Jesus, effect their prophecies and miracles 'in his name', and call him κύριε, κύριε. In 7.23 they are designated ἐργαζόμενοι τὴν ἀνομίαν. Granted that with ἀνομία Matthew apparently reproduces the LXX text of Ps. 6.9, but ἀνομία belongs to his favourite words, and besides he by no means assimilates the whole sentence in 7.23b to the LXX text: in ἀπόστητε ἀπ᾽ εμοῦ πάντες it is Luke, rather,

---

[1] Cf. R. Bultmann, *Syn T*, p. 95.

[2] Cf., above all, the Pastoral Epistles (I Tim. 4.1 ff.; 6.3 ff.; II Tim. 3.5, 13; Titus 1.15 f.), where it has hardly to do with libertines; cf. M. Dibelius, *Pastoralbriefe* (Handbuch zum NT, Tübingen), additional note on I Tim. 4 about the heretics in the Pastoral Epistles.

who reproduces the LXX text. The false prophets are thus clearly designated antinomians. The other marks agree with that: they fail to do the will of God (7.21), they yield only bad fruits (7.16 ff.). In this way in 5.17 ff. and 7.15 ff., Matthew has put the Sermon on the Mount in brackets, which are clearly directed against the antinomians, and thus he understands the whole Sermon on the Mount in relation to the question about the law.

Matt. 24.10 ff.

Matt. 24.10 ff. speaks of the same false prophets. As Matthew has already made use of Mark 13.9–13 in the missionary discourse, he gives here only a brief summary, yet from different viewpoints. For Matt. 24.10 f., Mark 13.12 and 22 provided the basis; 24.12 furnishes the thought of increasing unrighteousness during the Messianic Woes, which was current in apocalyptic teaching.[1] Matthew, however, uses these portions to characterise the experience of the congregation with the antinomian heretics, as belonging to the confusions of the End. The words associated with the antinomian struggle appear: ψευδοπροφῆται, ἀνομία, ἀγάπη, πλανήσουσιν, σκανδαλισθήσονται.[2] The false prophets here are not the same as in 24.24, but are the antinomian heretics again, who threaten the true life of the congregation.[3] Antinomianism is there once again most sharply condemned, in that its Satanic origin is exposed, for the confusions of the End are a last rearing of Satan's head. At the same time it is shown once again how important this problem is to the evangelist, when he shapes even the Apocalyptic Discourse under this viewpoint.[4]

III. THE INTERPRETATION OF THE LAW

1. *The significance of the love-commandment*

Despite the conclusion thus reached, that Matthew's understanding of the law is largely determined by his opposition to the antinomians,

---

[1] Cf. II (4) Esd. 5.2, 10; *I Enoch* 91.7; II Thess. 2.3; II Tim. 3.1 ff.

[2] σκανδαλίζειν belongs to the special vocabulary of Matthew: 14 times, Mark 8 times, Luke twice; σκάνδαλον: Matthew 5 times, Luke once.

[3] The opposite to ἀνομία is here ἀγάπη; that corresponds entirely with Matt. 22.34–40! Who are the 'many' whose love grows cold? Obviously simply 'most', the majority of the congregation. The expression must be interpreted in the light of Matthew's understanding of the Church, as it is expressed in 22.14 and 7.13 f.

[4] There is probably an allusion to the antinomians in 13.41 τοὺς ποιοῦντας τὴν ἀνομίαν; here as in 24.10 σκάνδαλον or σκανδαλίζεσθαι occurs in conjunction with ἀνομία; cf. J. Weiss, *Die Schriften des NT*, I, Göttingen, 1916³, *ad loc.*

this is by no means his only battle-front. Through the whole Gospel there likewise runs an opposition to Pharisaism and the Rabbinate. But if the struggle against the antinomians led Matthew to the defence of the irrevocable validity of the law, is it still at all possible for him to maintain a genuine opposition to the Rabbinate with regard to the question of the law? Must not that lead him to an understanding of the law which differs scarcely, if at all, from that of the Rabbinate, so that he can only accuse the Pharisees of not doing the law (rightly understood), that they are not in reality the pious people that they claim to be? Matthew himself raises this accusation with emphasis (3.7–10; 21.28–32, 33–46; 23.1–36). If it were so, his Christianity would be in fact 'nothing else than a strict Pharisaism purified from failure in practice'.[1] The evangelist, however, regards himself as in opposition to the Rabbinate also with regard to the understanding of the law. The discussion of the schools about the greatest commandment has become with him a contention (22.34 ff.). The great conflict between Jesus and the Pharisees in Matt. 12 arises, in the first half of the chapter, out of the question of Jesus' attitude to the commandment concerning the Sabbath (12.1–14).[2] The new interpretation of the law in 5.21 ff. also takes on, through 5.20, a direction opposed to the Pharisees, and 16.12 warns against the teaching of the Pharisees.[3]

The prominent place of the commandment of love in the first Gospel has been repeatedly noted.[4] In the light of the commandment of love in Matthew his opposition to the Rabbinate will become clear.

Matt. 22.34–40

Here again our interest is confined to Matthew's characteristic alterations, i.e. what the evangelist has done with the material he received.[5] Out of the discussion of the schools in Mark a contention

---

[1] Thus E. Haenchen, *ZTK* 48, p. 61.

[2] The attitude of Jesus to the Sabbath-question leads to the decision to kill him in 12.14. True, that is taken over from Mark, but it gains added weight through the piling up of the debate in ch. 12.

[3] Cf. Mark and above all Luke, who interprets the saying with reference to the hypocrisy of the Pharisees. E. Lohmeyer *ad loc.*: 'Matthew dogmatises, Luke moralises.'

[4] Cf. Matt. 5.43 ff.; 7.12; 22.34 ff.; 24.12; 19.19; cf. further the quotation from Hos. 6.6 in Matt. 9.13 and 12.7.

[5] G. Bornkamm ('Das Doppelgebot der Liebe', *Neutest. Stud. für R. Bultmann*, pp. 92 f.) has shown that Matthew can scarcely have had our present Markan text before him. That does not mean that within Matt. 22.34–40 editorial modifications by Matthew cannot be recognised, especially in 22.40. On Matthew's alterations cf. G. Bornkamm, *op. cit.*, p. 93.

has arisen: the Pharisees pose the question about the greatest commandment, to tempt Jesus. Wherein did Matthew see the element of temptation in this question? He cannot have seen it in the fact that Jesus might improperly displace some first commandment or other, might give the commandment of neighbourly love an improper precedence over the command to love God. Judaism nowhere shows that kind of scruple, but can, without any qualms, summarise the law in the commandment of neighbourly love. The slant of the text, however, points most markedly in another direction. The chief emphasis does not lie on δευτέρα ὅμοια αὕτη but in 22.40 on ὅλος ὁ νόμος and ἐν ταύταις ταῖς δυσίν, i.e. in the concentration of the whole law on one point, in which everything is contained. As the Rabbinic equivalent of κρέμαται means the exegetical deduction of a Halakah from a given portion of Scripture (תָּלוּי),[1] the meaning could be: the whole law and prophets can be exegetically deduced from the command to love God and the neighbour, they 'hang' exegetically on these. The emphasis would then lie only on the fact that the possibility exists of deriving the whole law from these; there would be no reference to the precedence of either. The objection to this is that it leaves entirely beyond comprehension wherein the element of temptation lies, but even more, that by μεγάλη καὶ πρώτη a precedence of these two over all others is expressed.

The Rabbinate also occasionally recognises a summary of the law in one or a few central commandments, but this summary, like the distinction between easy and difficult commandments, has no fundamental significance.[2] In principle each commandment is as important as the rest; in fact, for the Rabbinical understanding of the law there can be no question of raising one commandment above the others in importance. The Rabbinate stated this many times.[3] The danger

---

[1] Cf. Billerbeck, I, pp. 907 f., but above all the saying of Bar Qappara, Berakoth 63a: 'What is the smallest portion of Scripture on which all the regulations of the Torah hang (שכל גופי תורה תלוין בה)? In all thy ways remember him . . .'; further Hagigah 1.8: 'The Halakoth concerning the Sabbath . . . are like mountains which hang on a hair (בְּשַׂעֲרָה הַתְּלוּיִן) for there is little Scripture to support them but many Halakoth.'

[2] Cf. Hillel's statement Shab. 31a, Aqiba, on Lev. 19.18 (Sifra, Lev. 19.18); cf. W. Gutbrod νόμος, TWNT IV, p. 1051, E. Lohmeyer, Markus, ad loc.

[3] The distinction between easy and difficult commandments (מִצְוֹת קַלּוֹת and חֲמוּרוֹת) led to the distinction between important and less important commandments (מִצְוָה גְדוֹלָה and זְעֵירָא); cf. Billerbeck, I, pp. 901 f. Nevertheless the invariable tendency is to equate them, cf. Aboth 2.1b: 'Behave towards an easy

which arises from this can be seen even by the Rabbinate, but according to the formal understanding of the law there is no possibility of avoiding it.[1] In Mark already the summary in the love-commandment has a different meaning, namely a fundamental one.[2] The two commandments in Deut. 6.5 and Lev. 19.18 are not only the greatest, but the whole law and the prophets 'hang on them' 'like a door on its hinges' (Bauer on κρεμάννυμι). They are the basic norms, in the performance of which all others are performed, they are the essence of the law. The formal understanding of the law, according to which all the commandments are equally important and formally must be performed and can be performed, is thus abandoned (that applies also to the imperishable κεραία Matt. 5.18!). Only in this way can it be explained how Matthew could make a contention out of it.

If in this way the essence of the law is found in the love-commandment in Matt. 22.34–40, the question arises how far Matthew drew the consequences from this knowledge. Only in this way will it become clear how far he has here really left the Rabbinic understanding of the law.

According to G. Bornkamm,[3] Matthew raises the love-commandment to be the canon for the interpretation of the whole Torah. In what follows we shall enquire how far this is correct.

---

commandment (מִצְוָה קַלָּה) exactly as towards a difficult one (הַמּוּרָה); for you do not know what reward will be given for the commandments.' In Jer. *Kiddushin* 1.61b R. Abba bar Kahana said: 'The Scriptures make the easiest among the easy commandments equal to the hardest among the hard (השוה הכתוב מצוה קלה שבקלות למצוה חמורה מן תהמורוח).' *Tanḥuma* עקב 5b: 'Lord of the world, I am not afraid because of the important commandments . . . because they are important. On what account then am I afraid? On account of the small commandments, perhaps I should like to transgress one of them . . .' Further examples: cf. Billerbeck, I, pp. 902 ff., J. Abrahams, *Studies in Pharisaism and the Gospels* I, 1917, pp. 24 ff.

[1] Cf. the saying of Johanan ben Zakkai, Bab. *Hagigah* 5a: 'Woe to us that the Scripture attaches the same weight to the easy as to the hard (אוי לנו ששקל עלינו הכתוב).' On this see A. Schlatter, *Jochanan ben Zakkai*, Gütersloh, 1899, p. 37: '. . . (it) is significant in the saying, that it is not the difficult which is felt to be hard, but rather that the easy, which is in itself of little significance, is placed alongside the difficult by the Scripture, without differentiation. The question of the "great commandment" is there; Johanan rejects it absolutely, because the Scripture itself does not answer it.'

[2] Cf. E. Lohmeyer *ad loc.*; W. Gutbrod, *TWNT* IV, p. 1055; J. Abrahams, *ibid.*

[3] G. Bornkamm, 'Das Doppelgebot der Liebe', *op. cit.*, p. 93, cf. also 'End-expectation and Church', above, pp. 31 f.

Matt. 12.9–14

Matthew takes over the second polemical conversation about the Sabbath question from the Markan basis, but he introduces some characteristic modifications. In 12.10 he substitutes for the lying in wait of the Pharisees a direct, significantly worded question which asks what is allowed by the law.[1] Here again his interest in the question of the law is evident. In 12.11–12a an isolated saying about the Sabbath is inserted.[2] In Mark 3.1–5 the context is complete and does not need any such amplification. Why did Matthew insert it? The alteration in 12.12b does away entirely with the point of Mark 3.4 and takes away from the reply of Jesus something of its radical nature. Instead of that a positive rule for the behaviour of the congregation on the Sabbath is introduced with ὥστε ἔξεστιν, and the way is prepared for this by the question εἰ ἔξεστιν in 12.10. As this cannot be explained from the text which Matthew received, it must be regarded as having been done deliberately by him. Now the insertion in 12.11–12a can also be understood: if Matthew wanted in 12.12b a positive rule for the behaviour of the congregation on the Sabbath he needed a new basis for it, and this 12.11–12a now provides.[3] In the rule of 12.12b two things stand out: on the one hand it assumes that in the congregation the Sabbath is still kept, on the other καλῶς ποιεῖν (influence of Mark 3.4 ἀγαθὸν ποιῆσαι— κακοποιῆσαι), i.e. the love-commandment, is placed above the Sabbath commandment. Matthew thus knows very well how to draw the consequences from 22.40. The interpretation of the Sabbath commandment by the love-commandment leads to the limitation of the former and this is expressed in a positive rule in 12.12.

Matt. 7.12

Matt. 7.12 clearly shows the significance of the love-commandment as the principle of interpretation for the whole of the law and the prophets. The significance of 7.12 as a summary of the directions of the Sermon on the Mount was mentioned above.[4] Here it is only necessary to add that by 7.12 the directions of the Sermon on the

[1] On ἔξεστιν cf. Matt. 14.4; 19.3; 22.17; 27.6; Luke 14.3; Acts 16.21; 22.25, etc.; further A. Schlatter, *Matthäus*, p. 393.

[2] Cf. R. Bultmann, *SynT*, p. 12.

[3] It should be noted that Matt. 12.11 refers to an alleviation which was not generally recognised. As is well known, there was here a stricter and a milder course. Here Matthew appeals to the milder! Cf. Billerbeck, I, pp. 623 ff.; further *Dam.* 11.13.

[4] See above, p. 73.

Mount are once again interpreted, and that in the sense of the love-commandment. All the preceding directions of the Sermon on the Mount, which are concluded by 7.12, are thereby subordinated to the love-commandment. This is the ground and secret goal of all the commandments. Thus the interpretation[1] of Windisch also falls to the ground, for he deduces from the formal agreement with the saying of Hillel (*Shab.* 31a),[2] that the understanding of the law in the Sermon on the Mount remains entirely within the framework of the Jewish religion of law. The significance of the love-commandment for Matthew is seen once again in the Sermon on the Mount in 5.43 ff. By the saying about perfection in 5.48, 5.43–47 is denoted as the climax of the six antitheses. The perfection of the disciples is shown in their undifferentiating observance of the commandment of love towards friend and foe. That is the περισσόν (5.47) which distinguishes them. It follows from this that in connexion with the 'better righteousness' demanded in 5.20 the love-commandment is thought of most of all.

Matt. 23.23 is also concerned with the interpretation of the law. τὰ βαρύτερα τοῦ νόμου is clearly an editorial insertion, whereas in connexion with the 'Old Testament' combination of κρίσις, ἔλεος and πίστις the question arises whether this is the original form over against Luke 11.42, or the Old Testamental-Jewish expression of Matthew.[3] By the insertion of τὰ βαρύτερα τοῦ νόμου Matthew gives expression to a different valuation of the individual parts of the law: judgment, mercy and faith are expressly assessed by the evangelist as the weightier commandments and put before all others. Here, of course, it is not directly the commandment of love according to which the whole of the law is to be expounded but a somewhat larger circle of basic demands: judgment, mercy and faithfulness.[4]

15.16–20 is also concerned with the interpretation of the law. Matthew has reduced the catalogue of vices in Mark to commandments of the decalogue.[5] The ceremonial law is subordinated to these

---

[1] *Der Sinn der Bergpredigt*, p. 47.

[2] *Shab.* 31a: What you do not wish to happen to you, do not do to another. That is the whole Torah and all the rest is explanation; go and learn!

[3] The conclusion 'these ye ought to have done, and not to have left the other undone' is wanting in the text of Luke in D and Marcion. It is too much to conclude from this, however, that it was wanting in Q (Klostermann). It fits in entirely with the whole of the saying, which obviously stems from the Jewish-Christian congregation (E. Haenchen, *ZTK* 48, pp. 48 f.).

[4] On πίστις in Matt. 23.23 cf. below, p. 114.

[5] On 15.1–20 cf. below, pp. 86 ff.

commandments and the washing of hands is declined in their favour (15.20). The norm of interpretation is also here somewhat wider, even though the significance of the love-commandment is shown in the sharpening by Matthew of the accusation connected with the commandment concerning love of parents (15.5 f.): οὐ μὴ τιμήσει = 'he has no need to honour'. In all these cases it is the interpretation of the law by which Matthew differentiates himself from the Rabbinate; the love-commandment has become the deciding principle in the interpretation of it, even though a somewhat wider norm (15.19; 23.23) can come in alongside it.

Matt. 12.1–8

The understanding of 12.1–8 is more difficult, however widely recognised the influence here, too, of the love-commandment is. Again the Markan text is provided with modifications and additions. In 12.1 the evangelist has inserted ἐπείνασαν (cf. the parallelism of 12.3). He shows in this way that the freer sense of the Markan text, in which the absolute binding force of the law is no longer recognised,[1] cannot be upheld by him: the disciples did not wantonly break the Sabbath.[2] From this it follows again that in Matthew's congregation the Sabbath was still kept, but not in the same strict sense as in the Rabbinate. Thereby, however, Matthew renders the understanding of the section difficult—it means either: the disciples were in need and were therefore justified in breaking the commandment; but it could never be his opinion that God's commandments could generally be broken in time of need (cf. 10.32, 39; 16.24 ff.!). Or else: in the Rabbinate when life is in danger help may be given even on the Sabbath to the person concerned;[3] the disciples did just that kind of a work of necessity; they thus remained within what was allowed by the Rabbinate. But that completely contradicts the appeal to David, for he transgressed a completely different commandment![4] Further the accusation in 12.2 presupposes that hunger was not regarded as an adequate reason by the Pharisees. These difficulties have arisen because Matthew has inserted ἐπείνασαν. It is intended

[1] Cf. E. Lohmeyer, Mark, ad loc.
[2] Cf. G. D. Kilpatrick, Origins, p. 116.
[3] Cf. Billerbeck, I, pp. 623 ff.
[4] According to some Rabbinic passages (Billerbeck, I, pp. 618 f.; B. Murmelstein, Jesu Gang durch die Saatfelder, Angelos, 1930, p. 112) David's action did take place on the Sabbath, but no reference is made to this in Mark 2.25 f. = Matt. 12.3 f. (cf. Lohmeyer, Mark, ad loc., p. 64); it is not that David ate on the Sabbath, but that he ate the consecrated shewbread, that is emphasised.

to guard against the conclusion that *everything* is permissible on the Sabbath. On the contrary, the insertion must not be evaluated in such a way as to suggest that Matthew wished to remain entirely within the framework of the Pharisaic understanding of the law,[1] as was seen above. He will have understood the verses, then, in the following way—it is not, that need knows no commandment, but rather the question is: what is God's commandment? The Sabbath commandment is not intended in such an absolute way as to forbid the allaying of hunger. But even with this, the only possible explanation, the link with the evidence from David is only weak.[2]

In 12.5 Matthew has added another proof from Scripture, which at first agrees with the Rabbinic teaching that urgent Temple duty takes precedence over the Sabbath. In 12.6 the application is drawn from this: τοῦ ἱεροῦ μεῖζόν ἐστιν ὧδε, where undoubtedly Jesus is meant,[3] for in him the Messianic fulfilment and consummation has come and he is therefore more than the Temple. But the weakness of the comparison with Temple duty is that the plucking of the ears of corn cannot be regarded as urgent service of the Messiah. And how does this explanation fit in with the insertion of ἐπείνασαν in 12.1, which is designed to show that the disciples did not do it wantonly, but because of hunger? One can scarcely on that account regard the second proof from Scripture in 12.5 f. as a scribal construction of Matthew; it is more probable that it already lay before him and he sought to insert it here at an appropriate place.[4]

Not until 12.7 does Matthew provide his own interpretation by means of the quotation from Hos. 6.6, by which he also interprets the behaviour of Jesus in 9.9–13. It should be noticed first of all that in the quotation from Hosea in this context θυσία and ἔλεος can only be understood in an extended or derivative sense (in the case of each of the suggested interpretations). Commonly the contrast between ceremonial law and moral law is seen in it. But: the inferior assessment of the ceremonial law is foreign to Judaism.[5] Even Philo stresses that the ceremonial law must also be observed to the letter.[6]

---

[1] Thus B. W. Bacon, *Matthew*, p. 350.

[2] It would only be closer if by the Sabbath commandment and the eating of the shewbread a special group of commandments were intended: ceremonial commandments. But that is not said.

[3] Although μείζων is in some manuscripts, it must be a later alteration. Cf. on this 12.41 and G. C. Montefiore, *ad loc.*, p. 188.

[4] Cf. R. Bultmann, *SynT*, p. 16.

[5] Cf. the understanding of Hos. 6.6 in the Rabbinate: Billerbeck, I, pp. 499 f.

[6] Cf. W. Bousset, *Religion des Judentums*, 1926³, pp. 439 ff.

His marked nearness to Judaism makes it appear improbable therefore that Matthew meant this distinction. If ἔλεος refers to the moral law, to what should it refer here? The disciples have not exactly kept the moral law by plucking the ears of corn. As Hos. 6.6 is quoted in two places, in Matt. 9.13 and 12.7, and it is thus a favourite thought of Matthew's, 9.13 must be called upon to assist with the interpretation here. There, however, there is no question of opposition to the ceremonial law being meant. Nor can 12.7 mean the Pharisees ought to have shown ἔλεος to the disciples who plucked the ears of corn by not accusing them,[1] for that would mean assuming that after all the disciples had committed a sin (otherwise they would not have needed mercy but only justice), which is disputed in 12.5 as well as also expressly denied in 12.7 with the word ἀναίτιοι.[2] From this it follows that the quotation from Hosea in 12.7 is less a commandment than a statement about the true will of God, and thus denotes a dispensation, an emancipation. The saying 'I desire mercy and not sacrifice' thus means here in the first place that God himself is the merciful one, the gracious one, and that the Sabbath commandment should therefore be looked upon from the point of view of his kindness. Only in this way is there a real connexion with the use of the same quotation in 9.13: if Jesus does not shrink from a defiling association with sinners, it is because God himself is gracious and merciful, and therefore desires that we show mercy. The Rabbinical understanding of the law, which demands strict separation from sinners, is closely linked with the understanding of God as the one who makes demands. It is true that the Rabbinate can also say that the gift of the Torah is an act of grace, that God gave Israel the Torah out of his love;[3] but this love consists in the fact that he makes it possible for Israel to fulfil it. God remains primarily the demanding one. In 9.13 and 12.7, however, God is no longer primarily understood as the demanding one, but as the gracious one, the merciful one. The insertion of 12.7 means that Matthew regards the Sabbath commandment as subordinated to the kindness and mercy of God. By this means the content of the Sabbath commandment, however, is also determined, and it follows from this that the conduct of the disciples is defended in terms of the kindness of God.

[1] Thus E. Klostermann and B. Weiss (*Matthäusev.*, Göttingen, 1898), *ad loc.*
[2] Nor is it possible to understand by it that the Pharisees, instead of condemning the starving disciples, should have fed them (thus Montefiore); in that way the point would have been shifted, for it is connected with the validity of the Sabbath.
[3] Cf. *Aboth* 3.14; *Menakoth* 43b.

Matt. 18.12–35

The influence of the love-commandment is again especially clear in 18.12–35, though it is not there a commandment of the Old Testament but a regulation for the discipline of the congregation that is determined by the love-commandment. Here it is the construction above all that is the means by which Matthew interprets.[1] Is Matt. 18.15–17 the evangelist's own expansion on the basis of the Q-saying (Luke 17.3)? That is improbable, since 18.15–17 is not a unity in itself. The appeal to Deut. 19.15 is a later addition,[2] which obviously stems from Matthew himself, on account of his predilection for appealing to the Old Testament. But then the expanded form in 18.15–17 (except for 18.16b) came to him in that form.[3] In support of this is the fact that the tendency of 18.15–17 is opposed to that of the framework which Matthew erects. The expanded rule of Matt. 18.15–17 is not aimed so much as Luke 17.3 is at maintaining that the converted sinner should be forgiven, but at the exclusion of the sinner when all exhortations to repentance have proved fruitless. By the framework of 18.12–14, 19–20, 21–35, however, Matthew interprets the rule in the opposite direction: the one who has gone astray should be sought as the shepherd seeks the lost sheep, trusting in the promise of the hearing of prayer and the presence of the Risen One in the Church,[4] thinking of forgiveness received and the judgment to come. Out of the love which has been received (18.12–14) grows the obligation of love towards the brother who has gone astray;[5] the

---

[1] A. Schlatter already regards the whole of ch. 18 as grouped under the central concept of love (*ad loc.*, p. 543).

[2] The taking of one or two brethren is intended to strengthen the authority of the admonitions, as the advance from one to the whole congregation shows; what else could be the meaning in 19.15 of the emphasis on 'under four eyes'? I.e. the taking of one or two brethren was not originally motivated by Deut. 19.15. Further: of what are they to be witnesses? Of his sin, or of his unwillingness to repent?

[3] So also R. Bultmann, *SynT*, p. 141; E. Klostermann, *ad loc.*

[4] 18.18 may already have been preserved alongside 18.15–17; 18.19 is not only attached by the catchword (ἐπὶ τῆς γῆς), but in Matthew's mind has a factual basis. 18.20 promises the presence of him who as the faithful shepherd seeks the lost (18.12–14).

[5] This knowledge is important for the question of the motivation of the ethical conduct of the disciples in Matthew. Alongside the extended motivation of ethical behaviour through looking towards the judgment according to works, which Matthew to some extent took over from tradition, though he strengthened it considerably, there stands here the quite differently disposed motivation through looking towards the love which has been received. 18.14 is to be understood as the experience of the whole congregation, for the μικροί are not individuals who have

section ends—typically for Matthew—with the reference to the judgment.

It has thus been shown that the central meaning of the commandment of love is not only exhibited in 22.34–40, in that it appears there as the essence of the law, but that Matthew drew far-reaching conclusions from that. The love-commandment is for him the centre and the supporting basis for the whole of the law and the prophets, and therefore it is made the principle of interpretation. That is shown in various directions. First, the content of the conduct demanded by the law is determined by it; this is especially clear in the limitation of the Sabbath commandment by the commandment of love in 12.12. Again, the conception of God is itself determined by the love-commandment; God himself is primarily the Merciful, the Gracious, the Loving (9.13; 12.7). And finally, in 18.12 ff. the obligation to show love is motivated by the love which has been received.[1] In giving prominence to the commandment of love Matthew is no doubt ruled by the sayings of Jesus and Christian tradition, which generally gives a special place to the love-commandment, though in the individual writings in markedly different degree. As it here has to do with the editorial interpretation of the evangelist, however, Matthew here stands alone among the Synoptic writers. With the meaning of the commandment of love as the essence of the law the contrast to the Rabbinate is given. Matthew regards himself as separated from this not only by practice but also by teaching. He is linked with the Rabbinate in holding fast to the whole law; he parts from it in his interpretation. And not merely in the interpretation of particular questions, but this contrast goes already to fundamental depths and leads to a quite different understanding of the law.

2. *The range of the valid law for Matthew*

With the statement that Matthew's firm retention of the whole law

---

gone astray, but Christians as such, cf. below, pp. 121ff. Because it is not the will of the Father in heaven that one of the least should be lost, but he has sought the disciples as a shepherd the lost sheep, they also should seek the lost. In a similar way the admonition to be always ready to forgive is established by the parable of the unforgiving servant: the threat of judgment only follows here because of the ingratitude for forgiveness received (18.21–35).

[1] It is possible that Matt. 17.24–27 provides a further out-working of the love commandment in so far as it leads the congregation to observe precepts which in themselves are not regarded as binding. It is impossible, however, to speak with certainty here, since Matthew found 17.24–27 already in the tradition, with the result that it is difficult to say how far it agrees with his own interpretation.

unites him with the Rabbinate a question was anticipated which so far has not been at all adequately clarified. It is the question of the range of the law which was valid for Matthew.

A. *The relation to the Rabbinic Tradition*

Since in the Rabbinate the law was valid for the whole area of human life, Scriptural law, because of its lack of detailed regulations, was inadequate. Judaism, however, did not feel this lack so deeply, because alongside the Scriptural it had the oral law, the tradition. Tradition was of the same standing as the Scriptural law.[1] In both forms it was the law of Moses on Sinai that was handed on. The unwritten law was passed on in an unbroken chain of tradition from Moses to the Rabbis; this unbroken chain guarantees its authenticity.[2] To hold firmly to the law means, then, for the Rabbinate, as a matter of course, to accept the Rabbinic tradition as well.

Does the Rabbinic tradition also belong to the law to which Matthew firmly held? In 23.2 the authority of the Rabbis as teachers is expressly recognised and the conclusion drawn from that: everything which they say to you, do and observe. In the original meaning of the saying therefore the word 'everything' included the Rabbinic tradition. Since, however, Matthew found the saying in this form already, and he also transmits material which contradicts it, it may at least be questioned whether in using the word 'everything' he was also thinking of the tradition as well.[3]

Matt. 15.1–20

The attitude to the Rabbinic tradition is treated in more detail in Matt. 15.1–20. Again we pay attention to the interpretation, which the evangelist, by means of insertions, abbreviations and modifications, gives to the traditional material.[4] In Mark, in the first half the demand that the hands should be washed in accordance with the Rabbinic tradition, it is absolutely rejected (Mark 7.1–13). Mark 7.10–13 actually plays off one Old Testament commandment against another. Hence Kümmel writes: 'It is not the unwritten law, but the violating of the will of God by means of the letter of the Torah, that

---

[1] Cf. the reply of Shammai to the question: 'How many Toroth have you?': 'Two, the Scriptural and the oral Torah' *Shab.* 31a.

[2] *Aboth* 1.1; cf. further G. F. Moore, *Judaism in the first centuries of the Christian Era* (Cambridge, 1927), I, pp. 251–62; W. Bacher, *Die Agada der pal. Amoräer*, I (1892), p. 138.

[3] Cf. E. Haenchen, *ZTK* 48, p. 40.

[4] On the structure of Mark 7.1–23 cf. R. Bultmann, *SynT*, pp. 17 f.

Jesus is attacking here.'[1] But Mark, in any case, did not understand the saying in that way; he clearly regards it as an attack on the tradition (7.9!). On the other hand, Mark 7.15 ff. is not directed against the tradition, but against the Levitical law altogether.

What is the result in Matthew? In spite of the insertion of 15.12–14, Matthew has immensely tightened up the section.[2] He deletes the editorial explanation in Mark 7.3 f. with the reference to 'many other things' which the Jews observe: washings of cups, and pots, and brasen vessels (cf. Matt. 15.1). But the reason for this is presumably above all that such explanations are superfluous in a congregation which is familiar with Jewish customs (Klostermann). In Matt. 15.2 the drastic technical expression κοιναῖς χερσὶν ἐσθίουσιν (Mark 7.5) is avoided. Does this mean an alleviation, in so far as he avoids the sharpness of the question, perhaps because his congregation still observes the washing of hands? But Matthew also avoids the technical expression Korban (Mark 7.11), and in 15.20 (construction of Matthew) he uses the technical expression κοινοῦν. Nor is there any alleviation to be seen in the fact that in 15.2 Matthew uses παραβαίνειν instead of περιπατεῖν in Mark. By transposing Mark 7.9–13 before 6–8 Matthew unites into a compact discourse what was only loosely connected by καὶ ἔλεγεν αὐτοῖς in Mark (7.9). Hence there immediately follows the accusation of the Pharisees 'Why do they transgress the tradition?' the counter accusation 'Why do you transgress the commandment of God?' Since, however, 15.20 summarily asserts that eating with unwashed hands does not defile men, 15.3 ff. cannot be understood merely as a diversionary polemic, say in the sense of: remove first the beam out of your own eye, before you look for the splinter in the eye of the disciples. The washing of hands is not for Matthew, in fact, obligatory (15.20)! Thus 15.3 ff. is also intended to reject the binding force of the washing of hands. This is done—in agreement with the Markan original—by rejecting the binding force of tradition altogether. Matthew works out the setting of παράδοσις τῶν πρεσβυτέρων against that of the ἐντολὴ τοῦ θεοῦ more energetically; notice that παραβαίνειν is used twice in 15.2 and 3 and also the antithesis of 'God said' (in Mark: Moses!) and 'But ye say' (15.4 f.). Is not the rejection of tradition thereby still more underlined?

In 15.20 Matthew provides another reason for the rejection of the washing of hands, not formally, by attacking tradition as such, but

[1] *ZNW* 33, p. 124.
[2] Reduced by about one quarter of the Markan original.

on the basis of the interpretation of the law: it is something different that defiles the man (15.18 f., where the catalogue of vices, Mark 7.21 f., is reduced to commandments of the Decalogue). The same criterion is applied in 15.10 f., 15 ff. (= Mark 7.14 ff.) not only to one regulation of the tradition but to the whole Levitical law. The way in which Matthew understood these verses will be further investigated below; here the only matter of interest is the different reason given for rejecting the washing of hands: not because of the rejection of tradition altogether, but on the basis of the interpretation of the law.

There is still the insertion in 15.12–14 to consider. Matthew has inserted two isolated sayings in 13 and 14 by means of the editorial construction in 15.12. By πᾶσα φυτεία in 15.13 the Pharisees are meant rather than their regulations. The figure of planting was in general use in the Old Testament and in Judaism with reference to people.[1] The insertion of 15.12–14 means, however, a strengthening of the question of the law; for the Pharisees are condemned on account of the question of the law. The accusation that they are blind leaders of the blind strikes them at the heart of their effort,[2] for it means that they are blind to the actual will of God. Their blindness shows itself in the tradition of the elders with which they conceal the actual will of God.

It is not the omission of the washing of hands that defiles a man, but the transgression of the commandments indicated in 15.19. Matthew scarcely bases his rejection of the washing of hands on the rejection of the Rabbinic tradition, for elsewhere he impartially adopts tenets from the Rabbinic tradition or appeals to them. The interpretation of the law is rather for him the deciding criterion. In 23.23, where the extension of tithing to spices is a Rabbinic amplification of the law,[3] he adopts the Rabbinic tradition. The saying, which Matthew obviously adopted from Q, does not find fault with these amplifications, but only opposes the neglect of more important things because of them. That it is the true interpretation of the law

---

[1] Cf. E. Klostermann and Billerbeck, *ad loc.*

[2] ὁδηγοὶ τυφλῶν takes up one of the titles of honour (Rom. 2.19) claimed by the Rabbis (E. Haenchen, *ZTK* 48, p. 47). On this fact Kilpatrick's view that 15.1–20 is, through the addition of 15.12–14, more an attack on the Pharisees than on the unwritten tradition, collapses. On the contrary! The Pharisees are not attacked here as such, but because of their claim that they alone are the normative expositors of the law. But Kilpatrick rightly sees that Matthew does not oppose the oral tradition in itself and as a whole (*Origins*, p. 108).

[3] Cf. Billerbeck, I, pp. 932 f.

that is at stake he also shows in connexion with this saying by the insertion of τὰ βαρύτερα τοῦ νόμου.[1]

The basis of the discussion of the Sabbath in Matt. 12.11 is also similarly taken from the Rabbinic tradition,[2] and in 5.21, 43, the tradition is quite ingenuously quoted.

Thus Matthew does not reject the Rabbinic tradition in principle and as a whole. Matt. 15.3 ff. gives the basis taken over from Mark, while 15.20 shows the evangelist's own attitude: he does not start formally from a narrower conception of the canon, but from the interpretation of the law. In the interpretation, however, the love-commandment is decisive as was seen above. With this critical attitude as the deciding factor the whole idea of the Rabbinical tradition is, of course, broken through.

B. *The attitude to the ceremonial law of the Old Testament*

The saying in Mark 7.15 is not only directed against the tradition, but against the Levitical law as a whole. W. Brandt[3] has argued that the custom of the ceremonial washing of hands was originally motivated by the intention to protect food from defilement. On the one hand, however, Rabbinic discussion shows quite different motives,[4] and on the other, the purpose of this saying in Mark 7.15 must also be directed against the food laws as a whole. Matthew has reproduced the saying somewhat more briefly and with greater clarity by interpreting it in relation to the words which proceed out of the mouth; he has thus narrowed the meaning somewhat and thereby comes into collision with 15.19, but in his fundamental attitude he has altered nothing. Can he have overlooked that 15.11 is directed against the Mosaic law? But how can he have accepted this saying, after he has already appealed against the Rabbinic tradition to the validity of the Old Testament? That Matthew should have taken the saying in its full meaning, that the food laws, like the washing of hands should have lost their validity altogether, breaks down on his principle of the abiding validity of the law and the prophets, which would otherwise be decisively pierced with holes

---

[1] Matt. 23.25, on the other hand, does not belong here. According to 23.26 ποτήριον has become a figure for the man. 'J. Wellhausen thinks otherwise: the words τοῦ ποτηρίου καὶ τῆς παροψίδος are to be understood as genitives descriptive of τὸ ἔξωθεν: the vessels themselves are the outward. But this interpretation breaks down on the third person plural of γέμουσιν.

[2] Cf. Billerbeck, I, pp. 629 f.

[3] *Die jüdischen Baptismen* (Giessen, 1910), pp. 38 f.

[4] Billerbeck, I, pp. 695 ff.

here. Further: is a Jewish Christianity conceivable which in its battle for the law defends its validity most acutely, and yet abolishes the food laws? Hence Bacon[1] infers from 15.20 that in 15.1–20 Matthew is in principle only concerned with the washing of hands; he understands 15.11 as 'not to abolish but to subordinate the outward'. In support of Bacon's view is the fact that the summary in 15.20 speaks only of the washing of hands, and καθαρίζων πάντα τὰ βρώματα of Mark 7.19 is wanting.[2] But then it still remains for Matthew that what goes into the mouth does not defile the man. But such a Rabbi as Johanan ben Zakkai could have said the same thing, without thereby abolishing the commandment.[3] It follows that most probably Matthew is thinking here only of a subordination; there would then be a similar case of interpretation here to that in 23.23.[4]

A conservative attitude to the ceremonial law is also shown by the other passages we are to consider. Matt. 5.23 f. speaks of private sacrifice, 17.24–27 of the Temple tax. Both sayings are only possible in the situation before the destruction of the Temple. The Temple tax ceased with the destruction of the Temple. Admittedly the Romans continued to demand it as '*fiscus judaicus*' for the temple of Jupiter Capitolinus in Rome, but that cannot come into consideration here because of the relationship between the Temple and the υἱοί. In this way the section shows a clear consciousness of the special place of the congregation: they are the 'free sons' who only pay the tax so as not to give offence. Matthew has adopted both passages and he thereby shows that he had no objections in principle to them, but agrees with them.

---

[1] *Op. cit.*, p. 352; cf. E. Klostermann, *ad loc.*

[2] These difficult words can scarcely be linked with τὸν ἀφεδρῶνα. The simplest solution is to understand them as a parenthesis: 'whereby he pronounced all foods clean' (cf. E. Klostermann, E. Lohmeyer, *ad loc.*). Does this parenthesis stem from Mark (so Klostermann), or is it a later gloss (so Lohmeyer)? If Matthew found the words already in the text, he may have objected to their free attitude; he may, however, have omitted them simply as unintelligible.

[3] 'In your life, the corpse does not defile, nor does water make pure, but it is an ordinance of the King of Kings, God spoke: I have made a law, I have established an ordinance; no man is justified in transgressing my ordinance' (*Tanḥuma* [A], ed. Buber, Wilna, 1885, *Ḥuqqat* §26).

[4] Note here the tension which exists between the Jewish-Christian theology of Matthew and the attitude of Jesus to the law.

By his saying in Mark 7.15 Jesus abolishes the presuppositions of the whole ancient ritual with its practices of sacrifice and expiation. 'Expressed in another way: he abolishes the distinction which was fundamental for the whole ancient world, between the sacred, the holy place, and the profane' (E. Käsemann, *ZTK*, 1954, p. 146).

It has thus been shown that Matthew retains the ceremonial law, but it has undergone a reassessment under Christian motives. The same applies with regard to the Sabbath commandment. Matt. 12.1–8 and 9–14 had shown that the congregation of Matthew retains the Sabbath, but no longer so strictly as the Rabbinate.[1] It must still be observed, as 24.20 (μηδὲ σαββάτῳ) shows. Have we here a Matthaean addition,[2] or is this the original text, and Mark has made the omission?[3] Even in the latter case Matthew did not object to it, but more probably he himself has made the addition. What is the result of this as regards his attitude to the Sabbath commandment? To find this out we must briefly look at the Jewish practice in this question.

The older standpoint that it was better to allow oneself to be killed on the Sabbath than to desecrate it by fighting was given up already in the time of the Maccabeans (I Macc. 2.32 ff.; Josephus, *Ant.* 12.274 ff.), and Josephus expressly reports, that it is still their custom, when necessary (εἴ ποτε δεήσειεν), to fight on the Sabbath (*Ant.* 12.277). It is true that the thought primarily concerned defence, for which reason Pompey was not hindered by the Jews from building on the Sabbath the earthworks for the siege (*Bell.* 1.146), but then attack was also regarded as permissible on the Sabbath, as the edited formula of Shammai (*Shabbath* 19a) shows: 'if it has already begun, it is not necessary to break off [the siege of a city]. Thus spake Shammai: until it falls: even on the Sabbath.' Hence in the Jewish war the Jews frequently attacked, even on the Sabbath (*Bell.* 2.289 ff., 424, 456, 517).[4] It must be concluded from this that an escape on the Sabbath not only occurred frequently in the Jewish wars, but

[1] That the healing on the Sabbath in Mark 1.21–28 is wanting in Matthew is not significant. It is not omitted, for example, to relieve Jesus of a violation of the Sabbath, as 12.9 ff. shows. Mark 2.27 is wanting in Matthew. Was the saying too liberal for Matthew, was he afraid that it would strengthen the antinomian position? But it is also wanting in Luke, so that it is questionable whether it occurred in the text before Matthew.

[2] Thus Wellhausen, Allen, Bacon (*Matthew*, p. 320), Kilpatrick (*Origins*, p. 116). As Matthew does not think in 24.15–22 of the destruction of Jerusalem which lay behind him (note 24.29, εὐθέως), there is nothing to prevent this.

[3] Thus A. Loisy, *Les Evangiles Synoptiques*, 1907; J. Weiss, *ad loc.*

[4] When, on the other hand, John of Gischala (*Bell.* 4.99 ff.) explains to the Romans that he is forbidden both to carry weapons as well as enter into negotiations for peace on the Sabbath, that is nothing but a device of war, to gain time. On the same grounds the assertion of Josephus (*Vit.* 161) that he released his troops on the Sabbath cannot be quoted to the contrary, especially as the enterprise he led, with very limited forces, against Tiberias shows that he by no means abstained from an attack on the Sabbath.

also that it was no longer regarded as scandalous. Doubts about an escape on the Sabbath occur only once again in the saying of R. Eleazar ben Perata (*c.* 110), who was afraid to tell his questioners directly that they might escape on the Sabbath, but pointed them to Jacob, Moses and David who did escape on the Sabbath.[1] In *Tanhuma* (basic material goes back to R. Tanhuma *c.* 400) escape on the Sabbath is permitted (Billerbeck, I, p. 953).[2]

Does Matt. 24.20 mean that for the sake of conscience one should so pray because flight on the Sabbath is sin? For such a strict attitude, however, there are no longer any witnesses in contemporary Judaism. If one wished to maintain that Matthew held such a view it would mean that on the whole Sabbath question he adopted a stricter view than that known by the rest of Judaism. Against this Matt. 12.1–14 shows that his congregation observed the Sabbath, but not so strictly as the Rabbinate. E. Hirsch and A. Schlatter think, therefore, of dangers from the side of the hate-charged Jews; 'a Christian congregation fleeing on the Sabbath would have been as recognisable in Palestine as a spotted dog'.[3] The severe tension between Church and Judaism in Matthew's Gospel would make this addition intelligible. Or, however, the same attitude is meant as in 17.24–27: to give no offence. Thus Matt. 24.20 does not contradict the conclusions reached above in connexion with 12.1–14: the Sabbath is observed, but no longer as strictly as in the Rabbinate.

c. '*The Law and the Prophets*'

With this formula Matthew repeatedly summarises what he regarded as the valid law. This formula, which occurs frequently, otherwise often denotes the Old Testament as a whole.[4] There is reflected in this formula the fact that the Hagiographa were canon-

---

[1] W. Bacher (*Agada der Tannaiten*, I, 1903[2], p. 403), however, sees in this reply, not a doubt about escape on the Sabbath, but fear of occasioning annoyances by direct advice. The passage reads (*Tanhuma*, ed. Buber, Wilna 1885), מסעי 1: והיה מתיירא לומר להם ברחו בשבת. On the other hand, in the Berlin 1927 ed. מסעי 1: והיה מתירא לומר להם בשבת ברחו—he was afraid to say on the Sabbath, Flee! (cf. Billerbeck, I, p. 953).

[2] On the other hand, *Dam.* provides stricter regulations than the Rabbinate. According to *Dam.* 11.15 it is forbidden to protect one's own property (cf. G. Molin, *Söhne des Lichts*, Wien, 1952, p. 114). But *Dam.* 11.13 f. also forbids rescuing stock which has fallen into a pit, which Matt. 12.11 assumes to be generally allowed. Thus Matthew neither represents this stricter direction nor does he find it necessary to state his own position in opposition to it!

[3] E. Hirsch, *Die Frühgeschichte des Evangeliums*, II, p. 313.

[4] Cf. W. Gutbrod, νόμος, *TWNT*, IV, p. 1051; E. Klostermann on Matt. 5.17; Billerbeck, I, p. 240.

ised only towards the end of the first century. For this reason there is in the Talmud, not usually a twofold division but a threefold (Billerbeck, I, p. 240). For older times, however, 'law and prophets' simply means the Old Testament; one must not draw from that the conclusion that for Matthew the Hagiographa are to be regarded as excluded, as the frequent quotations from the Psalms show.[1] Thus the formula refers to the Old Testament, above all with regard to its imperative content. To this there corresponds a continuous appeal to the Old Testament in questions of the law (Matt. 5.18; 7.12; 9.13; 12.1–8; 15.1 ff.; 15.19; 19.1 ff.; 19.18; 22.40), often in discussion with the Rabbinate. Generally over against the antinomians the imperishable validity of the Old Testament is emphasised. But difficulties arise from the fact that Matthew at times takes a position in clear contradiction to the Old Testament. Does not 5.21–48 show that the law which is valid for Matthew is opposed to the Sinaitic law?

Of the six antitheses in Matt. 5.21–48, probably only those three which he adopted from Q were antithetically formulated by Matthew himself: 5.31 f., 38 ff., 43 ff. The others (5.21 f., 27 f., 33 ff.) were presumably already in an antithetic form when he received them, for in their case the antithesis without the thesis would be scarcely intelligible. Their antithetic character has been transferred by Matthew to the others, but that hardly reduces his responsibility. What is the meaning of these formulations? Who are the ἀρχαῖοι? Probably the generation that stood on Sinai.[2] The idea of the דורות הראשונים is very widespread in the Rabbinate, but the thought is generally of former generations of a considerable time ago.[3] What was said to those of old is accordingly the Torah.[4] But this is expressly quoted as a part of the tradition of the fathers: ἠκούσατε ὅτι ἐρρέθη. שמר and אמר are terms frequently used of belief in the tradition; ἠκούσατε means then: 'you have received as tradition', ἐρρέθη = 'it was taught as tradition'.[5] The Torah was thus received as a part of the tradition and in its traditional meaning. It is plain that the

---

[1] Cf. Matt. 5.5; 7.23; 13.35; 21.16; 27.43.

[2] Thus A. Schlatter, E. Klostermann, J. Wellhausen, J. Schniewind, ad loc.

[3] Cf. Billerbeck, I, pp. 253 f.; G. Dalman, Jesus-Jeshua, p. 71.

[4] W. Grundmann (Die Frage der ältesten Gestalt . . . der Bergpredigt, Weimar, 1939, pp. 6 f.) translates 'by those of old'; but in that case διά or παρά τῶν would be expected; cf. E. Klostermann, ad loc.

[5] It does not mean ἀνέγνωτε or γέγραπτα (Matt. 4.4, 6, 10; 12.3, 5; 21.16, 42; 22.31); cf. on this matter E. Klostermann, Billerbeck (I, pp. 253 f.), W. G. Kümmel (ZNW 33, p. 125), G. Dalman, Jesus-Jeschua, pp. 69 ff.

antitheses are not directed primarily against the Old Testament itself, but against the interpretation of it in the Rabbinate. This is supported by the heading in 5.20, which is now directed against the Pharisees and scribes, whereas previously 5.17–19 were directed against the antinomians. This result is similarly supported by 5.43. The saying from the tradition is here expanded by καὶ μισήσεις τὸν ἐχθρόν σου, which is nowhere to be found in the Old Testament. Abrahams[1] therefore explains this addition in the light of the Rabbinic phrase 'the text reads so and so; I hear from it so and so' (שומע אני ... תלמוד לאומר) which is constantly found in the exegetical terminology of Rabbi Ishmael at the end of the first century. Matthew means by it the exegetical understanding of the Rabbis which they put into the mouth of the text. Accordingly the antitheses are not directed primarily against the Old Testament itself, but against the Rabbinical interpretation of it.[2] It is in contrast to this that Jesus provides the true interpretation, 'I say unto you.' In fact, however, they are also directed against the Old Testament itself. Though Matt. 5.21 f., 27 f., 33 ff., provide only an outdoing of the prohibition, in 5.31 f., 38 ff., a direction, or rather, a concession, is not outdone but completely overthrown. The saying about divorce in Matt. 5.31 f. = 19.1–9 need not, it is true, be understood in Matthew's mind as a direct annulling of Deut. 24.1; for the addition παρεκτὸς λόγου πορνείας in 5.32 or μὴ ἐπὶ πορνείᾳ in 19.9 provides not only a weakening of the text as Matthew received it, but at the same time rescues Deut. 24.1 from total abolition: Deut. 24.1 is not, then, simply abolished, but by being interpreted in the light of Genesis 1 it is narrowed. The case is otherwise, however, with 5.38 ff.: here the Old Testament direction is completely overthrown, and the decisive verse is here obviously an editorial construction of Matthew. Thus what is at stake here also is the question of the right interpretation of the will of God; but this interpretation leads, in 5.38 ff., to a complete abolition of an Old Testament commandment.

Hence the attitude of Matthew to the Old Testament law is determined from two sides, corresponding to his double front against the antinomians and the Rabbinate. Against the antinomians he defends the abiding validity of the whole Old Testament law.

[1] *Studies in Pharisaism*, I, p. 16; cf. W. Bacher, *Die exegetische Terminologie d. jüd. Traditionsliteratur*, I, 1905, p. 189.

[2] Whether they do shatter this interpretation, or whether the Rabbinate did not at times go beyond the literal meaning of the commandments, is another question, which is not our concern here.

Against the Rabbinate, he emphasises the right interpretation of the law, which can lead him to contradict not only parts of the Rabbinic tradition but also individual commandments of the Old Testament itself. But in his conflicts with the Rabbinate he also appeals repeatedly to the Old Testament.

3. The radicalising of the demand of God and Discipleship

The attitude of Jesus to the law in Mark and Q is characterised by a marked radicalising of the demand of God. What has happened to this in Matthew? In some passages clear alleviations cannot be missed. In the contention about divorce (Matt. 19.3–9 = Mark 10.2–12) Matthew 'made an excellent formal correction',[1] but in effect he has thus taken the radicalism out of the discussion. 'For while in Mark, in opposition to the law and the Rabbis, Jesus radically condemns divorce, in Matthew the debate moves to the question discussed between the schools of Hillel and Shammai, about the adequate ground for divorce.' In the same sense Matt. 5.31 f. (cf. Luke 16.18) is toned down. Further, Matt. 12.12 denotes a toning down in comparison with Mark 3.4.

Yet alongside this Matthew also provides a marked radicalising of the demand of God. This is shown not only by 5.21–48 but also other passages. Matthew has expanded Mark 8.38b to a description of the judgment, in which the Son of man will reward everyone according to his $\pi\rho\tilde{\alpha}\xi\iota\varsigma$. By the context this $\pi\rho\tilde{\alpha}\xi\iota\varsigma$ is elucidated by the sayings about discipleship in Matt. 16.24–26. The works, according to which a man is judged in the judgment, are thus not determined by opposition to the antinomians alone (13.41) or by behaviour towards the neighbour (25.34 ff.: the love-commandment), but by suffering discipleship and the devoted life. *These* are the works that will be enquired about in the judgment.

Matt. 19.16–26

Is this also a case of toning down? This would be so if it could be established that there is here a development in the direction of the Catholic distinction between two levels of morality. Matthew's alteration in 19.17 and 21 is understood by most commentators as meaning that the evangelist wished to answer the question of how the two replies of Jesus are related to each other by saying that in addition to the universal obligations works of supererogation are demanded from the group of $\tau\acute{\epsilon}\lambda\epsilon\iota o\iota$, and to these belongs complete

[1] R. Bultmann, *SynT*, p. 27.

poverty as an Evangelical Counsel.[1] It is clear that the insertion of τέλειος in the first place gives the impression of a two-level morality, and so much the more as Matthew puts εἰ θέλεις τέλειος εἶναι in 19.21 in an exactly parallel contrast to εἰ δὲ θέλεις εἰς τὴν ζωὴν εἰσελθεῖν in 19.17. This interpretation, however, breaks down on a number of difficulties which it calls forth:

1. The question τί ἔτι ὑστερῶ in 19.20 refers to the attaining of eternal life[2] and not to a higher perfection. The answer in 19.21, however, must agree with this question.

2. The continuation in 19.22 ff. sees in what the rich man refuses to do the indispensable way to life and not a higher perfection—in that case Matthew would have had to have forgotten here what he had written in 19.21.

3. The conception of two levels of the Christian life—for the mass of Christians and for the perfect—is not found anywhere else in Matthew;[3] it rather contradicts his utterances elsewhere.[4]

(a) Since Matthew shows no kind of ascetic tendency in respect of property and wealth,[5] it is the ἀκολούθει μοι which is the decisive goal in 19.21, and this must on no account be overlooked. But discipleship is never in Matthew required of only a part of the congregation.[6]

---

[1] Thus E. Hirsch (op. cit., II, p. 311), E. Klostermann, J. Weiss, B. W. Bacon ('Jesus and the Law', JBL 47 [1928], p. 225). Opposed to these are Zahn, Schlatter, Schniewind, Loisy, ad loc.

[2] Cf. A. Loisy, ad loc.; E. Klostermann: 'Matthew's expansion is materially right.'

[3] J. Weiss and J. Wellhausen think they find such a distinction in Matt. 19.10 ff. and 10.40 ff. But 19.10 ff. does not say that those who are eunuchs for the sake of the kingdom of heaven represent a higher level of the Christian life (cf. H. von Campenhausen, Askese im Urchristentum, 1949, pp. 28 f.), and the resigned question of the disciples in 19.10 shows that they are not the people who would correspond with such a higher level. In 10.40 ff. J. Weiss and J. Wellhausen find the different levels of the Christian life expressed: apostles (10.40), prophets (10.41a), especially approved Christians, ascetics (δίκαιοι 10.41b) and the mass of μικροὶ οὗτοι the common μαθηταί (10.42). But this is contradicted by the combination and use of 'prophets and righteous men' as with reference to men of the OT, which is found only in Matthew (13.17; 23.29, 35; and 10.41), and thus forms one of his peculiarities. It is also contradicted by the slant of the text itself in 10.40–42, where from the major statement concerning the well-known rule about the reward for receiving a prophet or a righteous man is derived the reward for receiving a disciple. The emphasis lies absolutely on 10.42, that the very smallest help given to a disciple will find its reward (cf. 10.42: ... ἕνα ... μόνον ... ἀμὴν λέγω ὑμῖν).

[4] Cf. Matt. 23.8 ff.

[5] Luke differs, cf. H. von Campenhausen, op. cit., pp. 15 ff.

[6] Cf. G. Bornkamm, 'The Stilling of the Storm in Matthew's Gospel'.

(b) If there are two levels in the Church, the mass of Christians and the perfect, obviously the apostles must be reckoned on the higher level. But this is contradicted by the whole manner in which in Matthew the whole congregation is seen in the 'disciples'. It would be impossible to equate Church and disciples as Matthew does.

(c) τέλειος is found in the Synoptics in Matthew only (three times); in addition to 19.21 in 5.48. The latter must also be regarded as an alteration by the evangelist.[1] The requirement to be τέλειος in 5.48 applies to the whole congregation. If, then, the interpretation in terms of a two-level ethic thus breaks down, the question remains why, then, did Matthew alter the Markan original? He has expanded the answer of the rich man with the question: τί ἔτι ὑστερῶ; he thus expands it materially correctly in Mark's sense; yet another ἕν σε ὑστερεῖ would doubtless be disturbing. Yet this does not adequately explain the much fuller alteration (also 19.17). Such an explanation would, however, be provided if it could be shown that Matthew has a material interest in the notion τέλειος. That is, in fact, the case.

In Matt. 5.48 τέλειος denotes the new congregation in contrast to the τελῶναι and ἐθνικοί of 5.46 f. (the ὑμεῖς of 5.48 is emphatic; cf. E. Klostermann); it denotes them as the doers of the new interpretation of the law which Jesus has given. It is, therefore, immediately linked with περισσόν of 5.47, through which the doer of the law as interpreted by Jesus is distinguished from others, and likewise with περισσεύειν which in 5.20 is demanded in contrast to the righteousness of the Pharisees. One can thus say, in the first place, that τέλειος in 5.48 denotes the 'more' which distinguishes the doers of the teaching of Jesus from others; it is the mark of the congregation.[2]

---

[1] Matt. 5.48 = Luke 6.36 forms in Matthew the summary of the preceding section (οὖν). If the Matthaean form had stood in Q, Luke would have turned a good conclusion into a worse. But in the Luke-form it is the beginning of the next section; the alteration by Matthew, who made of it a concluding verse to what was said about loving enemies, or alternatively to the whole of 5.21–47, in this way becomes intelligible.

[2] It should be noted that τέλειος then means still more than δίκαιος, for it is not denied that the Pharisees are δίκαιοι, but the righteousness of the congregation must exceed that of the Pharisees. This corresponds with the fact that in the Rabbinate תמים is more than צדיק. It is so when in Sifre, Num. 12.5, §102, God calls Noah righteous when he speaks with him, but righteous and perfect when he speaks of him: אומר כי אותך ראיתי צדיק לפני בדור הזה ושלא אלה תולדות בפניו הוא נח נח איש צדיק תמים היה בדורותיו. In this matter the conception of righteousness in Matthew agrees with the Rabbinic one. The difference lies in the fact that this lower level of righteousness, which is no τελειότης is not sufficient for entrance into the kingdom.

There is nothing to prevent τέλειος in 19.21 being understood in the same way.

This use of τέλειος is found nowhere else in LXX,[1] the New Testament or the post-New Testament writings. On the other hand there is an analogous use of תמים in 1QS.[2] Characteristic of the use of תמים in 1QS is the following:

1. It is closely connected with the special law which the sect has. The sect differs from official Judaism in its interpretation of the law, which it regards as revelation,[3] and in various points it is stricter than that of official Judaism. Hence the emphasis that the whole law must be kept,[4] and the struggle against lying prophets who oppose this and teach defection from the law.[5] Anyone who observes this 'more' which distinguishes the sect's interpretation of the law from that of official Judaism, is תמים.[6]

2. In this way תמים becomes the special mark of the sect and its members, by which they are distinguished from official Judaism. Only those who belong to the community of perfection are the true people of God who inherit life.

This 'more' which תמים means in 1QS may appear mechanically quantitative as the more of a number of commandments.[7] If this is not the meaning of τέλειος in Matthew the reason is that the law is understood differently; it does not denote a 'more' in the sense of the quantitative or extensive, but the intensive. Thus in 1QS as in Matthew the Old Testament understanding of perfection (תמים, שׁלם) continues to be echoed in so far as it means total obedience, complete dedication to God: according to 19.21 τελειότης consists in discipleship.

---

[1] In the LXX τέλειος is generally a reproduction of words of the stems שׁלם and תמם. Perfection means here wholeness in the sense of entirety and undividedness. Thus above all in the frequent expression ἦν ἡ καρδία αὐτοῦ τελεία μετὰ κυρίου = היה לבבו שׁלם עם־יהוה, I Kings 11.4; 15.3, 14; 8.61; I Chron. 28.9 or Deut. 18.13, תמים תהיה עם יהוה אלוהיך, further Jer. 13.19; Ex. 12.5. There may be some influence of the Greek understanding of perfection in I Chron. 25.8 when the LXX translates 'master and pupil' (מֵבִין עִם־תַּלְמִיד) with τελείων καὶ μανθανόντων. Likewise Wisd. 9.6, where by the perfection, which is denied the man, it is not the 'wholeness' but the perfection of the idea which is meant. Thus with few exceptions the LXX reproduces by τέλειος the OT sense of תמים and שׁלם.

[2] Cf. 1QS 1.8 f.; 2.2; 3.3; 4.22; 5.24; 8.1, 9, 18, 20; 9.2, 5, 6, 8, 9, 19; 11.11, 17.

[3] Cf. 1QS 1.8 f.; 9.13, 19; Dam. 3.13 f.; 15.13.

[4] The passages are so numerous that a selection will suffice: 1QS 1.8; 8.1, 15; 9.13; 1.13 f.; 2.2; 3.10; 4.2; 3.8; 5.7; 6.15; 9.3, 9.

[5] 1QH 4.16, 20; 1QpHab. 10.9; Dam. 6.1 ff.

[6] 1QS 1.8 f.; 2.2; 4.22; 8.1, 20; 9.19.

[7] Cf., however, H. Braun, Spätjüdisch-häretischer und frühchristlicher Radikalismus, I, pp. 15 ff.

But only in so far as the conception of wholeness is present is the Old Testament understanding manifest. The close connexion with a new understanding of the law and the building of a front against those outside the community, whereby it becomes a characteristic of the community, are foreign to the Old Testament, but are found in 1QS.

Now a final misunderstanding which appears to stand in the way of this interpretation of τέλειος in 19.21 can be cleared out of the way. When it is seen how closely τέλειος in 5.48 is linked with the new understanding of the law it may at first sight be disconcerting that in 19.19 Matthew adds the commandment of neighbourly love—which is characteristic of the new understanding of the law—and thereby places it in an apparent opposition to τέλειος. This difficulty falls to the ground as soon as it is seen that the evangelist has done the same in 5.43, where he placed the commandment of neighbourly love before vv. 44 ff., which were taken over from Q, and enlarged it by an addition which—in his opinion—expresses the usual Rabbinic understanding: καὶ μισήσεις τὸν ἐχθρόν σου. As Matthew links the commandment of neighbourly love so closely with the new interpretation of the law (7.12; 22.40), it cannot be his intention in 5.43 ff. to add a further, second commandment to love the enemy, but he means thereby the intensifying of the commandment of neighbourly love. This can also be superficially understood, as 5.43 is intended to show. It follows that in 19.21 τέλειος is not opposed to the commandment of neighbourly love, but means its intensification. There occurs therefore in the double commandment of Jesus in 19.17 and 21 a similar case to the antitheses of the Sermon on the Mount. This also explains why the evangelist brings 19.17 into prominence by the introductory words εἰ δὲ θέλεις εἰς τὴν ζωὴν εἰσελθεῖν: it is to show the same identity of the old and the newly interpreted law which he so often emphasises.

It has thus been shown that in 19.16 ff. there is no development of a two-level ethic. 19.21 simply means the radicalising of the demand expressed in 19.17 f. Perfection is the decisive characteristic of the new community; only one who is τέλειος, who does the περισσόν, will enter into the kingdom. But 19.21 says perfection exists in discipleship. Corresponding to this, in 16.24 ff., Christians also will be judged in the final judgment according to the dedication of their lives and their suffering discipleship. Hence in Matthew discipleship is demanded of the whole congregation. In Mark not all who believe on Jesus enter into discipleship. The wish of the possessed man who was healed (Mark 5.18 f.) to enter into discipleship is turned down. Matthew omits these verses. The story of the stilling of the storm has become in Matthew a paradigm of discipleship.[1] The Church sees herself and what is happening to her in the disciples in the boat: discipleship is required of the whole congregation.[2]

The same is to be seen in the missionary discourse. Matthew bursts open the situation of a historical 'then' during the earthly activity of Jesus; Mark 6.12 is omitted: that the disciples carry out the missionary commission of Jesus is not reported. On the other hand, Matt. 10.17 ff. from the apocalyptic discourse (Mark 13.9–13) is inserted and 10.23 has in mind the time between the resurrection of Jesus and the parousia.[3] In that way the situation of the historical 'then' is left behind,[4] and the missionary discourse now speaks

[1] G. Bornkamm above, pp. 52–7.

[2] Matthew sees the Church in general embodied in the μαθηταί. This results in an altered use of μαθηταί: 1. Although Peter occupies a special place among the disciples (14.28 ff.; 15.15; 16.17 ff.; 17.24 ff.; contrast 21.20 and 28.7, cf. Mark), differentiations among the disciples are otherwise curtailed. The narrower circle of three or four intimate ones disappears in Matt. 9.23, 24.3 (= Mark 5.37, 13.3). Only in Matt. 26.37 (= Mark 14.33) and 17.1 (= Mark 9.2) are the 'three' taken over from Mark. Matthew is not concerned with distinguishing the 'three' but rather with abolishing the idea as when in 17.6 he says in a quite general sense οἱ μαθηταί and in 17.14 it is not the three who come to the other disciples (as in Mark) but the disciples as a whole who come to the multitude. In 26.17 ff. it is the disciples as a whole (not 'two' as in Mark) who are to prepare the Passover; cf. further Matt. 13.10 with Mark 4.10! 2. In addition there is a sharper differentiation between disciples and people in which the stiffened front of debate between the Church and Judaism after AD 70 is delineated; cf. Matt. 13.10 ff.; 12.49 f.; 23.1 (the disciples have to be named especially alongside the multitude; contrast Mark 12.37b); 16.24 (sayings about discipleship apply only to the disciples). It is in accordance with this that Matthew always speaks of 'their' synagogues (4.23; 9.35; 10.17; 23.34; 12.9; cf. G. D. Kilpatrick, Origins, pp. 110 f.).

[3] The decisive thing is that Matthew had to understand the saying thus. The original sense is uncertain. Between 10.23a and 10.23b there is no actual necessary connexion. 10.23b may have been handed down without 10.23a. B. H. Streeter (op. cit., p. 255) and C. G. Montefiore therefore assume a connexion between 10.23b and 10.5 f. The words 'Ye shall not have gone through the cities of Israel' would then refer to the mission, not to the flight. In that case 10.23a would be Matthew's construction, and the motive the same as in 23.34, where he has also inserted the reference to the flight from city to city. In this way he was able to make use of the saying.

[4] 10.5 f. appears to contradict this if one thinks with J. Weiss of a development: no mission to the Gentiles till after the resurrection (28.19). Against this, Matthew nowhere else makes a similar distinction between before and after the resurrection (cf. the 'understanding' of the disciples, see below, pp. 105 ff.). The most fruitful solution would be a material (not a temporal!) succession: in the matter of mission Israel always has precedence over the Gentiles. Hence before the resurrection of Jesus Gentiles appear repeatedly as recipients of salvation: 2.1 ff.; 8.5 ff., 11;

simply of the sending forth of the disciples. Still more, it is not a matter of sending out special missionaries but sending forth and persecution are essential for discipleship as such (10.24 f.). To be a Christian means to be sent forth, to be under way with the word, which is Jesus' own word, among an oppressed and broken people, which hates and persecutes the messengers. Hence it means the constant threat of fear which will again and again seize the disciples. For that reason the sayings about fear, confession and cross-bearing belong essentially for Matthew to the missionary discourse (10.26–39).

The imitation demanded of the disciples is suffering imitation.[1] Persecution and distress grow for the disciples immediately from their belonging to Jesus. That the disciple can experience no better lot than his lord is expressly emphasised in Matt. 10.25. Hence the disciple expects no reward in this age (19.29) but persecution, humiliation (5.10–12).

Since such meaning is attributed to discipleship in Matthew and it is so closely linked with perfection, the question arises whether discipleship is the way to perfection or is already 'perfection' itself. Since the thought of the Church is so strongly determined by the distinction between the many called and the few (in the judgment) chosen, one is disposed to think first of all of the way to perfection. This is contradicted, however, by the fact that Matthew does not use τέλειος in the Greek sense of the perfect ethical personality, but in the Old Testament sense of the wholeness of consecration to God, as the close relationship with the use of תמים in 1 QS shows. That discipleship itself is 'perfection' and not merely the way to it follows above all from the fact that the necessity of imitation in suffering is not grounded primarily on a goal envisaged in the future but on belonging to the suffering Son of man. The disciple can expect no better lot than what has happened to his lord: 'if they have called the master of the house Beelzebub, how much more shall they call them of his household'. This version of the saying taken from Q is

---

(8.28 ff.); 12.21; 15.22 ff.; 24.14. Also in Matt. 10 in spite of 10.5 f. the witness was to reach the Gentiles: in 10.18 Matthew adds καὶ τοῖς ἔθνεσιν to εἰς μαρτύριον αὐτοῖς (cf. Mark). Then in Matt. 10.5 f. and 15.24 can be seen the ties of the evangelist with his own people; in spite of rejection and persecution the Gospel belongs to them first of all.

[1] Cf. G. Bornkamm above, p. 30.

found explicitly only in Matthew (10.24 f.)![1] The exhortation to the
life of suffering discipleship in 16.24 ff. is preceded by Jesus' first
announcement of his own suffering in 16.21 ff., though this does not
speak explicitly of the suffering of Jesus ὑπὲρ ὑμῶν. Yet it is safe to
say that the suffering following of Christ by the disciples is a reply
to the suffering of Jesus.[2] Thus the judgment asks about confirmation
through testing: whether they have answered the Son of man who
gave himself up entirely for them with a complete dedication of life
and imitation in suffering.

Matthew clarifies what the congregation is commanded to do: in
the first place, in his interpretation of the law and in the second in the
demand for imitation. How are these related to each other? Do they
run alongside each other with no connexion or does each affect the
other? As the notion of perfection, which is for Matthew a decisive
mark of the congregation, is determined in 5.48 by the interpretation
of the law in 5.21–47 but in 19.21 denotes imitation, this requires a
close connexion. This becomes so much the clearer as in 5.48 and
19.21 τέλειος is contrasted with a superficial keeping of the commandments according to which even the love-commandment can be
rendered innocuous (5.43 and 19.19). In both cases it is a matter
of the radicalisation and intensification of the law. The following of

---

[1] In ch. V (below, p. 125) it will be shown that Matthew sees the proper work
of Christ in the establishing of the judgment of God. Since for Matthew the
condition of being a disciple is determined by belonging to the διδάσκαλος and κύριος
(10.24 f.), that means that doing the will of God is the entire essence and meaning
of being a disciple. To be a disciple means for Matthew doing the will of God.
This is shown especially by the alteration he has made to the apothegm about true
kinsmen (Mark 3.31–35 = Matt. 12.46–50). In Mark, Jesus looks round about
upon the ὄχλος and says: whosoever does the will of God is my brother. . . . In
Matthew Jesus stretched forth his hand towards his disciples: *They* are my
brethren, *for* whosoever does the will of God. . . . The differentiation from the
multitude is clear: the will of God is actually done in discipleship. Hence τελειότης
can become the mark of discipleship for Matthew, for the meaning and essence of
the discipleship to which Jesus calls men is that they do the will of God. Similarly
the designation of the disciples as the salt of the earth and the light of the world
(5.13 and 14, editorial!), and here the connexion with 5.11 f. should be noted. To
those who are persecuted for belonging to Jesus it is said: you are the light of the
world! Their ethical conduct through belonging to Jesus is also grounded here:
because they are the light of the world they must let their light shine (5.16).

[2] The ὑπὲρ ὑμῶν refers indeed to the whole humiliation of Jesus (in Matthew,
too!). It should be noted that Judaism knows no such severe standard of judgment
as 16.25–27 (Billerbeck, IV, p. 1037). In the light of such an exacting demand the
question must therefore be raised whether the dedication of life and imitation in
suffering which are asked about in the judgment should not be understood as the
reply to a gift bestowed.

Christ and radical fulfilment of the law are one and the same.

In this way the concept of following Christ is more closely defined. It is following the humiliated Son of man (in this is manifest the 'not yet' of the final actualisation of salvation: although the Risen Christ is present in the congregation [18.20; 28.20], the imitation is of the humiliated Christ). Imitation is expressed in obedience to the law as interpreted by Jesus. It should be emphasised yet again that we are dealing here with an editorial interpretation by Matthew, in which he characteristically differs from his fellow-reporters Mark and Luke.[1] For Matthew the following of the disciples behind the earthly Jesus in the historical 'then' through which they had to give up all earthly securities and attached themselves to Jesus has become an abiding figure for the necessary attachment of men everywhere to Christ. It has become a figure for the intimate belonging to Christ, for the obedience to his commandments which grows out of this and for the suffering, serving, love, dedication, lowliness that grow out of it.

It has been shown that Matthew differs decisively from the Rabbinate in his interpretation of the law. The Rabbinate is also concerned with the interpretation of the law. Rabbinic interpretation has a double task: in the first place it has to build a 'fence' around the Torah to protect it from injury; in the second, it has to provide an exegetical basis for the religious usage fostered in the congregation, so far as this is not explicitly prescribed in the Pentateuch. To this end the Rabbinate built up a series of hermeneutical rules to guarantee the legitimacy of the interpretation. That means that Rabbinic exegesis was determined throughout by formal criteria. The Rabbinate knows no interpretation deduced from a central point, such as the love-commandment is for Matthew, which, as was

---

[1] This identifying of imitation and obedience to the law as interpreted by Jesus is seen again in 11.28–30. R. Bultmann (*SynT*, pp. 159 f.) has shown that 11.28–30 was not originally linked with 11.25–27, it has rather the character of 'wisdom' and may be a modification of a saying from a Jewish wisdom writing. But in that case from whom does the modification stem? According to E. Hirsch (*op. cit.*, II, p. 285) and B. W. Bacon (*Matthew*, p. 290), 11.28–30 is a construction of Matthew. In favour of this is the fact that 11.28–30 is ruled by the thought of πραΰτης, which dominates the Christology of Matthew (cf. below, ch. V). In 11. 28–30 the κοπιῶντες καὶ πεφορτισμένοι are called. The double summons is addressed to them: come unto me (where Matthew is thinking of discipleship and imitation) and: take my yoke upon you. . . . Since the same promise is made for both summonses (11.28 ἀναπαύσω ὑμᾶς = 11.29 εὑρήσετε ἀνάπαυσιν) the summonses must also correspond to each other, both say the same thing: to take Jesus' yoke is not a second thing which is added to coming to Jesus, but is identical with it.

shown above, can be critically directed against individual command-ments of the Old Testament itself.

For Matthew the love-commandment became the principle of interpretation for the law. Alongside it is the imitation of Christ, which obviously also carries with it an interpretation of the law. Matthew thus interprets the law on the one hand by the love-commandment, on the other by the imitation. Do these two moments of interpretation stand alongside each other without any connexion, or are they rooted in a unity which lies at the back of them? To express it in another way: how does Matthew come to interpret the law on the one hand by the love-commandment and on the other by the imitation? This cannot be explained by the formal adoption of the synoptic tradition alone. The question therefore arises whether his understanding of the Christ event did not first modify the under-standing of the law which he brought from Judaism and lead to this interpretation by the love-commandment and the imitation. Of course, there lurks here in an especial degree the danger of wishing to read too much out of Matthew; but there are a number of indica-tions which support this assumption. Again it has entirely to do with traits in which Matthew characteristically differs from his fellow-reporters.

1. It is characteristic of Matthew to give prominence to the meekness, the πραΰτης of Jesus.[1] But meekness is also demanded of the disciples (emphatically!); thus 5.5; 18.1–10; 19.13–15; 20.20–28; 23.8–12. The editorial intervention of the evangelist can be seen especially in 5.5 and 18.1–10.[2] The link between the two is seen in 11.28–30, when Jesus as the πραΰς καὶ ταπεινὸς τῇ καρδίᾳ calls men to himself and invites them to take his yoke upon them. It is hardly likely that an ideal of meekness already in the evangelist's mind led him to portray Jesus according to it, for Matthew is not influenced in this emphasis by the traditions he received. The reverse is more probable: the demand for lowliness in the disciples was influenced by the lowliness of the Son of man.

2. The content of the concept of δικαιοσύνη in Matthew is derived from relationship with the humbled Son of man. Matthew himself has constructed the Beatitude of those who are persecuted for right-eousness' sake (5.10) according to the pattern of 5.11 f.[3] From this it

---

[1] On the meekness of Jesus cf. below, pp. 125 ff.
[2] On 5.5 cf. p. 124; on 18.1–10 cf. pp. 121 ff.
[3] Cf. R. Bultmann, *SynT*, p. 110.

follows: to be persecuted for righteousness' sake means the same as to be persecuted for Jesus' sake.

3. Originally 12.36 f. had a broad ethical meaning, but Matthew refers it to the words of the Pharisees who blaspheme against the Son of man, or alternatively the Holy Spirit resting upon him. The judgment according to works is not carried out according to a broad ethical principle which is indifferent towards the Christ-event. This is seen in 25.31–46 already, where the righteous have fed and clothed the Son of man unknowingly, but above all in 16.24–27 (16.27 is editorial!) where the disciples are judged in the judgment according to their imitation of Christ in suffering and their dedicated lives. When a man is judged in the judgment 'according to his works' that means he is asked about his relationship to Jesus Christ, to whom his works bear witness.

In all these passages the influence of Christology upon ethics can be seen. The assumption seems therefore justified that it is Christology itself that has led Matthew to the interpretation of the law by the love-commandment and discipleship, as has been shown above.

IV. ON THE ESSENCE OF BEING A DISCIPLE

For knowledge of the understanding of the law in Matthew it is necessary to know the essence of being a disciple, at least in its basic structure. Some marks have already been named: the relationship of the Christian to Christ is denoted figuratively by the concept of imitation. Therein both the close attachment and the obligation are established which underline the radicality of God's demand. A further characteristic of Christians is that they really do the will of God. This distinguishes the congregation from those outside, as was shown in connexion with the concept τέλειος and with reference to Matt. 12.46–50. But there still remains a series of concepts which are essential to the making of a disciple in Matthew and these must now be briefly considered.

1. Συνιέναι

In Matthew as also in Mark and Q the making of a disciple is based on the call of Jesus. Thus Jesus calls Peter and Andrew and the two sons of Zebedee away from their nets (Mark 1.16 ff. = Matt. 4.18 ff.), then he calls Matthew (Levi) the tax-collector from the place of toll (Mark 2.14 = Matt. 9.9). The same is contained in the saying about following him in Matt. 8.21 f. = Luke 9.59 f. But this calling of a man to be a disciple by the call of Jesus takes on a special note in Matthew through the 'understanding' which is given to the disciples. Matthew has omitted or interpreted differently all the passages in Mark's Gospel which speak of the lack of understanding on the part of the disciples. That makes it necessary for us to investigate more carefully the understanding of the disciples in Matthew.[1] Matthew has made alterations in the following passages or introduced the thought of 'understanding' in an emphatic way:

Matt. 13.14 f. οὐ μὴ συνῆτε, καὶ βλέποντες βλέψετε καὶ οὐ μὴ ἴδητε. ἐπαχύνθη γὰρ ἡ καρδία τοῦ λαοῦ τούτου . . . μήποτε . . . συνῶσιν: quotation from Isa. 6.9 f., added to Matt. 13.13 (= Mark 4.12).

13.19. ἀκούοντος τὸν λόγον τῆς βασιλείας καὶ μὴ συνιέντος is inserted into the interpretation of the parable of the sower; similarly

13.23. ἀκούων καὶ συνιείς.

13.51. The understanding of the disciples is ascertained by the question συνήκατε ταῦτα πάντα;

14.31 ff. Mark 6.52 is wanting: οὐ γὰρ συνῆκαν ἐπὶ τοῖς ἄρτοις, ἀλλ᾽ ἦν αὐτῶν ἡ καρδία πεπωρωμένη; the lack of understanding on the part of the disciples is transformed into the opposite—to adoring confession.

16.9. Mark 8.17 οὐδὲ συνίετε and the hardening is wanting.

16.12. τότε συνῆκαν substantiates the understanding of the disciples (as against Mark 8.21 οὔπω συνίετε;).

17.9 omits Mark 9.10: And they kept the saying, questioning among themselves what the rising again from the dead should mean.

17.13 τότε συνῆκαν substantiates again the understanding of the disciples.

17.23 omits Mark 9.32: but they understood not the saying (ἠγνόουν) and were afraid to ask him. Instead of that the sorrow of the disciples in Matthew shows that they did understand.

Further evidence is in the following: in Matthew 13.10 and 18 (= Mark 4.10 and 13) the interpretation of the parable of the sower

[1] The modification of the understanding of the disciples in Mark has already been treated by W. Wrede (*Das Messiasgeheimnis in den Evgl.*, Göttingen, 1913², pp. 157 ff.). But Wrede is solely interested in the negative side, in showing that Matthew no longer understood the Markan conception. Wrede fails to see that Matthew is moved by a new positive conception, which has quite different presuppositions and aims. It is true that he sees the difference between Mark and Matthew as between 'secrecy' and 'special knowledge' (p. 162), but in his view Matthew's alterations arise from the tendency to idealise the disciples as the legitimate representatives of the teaching of Jesus.

is not occasioned by a question of the disciples. In Matt. 13.34 Mark 4.34b 'privately to his own disciples he expounded all things' is omitted. Similarly in Matt. 17.4 Mark 9.6 'for he wist not what to answer' is omitted.[1] In the structure of Matt. 13 it is clear that it is precisely the συνιέναι that differentiates the disciples from the obdurate multitude. Matthew's alteration here is as clear as it is consistent. This is shown by:

1. The insertion of συνιέναι in 13.19, 23, 51. It is especially clear in 13.19, 23: the seed which has fallen on the path denotes those who have not understood the message of the kingdom, whereas on the contrary the yielding of fruit presupposes understanding.[2]

2. 13.10 ff.: the disciples do not ask about the meaning of the parables (they have no need to do), but why he speaks to the multitude in parables. For it is given to the disciples (sc. by God) γνῶναι τὰ μυστήρια τῆς βασιλείας,[3] which is brought into prominence by the expansion ἐκείνοις δὲ οὐ δέδοται and the addition of 13.12.

3. This is further shown by the insertion of 13.16 f. with the prominent position given to ὑμῶν,[4] which can only mean here: you are—in contrast to the obdurate multitude who do not understand—to be pronounced blessed because understanding is given to you disciples. Here seeing and hearing in 13.16 f. do not mean physical seeing and hearing (as originally, cf. Luke) but in an intensified sense understanding.[5]

---

[1] The lack of understanding on the part of the disciples in Mark 5.31 is also wanting in Matt. 9.21 f. but here it is only a matter of simple abbreviation. Wrede (p. 158) also points to Matt. 8.27, where in Matthew it is not the disciples but the 'men' who ask who is he whom the winds and the waves obey.

[2] Matt. 13.23 ὃς δὴ καρποφορεῖ, cf. Blass-Debrunner, §451, 4: 'who indeed'; Bauer: 'for he also bears fruit'; δή denotes the statement as something fixed, something settled; i.e., the consequence of συνιέναι is yielding fruit.

[3] Whether the plural μυστήρια is provided by Matthew it is not possible to say with certainty since Luke also has the plural; but at least it corresponds to the comprehensive meaning of the object of the understanding; the μυστήρια are obviously for Matthew doctrines; it is not only, as in Mark, the fact of the irruption of the βασιλεία that is intended (on Mark cf. G. Bornkamm, μυστήριον, TWNT, IV, p. 824).

[4] Similarly ὑμεῖς is emphasised in 13.18.

[5] 13.16 loses its original meaning in the Matthaean context. In Luke it was about 'what' was seen, about the difference in time between those who were privileged to experience the Messianic time and those who were not, but here it is about seeing with the eyes and seeing with the understanding. This is shown by the alteration in 13.16 through which the link with 13.14 f. is gained (instead of ἃ βλέπετε Matthew has ὅτι βλέπουσιν). The prophets and righteous men who through no fault of their own, and in spite of their longing, were not permitted to

4. It is in harmony with this that it is not necessary for Jesus to explain everything to the disciples κατ' ἰδίαν (Mark 4.34).[1] The disciples are distinguished from the multitude by the fact that they are given understanding while the multitude is obdurate. For this reason Mark 4.33b has to be deleted: καθὼς ἠδύναντο ἀκούειν—it contradicts the theory of obduracy; the multitude is now incapable of understanding. Hence Matthew inserts οὐκ ἐπέγνωσαν αὐτόν into the saying about Elijah (Mark 9.13 = Matt. 17.12): in its obduracy the multitude does not recognise that Elijah has returned in the Baptist.[2] In the light of this Matthew has altered all the other passages that refer to the understanding of the disciples, and that in the following way: 1. In some passages he entirely omits the reference to the disciples' lack of understanding: 17.4, 9, 23; 14.31 ff. Here also belongs the omission of Mark 10.32, where in ἐθαμβοῦντο . . . ἐφοβοῦντο there is an overtone of the disciples' lack of understanding (Matt. 20.17). In 14.31 ff. and 17.23 the lack of understanding is transformed into its exact opposite. 2. In other passages the lack of understanding on the part of the disciples is limited to a merely temporary, provisional one. Thus in 15.16 by the addition ἀκμήν; the lack of understanding about the saying concerning the leaven in 16.9 ff. ends in 16.12 with τότε συνῆκαν;[3] the request for the interpretation of the parable is fulfilled in 13.36, and in 13.51 understanding is explicitly substantiated. 17.13 also belongs here unless it counted with the preceding group because a temporary lack of understanding can only be inferred from τότε συνῆκαν, though it is

---

see are placed alongside the multitude who do not see because of their obdurate guilt, and in this way the grace granted to disciples in being permitted to 'see' is brought into still greater prominence.

[1] In 13.36 where, after all, the interpretation of the parable is introduced by a question put by the disciples, the understanding of the disciples is soon confirmed, in 13.51.

[2] Of course, it was less the multitude than its leadership which did this. Matthew simply uses the third person plural (as Mark). In this generalising description of the people as obdurate the later tense situation between Church and Judaism can be seen. Hence Matthew cannot completely carry through the thought that the Jewish multitude does not recognise anything (in Matt. 21.46 they hold Jesus at least for a prophet, in 21.9 they even do homage to him as the son of David; but it is questionable whether the evangelist regarded this as a contradiction of the theory of obduracy) but the intention to portray the multitude as obdurate as a whole is clear.

[3] The correction of Mark 8.17 ff. in Matt. 16.9 ff. is not so obvious as the other passages; we shall have to go into it in more detail below.

not suggested in any other word.[1] What is meant by 'understanding'?
For the most part Matthew reproduces this idea with συνιέναι
(13.13, 14, 15, 19, 23, 51; 15.10; 16.12; 17.13); but he also uses a
series of other expressions for designating this understanding or
alternatively not understanding: γνῶναι (13.11), βλέπειν and ἀκούειν
(13.13–17), παχύνω (13.15), ἀσύνετος (15.16), νοεῖν (15.17; 16.9, 11),
ἐπιγιγνώσκειν (17.12). The thought of 'understanding' cannot therefore be explained by a study of συνιέναι in the rest of the New Testament or in the LXX.[2] Matthew is here solely conditioned by Mark,
whose conception of the disciples' understanding he alters in a
characteristic way. Hence we are confined entirely to the statements
of Matthew himself.

Whereas in Mark the disciples remain completely devoid of
understanding until the resurrection of Jesus (Mark 4.13; 6.51 f.;
7.18; 8.17–21; 9.6, 10, 32; 10.32; cf. Wrede, pp. 101 ff.), in Matthew
understanding is already granted to them.[3] True it is by no means
complete and final, they are still often lacking in understanding,
hence in 13.36 and 15.15 a question about the meaning of a
parable or enigmatic saying can be put into their mouth, but Jesus
then gives them understanding and this is then explicitly stated. The
decisive evidence is the rejection of the thesis that Jesus generally had
to interpret all the parables especially for the disciples (Mark 4.34).
The object of συνιέναι is quite generally the Christian message as a
whole. Thus in 13.19 τὸν λόγον τῆς βασιλείας and in 13.23 τὸν λόγον.[4]

[1] One can also see in 26.8 an expression of the lack of understanding of the
disciples, but it is questionable whether Matthew understood the verse in that
way, for the disciples had long before understood, according to Matthew, that
Jesus would die (17.23!). He will rather have seen in it an expression of a mean
lovelessness.

[2] The use of συνιέναι in the LXX is anything but uniform: in most cases it
reproduces בין, and chiefly alongside that שׂכל; but even where it reproduces בין
the very thing that characterises it most of all in Matthew is missing; the only
exception is Isa. 6.9 f. On the very marked difference between this and the secret
knowledge of the Qumran-sect cf. H. Braun, op. cit., I, pp. 17 f.

[3] Only one passage appears to contradict this: the prohibition in 16.20 and the
connexion with the assurance of Jesus that it is only by virtue of a divine illumina-
tion that Peter has been able to utter such knowledge could lead to the inference
that the Messiahship of Jesus was a secret which had only just been opened to the
disciples. But W. Wrede (p. 156) has already shown that Matthew did not draw
this conclusion.

[4] Cf. Mark 4.15. Used absolutely ὁ λόγος is a technical term coined and frequently used by the primitive Church for the Gospel, cf. J. Jeremias, Gleichnisse,
p. 60. The addition of τῆς βασιλείας is characteristic of Matthew: cf. 4.23; 9.35;
24.14.

Thus the disciples generally understand the preaching and teaching of Jesus about the demand of God, about the teaching of the Pharisees, about forerunners, Messianic deeds of power, suffering, resurrection (15.16; 16.12; 16.9; 17.4, 9, 13, 23). The understanding of parables and enigmatic sayings is a special case.

In contrast to the συνιέναι of the disciples there is the καρδία πεπωρωμένη in Mark 6.52; 8.17 and in Matt. 13.15 ἐπαχύνθη ἡ καρδία (Isa. 6.9). Likewise συνιέναι is explained in more detail as 'seeing they see' and 'hearing they hear' (13.14 ff.). It is the indispensable presupposition of fruit-bearing (13.19, 23), as it is the absolute foundation of the Christian existence (13.16 f.). Hence συνιέναι does not denote any event which could have its basis in the natural reason of man; the disciples are not intellectually more gifted than the multitude which sees and does not see. The opposite to it is obduracy. It is an opening of the heart, an understanding of what God is now speaking.[1] But it is not only for the 'that' of the divine speaking, but also for the 'what'. It is the opening of the understanding for the revelation. Yet the human intellect is not excluded, since it also has to do with the understanding of parables. Understanding is no achievement of man, but is God's action on man, a gift. This is clearly stated in 13.11 with the addition of 13.12;[2] the same applies to the pronouncing of blessedness in 13.16 f., and through that the whole context of 13.10–23. For all that, the decision of man is not excluded; understanding is also recognition. As the opening of the understanding for the revelation recognition is now posited simultaneously. Thus in 13.15; 15.10; 16.9; 17.12, with the understanding an element of willing is also posited. But this remains completely in the background because prominence is given to understanding as a gift; it is an act of God on a man, as obduracy is God's judgment upon a man.

By consistently removing the difference according to Mark between the disciples before the resurrection of Jesus and after it,

---

[1] Cf. J. Schniewind on Matt. 13.23.

[2] This is not altered by the fact that by ὅτι in Matt. 13.13 instead of ἵνα in Mark 4.12 the thought of obduracy as the goal is weakened in Matthew and obduracy is given as the ground. For even Matthew sees in it, on the one hand the fulfilling of a divine necessity firmly established in Scripture (cf. G. Bornkamm, μυστήριον, *TWNT*, IV, p. 824), and on the other Matt. 13.34 f. shows that in the parables of Jesus Matthew saw the execution of judgment upon the people. But the decisive thing remains the augmented δέδοται in 13.11 f. There is no doubt the ὅτι indicates that it is a matter of guilty obduracy, and this is underlined by the addition of 13.12 (cf. T. Zahn, *ad loc.*, p. 475).

Matthew again here writes the situation of the Church into the life of the disciples during the earthly activity of Jesus. In this way he shows a quite different relationship to the historical past of the life of Jesus from Luke, as well as being different from Mark. Such an equating of the time of the Church with the time of the earthly activity of Jesus is not possible for Luke because of his historical interest and it is completely excluded by his pattern of salvation history, for according to this in the time of Jesus the timelessly valid salvation-time is portrayed, and the time of the Church as the afflicted Church is distinguished from this as a new epoch of salvation history.[1] Neither does Mark recognise such an equating of the time of the Church with the time of the life of Jesus. It is not right in this connexion to point to isolated sayings in which a question or a problem of the congregation is placed in the mouth of Jesus. Here it is rather a case of equating in time, which forms an element of the framework of the structure of the whole Gospel. Such an equating cannot hold for Mark because the disciples are completely lacking in understanding until the resurrection of Jesus; it is not till then that the scales fall from their eyes (cf. Mark 9.9 f., 32). Matthew is quite different! The hearer or reader of Matthew's Gospel is obviously intended by it to be made a contemporary of the historical Jesus, to be brought into the presence of Jesus.[2] This construction is obviously based on the presence of the Risen Christ in the congregation (18.20; 28.20); more will be said of this below.

There is yet another inference to be drawn from understanding in Matthew. The relationship of Matthew to Judaism has been repeatedly observed and depicted. On the one hand Matthew shows time after time a special nearness to the Rabbinate, so much so that E. von Dobschütz could see in him a converted Rabbi.[3] On the other hand, his debate with Judaism reached the height of passionate polemic.[4] It is true that the Church in Matthew seeks to keep fellowship with the Jewish nation, but the situation is tense; the Church is directly persecuted (5.10–12; 10.23; 23.34). Hence God's judgment is pronounced over the Jewish nation; the kingdom of God

[1] Cf. H. Conzelmann, *Mitte der Zeit*, p. 6.
[2] Hence the view of Marxsen (*Der Evangelist Markus*, Göttingen, 1956, p. 94) that in Matthew the proclamation of the Church is aetiologically read back into the history of Jesus and based there—'thus Jesus already proclaimed'—is false.
[3] 'Matthäus als Rabbi und Katechet', *ZNW* 27, 1928. Likewise B. W. Bacon (*Matthew*, p. 131), Kilpatrick (*Origins*, p. 137).
[4] Cf. E. Haenchen, *ZTK* 48, p. 59.

will be taken from them.[1] As this has been repeatedly described,[2] there is no need to go into it here. But 'understanding' adds something new to the subject—the problem of Israel rejecting its Messiah and thereby its salvation, so deeply felt and seen by Matthew alone alongside Paul. Matthew replies to it with the doctrine of the complete obduracy of the greater part of the Jewish nation. This obduracy is God's judgment and therefore guilty obduracy. Therefore in 13.13 instead of ἵνα a ὅτι has to be used; hence they remain blinded until the terror-stricken self-condemnation of 27.25. In this theory of obduracy again the situation of the congregation in the years after AD 70 is seen: the fronts against Judaism are now completely hardened. On the other hand, this also shows that for Matthew, to speak in Pauline fashion, no καύχημα can grow up over against Israel because of the message of salvation and the knowledge of Christ, for, that the disciples were given understanding rests on God's free grace.

2. Πίστις

On the basis of the emphasis on yielding fruit one must suppose either that πίστις plays no special part or that it is itself fashioned by the effort to do the will of God. In connexion with the remark of Jesus that he had not found such faith in Israel as he found in the heathen centurion (8.10) Matthew has added a saying about the rejection of Israel and the acceptance of the Gentiles. The intention is clear: the meaning of faith is brought into prominence; the Gentiles will be accepted on account of their faith, Israel will be rejected because of her lack of faith. What is meant by πίστις? Matthew has taken his πίστις-concept very largely from Christian tradition. It is trust in the fatherly kindness of God who cares for his creatures (Matt. 6.30 = Luke 12.28), who hears prayer (Matt. 17.20 = Luke 17.6; Matt. 21.20–22 = Mark 11.20–24); above all it is the trust which is directed to the ἐξουσία of Jesus and which experiences his wonder-working power (8.10, 13; 9.2, 22, 28 f.; 15.28). Thus πίστις denotes in the first place trust. Three times, with a slight variation, Matthew has added the formula 'As thou hast believed, so be it done unto thee' (8.13; 9.29; 15.28). The fulfilling of the promise which in 17.20 and 21.20 ff. is attached to trusting

[1] 8.11 f.: on account of their unbelief; 21.43: because they yielded no fruit.
[2] Cf. Kilpatrick, *Origins*, pp. 110 ff., A. Schlatter, *Kirche des Matthäus*, pp. 16 ff.

prayer is established in those cases by way of illustration. In this way πιστεύειν as trust is not simply adopted by the evangelist from tradition, but is especially emphasised. But alongside this emphasis on trust he also shows a characteristic modification in the πίστις-concept. If understanding denotes the openness of the understanding for the revelation, that drives us to the consideration of the relation between understanding and faith. Understanding is then obviously the presupposition of faith, if it does not extend its meaning still further and take over part of the function of πίστις. The alteration is clear in

Matt. 14.31–33

After the insertion of verses 28–31 about the attempt of Peter to walk on the sea, 14.32 returns to the Markan text (Mark 6.51). But now the accusation in Mark 6.52, 'For they understood not concerning the loaves, but their heart was hardened', is deleted; into its place comes an adoring confession (Matt. 14.33). Matthew cannot say that the disciples had not acknowledged the Messiahship of Jesus; hence Mark 6.52 has to be deleted. But the disciples (or rather Peter) in Matthew do not remain exempt from accusation: instead of hardness their little faith is condemned (14.31).[1] The alteration is clear: the disciples have understanding but they lack faith; it is significant that the two are separated, which is not the case in Mark. Although the words πίστις, πιστεύειν do not occur in Mark 6.45–52 the passage is concerned with the same subject. If the disciples had recognised the ἐξουσία of Jesus their knowledge would have been faith, and they would not then have been afraid. 'With the knowledge that the distributor of the food and the one who commands the storm and the waves acts with God's authority faith would have been established.'[2] This knowledge is a structural element of faith in Mark. It is different in Matthew: here they have this knowledge yet they lack faith. The knowledge of the ἐξουσία of Jesus is no structural element of πίστις here. The intellectual element which is contained in the πίστις-concept of Paul and John[3] and also in the editor of Mark is excluded from the πίστις-concept of Matthew and

---

[1] This alteration of 14.31–33 cannot be explained simply as conditioned by the insertion of 14.28–31. This insertion was only possible because in Matthew the disciples are regarded as 'understanding'. Nor was it in any way necessary to accuse the disciples of ὀλιγοπιστία. Cf. on this H. J. Held below, pp. 291 ff.

[2] H. J. Ebeling, *Das Messiasgeheimnis und die Botschaft des Markus-Evangelisten*, Giessen, 1939, p. 154.

[3] In Paul πίστις arises out of ἀκοή, in John faith, sight and hearing can be parallel, or rather, synonymous.

transferred to συνιέναι. In consequence πιστεύειν is emphasised again in 14.31 as 'trust'. The alteration is not unequivocal in

Matt. 16.5–12

In comparison with Mark 8.14–21 the point has completely changed. There the saying about the leaven is rooted entirely in testifying to the misunderstanding of the disciples: not only have the disciples failed to understand an enigmatic saying, but they have failed to recognise Jesus' ἐξουσία. Matthew deletes from Mark 8.17 f. the words οὐδὲ συνίετε; πεπωρωμένην ἔχετε τὴν καρδίαν ὑμῶν; ὀφθαλμοὺς ἔχοντες οὐ βλέπετε; καὶ ὦτα ἔχοντες οὐκ ἀκούετε; This deletion fits entirely into the framework of what we have already established: Matthew cannot say that the disciples have no συνιέναι. Instead of that the accusation of little faith is inserted again. But when Matthew has omitted οὐδὲ συνίετε and yet has not omitted οὔπω νοεῖτε, οὐδὲ μνημονεύετε τοὺς πέντε ἄρτους does not his alteration appear inconsistent? Is the omission of οὐδὲ συνιέτε and of the hardening simply an abbreviation? But against this it is far too constant a trait to be a coincidence in this passage, for everywhere else it is the result of a deliberate construction. And further, the conclusion is against it where instead of οὔπω συνιέτε there stands πῶς οὐ νοεῖτε ὅτι ... whereby the misunderstanding is purified, down to the words τότε συνῆκαν. But in this way the point has been completely altered from that in Mark: in Matthew the main point is not that the disciples had failed to recognise the ἐξουσία of Jesus but that for a time they had not understood an enigmatic saying. In that case Matthew obviously intends here the same alteration as in 14.31 ff., which, however (by allowing οὔπω νοεῖτε to stand), he has not quite consistently carried through.[1] Instead of the accusation of obduracy that of little faith is again introduced; the disciples have the decisive understanding, but they lack faith.

By excluding from the πίστις-concept the intellectual element included in Mark and transferring it to συνιέναι, πίστις is emphasised as trust by Matthew. πιστεύειν takes on more firmly a moment of willing.[2] Hence πιστεύειν can be equated with θέλειν: 15.28 γενηθήτω σοι ὡς θέλεις. That πιστεύειν and θέλειν here belong very closely together is not only shown by 15.28 itself but also Matt. 8.13, and 9.29,

---

[1] Probably οὔπω νοεῖτε in 16.9 as in 16.11 should be referred to the enigmatic saying; cf. J. Wellhausen's translation.

[2] πιστεύειν also contains in Mark a moment of willing (cf. H. J. Held below, p. 280), but in Matthew it is much more strongly emphasised.

where the formula runs ὡς ἐπίστευσας or κατὰ τὴν πίστιν ὑμῶν, γενήθητω ὑμῖν. From here the transition to two other passages is given, where πίστις, πιστεύειν denote obedience or alternatively faithfulness to the will of God, the law. In Matt. 21.32 (cf. 21.25 = Mark 11.31) the publicans and harlots 'believed' the preaching of the Baptist, who came ἐν ὁδῷ δικαιοσύνης, i.e. they repented and became obedient to his preaching of the law. Matt. 23.23 demands κρίσις (judgment), ἔλεος (mercy) and πίστις (faithfulness).[1] That πίστις should here be translated faithfulness has so far been generally accepted,[2] though it is mostly understood as faithfulness towards men. But this use would be unique in the whole of Matthew's Gospel; Matthew's interest lies elsewhere. One must therefore agree with G. Bornkamm, who understands it in the comprehensive sense of behaviour directed towards God, i.e. faithfulness to his will as stated in the law and the prophets.[3]

Since the intellectual element has been transferred to συνιέναι, πίστις denotes emphatically in Matthew, trust; it contains a strong element of willing, indeed it denotes obedience, faithfulness to the demand of God, the law. The interest which Matthew shows in the doing of the will of God also determines his conception of faith. πίστις never denotes for him the acceptance of a missionary message, the confession of a fellowship or a merely theoretical conviction. A conception of faith such as that of James 2.19 is completely strange to him.[4] In this the influence of the Old Testament conception of faith can be seen. האמין denotes in the Old Testament holding firmly to the covenant, to God's promise, to the law. This holding firmly means both trust and obedience. In this decisive characteristic the synagogue completely retained the Old Testament conception of faith. 'Faithfulness to God finds its concrete expression in faithfulness to the law. To be נאמן is therefore an essential mark of the devout

---

[1] Against the attempt to translate πίστις in 23.23 with faith is the fact 'that ἔλεος καὶ πίστις are so firmly linked by the OT that we may . . . scarcely separate them from each other here' (A. Schlatter, Der Glaube im Neuen Testament, Stuttgart, 1927⁴, p. 586). The demand for 'doing' in 23.23c would also hardly fit in with the translation 'faith'.

[2] Thus Schlatter, Haenchen (ZTK, 48, p. 48), Wellhausen, Klostermann, Zahn, ad loc.

[3] G. Bornkamm above, pp. 26f.

[4] On the conception of faith in the Epistle of James see below, pp. 160 ff. Faith is always for Matthew an obeying; it is not in any way contrasted with works, neither in the sense of James 2.14 ff. nor in the sense of Paul; indeed, it should be noted that Matthew knows nothing whatever of the Pauline conception of works.

person.'[1] Alongside faithfulness to the law there also stands in the synagogue trust in God's care, help, omnipotence and requital. Here also knowledge of the object of faith is no structural element of faith. In this respect Matthew is firmly determined by the Old Testament-Jewish conception of faith. Yet there is a difference, for πιστεύειν in Matthew always has συνιέναι as its presupposition and is impossible without it. There is nothing corresponding to this either in the Old Testament or in Judaism.[2] This complementariness of συνιέναι and πιστεύειν in Matthew rather presupposes the primitive Christian missionary preaching and the theory of the hardening of Israel.[3]

3. Conversion

Psychology is more firmly developed in Matthew than in Mark. This is shown by the link between πιστεύειν and συνιέναι. Both concepts clearly indicate the situation of Matthew's church. On one hand this is shaped by the hardening of the front against Judaism. The circle of those who belong to the Church is now more clearly differentiated from the rest of the Jewish nation; the latter is hardened whereas understanding is given to the Christians. On the other hand, there are now in the Church itself good and evil; but this distinction does not concern understanding but yielding fruit.[4] Hence the exhortation to the doing of God's will, which is also shown in the concept of faith. As Matthew's interest lies in yielding fruit, conversion also has not the heightened meaning which it has

[1] A. Schlatter, Glaube im NT, p. 15.

[2] The concept ידע cannot be brought against this, for ידע already denotes obedient recognition of God's might, his grace and his demand. Hence R. Bultmann can conclude that in John's Gospel πιστεύειν corresponds to ידע (TWNT, I, p. 713 [BKW Gnosis, p. 49]).

[3] It is possible that some light may fall from this upon the concept ὀλιγόπιστος, ὀλιγοπιστία (Matthew 5 times, Luke once). The expression corresponds to the Palestinian mode of expression, cf. H. J. Held below, p. 293. It is striking that Matthew never applies ὀλιγόπιστος to the multitude; they are ἄπιστος (13.58; 17.17). The disciples are constantly called ὀλιγόπιστοι (also in 17.20 ὀλιγοπιστίαν should be read with B, ℵ, syr^cur 1, 13, 23, 124, 346, against C, D, syr^sin, it, vg, and the Koine, which have ἀπιστίαν). Only in 17.17 could it be objected that ἄπιστος includes the disciples; but against this γενεά elsewhere always means the multitude. Obviously the preferential use of ὀλιγόπιστος with reference to the disciples is based on the fact that they have been given understanding. Little faith is then unbelief, for the disciple to whom the knowledge of Christ has been given.

[4] One may not read out of ὃς δὴ καρποφορεῖ in 13.23 that the yielding of fruit so necessarily follows understanding that understanding must have been lacking in those who are rejected in the judgment; rather 13.23 also recognises a difference in the yield of fruit, and this is exploited by Matthew, with the increasing numbers, in a hortatory sense as exhortation to the yielding of fruit.

in Luke.[1] In Luke the consequence of the increased interest is that conversion is split up into its component parts (H. Conzelmann, *op. cit.*, pp. 198 ff.): μετάνοια is the condition of ἄφεσις, and the latter is the presupposition of salvation. Conzelmann further thinks that a distinction should be made between μετανοεῖν and ἐπιστρέφειν as between change of disposition and of conduct. Conversion is linking up with the Church, ἄφεσις the once-for-all forgiveness in baptism. That conversion is not especially emphasised in Matthew is shown by Matt. 10.7: in the instruction connected with the sending out of the disciples the summons to μετάνοια can be passed over (cf. Mark 6.12); it is axiomatic and therefore not stressed. In Matthew no distinction is made between μετανοεῖν and ἐπιστρέφειν; obviously μετάνοια and ἄφεσις belong closely together. In the summary account of the preaching of Jesus and the Baptist one μετανοεῖτε suffices (3.2; 4.17). Further, one may not read out of 3.11 that Matthew denied the ἄφεσις ἁμαρτιῶν to the baptism of John,[2] for the evangelist especially emphasises the similarity between the preaching of the Baptist and Jesus (3.2; 4.17). The statement in Mark 1.4, however, that John's baptism produces ἄφεσις ἁμαρτιῶν had to be deleted, since in 3.2 Matthew emphasised the similarity between the preaching of Jesus and that of the Baptist. Now in 3.11 he tries to add the statement on John's baptism, but is already conditioned by the fight against the false security of the Pharisees (3.7–10), who look upon the forgiveness of sins in John's Baptism as a guarantee which makes them safe for the judgment and releases them from obedience.[3] One may scarcely, however, conclude from this that Matthew wished to deny the ἄφεσις ἁμαρτιῶν to John's baptism altogether. Matt. 3.7–10 shows the inseparability of repentance and good works, which admittedly was already in Q, but is also characteristic of Matthew.

Does conversion take place once-for-all or must it be constantly repeated in the life of the Christian? In passages like Matt. 3.2, 8, 11; 4.17; 11.20 f.; 12.41 a once-for-all turning about is no doubt in mind. These passages agree that in both the preaching of Jesus and that of the primitive Church what is in mind is a once-for-all

[1] μετάνοια μετανοεῖν: in Matthew 7 times, Mark 3 times, Luke 14 times; στρέφειν or ἐπιστρέφειν: Matthew twice, Mark once, Luke 4 times.

[2] But G. Bornkamm thinks one may (above, p. 15); J. Wellhausen on Matt. 3.15.

[3] It does not actually say that the Pharisees appealed to their baptism but to the fact that they were children of Abraham; but they came to baptism (3.7) and the warning about false security is linked with that.

turning about in face of the immediately imminent βασιλεία τοῦ θεοῦ.[1] But alongside this stands Matt. 18.3: conversion, turning about (ἐὰν μὴ στραφῆτε) means for Matthew 'to become as a child'. That it is not a matter of an unintentional, accidental change is shown by the whole structure of Matt. 18 with the prominence it gives to μικροί or alternatively παιδία.[2] Conversion is not here understood as a once-for-all joining of the Church, but it is an event constantly repeated in the Christian's life. This understanding of conversion, however, cannot be simply transferred to the other passages. Thus it is seen that Matthew has no uniformly constructed conception of conversion. He could do without it, as has been shown on the basis of συνιέναι and πιστεύειν in Matthew. What is important is that such an understanding of conversion as 18.3 was possible for him.

4. *Unbelief and sin of the disciples*

There is a widespread general view that the later standpoint of the Church also shows itself in Matthew in that he avoids reporting what is unfavourable to the disciples, by toning it down, passing over it, or simply twisting it round.[3] In this connexion E. Klostermann (additional note to Matt. 3.1) names the following passages: 8.26; 17.23; 20.20; 14.33; 16.9; 17.4, 9; 18.1; 19.23; 20.17; 26.43; 13.16 f. A further investigation yields the following: 17.23 (= Mark 9.32); 14.33 (= Mark 6.52); 16.9 (= Mark 8.17); 17.4 (= Mark 9.6); 17.9 (= Mark 9.10); 20.17 (= Mark 10.32); 13.16 f. (= Mark 4.13)—these have already been studied above; they are passages in which the lack of understanding on the part of the disciples in Mark is deleted; the disciples have understanding. But this is not a matter of a bias in favour of excusing the disciples, of deleting what is unfavourable to them, but it is a firm construction of the first evangelist which has a quite different background. For similar reasons 8.26 is untenable: that the disciples are not accused of unbelief but of little faith likewise corresponds to a quite firm conception. On the other hand, a clear and probably deliberate toning down occurs in Matt. 20.20 (= Mark 10.35): it is not the two

---

[1] Cf. J. Behm, μετάνοια, *TWNT*, IV, p. 997.

[2] On this see below, pp. 121 f.

[3] Thus J. Wagenmann (*Die Stellung des Apostels Paulus neben den Zwölf*, 1926, pp. 61 ff.) speaks of a sustained idealisation of the disciples in Matthew. Similarly W. C. Allen (p. xxxiii), W. Wrede (p. 160), H. von Soden (*Das Interesse des apostolischen Zeitalters an der evangelischen Geschichte*, Festschrift für C. von Weizsäcker, Freiburg, 1892, pp. 137 f.), C. G. Montefiore (on Matt. 18.1, p. 247).

sons of Zebedee themselves but their mother who, driven by the thirst for honour, puts the request. Thirst for honour is also the point in Matt. 18.1 f. In Matthew, Mark 9.34 is wanting: 'for they had disputed one with another in the way, who was the greatest'. In the absence of these words E. Klostermann sees similar toning down. Whether that is right is at least questionable, for the substance itself is completely sustained by Matthew. In Matthew the disciples themselves ask, and indeed not simply τίς μείζων, but who is greatest in the kingdom of heaven (i.e. of themselves, as 18.3 shows!). The reply of Jesus to this is still sharper than that in Mark. If it is at least questionable here whether one may speak of a toning down, one may still less in 19.23 and 26.43. In 19.23 Mark 10.24 is lacking. There the saying that it is difficult for rich men to enter into the kingdom of God is repeated in a somewhat more general form expanded to include all men. Even if this repetition stood in Mark's source—which in view of its absence from Luke is exceedingly dubious—one can hardly speak of a toning down, for the disciples refer the saying about the rich to themselves (19.25). Likewise, in the absence of Mark 14.40c 'and they wist not what to answer him' one can acknowledge an abbreviation, but scarcely a toning down, for the decisive accusation in 26.43 remains.[1]

Yet Matthew has five times inserted the accusation of the deficient faith of the disciples: 14.31; 16.8; 17.20; 28.17[2] and 21.20.[3] He has thus considerably strengthened the accusation of defective faith. He has also in 16.22 f. strengthened Peter's contradiction of the readiness of Jesus to suffer and also Jesus' correction of him in 16.23.[4] In 24.12 Matthew knows that in the congregation love grows cold. In 26.70 Matthew has depicted Peter's denial as still worse than Mark did: in Mark Peter is questioned by two people, in Matthew by three (26.71); he denies ἔμπροσθεν πάντων (26.70); that Matthew will have

[1] E. Klostermann names three further passages in which Matthew has inserted something commendable about the disciples. 16.12 and 17.13 again do not belong here, but to the thought of understanding in Matthew. He himself puts a question-mark after 16.17–19. His insertion cannot be explained as an expression of his desire to say something commendable about the disciples.

[2] ἐδίστασαν in the NT only in Matthew twice; on 28.17 see below, pp. 131 f.

[3] Cf. ἐθαύμασαν; the question: πῶς παραχρῆμα ἐξηράνθη in 21.20; and further 21.21a: ἐὰν ἔχετε πίστιν (cf. Mark). 21.21a (like 21.20) is a reformulation by Matthew; cf. E. Klostermann on 17.20.

[4] That Matthew understood Peter's conduct as disobedience is shown not only by the opposite case in 17.4, where he adds εἰ θέλεις because it is the task of the disciple to do the will of Jesus, but above all by the use of σκάνδαλον (cf. 13.41).

been thinking here of the prohibition of swearing in 5.33 ff. is shown by the many allusions to the Sermon on the Mount in the Passion story.[1] In 19.27 one might see simply a clarification in the addition 'what then shall we have'; but the fact that Matthew not only provides an affirmative reply by Jesus (19.28 ff.) but also by the parable of the labourers in the vineyard (20.1–16) a sharp warning,[2] shows that he wishes the addition to be assessed in a negative way. It characterises the desire of the disciples for rewards and this is what they are warned against.[3]

In all these passages the evangelist has brought the disobedience of the disciples still more strongly into prominence, or even inserted it. In comparison with this the one passage where the desire of the disciples for praise is really toned down (20.20) is of scarcely any weight at all. And the more so when a comparison with Luke is made in this matter. In Luke 9.22 Luke omits Peter's contradiction of the readiness of Jesus to suffer; whereas Matthew introduces the saying about the faith that removes mountains by the accusation of little faith (17.20) Luke does it by the devout prayer πρόσθες ἡμῖν πίστιν (Luke 17.5). Corresponding to this in Luke 9.37–43 the accusation because of the inability of the disciples to heal is omitted (Matt. 17.20). Only in Luke 9.54 does the revenge-seeking disposition of the disciples correspond with the passages mentioned above in Matthew.

[1] On the allusions to the Sermon on the Mount in the Passion story see below, pp. 143 ff.
[2] In 19.30 πολλοί cannot refer to the rich of 19.23, but only to 19.27 ff.; this is shown by the repetition in 20.16. Matthew thus wishes 19.30 to be understood in the light of 20.1–15: the 'first' are those whom the householder has sent to work in his vineyard. By their boasting of what they have earned and by their envy of their fellow labourers they can miss a share in the joy and the experience of the kindness of the lord. 20.1–15 is thus especially added by Matthew with 19.27 in mind!
[3] These are straightforward alterations in the presence of which it is hardly necessary to name the passages which show that Matthew not only takes over the failure of the disciples but even makes it clearer still. Whereas Luke omits the flight of the disciples at the arrest of Jesus (Luke 22.53), Matthew makes it clearer by the addition of μαθηταί in 26.56. In connexion with the anointing in Bethany he has also brought greater clarity: it is the μαθηταί who are indignant about the woman's service of love (26.8). The disciple's sword-blow in 26.51 is condemned in Matthew by Jesus. The editorial construction in 19.10 may be determined in its attitude by the intention to place by contrast the following saying about the eunuchs (19.12) in its true light. In any case the saying shows that Matthew had no hesitation about presenting the disciples in such a bad light as in 19.10: God's commandments are too difficult for them, they give in. Notice also the striking interpretation which Matthew gives to the story of the healing of the epileptic boy (17.14–21); cf. H. J. Held below, pp. 187 ff.

This calling of attention to the little faith and disobedience of the disciples in Matthew is illuminating; it shows that the constant exhortation to the doing of God's will, the constant threat of judgment according to works which will bring the final decision about eternal salvation, did not lead to the forgetting or concealing of the knowledge of the enduring sinfulness of the disciples. The constant attaching of importance to works does not lead to any leaning on one's own achievement. The following section will show this still more clearly.

5. *The disciples as* μικροί

That the constant threat of the judgment according to works does not drive the disciples according to Matthew to rely upon their works but as those who are empty before God to cleave to his grace is shown most clearly in Matt. 18. The interpretation which Matthew gave to the rule for the discipline of the congregation in 18.15–17 by the framework of 18.12–14 and 19–35 has already been shown. This exposition of the rule for the discipline of the congregation already shows that the congregation is aware that it owes its salvation to its Lord's seeking and pursuing, as the shepherd the lost sheep. It lives by virtue of a seeking and forgiving love. This is made still clearer by the fact that in Matt. 18 μικροί (or alternatively παιδία) becomes a designation of Christians. In 18.1–5 Matthew made compact the loose connexion in Mark between the ambition of the disciples and the saying about receiving the children, by omitting Mark 9.35, by introducing Mark 10.15 in a different form (= Matt. 18.3), and by his own construction of 18.4. In Mark the disciples quarrel over τίς μείζων; Matthew clarifies that: it is a matter of precedence in the βασιλεία τῶν οὐρανῶν and in harmony with that in 18.3 about entrance into the βασιλεία. Matthew thus makes out of the saying about humility in Mark a section about childlike behaviour as the condition of entrance into the kingdom of God. Only those who are converted and become as little children can enter into the kingdom of God. Conversion, and thus also becoming a disciple, means 'becoming like a child' (18.3). Hence the exhortation to humble oneself as a child (18.4); only such are counted great in the kingdom of God. The emphasis in 18.1–5 lies on this exhortation to the disciples to become like a child; the saying about receiving children recedes behind this. After the omission of Mark 9.38–41 there is then added the warning about σκανδαλίζειν ἕνα τῶν μικρῶν τούτων τῶν πιστευόντων εἰς ἐμέ in 18.6–9. To what does τούτων refer? Formally it is a link with the actual children in 18.5 or 2, but the addition τῶν πιστευόντων εἰς ἐμέ shows that Christians are meant, and not presumably believing children but Christians in general.[1] This transition from the actual child of 18.2 to the Christian in 18.6 has been made possible by Matthew's alteration in 18.1–5. Again Matthew has deleted Mark 9.49 f. and added a saying in 18.10 about despising a child. Originally the saying spoke of despising actual children but here, by the first evangelist's context the μικροί is referred to Christians.[2] The parable of the lost sheep follows and by means of 18.14 Matthew similarly refers this to the μικροί.[3] μικροί has thus become a designation for Christians.[4] There is a dispute about the point from which actual children are no longer meant, but, in the metaphorical sense, Christians. According to A. Schlatter and J. Wellhausen it is from 18.6, according to E. Klostermann and T. Zahn from 18.5 already (τοιοῦτο!). What is decisive is that for Matthew from the beginning it is transparent that the child stands for the essence of the disciple. The starting-point for this use of μικροί (or alternatively παιδία) is already given in Mark 10.15, but Matthew first develops the line more firmly. What is the essential thing about the μικροί (or παιδία) which makes them a figure of Christians? Sinlessness cannot be in mind, as 18.12–20 shows. According to 18.4 it is ταπείνωσις, but this is not understood as a virtue, since in 18.12–14 the disciples are exhorted to pursue the one who has erred, or been led away by sin, as the shepherd seeks the lost sheep. It is true that the mark of the μικροί is not that they have gone astray like a sheep, but rather the weakness and helplessness of the lost sheep. The disciples are thus the weak and lowly, helpless as regards their own salvation. But also, immediately over against this in Matt. 18 stands the fact that it is now entirely a matter of tearing out sin (18.8 ff.) and removing it from the congregation (18.15 ff.).

---

[1] Cf. J. Wellhausen, ad loc.: 'the μικροί are Christians as a whole, not a special section of them.'

[2] Cf. R. Bultmann, SynT, p. 145.

[3] 18.10 doubtless belongs to Matthew's special material; 18.14 is his own construction.

[4] Through the influence of Matthew in Matt. 18 μικροί is first made into a sustained designation of Christians. Hence in 10.42 also μικρῶν τούτων will not be the original form of the saying, but an alteration by the evangelist. On μικροί cf. O. Michel, ' "Diese Kleinen"—eine Jüngerbezeichnung Jesu', TSK 108, 1937/38, pp. 401 ff., who does not, however, examine the editorial moulding of this concept by Matthew.

If the disciples are designated as the μικροί in Matt. 18 a related view of the essence of discipleship is to be found in the first four Beatitudes in Matt. 5.3–6. This in no way contradicts the knowledge that the Beatitudes in Matthew give a kind of norm for the essence of what makes a disciple. According to Windisch[1] they actually denote the conditions of entrance into the kingdom of God; but that also applies to Matt. 18.3. Matthew constructs 5.3–10 in two similar strophes each of four Beatitudes.[2] Both strophes are constructed very largely alike. As the first strophe begins with the promise of the βασιλεία the second closes with it (5.3 and 10). In both strophes Matthew found three Beatitudes already, while a fourth was presumably added by Matthew himself.[3] The Beatitudes from Q (Luke 6.20 f.) are all in the first strophe, those of the second are obviously from the special Matthaean source. In both strophes the fourth Beatitude speaks of δικαιοσύνη. Similarly too, with regard to contents, 5.3–6 and 5.7–10 form two different groups.

In 5.3 Matthew has added τῷ πνεύματι. The πτωχοί (עֲנִיִּים) are even without this addition a religious concept. That Matthew makes this addition in spite of that can only mean that he is concerned to emphasise that it is not the materially poor but those 'who as regards their inner life, that is before God, in the feeling of their inability to help themselves, stand there as beggars' (E. Klostermann, T. Zahn).

In 5.6 Matthew has added καὶ διψῶντες τὴν δικαιοσύνην. Obviously this does not mean people who are at pains to make a constant effort, but those who long that God will pronounce upon them in the judgment the verdict 'righteous';[4] they long for the rightness of disposition

---

[1] *Der Sinn der Bergpredigt*, p. 63.

[2] A deletion of the πραεῖς Beatitude is not possible. It is true that its position in some MSS. is fluctuating. In D, 33, a, c, ff[1], g[1,2]h, k, l, vg, syr[cur], Clem., Orig., it stands before the Beatitude of those who mourn. But in no MS. is it missing. Its deletion therefore rests entirely on the dogma of the number of seven Beatitudes. Against this and in favour of its originality (not in the mouth of Jesus, but in the original Matthaean text) there are the following points: 1. that it fits admirably into the context between the first and fourth Beatitudes, 2. that it contains specifically Matthaean linguistic material and thought: πραΰς is found only in Matthew among the Gospels, and there three times; the thought of humility, above all in Christology, where Matthew interprets the Messianic secret in Mark in the light of this point of view (cf. Matt. 21.5; 12.15–21), is a favourite thought of Matthew. Hence 5.5 must be accepted as his construction.

[3]5.10 is presumably an excerpt from 5.11 f. (E. Klostermann, *ad loc.*); v. 5 is from Ps. 37.11.

[4] Cf. R. Bultmann, *Theology of the NT* (ET, London, 1952, 1955), I, p. 273.

which is acceptable with God.[1] They are thus those who lack righteousness, who can only be satisfied by the divine gift.[2]

In between these the third Beatitude in 5.5, following Ps. 37.11, fits well. The עֲנָוִים correspond to the πραεῖς, and the word is hardly distinguishable in meaning from עֲנִיִּים (E. Klostermann). But it is necessary here to pay attention to the use of πραΰς in Matthew.

πραΰς denotes Jesus' humble acceptance of his lowliness.[3] Hence 5.5 obviously differs from 5.3 by the element of acceptance: if it is there a matter of being empty before God it is here the humble acceptance of this relationship.

There can thus be seen a uniform direction in which Matthew interprets the Beatitudes from Q: it is the waiting, the lacking, the empty before God, the lowly, to whom the promise made.[4] Here also there follows the exhortation to the doing of God's will (Matt. 5.7–19).

It has thus been shown that the constant exhortation to the doing of God's will and the threat of judgment according to works has not

---

[1] According to G. Schrenk, δικαιοσύνη, *TWNT*, II, p. 200 [BKW *Righteousness*, p. 35], there is no need to think of the judging and saving δικαιοσύνη θεοῦ in the forensic eschatological sense. Schrenk obviously thinks that they do not long for God's judging and saving verdict, but for the rightness of their own disposition before the judgment of God. But then it should be noted that precisely here it is said that righteousness is bestowed upon them. Can this gift consist of anything other than that God pronounces them righteous in the judgment? Judaism also knows the forensic-eschatological concept of righteousness (cf. R. Bultmann, *op. cit.*, p. 273), only there righteousness is no longer regarded as grace, as saving righteousness, as it is in the OT.

[2] Thus J. Weiss, A. Schlatter, J. Schniewind, T. Zahn, *ad loc.*

[3] He is the βασιλεὺς πραΰς in 21.5 whose obedient acceptance of his humiliation the Passion story in Matthew especially emphasises. Jesus' command of silence and his withdrawal before the Pharisees is established in 12.15–21 on the lowliness of the παῖς of Isa. 42.1–4; cf. Matt. 11.28 ff. Jesus' humiliation is understood as obedience, i.e. as acceptance. For the references for this we must point to the next chapter.

[4] The Beatitude of those who mourn also fits well into this context. To what does the mourning of 5.4 refer? The interpretation in terms of mourning for the dead (thus Schlatter) is surely too narrow, and so is that in terms of one's own sin; mourning here surely means something more comprehensive. Hence E. Klostermann: mourning over the power of evil in the world. Clearly there is an allusion to Isa. 61.1–3: παρακαλέσαι πάντας τοὺς πενθοῦντας. In Isa. 61.1–3 the recipients of salvation are also wretched, broken in spirit, imprisoned, bound (both figurative expressions for material and inner need), mourning, heavy in spirit. Mourning thus here also characterises, in a series of concepts similar to those in Matt. 5.3 and 5 the attitude of the עֲנָוִים. This results in the first four Beatitudes presenting a closed series: it is the lowly, the empty before God, the waiting, who are pronounced blessed.

led in Matthew to the Christian relying on his own achievement; the disciples recognise themselves as empty before God, as the μιχροί, who live by the seeking love of the shepherd. What this means for the understanding of the law will also be investigated in the following chapter.

V. LAW AND CHRISTOLOGY

1. *The lowliness of Jesus, the* βασιλεὺς πραΰς *and the presentness of the Risen One*

If one asks about the understanding of the law in Matthew that means asking about the attitude of Jesus to the law in Matthew's Gospel. Matthew, however, does not seek to reproduce the attitude of the historical Jesus to the law, but he sees already in the earthly Jesus the risen Lord and hence shows rather the relationship in which the risen Lord stands to the law. It may therefore be assumed that a series of connecting lines will be found between Matthew's Christology and his understanding of the law and these will need to be exhibited if this is to be made clear.

This cannot mean that here the Christology, which has undergone a rich development in Matthew in comparison with Mark and Q, must be set forth as a whole. Only those traits of the Christology of Matthew which are important for the understanding of the law, will be studied. Something of this has had to be anticipated in the preceding chapters. The first thing that must impress is the strong emphasis laid on the lowliness of Jesus—despite the intensifying of his majesty.[1]

Matt. 12.17–21

In comparison with the Markan version Matthew has added to the two conversations about the Sabbath in 12.1–14 a summary report in 12.15–21 in which, on the one hand, he has strongly abbreviated the Markan original, and on the other has extended it by the quotation from Isa. 42.1–4. In this quotation he interprets

---

[1] On the intensifying of the majesty and deity of Jesus cf. the passages named by E. Klostermann (excursus on Matt. 3.1), in which human emotions of Jesus, cases of his inability to do something, instances where an intention of Jesus is not attained and cases of his ignorance, which mean that he asks seriously intended questions, are suppressed, in which miracles of Jesus are heightened and disrespectful questions put to Jesus are omitted. The supernatural birth in Matt. 1 also belongs here and the fact that Matthew can speak of angels of the Son of man (13.41; 16.27; 24.31). Further statements of this kind will be named in the following pages.

the withdrawing of Jesus from the Pharisees (12.15) and the command of silence (12.16) by the humility and lowliness of the servant of God, who will not strive and cry aloud and whose voice will not be heard in the streets.[1] His healings and his preaching activity are also shown to be a sign of the lowliness of the servant of God (12.20). In that Jesus thereby fulfils Isa. 42.1–4, his action, precisely in his lowliness, becomes an act of obedience. An analysis of 12.18–21 will support this.

The quotation in 12.18–21 is independent of the LXX as far as the conclusion, but it also differs markedly from the Massoretic Text. In 12.18 ἰδοὺ ὁ παῖς μου corresponds to הֵן עַבְדִּי in the Massoretic Text; but the continuation ὃν ᾑρέτισα, ὁ ἀγαπητός μου, ὃν εὐδόκησεν ἡ ψυχή μου departs markedly from the LXX as well as the Massoretic Text, Targum and Theodotion.[2] The words show a strong echo of the heavenly voice at the baptism of Jesus in Matt. 3.17 οὗτός ἐστιν (Mark = σὺ εἶ) ὁ υἱός μου ὁ ἀγαπητός, ἐν ᾧ εὐδόκησα, which Matthew has adopted from Mark 1.11. Did Matthew see in the words of the heavenly voice a quoting of Isa. 42?[3] At any rate the words of this heavenly voice must have been especially important for Matthew, since in connexion with the transfiguration of Jesus in 17.5, by the addition of ἐν ᾧ εὐδόκησα he also makes the words of the heavenly voice identical with those of 3.17. Then the variation in 12.18 would be explained as an expression of Matthew's desire to assimilate it to 3.17 and 17.5.[4] Hence by the word ᾑρέτισα he has drawn בחירי (LXX: ἐκλεκτός) out of the second half into the first. The variation cannot therefore be explained by some text or other which was to hand, but it corresponds with a conscious interpretation of the evangelist, who thereby links the quotation with 3.17 and 17.5.[5]

[1] This interpretation of the command of silence is already established by W. Wrede (op. cit., p. 155).
[2] Cf. the careful investigation by K. Stendahl, The School of St Matthew, pp. 108 ff.
[3] Thus K. Stendahl, pp. 109 f., who likewise explains the variation in Matt. 12.18 by the influence of Mark 1.11.
[4] The assimilation would be still clearer if one were to read in 12.18 with C, D, 1, 33, it. plerique, vg., Ir., Hil., ἐν ᾧ, but this is questionable; ℵ, B, 115, 244 have ὅν.
[5] In 18c K. Stendahl (p. 111) sees in ἀπαγγέλλειν a closeness to the Targum (יגלי = open, uncover, make audible, announce; cf. J. Levy, Chaldäisches Wörterbuch über die Targumim, 1867 on גלא), and likewise in the future θήσω (Targum אתין, imperfect, which according to Stendahl note 2 is always translated by the future). It is more probable, however, that Matthew uses ἀπαγγέλλειν for יוציא solely for reasons of clarity, while he has to use the future θήσω because the prophet is speaking of the coming Christ.

Equally striking are the variations in 12.19 οὐκ ἐρίσει οὐδὲ κραυγάσει. The οὐκ ἐρίσει can be explained neither from the Massoretic Text nor from the LXX.[1] On the other hand, it is entirely intelligible as an interpretation of Matthew: it clarifies his actual concern as he here adds the quotation. When the Pharisees decide to destroy him (12.14) Jesus withdraws (12.15). Matthew sees in this a fulfilment of Isa. 42 which he clarifies by reproducing οὐκ ἐρίσει. That shows, however, as a matter of course that he sees in the conduct of Jesus a sign of his humility and lowliness. In 12.19b ἐν ταῖς πλαταίαις is a translation of חַבּוּץ in the Massoretic Text. But 'the correct and natural translation is the adverbial one of the LXX' (Stendahl, op. cit., p. 113; the LXX has ἔξω). The variation from the natural translation of the LXX is again here best explained by the interpretation which the quotation is intended to give to the context: ἐν ταῖς πλαταίαις fits in better with the command of silence in 12.16. The meaning of the humility and lowliness of the 'servant of God' again goes so far that the quotation is especially shaped by it.

Finally the variations in 12.20 must be considered, although they first become important in a later context. 12.20a departs from the LXX but can be well explained as a translation of the Massoretic Text; more significant is the variation in 20b: ἕως ἂν ἐκβάλῃ εἰς νῖκος τὴν κρίσιν has no parallels, either in the Massoretic Text, Targum, Peshitta or the LXX.[2] Obviously it is a case of bringing together Isa. 42.3c לְאֱמֶת יוֹצִיא מִשְׁפָּט and 42.4b עַד יָשִׂים בָּאָרֶץ מִשְׁפָּט the part in between in 4a being passed over. But εἰς νῖκος cannot be explained in that way. E. Klostermann, T. Zahn and K. Stendahl find in it an influence from Hab. 1.4 יֵצֵא לָנֶצַח מִשְׁפָט. לָנֶצַח is frequently reproduced by εἰς νῖκος; it contains some influence from the Aramaic, where נצח means conquer.[3] But that does not yet answer the decisive question: Why has Matthew made this alteration? If it is a case of influence from Hab. 1.4, how did this influence come about?

[1] MT: לֹא יִצְעַק וְלֹא יִשָּׂא
    LXX: οὐ κεκράζεται οὐδὲ ἀνήσει
    Targum: לָא יִצוַח וְלָא יְכַלִי

[2] Isa. 42.3c–4b LXX: ἀλλὰ εἰς ἀλήθειαν ἐξοίσει κρίσιν. ἀνλάμψει καὶ οὐ θραυσθήσεται, ἕως ἂν θῇ ἐπι τῆς γῆς κρίσιν. Aquila and Theodotion: οὐκ ἀμαυρώσει καὶ οὐ δραμεῖται ἕως ἂν θῇ ἐν τῇ γῇ κρίσιν. Targum Jonathan: לקושטיה יפיק דינא : לא יהלי ולא ילאי עד דיתקין באראא דינא

Peshitta: b'qushta' n'pheq dina' la' nedh'akh w'la' n'taphteph 'dhama' dan'sim dina' b'ar'a'.

[3] Detailed statement of the material in A. Rahlfs, 'Über Theodotion-Lesarten im NT und Aquila-Lesarten bei Justin', ZNW 20 (1921), pp. 186–9.

A mistake on the ground that he was quoting from memory is excluded by the observations made above. Here also it can only be a matter of conscious alteration, of theological interpretation. In the context of ch. 12 there is no direct case, but it will be shown that the thought of 12.20b plays a significant role in the Christological conception of Matthew and recurs in different ways. This will be dealt with in the next section. Here 12.20a must be examined again. Since Matthew places the individual statements of the quotation from Isa. 42.1–4 in close relation to the activity of Jesus the question is of what he is thinking in connexion with the 'bruised reed' and the 'smoking flax'. The nearest relationship is to the sick in 12.15. But because of the close connexion between 12.20a and b 'till he send forth judgment unto victory', the thought cannot be only of the sick. It is rather in the comprehensive sense of the work of Jesus the Saviour for the lost, of πτωχοὶ εὐαγγελίζονται (11.5). Then similar expressions which characterise the situation of man and which are found only in Matthew catch the attention; men who are the object of Jesus the Saviour's work are designated in 9.36 as ἐσκυλμένοι καὶ ἐρριμμένοι, and in 11.28 as κοπιῶντες καὶ πεφορτισμένοι. The closest is the relationship to 9.36. Hence in 12.20a the thought is of Jesus the Saviour's activity in the comprehensive sense, of his acts of healing as well as his preaching.[1] Both are characterised by means of the quotation as the work of his humiliation.

By means of the quotation in 12.18–21 Matthew has especially underlined the humility and lowliness of Jesus. His withdrawing from the Pharisees, his command of silence, in fact his whole saving activity for the broken are signs of his lowliness, in which he proves himself the servant of God of Isa. 42. A similar underlining of his lowliness is provided by

Matt. 8.17

Here again a summary report (the text of Mark 1.32–34 is greatly shortened) is interpreted by the addition of a quotation:[2] in his healings Jesus shows himself to be the servant of Isa. 53; they are thus to be understood as a work of his obedience and his humiliation.[3]

---

[1] In connexion with the 'smoking flax' the emphasis is not on a remnant of the good that remains in man (E. Klostermann and C. G. Montefiore, *ad loc.*), but on the contrary, that the flax is only smouldering.

[2] Here Matthew keeps to the MT of Isa. 53.4 and disregards the LXX; at the same time the translation in Matt. 8.17 shows Matthaean linguistic usage, cf. A. Schlatter, *Matthew*, p. 282.

[3] Cf. G. Bornkamm above, pp. 36 f., and H. J. Held below, p. 262.

The same has already been seen with regard to 12.20 in so far as the bruised reed and the smouldering flax refer primarily to the sick of 12.15,[1] and here also in the healings as in his saving work as a whole the humiliation of Jesus is seen.

The insertion of 3.14 f. into the section on the baptism of Jesus also signifies an underlining of the humiliation of Jesus. More will be said of this in what follows; it is sufficient here to note that here again the humiliation of Jesus is brought into prominence.

These examples suffice to show that the lowliness of Jesus was in the forefront of Matthew's interest.[2] Matthew's characteristic designation of the attitude of Jesus as the humiliated One is πραΰς. By the quotation in

Matt. 21.4 f.

Matthew has completely fashioned the pericope on the entry into Jerusalem in the light of the thought of the πραΰτης of Jesus. It is well known that he takes the reshaping of the story of the entry on the basis of Zech. 9.9 so far that he duplicates the animal that is ridden in consequence of a misunderstanding of the parallelism in Zech. 9.9.[3] But what is decisive here is the way in which Matthew reproduces Zech. 9.9. Whereas the introduction in Matt. 21.5a is taken from Isa. 62.11, in the quotation from Zech. 9.9 Matthew follows the LXX exactly as far as ἔρχεταί σοι, and this agrees with the Massoretic Text.[4] But then צַדִּיק וְנוֹשָׁע הוּא = δίκαιος καὶ σώζων αὐτός is omitted, which is all the more surprising since Matthew shows a marked interest in Jesus as the δίκαιος who fulfils all righteousness

---

[1] If it is once appreciated that Matthew sees in the healings of Jesus an expression of his humiliation and obedience it will follow that the prominence frequently given to the fact that Jesus healed all (4.23; 8.16; 9.36; 12.15) will be seen not only as an enhancement of his deity but also an underlining of his obedience, the faithfulness of his serving.

[2] Hence A. Schlatter (*Theologie der Apostel*, Stuttgart, 1922², p. 81) sees a manifestation of the resignation and humiliation of Jesus not only in the quotations of 8.17 and 12.18 ff. but also in those of 2.15, 17, 23; 4.14; 13.35; 27.9. Matthew calls upon the Scripture above all when he wishes to set forth the resignation and humiliation of Jesus. In connexion with some of the passages mentioned it may well be asked whether the thought is primarily of the humiliation of Jesus, but on the whole one will have to agree with Schlatter's judgment.

[3] Who will straightway let the animals go? (21.3.) In Mark it is clearly Jesus (πάλιν ὧδε). In Matthew it is obviously otherwise: πάλιν ὧδε is deleted and δέ put in its place: the owners will let the animals go. The fact that it concerns the Messianic king, to whom unquestioning obedience belongs, also shapes this passage.

[4] MT: הִנֵּה מַלְכֵּךְ יָבוֹא לָךְ; LXX: ἰδοῦ ὁ βασιλεύς σου ἔρχεταί σοι.

(3.15).[1] Through this deletion πραΰς stands in the middle point, dominating the quotation. The only possible point in the omission is the emphasising of πραΰς. By Matthew's abbreviation of the account of the finding of the animal that is to be ridden (Mark 11.4 f.) the motive of the wonderful prediction of Jesus about the finding of the animal falls into the background. In this way the thought of the βασιλεὺς πραΰς steps in a dominating way into the centre. It now shapes the whole account of the entry. K. Stendahl (op. cit., p. 119) thinks that Matthew is here controlled by the Rabbinic exegesis of Zech. 9.9, in which 'poor and riding upon an ass' is frequently emphasised (cf. Billerbeck, I, pp. 842 ff.). But the passages collected by Billerbeck show that this exegesis belongs to a later period, so that Matthew could hardly have been influenced by it. The later date can be seen in the fact that Zech. 9.9 is interpreted in terms of the Messiah ben David in contrast to the Messiah ben Joseph, or alternatively, ben Ephraim.

The decisive thing for Matthew in reproducing Zech. 9.9 is that Jesus is πραΰς, he is the βασιλεὺς πραΰς. What is meant by that? Obviously above all his lowliness, his humiliation, the fact that the One who is destined to be the eschatological judge of the world, disclaiming his power and glory, enters here in lowliness on the way to the cross.[2] But in this lowliness there lies a moment of obedience, of humility, as the interpretation of the withdrawal of Jesus from the

[1] נוֹשָׁע denotes one who himself first received help (thus not = σώζων). Was this unacceptable to Matthew? But how could this objection to נוֹשָׁע fit in with the emphasis on lowliness and with 27.43? Fruther, נוֹשָׁע need not be understood in this sense only (cf. K. Elliger, Kleine Profeten II, ATD 25, 1951, p. 140), and Matthew does not hesitate elsewhere to prefer the LXX, when it agrees with his interests (cf. 12.21). The question then remains: Why has Matthew omitted these statements?

[2] Matt. 21.5 underlines the paradox that lies in the fact that the βασιλεύς, the king of Israel, comes as πραΰς. Further, Matthew alone reports the praise of the children (21.14–16) whereby the πραΰτης of Jesus is emphasised. The title βασιλεύς is applied to Jesus more frequently by Matthew than by Mark and Luke. In 2.2 already the 'new-born king of the Jews' is contrasted with Herod the king. In 25.34, 40 the 'Son of man'-'judge of the world' is designated as king. In the story of the Passion the title king is adopted from Mark in 27.11, 29, 37, and 42. The omission from Mark 15.9, 12 is understandable; when Pilate presents Jesus to the multitude with the question: Whom shall I release unto you?, Ἰησοῦν τὸν λεγόμενον χριστόν is the fitting designation. Matthew has also brought the paradox of the king in lowliness into prominence in the story of the Passion: in 27.29 he adorns the mocking scene by adding the sceptre, which heightens the element of grotesqueness; in 27.37 by the clarification Ἰησοῦς ὁ βασιλεύς: even this Jesus is king of the Jews.

Pharisees and his command of silence in 12.15 ff. show. In still one more place Jesus is designated by Matthew as πραΰς: 11.29. Here the statement that Jesus is πραΰς καὶ ταπεινὸς τῇ καρδίᾳ is closely linked with the yoke which Jesus offers those who come to him, i.e. the law. What is the relationship between the πραΰτης of Jesus and the law?

Alongside the emphasis on the lowliness of Jesus there stands a wealth of statements about his majesty. It is not our task here to go into them all; but *one* series of statements is especially important for the understanding of the law: they are the statements about the present dominion of Jesus and the presence of the Risen One in the congregation.

Matt. 28.16–20

Difficulties arise for analysis because there is no direct parallel to this section by means of which additions or alterations by Matthew might be recognised. A marked editorial encroachment by the evangelist must be reckoned with by virtue of its position as the conclusion of the Gospel. Besides, the section shows a series of Matthaean thoughts and linguistic peculiarities.[1] Nevertheless Matthew must, of course, have had before him a tradition about the appearing of Jesus to the disciples. How much in the section stems from tradition and what must be attributed to the editorial work of Matthew?

28.16 and 17 report with extreme brevity that the eleven disciples went to Galilee to the mountain where Jesus had appointed them and Jesus appeared to them there. Some tradition or other about this must have been before Matthew but that it was the lost conclusion of Mark and that he modified this is improbable.[2] The theme of the

---

[1] The following are instances of Matthew's linguistic usage: ἰδόντες — προσεκύνησαν, προσελθών — ἐλάλησεν, πορευθέντες — μαθητεύσατε — when two actions are linked in an event Matthew uses for the preparatory action the aorist participle before the aorist of the main verb (cf. A. Schlatter, p. 23); προσεκύνησαν (Matthew 13 times, Mark twice, Luke twice); ἐδίστασαν (only twice in the NT, in Matthew); προσελθών (Matthew 52 times, Mark 5 times, Luke 10 times); μαθητεύσατε (Matthew 3 times, otherwise only once in the NT, Acts 14.21); τηρεῖν (Matthew 6 times, Mark once, Luke none); ἰδού (ἰδού is not only a peculiarity of Matthew after a genitive absolute, but also occurs elsewhere over 18 times more in Matthew than in Mark and Luke together); συντέλεια τοῦ αἰῶνος (Matthew 5 times, elsewhere only in Heb. 9.26 with the plural τῶν αἰώνων); G. D. Kilpatrick, *Origins*, adds to these πορεύεσθαι, οὗ, οὐρανὸς καὶ γῆ, ἔθνος and ἐντέλλεσθαι.

[2] Thus most recently W. C. Allen, *ad loc.* He has in addition to postulate not only that the appearance of Jesus to the women (Matt. 28.9) occurred in Mark but that Mark further reported the following: how the women delivered the message to the disciples, the disciples did not believe them, thereupon Jesus appears

mountain may go back to Matthew[1] but it could also stem from the tradition (cf. Acts 1.12). The report about the appearance of Jesus (28.17 only καὶ ἰδόντες) is so short that the emphasis does not fall on the appearance itself but on the words of Jesus that follow. This makes all the more striking the fact that some doubted (28.17). Mark 16.14 and Luke 24.41 also report the doubt of the disciples but in their case it has quite a different meaning. In Mark 16.14 the disciples did not believe the message of those who had seen the Risen One. The unbelief is abolished by the doubters now seeing the Risen One for themselves. In Luke 24.41 some do not yet even believe when the Risen One appears. But the edge of their unbelief is removed by the explanation ἀπὸ τῆς χαρᾶς καὶ θαυμαζόντων: they do not believe their own eyes. Their unbelief is overcome by the request of Jesus for food, whereby proof is provided that they are not looking at a 'spirit' (24.39). In Luke, too, on both occasions the doubt is overcome by seeing the Risen One; there the only purpose of the doubt is to strengthen the proof of the resurrection mediated by sight and touch. Hence the naming of doubt in Matthew must also serve the purpose of the overcoming of this doubt through what is reported in the following verses.[2] But these verses do not provide any clearer seeing or observing, but the word of Jesus. The meaning therefore can only be that this doubt is overcome by the word of Jesus. One

---

to them, commands them to go to the mountain in Galilee, and then appears there not only to the eleven but to other disciples as well, some of whom doubted. But this requires the postulation of too much. The mention of the mountain cannot be explained in the way Allen does it; if so it would have had to be mentioned already in Mark 14.28 and 16.7. Why then should Matthew have omitted everything else from the Markan text? According to Allen (p. 303): because of his tendency to present the disciples in a better light. But not only has it been demonstrated above that this bias does not apply to Matthew but 28.17 contradicts it directly in that not only some of the wider circle of disciples (thus Allen) doubt but also some of the eleven. Moreover, B. H. Streeter rightly establishes that 28.16 ff. does not correspond at all with the pictorial description of Mark, even when one has Matthew's abbreviations in mind (op. cit., p. 343).

[1] Cf. E. Lohmeyer, 'Mir ist gegeben alle Gewalt', In memoriam E. Lohmeyer (Stuttgart, 1951), p. 24: 'It is the mountain which the reporter cannot or will not name; it is likewise in Matthew's Gospel obviously the place of the revelations of Jesus (5.1; 15.29; 17.1; 24.3 see also 14.23), as it is in the OT the place of the revelations of God.'

[2] E. Klostermann thinks that ἐδίστασαν refers to an historical recollection of Matthew; but in view of the pragmatic trait of the unbelief in the reports of the appearances this cannot in any case be the deciding factor; the mentioning of the doubt does not occur in an historical but in a theological interest (Mark 16.14; Luke 24.41; John 20.24 ff.). Matthew's peculiar reserve with regard to the appearance, which is only mentioned by the word ἰδόντες, is also very striking!

must therefore agree with O. Michel[1] when he sees here the problem
of the later Church, which seeks a new certainty about the Risen
One beyond the Easter appearance, since the appearance belongs to
tradition and to an event of the past. O. Michel compares John
20.29 with this, where the same question is concerned. In John the
hearer is directed to the understanding of faith itself, which can and
may do without the appearance. In Matthew the message of the
Risen One and obedience to this word is the way to the overcoming
of doubt. In this sense the mention of doubt in Matthew belongs to a
later time, and thus does not belong to the tradition. As it can only
be explained on the basis of the whole of Matt. 28.16–20 it should
probably be attributed to the evangelist.

The decisive weight of the section lies on the saying of Jesus in
28.18–20.[2] The connexion of the saying about revelation and authority in 28.18b with Dan. 7.14 has long been recognised.[3] Is it a case
of only an unwitting dependence on Dan. 7.14 or is it intended to
say that here the prophecy of Daniel is fulfilled?[4] The absence of the
usual formula of citation in Matthew need not contradict this; it
would be disturbing in the brief solemn concluding section.[5] The
deciding factor is the close combination of authority, dominion and
the recognition of this endowment by all nations. The conception of
the enthroning of the Son of man in Dan. 7.14 is here transferred to
Jesus. Hence it is not so much a matter here of the resurrection of Jesus
from the dead as of his exaltation and establishment as the eschatological ruler and judge of the world.[6] This exaltation happened at
Easter and the Risen One here makes it known to his disciples.

The Easter event means the exaltation and establishment of Jesus

---

[1] 'Der Abschluss des Matthäusevangeliums', *EvTh*, 1950/51, pp. 17 ff.
[2] Were verses 28.18–20 already in the tradition of the appearance in 16 f., as
received by Matthew? In view of the extremely short passage that is improbable.
O. Michel (p. 20) rightly assumes that the three members of the composition in
28.18–20 were originally independent. Matthew then put them together and
linked them as the conclusion of his Gospel. No departure of Jesus is reported; the
scene remains open. This also corresponds otherwise with Matthew's method of
composition (cf. the missionary discourse in Matt. 10, where the scene likewise
remains open).
[3] Thus Lohmeyer (*op. cit.*, p. 34), Michel (p. 22), Schniewind and Klostermann, *ad loc.* Dan. 7.14 LXX: καὶ ἐδόθη αὐτῷ ἐξουσία, καὶ πάντα τὰ ἔθνη τῆς γῆς
κατὰ γένη καὶ πᾶσα δόξα αὐτῷ λατρεύουσα· καὶ ἡ ἐξουσία αὐτοῦ αἰώνιος, ἥτις οὐ μὴ
ἀρθῇ, καὶ ἡ βασιλεία αὐτοῦ ἥτις οὐ μὴ φθαρῇ.
[4] Thus E. Lohmeyer, *op. cit.*, p. 34.
[5] Matthew has also assimilated 26.64 with ἐπὶ τῶν νεφελῶν τοῦ ὀυρανοῦ to Dan.
7.13 LXX, likewise without a formula of citation.
[6] Cf. E. Lohmeyer, *op. cit.*, p. 28; O. Michel, *op. cit.*, p. 22.

as the ruler and judge of the world. This cannot mean that Jesus already has the ἐξουσία but—before the συντέλεια τοῦ αἰῶνος—does not exercise it; otherwise 28.20b would be senseless. For Matthew the present is already under the kingly rule of Jesus Christ. This fact is all the more striking since Matthew throughout understands the βασιλεία τῶν οὐρανῶν as a future quantity.[1] Yet Matthew did not go on to make a terminological differentiation between the present kingly rule of Jesus Christ and the future βασιλεία τῶν οὐρανῶν.[2] There can be no doubt, however, in view of Matt. 8.23 ff.; 14.22 ff.; 28.18 ff. that for him the present is already under the rule of the Exalted One.

The exaltation of Jesus to be the eschatological ruler of the worlds provides the basis for the missionary command to go to all nations, which now follows (28.19 f.). The recognition of his rule is the aim of the missionary preaching. In the preaching the acceptance of his rule is offered to men; the rule of Jesus comes to men. In the command to baptise which follows, the triune ὄνομα has been the occasion of much hesitation. Whether Eusebius, who in his pre-Nicene writings regularly reproduces the wording of the passage without the baptismal command and without the trinitarian formula[3] can be counted as a witness to the text against it, or whether his text should be regarded as an abbreviation he himself made, is difficult to decide. More important in our context is the place and meaning of διδάσκειν in 28.20a. The disciples are to teach people to observe *everything* which Jesus commanded them.[4] In this way the significance of the commands of Jesus, of the law, is once again underlined in the last verses of the Gospel. The teaching of his commandments is by no means only a precondition of baptism but characterises the preaching as a

[1] There is widespread agreement today that the βασιλεία is a future quantity; cf. above all K. L. Schmidt, βασιλεία, *TWNT*, I, p. 562 ff. [BKW, *Basileia*, pp. 22 ff.] and on Matthew G. Bornkamm above, pp. 34 and 44.

[2] In 13.41–43 a distinction is made between the kingdom of the Son of man and the kingdom of the Father. Since according to 24.31 the gathering of the elect takes place at the parousia, the kingdom of the Son of man in 13.41 must precede the parousia. Then it presumably = Church (cf. G. Bornkamm above, p. 45; C. H. Dodd, 'Matthew and Paul', *New Testament Studies*, 1954², pp. 55 ff.). But 16.28 and 20.21 speak of the kingdom of the Son of man or alternatively Jesus, after the parousia. How are these two statements related to each other? At least it must be said that for Matthew the rule of Jesus begins with his exaltation (28.18). Dodd (*op. cit.*, p. 56), in conjunction with R. H. Lightfoot, can therefore speak of the Christophany in 28.16 ff. as a kind of proleptic parousia.

[3] Cf. F. C. Conybeare, 'The Eusebian form of the text Matt. 28.19', *ZNW*, 1901, pp. 275 ff., also J. Wellhausen and E. Klostermann, *ad loc.*

[4] τηρεῖν and ἐντέλλεσθαι correspond to the linguistic usage of Matthew (cf. above); attention was already drawn to the significance of πάντα on pp. 71 ff.

whole. The making-of-disciples occurs through baptism and the teaching of his commandments. The weight that falls in this connexion on the teaching of his commandments becomes still clearer by a comparison with the related missionary command in the Markan conclusion: there faith is spoken of in connexion with baptism, in Matthew with the commandments of Jesus! As it was concluded above that in the preaching the kingly rule of Jesus Christ comes to men, this can now be expressed precisely by saying that this preaching means the teaching of his commandments, of the law. In the preaching of the law, therefore, the kingly rule of Jesus Christ comes to men. The evangelist concludes with the promise of 28.20b. The words ἐγὼ μεθ' ὑμῶν εἰμι denote here not only the help and protection of Jesus in the carrying out of the missionary task, but the abiding presence of Jesus in the congregation.[1] There is no need for a farewell; the Risen One remains present in the congregation. Did the evangelist find the statement already in the tradition or is it his own construction? The latter is always possible since the thought of the presence of Christ in the congregation is found elsewhere in his Gospel (among the Synoptics only in Matthew). Here above all 18.20 must be mentioned, a saying which Matthew obviously adopted from his special source and incorporated into the framework for the ordering of the congregation in 18.15–17. The presence of Jesus in the congregation is here described as analogous to the presence of the Shekinah (cf. *Aboth* 3.2); the place of the Torah is taken by the ὄνομα of Jesus; the place of the Shekinah by Jesus himself. Matt. 1.22–23 should also be mentioned, where the quotation from Isa. 7.14 is due to Matthew, as the introductory formula shows.[2] Matthew has added to the quotation: ὅ ἐστιν μεθερμηνευόμενον μεθ' ἡμῶν ὁ θεός. In Jesus God himself is with the congregation, is present in the congregation. The beginning of the Gospel thus corresponds with its end in 28.20. Finally, attention should also be directed to the meaning of the story of the storm at sea in Matthew (8.23 ff.). The interpretation of the journey of the disciples in the storm on the sea

---

[1] So in the OT with reference to God's presence Gen. 28.15 and Judg. 6.12 f.; cf. E. Klostermann, E. Lohmeyer (p. 42). The close connexion with 18.20 shows that in Matt. 28.20 the divine support is not referred to in a merely figurative sense.

[2] On the introductory formula of the so-called reflective quotations cf. 2.15, 17, 23; 4.14; 8.17; 12.17; 13.35; 21.4; 27.9. G. D. Kilpatrick (*Origins*, pp. 57 and 93) thinks the introductory formula in 1.22 should be placed before 1.21, where he sees a quotation from Ps. 130.8. K. Stendahl (*op. cit.*, p. 98) rightly rejects this attempt as the Hebrew equivalent of σώσει in Ps. 130.8 is not ישׁע but פדה.

with reference to discipleship, and thus to the boat of the Church, presupposes that as Jesus is in the ship with the disciples so he is also present in the Church.

In the Church the Son of man exalted to be the eschatological ruler is present. She lives by his presence. The presence of Jesus in the congregation means for her sustenance and salvation in all the storms that break around her (8.23 ff.), gives her persistence in seeking the lost, since he is present among them, who like a shepherd seeks the lost sheep (18.20 in the context of 18.12–19, cf. above, p. 84); it means for her the presence of the forgiveness of God (1.21 ff.). In what way is this presence of the Risen One mediated to the congregation? It has already been pointed out that Matthew has consistently imported the present situation of the Church into the life of the earthly Jesus and his disciples (cf. above pp. 100 f. and 111). It was conjectured there that this equating of the Church with the disciples is connected with the presence of the Risen One in the congregation. This conjecture is confirmed by 28.16–20. The mention of doubt in 28.17 shows the question of the later congregation after a new Easter certainty, since the vision of the Risen One belongs to tradition and to the past. To see and talk with Jesus sojourning on earth is no longer possible. The doubt of the disciples is overcome by the saying of Jesus that follows, that makes known to them his exaltation and rule and gives them their commission. That means for the congregation that it is not the seeing of the Risen One that brings the Easter certainty and not the physical converse with the earthly Jesus, but the word of the proclamation. But in Matthew this proclamation is by the same token preaching of the commandments of Jesus, of the law. From this it follows that the preaching of the law occasions the presence of the Risen One in the congregation.

The close connexion between the presence of the Risen One and the law calls for a comparison with Judaism's concept of the Shekinah. In Judaism also the presence of the Shekinah is bound to the Torah. Thus *Aboth* 3.2 (cf. 3.6): R. Hananiah ben Teradion (died *c.* 135) said, שְׁנַיִם שֶׁיּוֹשְׁבִין וְעוֹסְקִין בְּדִבְרֵי תוֹרָה שְׁכִינָה בֵּינֵיהֶן. The presence of the Shekinah is dependent on the occupation of a man with the Torah, i.e. on the study of the law, which involves, however, the doing of the Torah.[1] But in Matthew the presence of Christ is not a

---

[1] Cf. the dispute about the precedence of doing over study, W. Bacher, *Die Agada der Tannaiten*, I, 1903[2], p. 296.

consequence of obedience to the law, but comes to a man with the proclamation of the word, which indeed is the proclamation of the law. The way in which God's action here precedes human obedience has been made clear under the concept of συνιέναι.[1]

2. *The establishing of the judgment of God*

Still more striking and more important is another trait in the interpretation of the activity of Jesus by Matthew: Jesus is the Sinless One, the Righteous One who fulfils all righteousness, who does the will of God entirely. The statement of A. Schlatter about the Church in Matthew should be accepted: 'her judgment about her conduct, that she consists of those who do God's will is entirely one with her judgment about Jesus, that he did God's will and worked God's works.'[2] Passages which support this run through the whole Gospel; these must now be presented and what they say made precise.

Matt. 3.14 f.

The alterations which the Markan text has undergone in Matt. 3.16–17 can for the time being be ignored. Here what is chiefly of interest is 3.14–15. But the alterations in 3.13 must also be considered now: the baptism of Jesus is prepared for in much more detail in 3.13 than in Mark and Luke: Jesus comes to the Baptist with the *intention* of being baptised.[3] The will of Jesus to be baptised is emphasised. This is brought about by the insertion of 3.14–15 by Matthew.[4] The insertion springs from reflexion on how Jesus could submit to baptism. E. Klostermann enumerates three scruples which could have led Matthew to make this insertion: (*a*) Jesus already has the Spirit, what could the incomplete water-baptism do for him? (*b*) The

---

[1] It is true that the Rabbinate is also familiar with statements which seem to break through the dependence of the presence of the Shekinah on obedience to the Torah. Thus the statement of R. Simon ben Joḥai (*c.* 150), *Meg.* 29a: 'Go and see how beloved the Israelites are by the Holy One, blessed be he, for everywhere where they were sent into banishment the Shekinah was with them. They were sent into banishment into Egypt: the Shekinah was with them . . .'; cf. *Sifre*, Num. 35.34. The Shekinah also accompanies the Israelites into the Diaspora and is still with them even when they are unclean. But the great majority of passages bind the presence of the Torah firmly to obedience to the Torah. Thus *Sotah* 48b, *Sifre*, Deut. 18.12, §173, *Shabbath* 30b, further references in Billerbeck, I, pp. 794 f.

[2] *Die Kirche des Matthäus*, p. 32.

[3] τοῦ βαπτισθῆναι ὑπ' αὐτοῦ in the sense of 'to submit himself to baptism', cf. Blass-Debrunner, §314.

[4] The linguistic usage of Matthew is seen in λέγων (112 times in Matthew; cf. A. Schlatter, *Matthäus*, pp. 16 f.); ἀποκριθεὶς εἶπεν (cf. J. Jeremias, *Gleichnisse*, p. 65); πληρῶσαι, δικαιοσύνη, τότε; in 3.15 it is questionable whether αὐτῷ should be read with B and the Ferrar group, or πρὸς αὐτόν with ℵ C and most Koine texts.

sinlessness of Jesus calls for no baptism of repentance. (c) May the 'stronger' subordinate himself to the unworthy Baptist? The third ground must be rejected as not in keeping with the text since it renders the Baptist's question innocuous and makes it an expression of a beautiful modesty. Matthew is concerned with an eminently theological question as the extremely problematical expression πληρῶσαι πᾶσαν δικαιοσύνην shows. In consequence of this weakening of the theological importance of the words, δικαιοσύνη is understood as δικαίωμα;[1] according to this interpretation the baptism of John is a regulation of God for the whole nation, to which Jesus must also submit himself as to every ordinance of the divine law. But that would not only completely contradict the use of δικαιοσύνη in Matthew,[2] the insertion of 3.14 f. would also be made senseless by it, for baptism would then become a purely formal act, a ceremony which a man fulfils because it is commanded. But the fact that Matthew was troubled by the baptism of Jesus and therefore inserted 3.14 f. presupposes that he did not understand baptism as a mere ceremony, a legal order.

G. Bornkamm[3] rightly understands the insertion in the light of its connexion with 3.11 f. It concerns a problem of salvation-history and the Baptist's question means: 'Now my time is past and the time of thy, i.e. Messianic, baptism has come, the time when thou art the baptiser and I am the candidate for baptism. "I have need to be baptised of thee—and comest thou to me?" ' If the question is so understood the reply of Jesus in 3.15 receives its meaning: Suffer it now! for thus it becometh us to fulfil all righteousness.[4] This fulfilling takes place in the adoption of baptism: in that the Messianic judge of the worlds and the Messianic baptiser himself becomes a candidate for baptism, humbles himself and enters the ranks of sinners. By this means he fulfils 'all righteousness'.

δικαιοσύνη belongs to Matthew's linguistic usage.[5] It is a case of a

[1] So T. Zahn, E. Klostermann; the same sense, without emending the text to read δικαίωμα is found in W. C. Allen, C. G. Montefiore, Bauer (s.v., §2a).

[2] δικαιοσύνη can never be understood in Matthew in the formal sense of a legal order; cf. 5.6, 10, 20; 6.1, 33.

[3] 'Die neutestamentliche Lehre von der Taufe', TB 1938, p. 44.

[4] The expression πρέπον ἐστὶν ὑμῖν can hardly be understood as a plural of majesty; it rather links Jesus and the Baptist: the Baptist is a Christological organ (G. Bornkamm, art. cit., p. 44, note 8). πρέπον ἐστὶν shows that the conduct of Jesus is not a case of accommodation but of an obligation, a divine 'Must' (δεῖ). The evangelists also give prominence to this divine Must elsewhere, especially in the Passion story; Matthew has repeatedly strengthened it (26.1 f., 18).

[5] Seven times in Matthew, elsewhere in the Synoptics only in Luke 1.75.

completely uniform use: it denotes the conduct of a man which is in agreement with God's will, which is well pleasing to him and right, rightness of life before God.[1] Thus in Matt. 5.20: the conduct demanded of the disciples. In 5.10 it is this action of the disciples on account of which they are persecuted. Similarly in 21.32 and 6.1 it denotes the conduct demanded of men.[2] Nor is 5.6 an instance of a different use.[3] 6.33 is more difficult. Matthew has added to ζητεῖτε πρῶτον τὴν βασιλείαν the phrase καὶ τὴν δικαιοσύνην αὐτοῦ. The word αὐτοῦ applies to βασιλείαν as well as δικαιοσύνην and must refer right back to the heavenly Father of 6.32. The reference then to the 'righteousness of God' is striking. However much this echoes a Pauline mode of expression it means something different here: it obviously means here the rightness which God demands (James 1.20 speaks of δικαιοσύνη θεοῦ in this sense). Only in this way does 6.33 fit in with the whole attitude of Matthew's Gospel. The meaning is then clear: Matthew cannot speak of the kingdom of God without thinking of the righteousness which obtains in it. To seek the kingdom means: to do the righteousness on the fulfilling of which admission to the kingdom depends. In 5.20 δικαιοσύνη is also attributed to the Pharisees. This shows the Old Testament-Jewish usage (which is seen above all in the contrasting pair δίκαιος—ἁμαρτωλός Matt. 5.45; 9.13; 1.19 and is found generally in the Synoptics); according to this he is denoted righteous who, in contrast to the 'sinner', is predominantly righteous. The Rabbinate developed this usage further in the formal sense that judgment is made according to the majority of the instances of the fulfilling of the commandments. In the light of this he is already צדיק who can show only one more instance of the fulfilling of a commandment than the number of transgressions.[4] Although the Jewish use of δικαιοσύνη is adopted by Matthew, the differentiation between different levels of righteousness is finally abandoned in that it is only to the τέλειος, whose righteousness far exceeds that of the Pharisees (in the Rabbinic sense thus the תמים) that the kingdom is granted. That is, for entrance into the kingdom a complete righteousness is required. A further difference from the Rabbinate lies in the

[1] Cf. G. Schrenk, δικαιοσύνη, *TWNT*, II, pp. 200 f. [BKW *Righteousness*, pp. 35 f.].
[2] In 6.1 not = ἐλεημοσύνη (as frequently in late Judaism), but as a heading for all the 'pious exercises' in 6.1–18, where the giving of alms is only one thing among others.
[3] Cf. above, pp. 123 f.; further G. Schrenk, *TWNT*, II, p. 200 [*Righteousness*, p. 35].
[4] Cf. Billerbeck, IV, p. 1037.

fact that this righteousness is not only a demand but at the same time an eschatological gift, 5.6; 6.33.[1] Righteousness is both things at the same time: demand and eschatological gift. These two sides do not fall apart but are very closely linked in both strophes of the Beatitudes: those who are pronounced blessed on account of their hungering after righteousness, who can thus receive righteousness only as a gift (5.6), are the same as those who for the sake of righteousness, i.e. on account of their doing of righteousness, are persecuted (5.10). Righteousness and grace do not therefore fall apart, as in the Rabbinate, but are one.[2] This understanding of righteousness is obviously closely connected with 3.15. That righteousness is at the same time a demand and an eschatological gift has its basis here. Similarly there may be a connexion between πᾶσαν δικαιοσύνην in 3.15 and the fact that a complete righteousness is required for entrance into the kingdom.

Jesus fulfils all righteousness by his humiliation in that he enters the ranks of sinners. G. Bornkamm can see no reason to introduce here the question raised in the Gospel of the Hebrews about the sinlessness of Jesus. In fact nothing is said about it in 3.14 f. But that is not to say that it was not concerned with the question how the Messianic judge of the worlds (and that includes his sinlessness) can place himself through baptism in a line with sinners. 'That means nothing but: by baptism Jesus enters on the way of the Passion and resurrection.'[3] In doing this Jesus fulfils 'all righteousness'.[4] In the

---

[1] On 5.6 cf. above, pp. 123 f. In 6.33 it may be that the thought of righteousness as a gift may not have been in the foreground in connexion with the insertion but it is implicitly contained in it. 'Righteousness is here linked very closely with God and his rule, again as a pure gift like everything connected with the βασιλεία' (G. Schrenk, *TWNT*, II, p. 200, [*Righteousness*, p. 35]). This is contained in προστεθήσεται: food 'will be added' to the βασιλεία and to δικαιοσύνη (cf. A. Schlatter and J. Schniewind, *ad loc.*). Yet it is too hazardous to deduce from this, as Schniewind does, that righteousness and the kingdom are bestowed already now, in the present. That would be overpressing the text since the interest in 6.33 is primarily in seeking after righteousness, i.e. in doing righteousness.

[2] On the Rabbinic distinction between the attribute of justice and mercy in the nature of God cf. E. Sjöberg, *Gott und Sünder im paläst, Judentum*, 1938; further H. Cremer, *Die paulin. Rechtfertigungslehre im Zusammenhang ihrer geschichtlichen Voraussetzungen*, 1899. The decisive thing is that for Matthew the two things belong immediately together: the doing of righteousness and righteousness as a gift.

[3] G. Bornkamm, *TB*, 1938, p. 45. H. W. Bartsch ('Die Taufe im NT', *EvTh*, 1948/49, pp. 89 f.) goes too far, however, when he deduces: 'The baptism is not only a pointer to the atoning deed of Christ that was to follow, but is the sacramental execution of his death and resurrection.' That is to import the baptismal teaching of Rom. 6 into Matthew. Matt. 3.15 does not say that Jesus now, in his baptism, fulfils all obedience which he has ever to accomplish.

[4] πᾶσαν δικαιοσύνην does not mean 'the righteousness of all' or 'righteousness for

context of Matthew's Gospel a special emphasis lies upon πᾶσαν; it has to do with the whole will of God, with the whole righteousness. But this righteousness is not understood legally; Jesus fulfils it precisely in that he, as the Messiah-'judge-of-the-worlds', humbles himself and enters into the ranks of sinners, acts for sinners. The unity of righteousness and mercy demonstrated above has its Christological basis here.

Matt. 12.20

Still more instructive for Matthew's conception is 12.20. It has already been shown that in the quotation from Isa. 42.1–4 there is not merely a translation but a theological interpretation. Here the alteration in 12.20 is important: ἕως ἂν ἐκβάλῃ εἰς νῖκος τὴν κρίσιν. As with the other two alterations (12.18 ἀγαπητός, 12.19 ἐρίσει) this cannot be explained on the basis of available texts but must be understood as a theological interpretation. The sentence thus reproduces a thought which is especially important to the evangelist, and the more so since there is not, as in the case of the other two alterations, any direct occasion given in the context. In 12.20 the vocation of the servant of God is named: to bring judgment to victory. That is the goal of his activity, his final comprehensive commission: the complete establishing and carrying out of judgment. More is meant by this than the carrying out of judgment in the associations of human life. It is rather a matter of the carrying out of the judgment of God with regard to men, to the world. It is a matter of the complete establishing of the will of God, of the judgment of God. It is clear in the context of 12.18–21 that this is the proper and decisive vocation of the servant of God; all other statements are subordinated to this statement. This establishing of the judgment of God is described in 12.20b as an act of power (ἐκβάλῃ εἰς νῖκος). At the same time, however, it is a work of the humiliated One, it is grace and is fulfilled in the saving work of Jesus for the 'bruised reed' and the 'smouldering flax'. For this reason the Gentiles will hope in his name (12.21). This definition of the work of Christ is characteristic for Matthew: the chief emphasis lies on the fact that Christ establishes the judgment of God.

Matt. 4.11

The story of the temptation in Matthew should also be seen in this

---

all', although there is contained in the baptism of Jesus that he does this for sinners, that he fulfils all righteousness for them.

context. This is shown by the evaluation which Matthew gives to it in 4.11. The ministering angels have obviously been taken over from Mark.[1] If their original meaning was to provide nourishment for Jesus during the forty days, in Matthew they have a different function: after Jesus has withstood the temptation, fulfilled God's will and in doing so conquered the devil, *then* the angels come and minister to him. Their ministries are here the answer to the conquering of the devil by Jesus; in them they recognise him in his Messianic vocation. In this way Matthew underlines that this obedient fulfilling of the will of God and overcoming of the devil constitutes the Messianic vocation of Jesus.

Matt. 6.10

For the third petition of the Lord's Prayer cf. above p. 70. If it is the Messianic vocation of Jesus to establish the judgment of God this petition corresponds completely with it. It is not an expression of resignation but the petition for precisely this carrying out of the judgment of God.

Matt. 28.18–20

In the conclusion of Matthew there are also echoes of this thought. The missionary command, which is based on the exaltation of Jesus to be the eschatological judge of the worlds, culminates in the command that the disciples should teach all nations to observe what Jesus had commanded them. The missionary preaching is at the service of the establishing of the commandments, of the judgment of God. It is important that here as in 12.18–21 three moments stand together: (*a*) the establishing of the judgment of God, (*b*) the promise of grace (28.20b) and (*c*) the world-wide validity for all nations (28.19 = 12.21). But what is new here is that this establishing of the judgment of God is not yet completed with the Passion and resurrection of Jesus. The βασιλεία has not yet come, not till it does will God's will and judgment have come to victory (cf. also the close link between the second and third petitions of the Lord's Prayer). Yet the present is not devoid of relation to this future of the complete establishing of the judgment of God. In the recognition of the rule of the Risen One, for which the preaching calls, the judgment of God is already being (in part) established. The Risen One is present in the congregation, and works and rules in her.

[1] Cf. R. Bultmann, *SynT*, p. 254.

The Passion of Jesus

If Matthew sees the work of Christ above all from the point of view of the establishing of the judgment of God that must also appear in his portrayal of the Passion. For Matthew's alterations in comparison with the parallel passages the following is significant: the meaning of the event as an action of God is especially emphasised. It is already so at the beginning of the Passion story in 26.2, by the further repetition of the prophecy of suffering: the event now beginning takes place under the inescapable δεῖ of the divine decree. ὁ καιρός μου ἐγγύς ἐστιν in 26.18 has the same purport. The remarkable events at the death of Jesus are enormously enhanced in 27.51 ff. Similarly the resurrection of Jesus as an act of God is underlined by the apologetic passages in 27.62 ff. and 28.11 ff. The majestic predicates of Jesus are also enhanced—precisely in the story of the Passion: in connexion with the mocking in 27.40 εἰ υἱὸς εἰ τοῦ θεοῦ is added; in 27.43 εἶπεν γὰρ ὅτι θεοῦ εἰμι υἱός; at the mocking by the soldiers in 27.27 ff. a reed is put in his hand as his royal sceptre; in 26.17-19 the word of Jesus to the householder in whose house he plans to observe the Passover also bears in Matthew the clear stamp of a sovereign word of command. G. Bertram rightly judges: there is 'attributed to the host an absolute assessment of the Person of Jesus such as was only possible for the cultic congregation'.[1] The majesty of Jesus is shown at his arrest—he is the one who without any question could command legions of angels.

If in these editorial passages the evangelist has emphasised and brought into prominence the importance of the event, that it is the Lord, the Son of God who here suffers and dies,[2] by that very fact the humiliation is emphasised, for the contrast is heightened by it.

A further trait stands out still more prominently: the humiliation of Jesus is voluntary[3] and therefore an act of *obedience*. Jesus' obedient fulfilling of the will of God is strongly emphasised. The prophecy of suffering in 26.2 and ὁ καιρός μου ἐγγύς ἐστιν in 26.18 serve the same end. The καιρός of Jesus is the hour determined for him by God, the hour of God's eschatological action, the hour of his death and resurrection. Jesus consciously lays hold of 'the καιρός appointed for

---

[1] *Die Leidensgeschichte Jesu und der Christuskult*, Göttingen, 1922, p. 23.

[2] Cf. N. A. Dahl ('Die Passionsgeschichte bei Matthäus', *New Testament Studies*, 1955/56, p. 25) who comes to a similar result: 'The hearers of Matthew's account know . . . the whole time that the crucified is the resurrected.'

[3] So also Dahl, *ibid.*

him by the will of God . . . in free submission'.[1] The freedom of the
action of Jesus at his arrest is emphasised by the saying about the
legions of angels in 26.53.[2] Because his suffering is voluntary it is an
act of obedience. In this Jesus shows himself to be the one who by his
action in suffering and dying fulfils 'all righteousness' (3.15). This is
shown by a number of instances of the emphasising of his obedience
and his righteousness in the Passion story, which contain in part
allusions to the Sermon on the Mount. Thus in Gethsemane Jesus
prays word for word the third petition of the Lord's Prayer (26.42).[3]
That he is innocent (ἀθῷος)[4] is repeated (27.4, 24). Pilate's wife calls
him δίκαιος (27.19).[5] It is in line with this that the enemies of Jesus
in the Passion story transgress the commandments, and Peter, too.
Jesus forbade the oath altogether but the high priest misuses it even
for condemning Jesus,[6] while in his reply Jesus has nothing to do with

---

[1] G. Delling, καιρός, *TWNT*, III, p. 462. What Matthew's intention is here
becomes much clearer when the whole section of 26.17–19 is considered. In Mark
the emphasis is on the prophetic foreknowledge of Jesus (cf. E. Klostermann, *ad
loc.*). Matthew tightens up the account so much that this trait is completely suppressed. I cannot agree with Dahl's view (*op. cit.*, p. 20) that by his omissions
Matthew here assumes that his readers were acquainted with the Markan account.
His alterations are too great for that: the aim in contrast to Mark is quite a different one; the emphasis does not rest any more upon the wonderful foreknowledge
of Jesus, but entirely on his obedient seizure of his καιρός.

[2] Cf. G. Bertram, *op. cit.*, p. 52. R. Gutzwiller (*Jesus der Messias, Christus im
Matthäus-Evangelium*, Zürich, 1949, p. 318): 'The voluntariness is also seen in the
fact that Jesus knows his betrayer and warns him for a last time.'

[3] The prayer of Jesus in 26.42 is Matthew's construction. In its interest he has
abbreviated the first prayer in 26.39 in comparison with Mark 14.35 f. From this it
follows that Matt. 6.10 has not been constructed in the light of 26.42 but on the
contrary, 26.42 in the light of 6.10. Of course 26.42 shows the thought of submission to God's will, whereas 6.10 prays for the carrying out of God's will on
earth; but the two thoughts are not necessarily mutually exclusive (cf. T. Haering,
'Matt. 11.28–30', in *Aus Schrift und Geschichte*, Festschrift für A. Schlatter, 1922,
p. 12: OT and NT linguistic usage does not know this distinction). It would remain
inexplicable why Matthew should construct the second petition in Gethsemane
word for word after 6.10 unless it were intended to be a reminder of the petition in
the Lord's Prayer.

[4] The self-cursing of the Jews in 27.25, 'His blood be on us . . .' itself proves
the innocence of Jesus.

[5] δίκαιος has here hardly the Greek meaning 'a just man in the sense of the
concept of virtue' (G. Schrenk, δίκαιος, *TWNT*, II, p. 189) [BKW *Righteousness*,
p. 20], but as elsewhere in Matthew the OT-Jewish sense. Jesus is for Matthew
the exemplary Just One!

[6] Only in Matthew does the high priest adjure Jesus. ἐξορκίζω does not mean
here adjure in the sense of 'ask urgently', which would be senseless, but in the sense
of 'cause him to swear'. On the legal practice of swearing in the Rabbinate cf.
E. Klostermann, *ad loc.*, Billerbeck, I, pp. 1005 f., J. Schneider, ὁρκίζω, *TWNT*,
V, p. 466. The difficulty that an oath is demanded of Jesus is sufficiently explained

an oath.[1] Prominence is also given to fact that at his denial Peter swears (26.72). These insertions which are not occasioned by anything in the Markan text,[2] can only be understood in the light of Matt. 5.33 f. Jesus taught that it is the will of God that there should be no swearing at all. He himself is the Righteous One who fulfils God's commandments while his enemies and also Peter in his denial transgress God's commandment.[3] The fact that according to Matt. 26.15 Judas betrays Jesus out of avarice brings out the contrast to δωρεάν, which was the mark of Jesus.[4] Is the saying to the disciple who

if one thinks, not of the historical probability but of the theological intention of Matthew, who has 5.33 in mind.

[1] On the difficult question of σὺ εἶπας cf. above all G. Dalman, *The Words of Jesus* (1930², pp. 253 ff.) ET¹, 1902, pp. 309 ff.; J. Abrahams, *Studies in Pharisaism*, II, pp. 1–3; A. Merx, *Das Evangelium Matthäus*, Berlin, 1902, pp. 382 ff. 391 ff. The explanation of σὺ εἶπας in 26.64 has mostly been disastrously amalgamated with the question of the Messianic consciousness of the historical Jesus and his reply before the judgment. J. Weiss, C. G. Montefiore and E. Klostermann, who understand σὺ εἶπας in an evading sense, deduce from this that Jesus did not claim to be the Messiah, while those who represent the Messianic confession, on the other hand, are at pains to prove that there is in σὺ εἶπας the formula of an oath (thus B. Weiss, J. Schniewind, *ad loc.*, Billerbeck, I, p. 1006). Since σὺ εἶπας in 26.64 is an editorial alteration of Matthew over against ἐγώ εἰμι of Mark 14.62 the question of the confession of Messiahship by the historical Jesus should be *here* at least completely eliminated. Billerbeck's view that σὺ εἶπας is a direct oath is untenable; he can furnish no kind of evidence for it, but deduces it solely from the fact that Jesus made his reply on the basis of an adjuration. Billerbeck is right in so far as Matthew undoubtedly understood the reply as affirmative (cf. 27.43!), but the alteration in comparison with Mark remains inexplicable in this way. The other side see in σὺ εἶπας a moment of evasion. It is very questionable whether the answer of Bar Qappara *Kilaim* 32b אמריתן אתון Jer. *Ketuboth* 35a אתון אמרתון may be quoted as a parallel (cf. A. Schlatter, *Matthäus*, p. 741; Billerbeck, I, p. 990; A. Merx, p. 382; J. Abrahams, pp. 1 f.). If it is called as evidence there is no escape from a formal evasion. Merx (p. 383) shows that for the *Apostolic Constitutions* 142.8 (Lagarde) σὺ εἶπας in Matt. 26.25 does not have the direct meaning 'Yes'. For Matt. 26.63 f. the double editorial alteration must be noticed: the high priest's question has been made into an adjuration and the reply of Jesus runs σὺ εἶπας instead of ἐγώ εἰμι. In view of this double alteration the explanation of A. Merx and J. Schneider (ὁρκίζω, *TWNT*, V, p. 466) is the most probable: Jesus will have nothing to do with an oath, he rather makes a simple declaration which contains his witness to Messiahship.

[2] μετὰ ὅρκου in 26.72 is particularly disturbing in view of ἤρξατο καταθεματίζειν καὶ ὀμνύειν following in 26.74.

[3] It cannot be concluded from 23.16–22 that Matthew regarded only false swearing as forbidden and not swearing altogether (5.33 ff.). It is true that Matthew probably found 5.33 ff. already in the tradition and that is still more certain of 23.16–22, which can only have been constructed before the destruction of the Temple. 23.16–22 is, however, no command for the Church, but an accusation against the Pharisees.

[4] Cf. A. Schlatter, *Matthäus*, p. 738.

is laying about him with a sword: 'put thy sword into its place; for all they that take the sword shall perish with the sword' (26.52) also intended to call Matt. 5.39 μὴ ἀντιστῆναι τῷ πονηρῷ to mind? Granted it diverges from his statement in 5.39, but here as there defencelessness is required of the disciples before their enemies. Jesus is to the end the one who trusts in God (27.43), his lowliness and humility are strongly underlined (cf. above). In order to exclude every thought of blemish or sacrilege on the part of Jesus the accusation in Mark 14.58 is also altered: Jesus had said he would destroy the Temple and within three days build it again. According to Matt. 26.61 Jesus did not speak of a desire but of the power he had to do it.[1]

What follows from this for the interpretation of the death and resurrection of Jesus in Matthew? P. Vielhauer has rightly said that in Matthew the Passion of Jesus is portrayed as a Christological revelation.[2] But what does that mean? The Innocent One, the Righteous One dies; but not in the sense of an error of justice or of an infamous judicial murder, nor even to magnify the guilt of the Jews thereby, but as a profoundly necessary event in God's plan of salvation. For it is the Lord, the Son of God (emphasised!) who dies here and his exaltation to be the eschatological ruler necessarily follows upon his death.[3] In this way the suffering and dying of Jesus becomes in a paradoxical way the very revelation of him as ruler, as Lord, as βασιλεὺς πραΰς (note ἀπ' ἄρτι 23.39 and 26.64, which empha-

[1] Are the special words of Jesus to Judas in Matthew (26.23, 25, 50) also to be understood as exhortations and warnings intended to set forth Jesus as the good shepherd (Matt. 18.12–14; cf. 26.31) who to the end goes after the lost? Whereas Mark 14.20 only says that one of the small circle of disciples will betray him, Matthew makes of it an identification of the traitor (26.23 ὁ ἐμβάψας . . . οὗτος). In 26.25 Matthew inserts the question of Judas, which Jesus answers in the affirmative (σὺ εἶπας is also here again evasive, but affirmative: cf. Klostermann on Mark 15.2). It is hardly possible to translate ἑταῖρε ἐφ' ὃ πάρει in 26.50 with any certainty. We must either assume that it is an ellipse or a case of corruption of the text. Hence probably either '(do) what you are here for' (Schlatter, Holtzmann) or '(dost thou kiss me) for such an end?' (Schniewind, Klostermann, Wellhausen). Wellhausen: 'do you kiss me does not need to be said because the kissing actually takes place there at that moment.' If these three passages are not accepted as warnings they still denote in any case the Majesty of Jesus who knows the traitor and is master of the situation. I.e. they again underline the freedom of Jesus and at the same time his obedience.

[2] *EvTh*, 1952/53, p. 482; cf. R. H. Lightfoot, *History and Interpretation in the Gospels*, London, 1935, p. 164.

[3] The resurrection of Jesus is understood above all as his exaltation; cf. above, p. 133 f.

sises the significance of the moment as one of salvation-history, and precisely in the direction of the revelation of Jesus as Lord). For Matthew the Passion of Jesus is not merely the gateway to glory, but the Passion and resurrection are two sides of one event in which Jesus takes the place of sinners and 'fulfils all righteousness', brings God's judgment to victory.

Matthew adopted the interpretation of the death of Jesus as an atoning sacrifice for sins from tradition. This interpretation, which presumably arose earlier in the primitive Church,[1] is expressed in the statements and formulae in which the suffering and death of Jesus are denoted as taking place ὑπὲρ ὑμῶν (or πολλῶν, τῶν ἁμαρτιῶν). The sayings which Matthew adopted from Mark 10.45 and 14.24 belong here. The taking of the place of sinners by Jesus is presupposed in Matt. 3.15. But Matthew not only adopts the thought of the atoning sacrifice but at the same time he interprets it, and indeed in the sense that the forgiveness of sins through the substitutionary sacrifice of Jesus does not mean any invalidating of the will of God, of the law, but means precisely the establishing of it. But this establishing of the will of God means grace, forgiveness; or better —grace and forgiveness mean precisely the establishing of the judgment of God.

Matt. 5.17 and 18c

When Matthew thinks of the work of Christ the foremost thought in his mind is thus that Christ establishes the will of God, the judgment of God. Obviously Matt. 5.17 and 18c belong to this context. In correspondence with the context πληρῶσαι takes place in the teaching of Jesus. But πληρῶσαι does not mean here what is said in the law is modified or clarified, but rather πληρῶσαι signifies a more comprehensive event: the teaching of Jesus is concerned with the establishing of the law, of the will of God. Hence it is unthinkable for Matthew that the law should be abolished by the death of Jesus even when he sees in the life and death of Jesus the πληρῶσαι πᾶσαν δικαιοσύνην (and that in the place of sinners! 3.15). The complete establishing of the will of God is also the concern of 5.18 (ἕως ἂν πάντα γένηται) whereby the goal, the aim is exhibited for the sake of which the law must remain valid.

In this way there is given to the law a firm reference to the Messianic work of Christ. In the case of Matthew the question may properly

---

[1] Cf. R. Bultmann, *Theology of the NT*, I, pp. 46 f.

be asked, why the law was given. In Judaism this question was not possible. The Jew can ask why the world was created and can answer: for the sake of the law; but he cannot ask why the law exists.[1] That this question is asked in Matthew is shown by Matt. 12.5–8, and further by the critical function exercised by the love-commandment. In 5.17–18 Matthew's reply is: it is an instrument of the eschatological execution of the will of God, which the work of Christ is. That is, however much the law is the will of God it still cannot be simply equated with the will of God, the carrying through of which is the work of Christ; the will of God is superior to the law as its goal (5.18 ἕως ἂν πάντα γένηται), the law serves it.

It has thus been shown that Matthew adopts the thought of the atoning sacrifice of Christ and interprets it as meaning that this grace is actually the establishing of the judgment, the righteousness of God. In his living and dying Jesus obediently fulfils all righteousness, hence for Matthew the law cannot be abolished. The proper work of Jesus is the establishing and carrying through of the will of God, of his judgment, of his righteousness. He does that by his teaching and as the πραΰς, the Meek One, who fulfils all righteousness in the place of sinners;[2] at the same time it is plain that the establishing of the judgment of God has to do with a deed of power, as 12.19 f. ἐκβάλῃ εἰς νῖκος τὴν κρίσιν shows; in 28.18 ff. it is the act of the one who has been exalted to be the eschatological ruler. It cannot be said with

---

[1] Cf. *Genesis Rabba*, §1: R. Bannaah said: the world and what it contains was created only for the sake of the law: cf. *Aboth* 2.8, and *Assumption of Moses* 1.12, where instead of '*plebem*' '*legem*' should be read with C. Clemen (*Die Apokr. u. Pseudepigraphen des Alten Testaments* . . ., ed. von Kautzsch, 1900, II, p. 319): 'He created the world for the sake of his law.'

[2] From here it is possible to understand the striking statement that the taking of the 'yoke' of Jesus brings ἀνάπαυσις (11.28–30). By κοπιῶντες καὶ πεφορτισμένοι it is not those burdened with sin but those burdened with the severe demands of the Pharisaic conception of the law who are meant (cf. Klostermann, Schlatter, Wellhausen, Schniewind, *ad loc.*), and further it is not the casuistry of the Rabbinic tradition that is in mind, which Matthew rejects on principle, but the Rabbinic understanding of the law. In what sense can Matthew say that Jesus' yoke (= law) is χρηστός and ἐλαφρός with the result that it brings refreshment? Jesus' interpretation of the law did not provide any alleviation but rather a sharpening of the demand of God. As the ground of the refreshment a statement is made in 11.29b about Jesus and in 11.30 a statement about his kind of yoke, i.e. his yoke is χρηστός and ἐλαφρός because Jesus is πραΰς καὶ ταπεινὸς τῇ καρδίᾳ. But Jesus shows himself to be πραΰς in that he, as the Messianic judge of the worlds enters the ranks of sinners, submits to baptism and so, on behalf of sinners goes the way of the cross. The yoke of Jesus is easy and light because Jesus acts for sinners, because the yoke of Jesus does not throw a man upon his own efforts but rather brings him into fellowship with the πραΰς.

certainty how Matthew conceives the establishing of the judgment of God by the Risen One. He may be thinking on the one hand of the presence of the Risen One in the congregation, who seeks the lost, restores him and leads him into the way of obedience (18.12 ff.); on the other hand, he may be thinking of his coming for the judgment. The decisive thing is first that in the thought of the eschatological salvation and its establishment by Christ the ruling thought which occupies the foreground is that it is concerned with establishing the judgment of God, and second that this establishing of the judgment of God is a saving thing for which the broken may look in hope. The question remains: Whence does it come that when Matthew thinks of the work of Christ it is the establishing of the judgment of God that stands in the foreground? Concentration on this point is only found in Matthew in the New Testament. Of course, salvation is always implicitly thought of as an establishing of the judgment and the righteousness of God as well; but the interest is not so focused on it as in Matthew.[1]

Where does this emphasis in Matthew come from? It cannot be explained as coming from the Rabbinate alone, though it is true that in the Rabbinate eschatological salvation is always somehow concerned with the judgment of God. The absolute validity enjoyed by the Torah inevitably determined, too, the conception of the time of salvation, of course. In the days of the Messiah the theatres and circuses of the Roman empire will be transformed into halls for teaching the Torah. The Messiah will study and teach the Torah; he will make the 'bases' of the law of Moses plain.[2] The evil impulse will be purged out of the heart, and some obviously also believed that Israel would be pure from sin in the days of the Messiah.[3] To this extent it can be said that the days of the Messiah bring an establishing of the judgment of God. This, however, is not conceived at the same time in terms of healing and forgiving. Where the Rabbinate expects redemption in the days of the Messiah it is thinking of something different: of the destruction of the enemies of the people of

[1] In Paul, for example, interest lies much more in the fact that Christ has brought καταλλαγή but not so much on the fact that he brings the establishing of the judgment of God. One can also scarcely point to the eschatological preaching of Jesus here. If all eschatological expectation in his case can be summarised by saying 'that God will then rule' (R. Bultmann, *Theology of the NT*, I, p. 5), such a fine differentiation is difficult to carry through. With Jesus something different is in the foreground, namely that God's rule is immediately imminent.

[2] Billerbeck, IV, p. 883.

[3] Billerbeck, IV, p. 882.

Israel (above all of the world power of Rome), of a brilliant rule of Israel to whom all other nations pay tribute,[1] of the return of the conditions of paradise. The Torah is only bound up with this in so far as in the last resort these conditions again are made to depend on obedience to the Torah. Above all it should be observed that after the destruction of Jerusalem the expectation of the days of the Messiah loses considerably in meaning for the religious life and recedes behind the 'ōlam habbā', which alone brings the real consummation of salvation (after the final judgment).[2] The foreground of the expectation is taken over by the final judgment and the judgment immediately after death. But there it is a matter of pure *justitia distributiva*, of recompense in each case according to the majority of the works. Hence the accent in Matthew cannot be explained with reference to the Rabbinate alone.

In the Pseudepigrapha also eschatological salvation has to do with judgment and righteousness. Here to a great extent the days of the Messiah already bring the absolute consummation of salvation.[3] The Messiah is distinguished by his righteousness,[4] he is *the* righteous one.[5] Hence he will judge righteously in his kingdom; righteousness will reign, unrighteousness and sin disappear.[6] But in the foreground of the expectation stands the destruction of the enemies of Israel and of sinners[7] and thereby the establishing of the reign of the people of Israel and the inception of the conditions of paradise.[8] The establishing of judgment and righteousness comes out most strongly in *Ps. Sol.* 17. The Messiah will bring a holy people together whom he will rule with righteousness (17.26), he will make Jerusalem pure and holy (17.30) so that no wrong will be done among them (17.32); further, he watches over the Lord's flock faithfully and well and does not permit one of them to faint in the pasture (ἀσθενῆσει 17.40). Has this influenced Matthew? But what it means the Psalm makes quite

---

[1] Billerbeck, IV, p. 881.

[2] Billerbeck, IV, p. 817.

[3] The later development, that the earthly Messianic kingdom does not bring the absolute consummation of salvation is seen already in *I Enoch* 71, 2 (Slav.) *Enoch, Assumption of Moses,* Syr. *Baruch* and II (4) Esdras.

[4] Cf. *Test. Judah* 24; *I Enoch* 46.3; 49.2; 62.2; 71.14; *Ps. Sol.* 17.32.

[5] Cf. *I Enoch* 38.2; 39.6; 46.3.

[6] Cf. *Test. Judah.* 24; *Levi* 18; *I Enoch* 39.6; 49.2; P. Volz, *Die Eschat. d. jüd. Gem. im neutest. Zeitalter,* 1934, p. 218.

[7] Cf. Syr. *Baruch* 72; *Or. Sib.*, III, 653 f; *Ps. Sol.* 17.22 ff.; II (4) Esdras 11–12; *I Enoch* 52 f.; 56.

[8] *I Enoch* 58.2 is significant for the underlying atmosphere: 'Blessed are ye righteous and elect for your lot will be glorious!'

clear: the Messiah brings it about by instruction (παιδεῦσαι 17.42), by righteous judgment (17.26, 29, 43), by the destruction of sinners (17.22, 23, 24, 25, 36). This establishing of judgment is not understood in the radical sense of forgiveness. It is true that *Ps. Sol.* 9.7 says, Whose sins shalt thou forgive if not those of sinners? and 18.3 says God's judgment is full of mercy (μετὰ ἐλέους), but that is then immediately restricted again by saying that God does not punish (9.7 οὐκ εὐθυνεῖς) the sins of the righteous, and his judgments are μετὰ ἐλέους because they serve a pedagogical purpose, as discipline (παιδαία 18.4).[1] It is also true that in *Ps. Sol.* 17 otherwise the petitioner's hope is primarily directed towards the destruction of his enemies.

In the same way in the expectation of the time of salvation is the establishing of the judgment of God. It is the absolute work of the Messiah to create משפט and צדקה on the earth.[2] This thought is directly in the forefront in Isaiah.[3] Has Matthew here been influenced by the exegesis of Isaiah? Isaiah certainly occupies a large place among the quotations in Matthew,[4] and the decisive passage in 12.18 ff. is a quotation from Isaiah 42. But precisely here Matthew alters the Isaiah text at the decisive point and the alteration cannot be explained in terms of textual variations or other translations. Thus Matthew had already had the thought and it is very unlikely that he derived it from Isaiah.

The congregation of the Ain-Feshcha Scrolls and the congregation of the new covenant linked with it in the land of Damascus believed that they lived directly in the end-time. Here the establishing of the judgment of God obviously stood entirely in the foreground of the expectation.[5] This is already seen in the fact that the end-time is characterised by the appearance of the teacher of righteousness (*Dam.* 6.11). The dualism between the spirits of light and darkness which rules the present will be overcome at the end: God has set an

---

[1] Cf. on this point H. Cremer, *Die paulin. Rechtfertigungslehre im Zusammanhang ihrer gesch. Voraussetzungen*, 1900², pp. 123 f.; H. Braun, 'Vom Erbarmen Gottes über den Gerechten, zur Theol. der Ps. Sal.', *ZNW*, 1950/51, pp. 1–54, especially 44 ff.

[2] Jer. 23.5 f.; Isa. 9.6; cf. H. W. Wolff, 'Herrschaft Iahwes und Messiasgestalt im AT', *ZAW*, 1936, p. 182.

[3] Isa. 1.26 f.; 2.3 f.; 4.3 ff.; 9.6; 10.22; 11.3 ff.; 28.17; 29.18 ff.; 30.18 ff.; (32.1); cf. in Deutero- and Trito-Isaiah: 42.4; 45.8; 60.17 f., 21; 61.11.

[4] But Isaiah along with Psalms is also most quoted elsewhere in the NT.

[5] Cf. *Dam.* 1.12; 4.4, 10 f.; 6.11; 19.10; 20.26; 1QH 3.28 ff.; 4.20, 25; 1QpHab. 5.3 ff.; 10.4, 13; 11.1; 13.3; 1QS 4.7 f., 12,18 f.; 5.12 f., 19; 8.10.

end to the existence of corruption and at the time of visitation will destroy it for ever.[1] Then the truth which is destined for the world will be victorious.[2] God will cleanse a part of mankind by his Holy Spirit from all infamous deeds and blot out every spirit of corruption from their midst.[3] Here also paradisal conditions[4] and glory are expected, but so far as can be judged up to the present these expectations recede behind the establishing of the judgment of God; indeed 1QH 10.12 can say that God does all this solely for his own glory (רק לכבודכה עשיתה כול אלה). It follows from the whole character of the sect that the establishing of the judgment of God had to stand in the foreground of its expectations for the future. For the very thing which separated them from official Judaism was that they had to accuse their enemies of falsifying God's law and impeding it. From this it follows directly that the establishing of the judgment of God necessarily occupied the foreground in their conception of eschatology. The difference from Matthew is seen first in the dualism and then in the fact that the Messiah recedes into the background; it is God who acts.[5]

It has thus been shown that with his thought of the establishing of the judgment of God Matthew in the first place stands in the general framework of Jewish expectation. This thought stands directly in the foreground of the expectation only in Isaiah and the sectarian writings. There are, however, several difficulties in the way of a direct influence from these: against Isaiah—at the decisive point precisely Matthew has made an alteration; against the sectarian

---

[1] 1QS 4.18.

[2] 1QS 4.19: ואז תצא לנצח אמת תבל, compare with that Matt. 12.20 where according to Schlatter, Zahn, Klostermann and Stendahl εἰς νῖκος corresponds to לנצח. The difference from Matthew is seen first in אמת, in which the dualistic terminology is seen (yet cf. 1QH 4.25 ותוצא לנצח משפטם), and second it is God himself who acts and not the Messiah.

[3] The many passages which promise destruction to the godless, the wicked, etc., but salvation to the children of light, the members of the congregation, correspond with this: Dam. 1.12; 4.4; 19.10; 20.26; 1QpHab. 5.5; 9.6; 10.4, 13; 13.3; 1QS 4.7 f., 12; 5.12 f., 19. According to 1QpHab. 5.4 and 1QS 8.10 the members of the congregation will even take part in the judgment.

[4] According to 1QS 4.23 after the last judgment the children of light will possess 'all the glory of Adam'; in 1QM 12.14 Zion is promised that the possessions of all nations will be brought to her and their kings will serve her.

[5] It is obviously also regarded as a saving, forgiving event, for in 1QS and 1QH righteousness and grace are not yet splitting apart; it is precisely from the righteousness of God that the petitioner expects the forgiveness of sins 1QS 11.3, 5, 12–14, although he knows he is in sin from his mother's womb to old age 1QH 4.29 f. The צדקות of God are his proofs of salvation.

writings because of the dualism and the receding place of the Messiah. On the other hand, the latter point another way: the emphasising of the judgment of God is a consequence of the attitude to the law and to the enemies who falsify the law or even abolish it. It is from this angle that Matthew's emphasis can be most easily explained.

3. *Is Christ the giver of a* nova lex?

A number of exegetes hold that in Matthew Jesus is depicted as the giver of a *nova lex*. Thus B. W. Bacon explains: 'To Matthew's mind the Christian message is a promulgation of the *nova lex*, i.e. the Torah of Moses amplified and spiritualised by Jesus.'[1] G. D. Kilpatrick accepts Bacon's opinion: 'Bacon has convincingly developed the view that the Gospel is the new Law and that the fivefold division of chapters 3–25 is a deliberate imitation of the Pentateuch. The mountain of the sermon on the mount is meant to recall Sinai and Jesus is himself a greater Lawgiver than Moses.'[2] On the other side such a view can be put forward as that of G. Bornkamm: 'It must be observed that in Matthew's Gospel there is no idea of a *nova lex* and cannot be.'[3]

The concept of the *nova lex* may here have a twofold content. It can, in the first place, mean that the activity of Jesus includes the proclamation of a new law; in this way the preaching of Jesus in the Sermon on the Mount is made parallel or antithetical to the giving of the law through Moses on Sinai. The law which holds for the Christian is then a new, better, different law than the law of Sinai which holds for the Jews. It is so, for example, in Hermas, Barnabas and Justin.[4] In the second place it can mean that the Gospel itself is understood as a law, in a legal way. This is clearest in Hermas.[5] In this case the concept of the law becomes more or less absolute and

---

[1] *JBL*, 1928, p. 223. He continues: 'On this point agreement of expositors is so general that we need hardly expatiate upon the points already adduced.' J. Wellhausen and J. Weiss on Matt. 5.17 f. also designate Jesus as the new lawgiver. J. Schniewind, p. 38: 'The Sermon on the Mount is the new law of the Messianic king'; cf. further C. G. Montefiore on Matt. 5.17 f.

[2] G. D. Kilpatrick, *Origins*, pp. 107 f.

[3] See above, p. 35, note 2.

[4] Herm. *Sim.* 5.6.3; 8.3.2; *Barn.* 2.6; Justin *Dial. c. Tryph.* 11.4; 14.3; 18.3; Barnabas, in fact, can equate it with the law of Moses, but only by using allegory to alter its meaning and by denying to the Jews right understanding and the covenant altogether.

[5] Herm. *Sim.* 5.6.3; 8.6.2; *Mand.* 4.1.11; 4.3.1–7; *Vis.* 2.2.5.

takes its place independently alongside the gift wrought through the death of Christ. The law is then understood in a way that does not differ fundamentally from that of Judaism: as the way of salvation in the strict sense. The way of achievement can, it is true, be interrupted by repentance but after that the person depends again upon himself and his achievement. These two statements of the case concerning the *nova lex* often go hand in hand, but do not necessarily stand side by side. Hence when reference is made to a *nova lex* in Matthew two things may also be meant. According to J. Schniewind, Jesus brings the new Messianic Torah; but he does not mean by that that in Matthew the Gospel is understood as law (= legally). B. W. Bacon and G. D. Kilpatrick, on the other hand, obviously think both are correct.

The thesis that Jesus, as a second Moses, founds a new law, the Messianic Torah, is based to a large extent on the opinion that the old synagogue expected a new Torah from the Messiah. According to P. Billerbeck, whose views obviously exercised a great influence,[1] Judaism expected in its Messiah not only a teacher of the Torah but 'the expectation went so far that there was mention made of a new Torah which the Messiah would found and which was even designated as "the Torah of the Messiah".' But Billerbeck himself so limits this that it does not mean that the old Torah of Moses will be superseded and be expanded by additions: 'no, the new Torah of the Messiah will be the old Torah of Moses; but the Messiah will interpret the old Torah in a new way. By interpreting its bases he will bring to light the wealth of its divine thoughts, will make prominent all the treasures of knowledge which lie concealed within it, will solve all its riddles the solution of which was withheld from earlier times.' This limitation must be taken still further and made still firmer. All the passages quoted by Billerbeck in support of the new Messianic law belong to a considerably later time and cannot be quoted with reference to the first century after Christ.[2] But for the later period

---

[1] Excursus on Jesus' Sermon on the Mount, Billerbeck, IV, pp. 1 ff.

[2] The oldest passage mentioned by Billerbeck, Targum Jonathan on Isa. 12.3, does not belong here. It says there: ותקבלון אולפן חדת בחדוא מבחירי צדקא you will receive with joy a new teaching from the elect pious ones. But this 'new teaching' is received from 'the elect pious ones', and thus it is not the new Torah of the Messiah! The other passages are from a very late period: *New Pesiqta (Beth ha-Midrasch* ed. Jellinek, 1853 ff., vi, 63, 13 ff.) arose after the ninth century (cf. H. Strack, *Einleitung in Talmud u. Midrasch*, 1921[5], p. 209); Alphabet of R. Aqiba (*Beth ha-Midr.*, iii, 27, 29) probably in the same period (according to *Encycl. Judaica*, II, p. 452, later than the great Midrash works, but not before the tenth–

also one can scarcely speak of a 'Torah of the Messiah'. The expression 'Torah of the Messiah' is found in Midrash Qoh. 11.8. There it says משיח תורה שאדם למד בעה"ז הבל היא לפני תורתו של. The Torah which a man learns in this world is compared with that of the Messiah, i.e., however, it means the *knowledge* of the Torah which is as nothing compared with knowledge of the Torah which the Messiah has or teaches. The expression תורתו של משיח does not mean that the Messiah is the giver of the Torah.[1] This is further supported by the older parallel to it in Midrash Qoh. 2.1: R. Hiskia said in the name of R. Simon bar Zabdai:[2] התורה שאת למד בעוה"ז הבל היא לפני תורה שבעולם הבא כל. The saying continues: 'for in this world a man learns the Torah and forgets it again, but what is written about the future world? I will put my teaching in your inward parts.' Both sayings say the same thing: it concerns the knowledge of the Torah which in this world is nothing in comparison with the future. Nothing is said about a 'new Messianic Torah'. There remain the passages which speak of a תורה חדשה. In the older of them, *Leviticus Rabba* 13 it states: The Holy One, Blessed be he, has said: a new Torah (תורה חדשה) will go out from me, a renewal of the Torah (חדוש תורה) will go out from me. What is meant by that is given by the context: the slaying of Leviathan and Behemoth, which is to take place in 'ōlam habbā' contradicts the present explanation of the Torah in which it is ritually forbidden. According to תורה חדשה this contradiction will be done away. One must therefore think of a new

---

eleventh centuries); *Lev. Rabba* 13 at the earliest in the seventh century (*Encycl. Judaica*, X, p. 897); Midrash Qoh. 11.8 arose after *Lev. Rabba*. Only in *Lev. Rabba* 13 is reference made to an older tradition, that of R. Abin bar Kahana, a Palestinian Amoraan of the third generation (cf. *Encyc. Judaica*, II, p. 646). According to H. J. Schoeps (*Aus frühchristlicher Zeit*, Tübingen, 1950, p. 224) the apocalyptic writings already presuppose the cessation of the validity of the law in the Messianic kingdom, but he can produce no passage in evidence of this, but only quotes A. Schweitzer's *The Mysticism of Paul the Apostle*, according to which it is nowhere maintained in the late-Jewish apocalypses that the law remains in force in the Messianic kingdom, and existence in the Messianic kingdom is not depicted as existence in complete fulfilment of the law. The latter would break down on *Ps. Sol.* 17. That the law still remains in force in the Messianic kingdom is included in the statements about the eternal validity of the law (*I Enoch* 99.2; *Baruch* 4.1; II (4) Esdras 9.37; Wisd. 18.4; Syr. *Baruch* 77.15 f.; Ecclus. 24.9). The statements of Justin about the new law (*Dial.* 11; 19; 21; 34) cannot be assessed as sources for contemporary Judaism. Justin appeals in connexion with the new law to Isa. 51.4–5 and Jer. 31.31 f., but to no Judaistic witnesses.

[1] Cf. on this *Genesis Rabba* 94: בתורתו של רבי מאיר... 'in the Torah (scroll) of R. Meir . . .' The genitive-connexion need not denote a giver of the law.

[2] Palest. Amoraan of the third generation (*Encycl. Judaica*, II, p. 684).

interpretation of the Torah by which the contradiction will be abolished. That is fundamentally no different from what the Rabbinate also does by its interpretation.[1] P. Billerbeck himself interprets the passage as follows: 'The opinion is that in the future world, on the basis of the new interpretation of the Torah, eating of animals not ritually slain will be permitted.'[2] Hence in the other passage in the New Pesiqta one should also think only of a new interpretation of the Torah, not of a new Torah itself.[3] No other understanding is possible in view of the Jewish faith in the eternal validity of the law of Moses. On the passages cited by Billerbeck (IV, p. 2 under f) in this connexion compare also *Deut. Rabba* 8.6 on Deut. 30.12—Moses said to them: So that you may not say, 'Another Moses will arise and bring us another Torah from heaven', I have long made known to you: the Torah is not (any longer) in heaven! In so far as more is meant by the Torah of the Messiah than a new interpretation of the old Torah, which, however, is also fundamentally possible in the Rabbinate, one cannot speak of such an expectation in the later period either.[4] On the

---

[1] One might compare the story of Hananiah b. Hiskia b. Garon, who by exegesis overcomes the contradictions between Ezekiel and the Pentateuch and thereby saved Ezekiel from apocryphysing (W. Bacher, *Die Agada der Tannaiten*, I, p. 19). חדש and חדוש are both in the Tannaitic and Amoraan periods technical terms for putting forward a new Halakah, which is intended to be an altogether legitimate interpretation of the Sinaitic law; cf. W. Bacher, *Die exegetische Terminiologie der jüdischen Traditionsliteratur*, I, p. 56, II, p. 64 (here above all *Ruth Rabbah* on 4.1: he did not know that the Halakah had already been renewed נתחדש הלכה; similarly 4.5).

[2] Billerbeck, IV, p. 1163.

[3] *New Pesiqta* (*Beth ha-Midr.*, vi, 63, 13 ff.): God delivers the 'grounds' of the new law טעמי תורה חדשה which he will hereafter give to Israel through the Messiah. Here also the new interpretation is meant by תורה חדשה. Similarly Alphabet of R. Aqiba (*Beth ha-Midr.*, iii, 27, 29).

[4] M. Löwy (*Monatsschrift f. Gesch. u. Wiss. d. Judentums*, 1904, p. 324) appeals for the cessation of the law in the days of the Messiah to *Eduyoth* 8.7, where it is reported of Johanan ben Zakkai, Elijah will not come to pronounce for impure or pure but to remove those (families) brought near by force and to bring near those who have been removed by force. But this saying is not intended to make any statement about the duration and scope of the validity of the law, but refers to actual acts of violence by one Ben Zion in the land east of Jordan, which Elijah when he returns will have to put an end to (cf. A. Schlatter, *Jochanan ben Zakkai*, p. 45). H. J. Schoeps (*Aus frühchristlicher Zeit*, pp. 223 ff.) also appeals to the following passages: *Sanh.* 97a; *Shab.* 30a, 151b; *Kilaim* 9.3 and *Niddah* 61b. When in *Sanh.* 97a world history is divided into three periods—2,000 years waste and void, 2,000 years of the Torah and 2,000 years of the Messianic kingdom—this is not intended to make any statement about the duration of the validity of the law as the context clearly shows; it has to do solely with the question: When will the Messiah come? According to *Shab.* 30a, 151b; *Kilaim* 9.3 the dead are free from the law. Again this does not mean any limitation of the validity of the law but solely con-

contrary, in the New Testament period already the Messiah is awaited as the great teacher of the Torah, as P. Seidelin's investigation of the Messianic expectation in the Isaiah Targum has shown.[1]

As the basis for the view that in Matthew Jesus is depicted as the bringer of a *nova lex*, as a new lawgiver, as a second Moses, B. W. Bacon and G. D. Kilpatrick point above all to the Moses typology in Matthew. The story of the childhood of Jesus especially is portrayed after the pattern of the Moses-legend,[2] according to which the prophecy of the birth of the deliverer was the occasion for Pharaoh to have all the children of that year put to death. The mention of Egypt in 2.13 also inevitably reminds the hearer of the Moses stories, and Matt. 2.20 is taken over almost word for word from Ex. 4.19. This fashioning of the story of the childhood of Jesus after the pattern of the Moses-legend is not, of course, in the first place the work of Matthew, but was already before him when he wrote; Matt. 2.20 = Ex. 4.19 can, however, be attributed to him. A. Schlatter and J. Jeremias also find in 4.2 an influence from the Moses typology; here the addition of 40 nights is due to the 40 days in Ex. 34.28 and Deut. 9.9, 18. It is possible that the mountain of the Sermon on the Mount is meant as a reminder of Sinai. But then the question arises: in what sense? Does it mean that Jesus is depicted as a second Moses, as the giver of a new Torah? For the Judaism of the time this inference by no means necessarily follows. The reminder of the mount on which the law was given means rather that here the right interpretation of the Sinai law is provided. Thus Joshua ben Hananiah

cludes that the dead cannot and need not fulfil the commandments. Out of the sentence that a shroud may be made out of a mixed cloth R. Joseph (*Niddah* 61b) deduces that in the future world the practice of the commandments will cease. In the light of the context W. Bacher (*Die Agada d. babyl. Amoräer*, Berlin, 1878, p. 105, note 23) maintains that this refers to the ceremonial law only and in what follows the opinion of R. Joseph is contradicted. Nothing whatever is said in this context about a Torah of the Messiah or a new Torah which God will give. We do not mean that all Rabbinic statements may be forced into one mould; differences remain; in Midrash on Ps. 146, §4 (according to Billerbeck, II, p. 702) there is also the expectation that the ceremonial law will cease—but there again this is contradicted in what follows. The question is rather what is the decisive note in the Rabbinic expectation. It is difficult to deduce from the evidence that there is to be a new Torah, another Torah, or even the cessation of the Torah in the Messianic time. Such a thought is quite impossible for the Jew, who believes that God himself studies the law three hours daily (*Abodah Zarah* 3b).

[1] 'Der Ebed Jahwe und die Messiasgestalt im Jesajatargum', *ZNW*, 35, 1936, pp. 194 ff.

[2] Cf. J. Jeremias, Μωϋσῆς, *TWNT*, IV, p. 875; A. Schlatter, *Matthäus*, p. 32; E. Klostermann, p. 12; Billerbeck, I, p. 78.

said when he kissed the stone on which Eliezer ben Hyrcanus sat when he gave his lecture on the law: 'This stone is like Mount Sinai, and the one that sat upon it like the ark of the covenant.'[1] For the contemporary hearer the reminder of Sinai could only mean that here the Sinai law was really taught. In 19.1–9 the original order of God is set over against the Mosaic command about the bill of divorcement. But Matthew could scarcely be understood here as meaning that the Mosaic law should be degraded, he means that the Mosaic law should be radicalised, its proper meaning brought out.[2] Whereas Mark 7.10 introduces a commandment of the decalogue with the words 'Moses said' Matthew substitutes: God said (Matt. 15.4). The law of Moses is for him unquestionably the law of God, and also for the Church. Jesus' interpretation of the law and his commandments are not in opposition to the law of Moses but are rather again and again based on the Old Testament (12.1–7; 15.1–20; 19.1–9). The law which holds in the Church is identical with the 'law and the prophets'. Hence the Moses typology can only be intended to confirm the teaching of Jesus as genuine teaching from Sinai.

It could be objected that in the antitheses of the Sermon on the Mount the teaching of Jesus is contrasted with the law of Sinai and opposed to it. The analysis above has shown, however, that Matthew is less concerned to set the teaching of Jesus in opposition to the law of Sinai than to the Rabbinic interpretation of it. It is true that in 5.38 f. the Sinai commandment is actually abolished by the teaching of Jesus,[3] but the question is whether that is the whole intention of 5.21–48, which is clearly directed according to 5.20 against the Rabbinate, and in 5.43 a commandment of the Old Testament is commented on with Rabbinic exegetical terminology as it was understood in the Rabbinate. 11.28–30 speaks of the ζυγός of Jesus,

---

[1] *S. of S. Rabba* on 1.3 (Joshua was a pupil of Johanan ben Zakkai and thus belonged very closely to the same period as Matthew): האבן הזאת דומ' להר סיני וזה שישב עלי' דומ' לארון הברית. Cf. W. Bacher, *Die Agada d. babyl. Amoräer*, p. 101: Joseph bar Ḥiyya was called 'Sinai' because he had a comprehensive knowledge of the whole traditional teaching which was revealed on Sinai.

[2] Note the alteration of Mark 10.1–12 in Matthew. Matthew does not say: Moses ἔγραψεν ὑμῖν because of the hardness of your hearts but: Moses ἐπέτρεψεν ὑμῖν 'suffered' you because of the hardness of your hearts. Besides, by the toning down in Matt. 19.9 (μὴ ἐπὶ πορνείᾳ) in comparison with Mark 10.11, the Mosaic law about the bill of divorcement is saved from completely losing validity.

[3] It should be remembered in this connexion that even in the Rabbinate—paradoxical as it may appear—the abolition of the commandments of Sinai is actually possible; cf. Billerbeck, I, pp. 717 f.

of his φορτίον, which brings refreshment to the πεφορτισμένοι, i.e. to those who bear the burden of the Rabbinic conception of the law. Here, too, it is difficult to see any justification for inferring a *nova lex*, since the ζυγός of Jesus does not indicate a new content but a new understanding of the law. The front is again drawn up against the Rabbinate. Above all the repeated emphasis in Matthew that the valid law is identical with the νόμος καὶ προφῆται (5.17; 7.12; 22.40) must be called to mind here. What is justified in talk about a *nova lex* consists in the fact that Matthew does not share the understanding of the law in the Rabbinate but rather opposes the Rabbinate face to face. But it would still not be correct to speak of a *nova lex* because the identity with the law of Sinai is so strongly emphasised.

Nor can one speak of a *nova lex* in Matthew in the second sense, that the Christian message has become a law. This question has already been repeatedly considered in the preceding paragraphs and does not need to be described here again. The constant threat of judgment does not yet in Matthew lead to the Christian trusting to his own achievement; the disciples are the μικροί. The law and the saving deeds of Christ in his death and resurrection do not fall apart, but are closely bound together by the concern of Matthew for the establishing of the judgment of God. But one may perhaps say that the emphasising of works, of judgment according to works and the kind of attack on the Pharisees in Matt. 23 did further the development of the ancient Church in the direction of the *nova lex*, and this is closely connected with the fact that Matthew was the most quoted of all the Gospels in the ancient Church.

VI. THE ANTINOMIANS IN MATTHEW

There still remains the attempt to sketch somewhat more exactly the antinomians whom Matthew opposed. These opponents in the face of whom Matthew emphasises the abiding validity of the law are clearly seen in Matt. 5.17 ff.; 7.15 ff. and 24.11 ff. They dispute that the law and the prophets still hold for the Church. For this reason Matthew lays particular emphasis upon them. From 5.17 it follows that the opponents did not dispute the validity of the Old Testament altogether; in the past the law and the prophets rightly held, but Christ has abolished the law and the prophets; since the coming of Christ their validity is ended. The same is shown by Matthew's alteration in 11.13 where in the text before him the unacceptable

sentence for him ran: 'the law and the prophets were until John'.
This sentence already occurred in Q, but Matthew must have seen in
it the opinion of his opponents.[1]

Hence at times the enemies against whom Matthew fought have
been regarded as a Pauline group. According to H. J. Schoeps[2] the
ἐχθρὸς ἄνθρωπος in 13.24–28 refers to Paul. That breaks down,
however, on the interpretation which the evangelist himself gives to
the parable in 13.39: the enemy is the devil. H. J. Holtzmann and
J. Weiss characterise the opponents as ultra-Paulinists.[3] The thought is
suggested by the Pauline thesis: Christ is the end of the law (Rom.10.4.)[4]

A comparison with the libertines opposed in James 2.14–26 leads
us somewhat further. In this section, developed in the style of a dia-
tribe, a group is attacked which appeals to its faith and discounts
good works. The attitude of the opponents is already shown in 2.14.
The author of the Epistle of James (here simply called James, without
intending any reference to the question of authorship) poses the
question concerning such a man: Can faith save him? (2.14). James
cannot be concerned here about a 'theologically narrow conception
of faith'[5] but the common meaning of the word faith is intended, as
in 2.1: the faith in Christ which appertains to every baptised person.
'Faith' without works is dead for James; it is just as fruitless as bene-
volent words without any actual help (2.15 ff.).[6] 2.18 brings forward
an objection by means of which the author desires to clarify his meaning.[7] Difficulty arises because the objector attributes works to himself
but faith to the other person. This difficulty can most easily be removed by explaining σύ and ἐγώ as unstressed in the sense of 'the
one—the other',[8] as Dibelius does. The apportioning of faith and
works to thou and I is then incidental. What is opposed is a sophisti-
cal separation of faith and works in general. James summons his
opponent to show his faith without works, whereas he will show his

---

[1] Cf. above, pp. 62 ff.

[2] *Theologie und Geschichte des Judenchristentums*, pp. 120, note 1, 127, note 1.

[3] H. J. Holtzmann, *Lehrbuch der neutestamentlichen Theologie*, I, 1911², p. 508;
J. Weiss on Matt. 5.17 ff.

[4] R. Bultmann (*Theology of the NT*, I, p. 54) regards it as possible that in 5.19
ἐλάχιστος may refer to Paul; but 5.19 was already in the text used by Matthew.

[5] Cf. M. Dibelius, *Der Brief des Jakobus*, 1921, *ad loc.*

[6] 2.15 is not an illustration from life, but a comparison: the middle term is
unfruitfulness (M. Dibelius, *op. cit.*, p. 142).

[7] The objection comprises only 2.18a. 18b already provides the reply: cf.
M. Dibelius, *op. cit.*, p. 144.

[8] Cf. also A. Meyer, *Das Rätsel des Jak.-Briefes*, 1930, p. 92, note 3, and G.
Eichholz, *Jakobus und Paulus*, 1953, p. 44.

faith by means of his works. For James it is self-evident that his opponent will not be able to provide this proof and for this reason he himself undertakes a test of this kind of faith. Care must be taken not to deduce too much about the opponents' conception of faith, or the author's, from 2.19. James does not give here an exact description of his opponents' faith or his own.[1] But it can be seen here on what native earth the author stands: what he is most concerned about here is to apply that formulation of the monotheistic faith with which Judaism was familiar from Deut. 6.4–9. So much, however, is clear from 2.19: πίστις denotes the same common understanding of faith as was assumed above; it is the acceptance of a missionary message, the confession of a fellowship; πίστις has possibly faded to a theoretical conviction. 2.20–23 provides the Scriptural evidence by the example of Abraham. It is obvious that the opposite side itself had appealed to Abraham. James protests against an Abraham in whom works were displaced. For him Genesis 22 follows immediately after Genesis 15 and this confirms for him the inseparability of faith and works. In his manner of proving he is obviously influenced by the Judaistic tradition about Abraham, but in spite of that he differs from the Jewish exposition of Gen. 15.6. For Judaism Abraham's faith is regarded as a work and is therefore counted as righteousness. Faith and work are not separated in Judaism.[2] Such a direct unity of faith and work is no longer possible for James, however; that is the consequence of the thesis of his opponents. He therefore seeks to show that ἡ πίστις συνήργει τοῖς ἔργοις αὐτοῦ, καὶ ἐκ τῶν ἔργων ἡ πίστις ἐτελειώθη.[3] In order that he should be pronounced righteous works had to be added to Abraham's faith.

One cannot therefore avoid seeing behind the opponents attacked here the Apostle Paul, whatever the distance. It is true that the line of argument in 2.14–26 is a long way from striking Paul, since it has not understood the Pauline contrast between πίστις and ἔργα and indeed does not know it at all.[4] But: 'none of the interpreters of the Epistle of James has succeeded in presenting a historically credible figure in

[1] Cf. M. Dibelius, op. cit., p. 148.
[2] Cf. M. Dibelius, op. cit., pp. 151, 157 ff.; A. Meyer, op. cit., pp. 135 ff.
[3] James is concerned about the co-working of the two entities. 2.24 shows that the two factors were not of equal importance for James. One may not read out of ἐτελειώθη, however, that faith only really becomes faith through works; in connexion with 'perfection' he is thinking of the goal towards which both faith and works are working: the righteousness of Abraham.
[4] Paul would also have agreed with the statement that faith without works is dead; for Paul πίστις is at the same time ὑπακοή.

the first or second century as a probability, apart from the one Paul, who represented something like "faith without works".[1] The example of Abraham, which the opponents obviously brought forward in their argument, also points in the same direction. It is, in fact, 'still only the shadow of Paul, or even of a Paul who has become formalised',[2] but this group cannot be explained on any other basis.

Matthew's πίστις-concept stands in sharp contrast with that of James 2.14–26 as we have seen it in the debate with his libertine opponents. The above investigation has shown that πίστις in Matthew unquestionably means a willing and obeying; it means trust. Matthew's conception of faith is very close to the Old Testament-Jewish one. He knows no πίστις in the common sense of the Christian faith as the acceptance of a missionary message or even of a merely theoretical conviction. From this it follows that the antinomians of Matthew cannot have appealed to their πίστις in support of their neglect of works in the way the libertines of the Epistle of James did. Otherwise πιστεύειν = obey could not have been so straightforward for Matthew. From this it follows further that one can hardly see a Pauline group in the antinomians of Matthew, for in that case one would have to expect that they would make πίστις the basis of their attitude. There is, however, no trace of this; they do not appeal to πίστις, but to the fact that since the coming of Christ the validity of the law is at an end.

There is a further factor. A group which represents the view that the law has no validity for the Church is unthinkable in the area of Judaism, in Jewish Christianity. It must concern Hellenistic Christians. With this the portrayal of these people in Matt. 7.21–23 agrees. In his description of the judgment in 7.22 Matthew has made a significant alteration in comparison with Luke 13.26. Through the link with 7.21 (= Luke 6.46) those who defend themselves at the judgment are those who have not done the will of God. The same people are meant as those against whom a warning is issued as false prophets in 7.15–20 and who are characterised as doers of lawlessness in 7.23. These appeal at the judgment to the fact that they have prophesied in the name of Jesus, have driven out devils and performed many miracles.[3] They appeal to their *charismata*. It is true

[1] G. Kittel, 'Der geschichtliche Ort des Jak.-Briefes', *ZNW*, 1942, p. 95.

[2] G. Eichholz, *op. cit.*, pp. 40 f.

[3] τῷ σῷ ὀνόματι doubtless does not simply mean 'in thy commission' but instrumentally 'in thy power', H. Bietenhard, ὄνομα, *TWNT*, V, pp. 276 f.; cf. W. Heitmüller, *Im Namen Jesu*, 1903, p. 58.

that prophecy and the working of miracles are also found in the Palestinian primitive Church and there are no specifically Hellenistic ideas in προφητεύειν, δαιμόνια ἐκβάλλειν and δυνάμεις ποιεῖν (though these derive from the non-Hellenistic editor), but this speech in their own defence is only possible among Hellenistic Christians; for the appeal to *charismata* here occurs precisely because of a lack of good works. The combination with 7.21 means that the accused were of the opinion that they had in their *charismata* a sufficient substitute for their lack of works.[1]

Although in the antinomian opponents we have to do with a Hellenistic group the question at issue is no longer the same as in the original disputes about the law in the forties and fifties. It is not possible to point to any particular part of the law on which the struggle turned in Matthew, such as circumcision, for example, or food laws. The fact that there is no mention of circumcision in Matthew may be explained on the basis of the material of the tradition which lay before him. But the abandon with which Matthew adopts the saying about defilement through food (Mark 7.15 = Matt. 15.11) shows that he was not concerned about the question of food laws. It must perhaps be inferred from 15.11 that Matthew himself no longer belongs to the strict Jewish-Christian wing which demanded that the Gentile Christians should adopt the ceremonial law with its commandments concerning food. Matthew did lay emphasis on the observing of the Sabbath, even though he differed from the formal, rigorist attitude of the Rabbinate in placing the love-commandment above the Sabbath commandment. But can the question of the Sabbath commandment have been the point at issue with the antinomians? The mood of Matthew's Gospel points in another direction. Matthew *generally* emphasises the abiding validity of the law and the prophets for the Church. According to 7.16–20 the opponents are recognised by their bad fruits and according to 24.12 they cause love to grow cold. The constant threats of judgment are also attuned to this note (25.31 ff.; 13.36 ff.; 16.27; 3.7 ff.). Hence the opponents can best be denoted as libertines.[2]

Difficulties do arise, however, from the fact that where we hear of

---

[1] This thought is not possible in Judaism. The only question that can arise there is whether miracles are a sufficient legitimation for a prophet who permits transgression of the Torah or parts of it (*Sanh.* 90a; further Billerbeck, I, pp. 726 f.), but the thought of an appeal to miracles in the judgment as a substitute for the fulfilling of the commandments does not arise, in my opinion.

[2] Hence B. W. Bacon, p. 348, rightly speaks of a Hellenistic libertinism.

libertines in Hellenistic Christianity there are always somehow Gnostic influences present. Can we, then, say that Matthew is opposing a Gnostic group? B. W. Bacon[1] thinks of Gnostics in connexion with the false prophets, such as Dositheus, Simon Magus, Menander and Elkesai. There is, however, no trace of this in Matthew. Matthew's Gospel is not anti-gnostic but rather ungnostic.[2] Its constant appeal to the Old Testament presupposes that such a line of argument will be clear to his opponents, and this means that they cannot reject the Old Testament altogether. Unless we are to assume therefore that Matthew completely misunderstood his opponents we must at least say that they did not represent any gnosticism in the serious sense.

Thereby the possibilities of stating something certain about these opponents are exhausted. More cannot be said. Matthew opposes a group who appeal in support of their libertinism to the fact that Christ has abolished the law; these opponents rely on their *charismata*, their spiritual gifts, but not on their πίστις. There is no anti-gnostic polemic in Matthew. But the knowledge of this battle-front is important for the understanding of Matthew's Gospel. The constant exhortation to do God's will, to yield fruit, and the threat of judgment according to works takes on in this way a different look, because that to which it specifically refers is thus given.

[1] B. W. Bacon, pp. 73 f. Cf. J. Weiss, *Das Urchristentum*, 1917, p. 586 [ET *Hist. of Primitive Christianity*, p. 759].

[2] In Matthew there is no soul without body, and also in referring to the final destiny of a men he speaks of their bodies (5.29; 10.28, cf. 27.52). But is that anti-gnostic? Or is it not simply OT-Jewish?

MATTHEW AS INTERPRETER OF THE MIRACLE STORIES

Heinz Joachim Held

IN HIS BOOK on the Synoptic problem P. Wernle called Matthew's Gospel a 'retelling' of Mark's Gospel.[1] On the basis of the so-called two-source theory this judgment is entirely logical. It explains the striking evidence of the close relationship between the two Gospels. This explanation, however, immediately raises new questions. How are we to account for the fact that Matthew does not simply hand on the tradition as he receives it but retells it? What causes him in countless passages, in great matters and in small, to take a way of his own? The following investigation is offered as a contribution to these questions. We select the miracle stories in order to show that the evangelist Matthew in reproducing them must be understood as an interpreter with a definite goal in mind.

First of all we shall enquire about the intention which governed the evangelist in retelling the individual miracle stories. In this connexion the Synoptic parallels of Mark and/or Luke will be drawn on for the purposes of comparison (I). Our next concern will be to recognise the peculiar characteristics of the form of the Matthaean miracle stories and to assess their significance for the evangelist's interpretation (II). Next this interpretation will be unfolded from two positive points of view, Christology and faith (III and IV). In conclusion the result will be summed up on the background of the problem of tradition and interpretation (V).

I. THE RETELLING OF THE MIRACLE STORIES BY MATTHEW

Looked at as a whole the re-presentation of Mark's Gospel by the evangelist Matthew is ruled by two general characteristics: on the

---

[1] P. Wernle, *Die synoptische Frage*, Freiburg, 1899, p. 161.

one hand by the expansion or the insertion of discourse material, and on the other the abbreviation of the narratives. This second point of view, of abbreviation, applies above all to the miracle stories which —apart from the Passion story—contain the greater part of the purely narrative parts of Mark's Gospel. This gives the impression at first that the first evangelist did not attach much importance to the narratives about Jesus. Thus J. Wellhausen, for example, summarises his impression of the revision of the stories as he received them by Matthew as follows: '. . . the actual material of the narratives he only repeats in detail in the Passion; generally he does not lovingly expand it but compresses it and only uses it as an occasion for his own purposes. The stories of the man sick of the palsy, the demon-possessed man of Gadara, Jairus, the dumb epileptic have been particularly weakened by abbreviation. There are also many details elsewhere which have been passed over as insignificant and this has not always happened without injury to the sense.'[1]

The question remains, however, whether the abbreviation of the narratives and in particular the miracle stories by Matthew can be called a loveless treatment. G. Bornkamm shows by means of the stilling of the storm in Matthew's Gospel that the evangelist exercises great care in reproducing this miracle narrative. Indeed he shows himself to be not only a person handing on the story but also an 'exegete' of it.[2] Since a number of details of the narratives in Mark are omitted the question arises whether this pattern of abbreviation may not be a means of interpretation. One feels that something of an answer to this question is provided when H. Greeven in an investigation of the healing of the paralytic according to Matthew concludes that the 'abbreviation of the expansive Markan narrative' takes place 'in the interest of concentration on what is essential' (on Matt. 9.3 and 4).[3] In a similar way the healing of the blind man of Jericho (Matt. 20.29–34) gains a really germane compactness by the abbreviation of Mark 10.49–50: 'a prelude or interlude which contributes nothing to the actual point is omitted'.[4] Something similar can be seen in the narration of the preparation for the Passover meal (Matt. 26.17–19). Hence H. Greeven sees in the

---

[1] *Einleitung in die drei ersten Evangelien*, Berlin, 1911[2], p. 50.
[2] Cf. above, p. 55.
[3] H. Greeven, 'Die Heilung des Gelähmten nach Matthäus', *Wort und Dienst*, Jahrbuch der Theol. Schule Bethel, 1955, p. 69.
[4] *Ibid.*, p. 74.

abbreviation of the narratives a well-considered measure adopted by Matthew, 'of compression for the purpose of reaching the essentials more quickly'.[1] Thus, far from intending to damage the sense, this measure is directly intended to direct attention to the major point. It is obviously a means of interpretation. It must, of course, be investigated whether this thesis is sustained in detail with reference to the miracle stories of Matthew's Gospel.

The proof that the abbreviation of the miracle stories serves the interests of interpretation can only be supplied by making clear at the same time in each individual case the purpose of this interpretation. This is expressed not only in what remains after the abbreviation but even more in the setting of the miracle story under consideration in the framework of the Gospel and also in the wording of the text of the pericope in Matthew in contrast to that in Mark. Hence it will be necessary, by a comparison of the versions of the two evangelists with regard to abbreviation, setting and wording, to work out the Matthaean interpretation of the miracle stories. A look at the Gospel of Luke may well help us to discover the uniqueness of the first Gospel.

Of course we are not concerned with 'explaining' as fully as possible the deviations of the two later evangelists from our text of Mark. It is certainly true that we have to reckon 'with the carelessness of popular journalism'.[2] In addition many abbreviations will be due to the removal of elaborations of language and of prolixities of style. Yet such an explanation does not really satisfy in the light of the observation that Matthew shows no interest in descriptive details in the miracle stories.[3]

It would be extremely difficult, in view of the far-reaching abbreviation of the narrative of the casting out of demons in Gadara (Matt. 8.28–34), for example, and of the story of the raising of Jairus's daughter (Matt. 9.18–26), to speak of the carelessness of popular journalism. Above all, the healing of the woman with the haemorrhage (Matt. 9.20–22) gives the impression that Matthew has substituted a concise and clear report for one which in Mark is obscured by detail. Everything that is accidental is omitted, only the main line is worked out. In actual fact one can hardly speak of a real

[1] *Ibid.*, p. 74.
[2] Thus J. Schniewind, 'Zur Synoptikerexegese', *TR*, N.F. 2, 1930, p. 139.
[3] Examples of this in P. Wernle, *Die synopt. Frage*, pp. 151–8, and in W. C. Allen, pp. xvii f.

story any more. We have here no variegated picture, bewildering by reason of its diverse scenes, so to speak, but a simple outline drawing. How far this is a case of a planned and significant presentation we shall see later. Certainly it is not a matter of carelessness in this instance. It looks very much more as though the abbreviating is done in the interest of concentration on what is essential and must consequently be regarded as a means of interpretation.

The retelling of the miracle stories in Matthew's Gospel takes place, of course, not only with the help of abbreviation. On four occasions the evangelist inserts something new into the pericope which he received (Matt. 8.11, 12; 8.19–22; 14.28–31, and 15.22–24). That he does this out of the joy of telling a story is ruled out by his method of presentation elsewhere, including these four miracle stories, which is far removed from anything of a novelistic nature. These expansions also serve rather as a means of interpretation.

This is the way J. Wellhausen assesses the report of the walking of Jesus on the sea: 'In Matthew meaning is given to the miracle by an episode which is inserted.'[1] A. Schlatter also ascribes to this same scene of Peter walking on the sea a 'didactic power'.[2] If the stilling of the storm is interpreted by Matthew as a paradigm of discipleship,[3] then the placing of the two conversations about discipleship immediately before it can be nothing other than a means of this interpretation. How far this also applies to the insertions into the story of the centurion of Capernaum and the Canaanite woman remains still to be determined. In any case, however, the thesis that the expansions are also made in the interests of interpretation will only hold good if other observations on the transmitted wording of the pericope also point in the same direction.

Finally, there is the question why in his retelling of the Gospel of Mark Matthew omits some of the miracle stories altogether. Whether this may be a matter of chance or whether other grounds may be conjectured will depend not least on observations which can be made on the retelling of other miracles by Matthew.

A. *Abbreviation as a means of interpretation*

We are not yet in a position to present the interpretation of the miracle stories as a whole by the evangelist Matthew. Our immediate

[1] *Einleitung in die drei ersten Evangelien*, pp. 50 f.
[2] *Markus, der Evangelist für die Griechen*, Stuttgart, 1935, p. 133.
[3] Cf. G. Bornkamm above, pp. 56 f.

task is simply to show how the abbreviation of particular narratives works out some particular theological theme, or more exactly, brings it into greater prominence than is the case in Mark. The themes of interpretation under consideration are Christology, faith, and discipleship. It is obvious that they may not and cannot be taken in any mutually exclusive sense, for they not only overlap in actual content but they occur in each single story overlapping each other in some way or other. The themes mentioned thus simply indicate the prevailing interest in the retelling of a miracle story.

1. *The theme of Christology*

The first pericope that calls for consideration here is the healing of the leper (Matt. 8.2–4). It is examined in detail, however, in another context.[1] All we need say at this point by way of anticipation is that by his concise rendering Matthew brings out with particular impressiveness the powerful majesty of Jesus.

Matt. 8.14–15

The healing of Peter's mother-in-law is told on the whole in the same way by Matthew as by Mark (Mark 1.29–31). The abbreviations of the first evangelist relate to specific details of a narrative kind. Thus the clause καὶ εὐθὺς λέγουσιν αὐτῷ περὶ αὐτῆς (Mark 1.30b) is omitted, while instead of the vividly presented action of Jesus καὶ προσελθὼν ἤγειρεν αὐτὴν κρατήσας τῆς χειρός (Mark 1.31a) only the brief expression καὶ ἥψατο τῆς χειρὸς αὐτῆς (Matt. 8.15a) is used. This last contraction in expression may be for stylistic reasons only, i.e. may be more or less superficially occasioned. The omission of the intimation to Jesus of the need cannot, however, be explained in this way, especially as it is quite striking, for on it depends the fact that this is the only time in Matthew's Gospel that Jesus of himself takes the initiative in a miracle of healing.[2]

In fact the open-minded reader of the Matthaean narrative gains 'the impression that Jesus entered the house *alone*'.[3] The disciples are not mentioned, although the use of the expression εἰς τὴν οἰκίαν Πέτρου (Matt. 8.14) makes the presence of Peter and his brother probable. Further there is no mention of the 'people' of Mark 1.30b (= Luke

---

[1] Cf. below, pp. 213 ff. and 255 f.

[2] Elsewhere, not only in Matthew's Gospel but in the whole Synoptic tradition, Jesus only heals when people come to him or expressly ask him (exception Luke 7.11–17). The expulsions of demons do not come in for consideration here, as they are not healings in the actual sense of the word, but exorcisms.

[3] E. Klostermann, *ad loc.*, p. 75.

4.38b). The less important people are absent and everything points to the fact that Matthew's interest is concentrated on the major figure alone, namely Jesus.

This is clear in the first place from the fact that purely as a matter of grammar Jesus (ὁ 'Ιησοῦς Matt. 8.14) is the only subject in the incident of the healing. The change of subject which gives a certain liveliness to Mark's account (and Luke's) is deleted: Mark 1.29 Jesus, 1.30a the mother-in-law, 1.30b 'they', 1.31 Jesus. Instead of this we read in Matthew: καὶ ἐλθὼν ὁ 'Ιησοῦς ... εἶδεν ... καὶ ἥψατο τῆς χειρὸς αὐτῆς. The further course of the narrative betrays that the occurrence takes place only between Jesus and the mother-in-law, for the concluding sentence reads: καὶ διηκόνει αὐτῷ (Matt. 8.15b) instead of διηκόνει αὐτοῖς (Mark 1.31b = Luke 4.39b). Finally the incorporation of this miracle story into the section Matt. 8.2–17 points to a Christological purpose. Three miracle stories stand here alongside each other and they reach their clearly recognisable conclusion in the summary report and the quotation from the Old Testament in Matt. 8.16–17. Jesus in his healing activity is here shown to be the fulfiller of the prophetic prediction. There he was announced as the one who would free us from our sicknesses. Corresponding to this, Matt. 8.14–15 presents him as answering of his own accord this call laid upon him by God. The Matthaean picture 'brings into prominence . . . the view of the Master who sees sickness and need where they are to be found'.[1]

The abbreviation of the Markan version by Matthew has thus no merely formal causes. It goes hand in hand with a substantial revision and can best be understood as a means of interpretation. The theme of this interpretation, Jesus as the healer of the sick, is also intended by Mark so that by his abbreviated and compressed revision Matthew simply brings more clearly to expression a theological thought which is already present.

Luke, on the other hand, in his presentation (Luke 4.38–39) follows Mark very exactly, not, of course, without clarifying in his own way certain statements. Thus he speaks expressly of a request to Jesus (4.38 ἠρώτησαν instead of Mark 1.30 λέγουσιν) and emphasises the seriousness of the fever (4.38 . . . ἦν συνεχομένη πυρετῷ μεγάλῳ). Jesus acts towards the sickness as he does in driving out demons in that he 'rebukes' the fever (4.39 ἐπετίμησεν τῷ πυρετῷ). This all results in a different picture from that in Matthew. The marks of his

[1] E. Lohmeyer, p. 159.

revision—omission of all subordinate details and concentration on the major person—are not found in Luke. In his case the emphasis is much more upon the miraculous deed of Jesus.

Matt. 8.16–17

In Mark this summary report of the healing activity of Jesus (1.32–34) forms the conclusion of the first day in Capernaum which portrays the activity of Jesus programmatically so to speak (Mark 1.21–39). Hence it also has there a real task of narration, as can be seen from the continuation in Mark 1.35–38 (the going out of Jesus in the early morning), which is exactly the same in Luke (4.42). Above all the information in Mark 1.33 καὶ ἦν ὅλη ἡ πόλις ἐπι συνηγμένη πρὸς τὴν θύραν shows that what happened there and then is in mind—Jesus in the house of Peter.[1] In Matthew, on the other hand, this summary report no longer refers solely to the healing activity of Jesus on the evening of a day in Capernaum, although in his case also the place (Matt. 8.5) and the time (Matt. 8.16) are firmly retained; on the contrary all concrete traits are missing, so that we are given a bare and merely summary sketch which gains its significance within the composition of Matt. 8.2–17. It serves not only as an introduction to the quotation from Scripture but provides the concluding stroke to the three miracles already reported: what the particular examples have portrayed is now stated comprehensively and in general. Thus we have here a summary in the proper sense of the word, bringing out the essence of what has gone before. It is certainly not fortuitous that in the formulation καὶ ἐξέβαλεν τὰ πνεύματα λόγῳ (Matt. 8.16) Matthew alludes to the saying of the centurion: μόνον εἰπὲ λόγῳ (Matt. 8.8). This confirms the summarising character of the concentrated report. It becomes a statement about the power of Jesus by his mere word. Finally, in this context the use of the word πάντας (Matt. 8.16) can be understood. The purpose of it is less to enlarge the number of miracles[2] than to make a general and doctrinal statement to open up the way for the quotation from the Old Testament. If Jesus heals all who are brought to him, that corresponds to the actual fact in the Synoptic healing stories that everyone who turns to Jesus for healing receives it. Quite clearly—and this would best correspond with the planned layout

[1] If Mark 1.33 is an insertion by the evangelist that shows all the more clearly that the summary is not systematically conceived but biographically.

[2] The emphasis on the little word 'all' obviously belongs to the way in which Matthew reports summaries of events, cf. 4.23; 9.35; 10.1.

of Matt. 8.2–17—the summary report speaks less about individual deeds of Jesus at a particular place and time than about his healing activity generally, and the quotation from Isa. 53.4 in Matt. 8.17 is intended to interpret all his works of healing.

Matt. 8.28–34

The expulsion of the demons of Gadara is an illuminating example of the way in which the evangelist Matthew puts a brief report in the place of the richly expanded description of Mark. This is a place at which it should be particularly plain whether the incisive abbreviations serve the ends of interpretation.

The most striking thing is the complete absence of the concluding section of Mark 5.18–20 in which the person healed asks if he may remain with him. And further: there is not a word about the healing itself in Matthew.[1] Mark relates that the people of the city come to Jesus and see the healed man and in this way the miracle wrought on the man concerned is established (Mark 5.15 . . . καὶ θεωροῦσιν τὸν δαιμονιζόμενον καθήμενον ἱματισμένον καὶ σωφρονοῦντα, τὸν ἐσχηκότα τὸν λεγιῶνα . . .).

The report in Matthew, on the other hand, reads (8.34): καὶ ἰδοὺ πᾶσα ἡ πόλις ἐξῆλθεν εἰς ὑπάντησιν τῷ Ἰησοῦ καὶ ἰδόντες αὐτον . . . , namely Jesus.[2] This can only mean: no interest is attached to the person healed nor to his wish to follow Jesus. In agreement with this the expansive and very detailed description of the terrible nature of this case of possession (Mark 5.3–5), which provides the contrast to the demonstration of the healing of the man possessed,[3] is omitted. At this point Matthew has a brief and peculiar statement the meaning of which is not altogether clear (Matt. 8.28): . . . χαλεποὶ λίαν, ὥστε μὴ ἰσχύειν τινὰ παρελθεῖν διὰ τῆς ὁδοῦ ἐκείνης.

In spite of these considerable abbreviations the basic structure of a miracle story is not damaged. The exposition (Matt. 8.28) makes clear the magnitude and danger of the sickness. Then (in Matt. 8.29–32a) the 'technique' of exorcism is seen and the grotesqueness of the bargaining of the demons with Jesus is retained, although it is abbreviated. The reality of the miraculous deed is shown by the plunging of the herd of swine into the sea (Matt. 8.32b), whereas the

[1] E. Lohmeyer draws attention to this on p. 166.

[2] Since Matthew speaks not of one but of two possessed men, the αὐτόν can only refer to Jesus.

[3] Luke above all heightens this contrast in that he not only mentions that the healed man was properly dressed (Luke 8.35 = Mark 5.15), but expressly states that he was previously naked (Luke 8.27: καὶ χρόνῳ ἱκανῷ οὐκ ἐνεδύσατο ἱμάτιον).

effect of this extraordinary miracle on the people is expressed at the end (Matt. 8.33–34). The impression given on the whole is that Matthew preserves the essential elements of the Markan narrative. What he omits are the descriptive non-essentials. Instead of them he gives something in the nature of an unadorned sketch. In this procedure we recognise once more the interest of the evangelist, to lay the emphasis upon essentials.

The omission of some of the scenes by Matthew itself produces a firmer concentration on the person of Jesus in his account. The Christological interpretation of this pericope by Matthew is seen most clearly in the cry of the two possessed men (Matt. 8.29): ἦλθες ὧδε πρὸ καιροῦ βασανίσαι ἡμᾶς. Behind the corresponding words in Mark's Gospel (Mark 5.7): ὁρκίζω σε τὸν θεόν, μή με βασανίσῃς there obviously lies an oath of protection from Jesus by the demon.[1] Luke regarded this attempt at counter magic as a request of the demon to Jesus (Luke 8.28): δέομαί σου, μή με βασανίσῃς. But neither the interpretation in the sense of a request[2] nor that in the sense of coercion of the spirit does justice to the alteration of the words of the demons by the first evangelist, for they contain no expression of a request. Not until Matt. 8.31–32 is an express request by the demons and an acceding reply by Jesus reported. Previously the first words of the demons τί ἡμῖν καὶ σοί, υἱὲ τοῦ θεοῦ; could best be understood as a defence against a threat, analogous to the adjuring words of the demons in Mark 1.24 and 5.7, which also contain this formula. In this particular case, however, it is quite clear that Matthew is not placing the chief emphasis, at least, on the interpretation in terms of a formula of protection. It is probable that he came to the words of the demons in Matt. 8.29 by combining the words of the demons in Mark 1.24 and 5.7, for the sentence about his coming refers to the first passage and the word βασανίζειν derives from the second. It is noteworthy, however, that in both cases the evangelist passes by the actual words of adjuration, in Mark 1.24 οἶδά σε τίς εἶ and in Mark 5.7 ὁρκίζω σε τὸν θεόν. The parallels in the papyri dealing with magic are most convincing precisely for these expressions.[3] When Matthew passes them entirely by and only uses

---

[1] Cf. O. Bauernfeind, *Die Worte der Dämonen im Markusevangelium*, Stuttgart, 1927, p. 28.

[2] Thus O. Bauernfeind, *op. cit.*, p. 100.

[3] The formula οἶδά σε τίς εἶ has many similarly sounding parallels in magical sayings, as O. Bauernfeind, *op. cit.*, pp. 14 ff., establishes with examples. Further ὁρκίζειν is used in the sense of taking an oath, cf. the magical formula used for the

the statement about the 'coming', i.e. the mission of Jesus, it is clear that he does not wish to depict the demons as trying to exercise counter-magic, but he is putting a Christological statement into their mouths.[1] Jesus has come to deliver the demons to the judgment of torment before the 'time', before the final irruption of the rule of God.

The whole of the remainder of this retelling of the exorcism of the demons plainly serves the purpose of illustrating the truth of this Christological statement. Whether the words of the demons are understood as a question or a statement is quite unimportant in this connexion. In the one case the narrative that follows provides the affirmative answer, in the other it serves as a confirmation. Hence the fact of the exorcism of the demons alone is reported and the reality of it brought to view. It is understandable that no interest is taken in the healing or in the people healed. The theme is the destruction of the demons, and Matthew expressly confirms that they died in the waters.[2]

Thus the wording of this pericope in Matthew's Gospel shows quite clearly that the marked abbreviations are means of interpretation and they direct attention to the Christological statement. A Christological interest certainly underlies the Markan narrative, too. Jesus is the subduer of demons whom none could master (Mark 5.4); indeed the demon submits at the sight of Jesus at a distance (Mark 5.6). 'The power of Jesus is recognised as a matter of course.'[3] Matthew thus finds the principle of his interpretation in Mark

---

awakening of a corpse, which P. Fiebig (*Antike Wundergeschichten zum Studium der Wunder des NT*, Bonn, 1921, p. 27) prints, and the magical saying which O. Bauernfeind (*op. cit.*, pp. 24 f.) quotes. The passage quoted in support of the 'coming' and for βασανίζειν in the sense of 'exercising heightened coercion of the spirit' (O. Bauernfeind, pp. 18 and 25) does not require a magical interpretation of the corresponding expressions in Mark 1.24; 5.7; Matt. 8.29.

[1] R. H. Lightfoot, *The Gospel Message of St Mark*, Oxford, 1950, p. 21, contends emphatically for the understanding of Mark 1.24 in the sense of a programmatic Christological statement: Thou hast come to destroy us! Cf. also W. Wrede, *Das Messiasgeheimnis*, p. 128: 'Every confession of this kind (of the Messiahship of Jesus by demons) is a *witness* for Jesus; in the eyes of the narrator as of the reader he receives attestation thereby' and M. Dibelius, *Formgesch.*, p. 52 [ET², p. 55]: Mark 1.23 ff. is in the mind of the old narrator a 'confirmation of Messiahship'.

[2] K. Bornhäuser (*Das Wirken des Christus durch Taten und Worte*, Gutersloh, 1921, p. 81: it is not the pigs that die but the demons) and E. Lohmeyer (p. 166: the death of the demons sounds more solemn than in Mark) draw attention to this particular trait of Matthew.

[3] E. Lohmeyer, p. 95.

already; in his case alone, however, there is to be seen an almost exclusive concentration on the Christological element.

With regard to the range and detail of the story Luke agrees essentially with Mark (Luke 8.26–39). At different points, however, he elucidates the account of the occurrence, sometimes with a devotional turn.[1] Yet no deliberate shaping of the tradition can be recognised in his work.

Matt. 9.2–8

The most striking peculiarity of Matthew in the healing of the paralytic is to be found in the omission from his account of the exhibition of faith shown by those who carried the sick man (Mark 2.3 and 4, and Luke 5.18 and 19). This supremely pictorial scene provides the best possible basis for the clause which Matthew also contains: καὶ ἰδὼν ὁ Ἰησοῦς τὴν πίστιν αὐτῶν . . . (Mark 2.5; Matt. 9.2; Luke 5.20). And thus—in the words of J. Weiss—it belongs 'to the greatest riddles of Gospel criticism how Matthew could deny himself the use of these living details'.[2] When A. Schlatter precisely in this passage finds confirmation of his view that Mark elucidates Matthew as the oldest evangelist[3] this is at first very illuminating. When one seeks, however, to explain the whole Markan pericope as a new relating of the Matthaean version this thesis becomes less probable. This applies particularly to the conclusion of the story. Matthew writes (Matt. 9.8): . . . καὶ ἐδόξασαν τὸν θεὸν τὸν δόντα ἐξουσίαν τοιαύτην τοῖς ἀνθρώποις. What convincing ground can be established for the view that Mark has rejected this sentence which expressly refers to what in his version, too, is the overriding major question concerning authority to forgive sins, and that instead of this proffers a conclusion expressing amazement which has no clear connexion with this theme and which in principle would suit any miracle story: . . . ὥστε . . . δοξάζειν τὸν θεὸν λέγοντας ὅτι οὕτως οὐδέποτε εἴδαμεν (Mark 2.12)? Besides, it is not comprehensible why Mark should have broken up the well-fashioned narrative

[1] The following may be regarded as instances of his elucidations: Luke 8.26 ἥτις ἐστὶν ἀντιπέρα τῆς Γαλιλαίας; 8.27 ἀνήρ τις ἐκ τῆς πόλεως . . . καὶ χρόνῳ ἱκανῷ οὐκ ἐνεδύσατο ἱμάτιον; 8.29 ἠλαύνετο ἀπὸ τοῦ δαιμονίου εἰς τὰς ἐρήμους; 8.37 φόβῳ μεγάλῳ συνείχοντο. A devotional note echoes in the expressions Luke 8.31 εἰς τὴν ἄβυσσον ἀπελθεῖν; 8.35 . . . παρὰ τοὺς πόδας τοῦ Ἰησοῦ (c.f. Luke 10.39) and 8.36 ἐσώθη.

[2] Das älteste Evangelium, Göttingen, 1903, p. 156.

[3] A. Schlatter, Matthäus, p. 297, on Matt. 9.2: 'The brevity of this account, which points to some kind of event which manifested the faith of the bearers, demanded an explanation, and this is not lacking in Mark.'

of Matthew. This argument is based upon observations which concern the form of the pericope in both evangelists.

From the point of view of form-criticism Mark 2.1–12 contains a double structure. It contains a healing miracle with traits of style appropriate to it (Mark 2.3–5a, 11–12) and embedded within it a controversial discourse of Jesus with the scribes about authority to forgive sins (Mark 2.5b–10). In its present form in Mark the story combines two themes which are both fully brought out. On the one hand the controversial question is decided in favour of Jesus through his mighty deed. On the other, however, the miracle is reported in considerable detail: how the path to the giver of help is made (Mark 2.3 and 4), how the latter carries out the expected miracle (Mark 2.5a, 11) and how the healing occurs and the on-lookers praise God (Mark 2.12).

In the Matthaean narrative the element of the miracle story recedes markedly into the background. It is 'written around a clear and dominating centre-piece, the saying about the sin-forgiving power of the Son of man'.[1] That this is what Matthew is concerned about is shown by the conclusion of his story (Matt. 9.8) in which the catch-word ἐξουσία is taken up again from Matt. 9.6. In this way, however, the conclusion of the miracle story, which in Mark shows no kind of connexion with the central piece,[2] namely the controversial discourse, is subordinated to the theme of this very centre piece and made subservient to it. Thus the glorifying of God no longer refers so much to the miracle itself as to the power of Jesus to which it witnesses, namely to forgive sins. In this context it is understandable that the eyewitnessing of the multitude (Mark 2.12 ἔμπροσθεν πάντων and εἴδαμεν) which is strongly accentuated in Mark is only mentioned incidentally by using the word ἰδόντες (Matt. 9.8) in Matthew.

At the beginning of the pericope the well-known abbreviation occurs. In the light of the wording of the conclusion, which resumes the theme of authority to forgive sins, this is seen to be entirely appreciable. The omission of those living details (Mark 2.3 and 4) makes the opening verse (Matt. 9.2) an introduction in the strict sense, not, of course, to a miracle story as in Mark, but to the controversial discourse of 9.3–6. As·the conclusion resumes the major

---

[1] E. Lohmeyer, p. 169.

[2] This fact must be understood as a confirmation of the form-critical analysis of the pericope's double nature; cf. R. Bultmann, *SynT*, p. 14; E. Lohmeyer, *Markus*, pp. 50 ff., and V. Taylor, *The Gospel according to St Mark*, London, 1953, p. 192.

theme of this controversial discourse once more, the introduction already prepares the way for it (Matt. 9.2 θάρσει, τέχνον, ἀφίενταί σου αἱ ἁμαρτίαι). In this way, however, the new relating of the healing of the paralytic by Matthew is seen to be a well-thought-out construction on the basis of the saying of Jesus about his authority to forgive sins.[1] The elements of the miracle narrative are either deleted or made ancillary to this saying. At the same time the controversial discourse has subjugated those parts of the pericope which originally portrayed a miracle story on the usual lines.

The arrangement of the three controversial discourses in Matt. 9.2–17 shows that Matthew very carefully associates the controversial questions with their typical advocates. The protest of the scribes comes about as a result of a theological consideration (Matt. 9.3); the objection of the Pharisees is directed against the conduct of Jesus (Matt. 9.11), and the fact that the disciples of Jesus do not fast brings the disciples of John into the arena. In this way we are provided with the answers of Jesus to those groups of the people who are closest to him.[2] From this angle it is obvious that Matt. 9.2–8 is not so much concerned with the miracle itself as with the controversial question about the forgiveness of sins with which it deals.

In this way the text, form and arrangement of this story of healing in Matthew make it clear that the abbreviations fit in with the interpretation of the story from the point of view of the saying about the forgiveness of sins. As this also stands in the centre in Mark and is confirmed by the miracle, the judgment holds concerning Matthew's compilation that he introduces nothing new. He develops most clearly what has already been established as the major theme, and in the process revises the miracle story in the light of it.

Luke, on the other hand, narrates essentially in the same way as Mark (Luke 5.17–26). Admittedly his peculiarities are clearly seen in the emphasis he gives to the miracle story. Thus right at the beginning as a kind of heading he places the sentence (Luke 5.17): καὶ δύναμις κυρίου ἦν εἰς τὸ ἰᾶσθαι αὐτόν. He brings out the suddenness of the healing by the word παραχρῆμα (Luke 5.25), which belongs as much to the subject of Hellenistic miracle healings as the concept παράδοξον (Luke 5.26).[3] The reaction of the on-lookers to the

---

[1] Cf. the analysis of the form by E. Lohmeyer, pp. 167 f.
[2] Cf. A. Schlatter, *Matthäus*, p. 297.
[3] Cf. O. Weinreich, *Antike Heilungswunder*, Giessen, 1909, pp. 197–9. The abruptness with which the miracle follows is not emphasised at all in Matthew (9.7) and is hardly noticeable in Mark, as the word εὐθύς (Mark 2.12) is so frequently used

miracle is brought out particularly strongly (Luke 5.26): καὶ ἔκστασις ἔλαβεν ἅπαντας, καὶ ἐδόξασαν τὸν θεόν, καὶ ἐπλήσθησαν φόβου λέγοντες ὅτι εἴδομεν παράδοξα σήμερον.

The new relating of the story by Luke is informative in still another respect. Right at the beginning the Pharisees and teachers of the law are introduced (Luke 5.17) so that the transition from the miracle story to the controversial discourse does not find the hearer quite so unprepared as in Mark 2.5–6 and does not face him with such a sudden change of person. This indicates the pains taken to pass on the originally non-unitary pericope as something quite new, pains which are also visible in Matthew, though he subordinates the one theme to the other. Luke, on the other hand, places both as of equal standing alongside each other, as the beginning of his pericope shows (Luke 5.17). In the light of this observation, too, it is improbable that Mark should have expanded the account of Matthew or destroyed its austere form.

2. The theme of faith

The intention of making statements about faith determines the abbreviations of Matthew in two miracle stories. Significantly they are placed alongside each other in Matt. 9.18–31. The second of these pericopes, the healing of the blind men in Matt. 9.27–31, which is peculiar to Matthew, will be investigated along with that of the healing of the blind men of Jericho in Matt. 20.29–34 at the beginning of the next chapter.[1] It is sufficient here to draw attention to the fact that Matthew not only retells the story of the healing of blind Bartimaeus from Mark 10.46–52 in 20.29–34 but that he presents it yet again in an entirely new form in Matt. 9.27–31 as he develops the theme of the faith which receives the miracle (Matt. 9.28–30).

Matt. 9.18–26

In a similar way to the narration of the exorcism of the demons of Gadara (Matt. 8.28–34) the evangelist Matthew has again sharply abbreviated in this story. One has the impression still more than in the other instance that he has only retained the naked skeleton of what Mark (Mark 5.21–43) reports.

This applies above all to the healing of the woman with the haemor-

---

in the second Gospel that it appears to bear the smoother meaning 'afterwards'. It is Luke who, by using the word παραχρῆμα first rightly brings home the miracle's sudden occurrence.

[1] Cf. below, pp. 219 ff.

rhage (Matt. 9.20–22).[1] The detailed description of the seriousness of her sickness (Mark 5.25–26) is compressed into the parsimonious expression: καὶ ἰδοὺ γυνὴ αἱμορροοῦσα δώδεκα ἔτη (Matt. 9.20) and the extremely vivid scene of Mark 5.29–33 in which the woman healed seeks to conceal herself in the crowd but cannot conceal herself from Jesus is omitted altogether. The crowd, an important requisite of the narrative in Mark, is omitted, although the formulation in Matt. 9.20 . . . προσελθοῦσα ὄπισθεν ἥψατο τοῦ κρασπέδου τοῦ ἱματίου αὐτοῦ silently presupposes it as part of the setting. According to Matthew's account the occurrence takes place purely between Jesus and the woman alone. Even the disciples, who according to Matt. 9.19 accompany Jesus on the way and in the narrative of Mark 5.31 ask a question, have completely disappeared from the picture. We have before us only the meeting of a sick person with Jesus, without being given any intimation regarding place, or time or the closer circumstances. Obviously they are inessential for the real point of the story. What Matthew is concerned about, however, is made clear by the saying about saving faith (Matt. 9.22). At the same time it contains the theme of Matthew's retelling of the story, for of the details of Mark's presentation of the story only the behaviour of the woman towards Jesus remains, what she did and what she thought (Matt. 9. 20b and 21)—the things by which her faith becomes known. Of Jesus himself there is solely reported what attitude he adopts towards the faith of the woman. He replies to it by delivering her by his word and deed (Matt. 9.22). In this way the healing of the woman with the haemorrhage is made by Matthew entirely ancillary to the saying of Jesus which this story contains: ἡ πίστις σου σέσωκέν σε. (Matt. 9.22.) The abbreviations are again here seen to be means of interpretation in that every detail which does not strictly belong to the theme is omitted. The intention of Matthew's retelling of the story is not really to narrate but to give instruction about the matter indicated by the saying of Jesus.

The story of the raising of the daughter of Jairus is likewise markedly abbreviated. Thus there are lacking in Matthew such typical motives of a miracle story as 'heightening by drawing attention to the magnitude of the task', the 'magical word' (Mark 5.41) and the demonstration of the reality of the restoration (Mark 5.43b).[2] In this way it can be seen how little in this case the evangelist

[1] Cf. below, pp. 215 ff.
[2] Cf. R. Bultmann, SynT, p. 214.

is concerned about a careful reproduction of the narrative of the miracle. What he is concerned about is made clear by the only real alteration which he makes in comparison with Mark (Matt. 9.18):
. . . ἰδοὺ ἄρχων εἷς προσελθὼν προσεκύνει αὐτῷ λέγων ὅτι ἡ θυγάτηρ μου ἄρτι ἐτελεύτησεν. ἀλλὰ ἐλθὼν ἐπίθες τὴν χεῖρά σου ἐπ' αὐτὴν καὶ ζήσεται. Here the word ἐτελεύτησεν is 'not only a simple contraction, but a heightening of the narrative, not of the miracle itself . . ., but of the faith of the ἄρχων, who at the same time begs for the restoration of life'.[1] We are thus shown not a faith which is harassed and in need of consolation (as in Mark 5.36) but one which even in the face of death itself holds firmly and confidently to Jesus. Again everything takes place between the believer and Jesus. Neither the disciples nor the crowd nor even the parents of the child play any part in the story that follows. It sounds exactly like a fulfilment and confirmation of the faith expressed by the imploring father at the beginning. The few details which Matthew provides in his presentation serve more or less to prove how Jesus fulfils the request of faith: he comes, touches the dead child, and she stands up alive again (cf. Matt. 9.18 with Matt. 9.23–25). Thus in this instance, too, we see not really a miracle story but a teaching narrative about faith.

This situation is confirmed by the arrangement. Matthew has placed the double story of 9.18–26 alongside the healing of the two blind men, in which the question about faith occurs in the middle (Matt. 9.27–31). In this context our only concern is with the healing formula of Jesus by which he carries out the healing of the blind men (Matt. 9.29): κατὰ τὴν πίστιν ὑμῶν γενηθήτω ὑμῖν. This statement of Jesus describes exactly the content of both miracle stories told in Matt. 9.18–26. Both people, the ἄρχων and the woman with the haemorrhage, are rewarded according to their faith. Thus it is seen not only that all three miracle stories are closely bound together with regard to content but also that the stories of the woman with the haemorrhage and of the restoration to life must, in fact, be understood as examples to illustrate genuine miracle-faith.

A glance at Luke (Luke 8.40–56) provides the usual picture. He tells the story essentially in the same way as Mark, but again adds new details. Thus he knows that the daughter was an only child (8.42); he mentions the name of a disciple (8.45) and fashions the

---

[1] E. Klostermann, pp. 82 f. Cf. B. W. Bacon, *Matthew*, p. 193: 'Jairus evinces from the outset an incredible degree of faith by coming to ask from Jesus an unheard-of miracle.'

scene between Jesus and the healed woman more clearly (8.47). He introduces elucidations into the story to clarify statements, as, for example, in 8.50 . . . καὶ σωθήσεται, 8.53 εἰδότες ὅτι ἀπέθανεν and 8.55 καὶ ἐπέστρεψεν τὸ πνεῦμα αὐτῆς to bring out the miracle of the restoration of life. Finally, there again occur traits which bring the narrative close to Hellenistic miracle stories. To the typical trait of the suddenness of the occurrence of the miracle (παραχρῆμα 8.44, 47, 55) and the reference to the incurability of the sickness for human physicians (8.43; cf. Mark 5.26) there comes the similarly characteristic report that the person healed comes and tells of the miracle to all the people (Luke 8.47b).[1] The third evangelist thus here, too, brings the miraculous character of the occurrence into prominence.

3. The theme of discipleship

Only in a very few of the miracle stories in the Synoptic tradition do the disciples play any part. They are found above all in the stories of the feedings and in the Lake stories (Mark 6.35 ff. and par.; Mark 4.35 ff. and par.; 6.45 ff. and par.). Since both Lake stories, however, are instances of expansions, the reports of the miraculous feeding alone call for consideration here where we are dealing with abbreviations.

In most of the healing stories the disciples do not appear at all. In the double story of the woman with the haemorrhage and the raising of Jairus's daughter they are actually mentioned, but they have no essential significance. Only in the healing of the epileptic boy (Mark 9.14 ff. and par.) do they form an indispensable part of the narrative.

Matt. 14.15–21

The abbreviations of this first story of feeding in the first Gospel are not so striking in comparison with Mark as the miracle narratives already discussed. Yet they give to Matthew's account a greater compactness and 'solemnity' in comparison with the original and colourful version of the second evangelist.[2]

---

[1] Cf. O. Weinreich, Antike Heilungswunder, pp. 195 f., on the futility of the physician's art, pp. 197 f., for the suddenness of the miracle's occurrence, and pp. 108 f., 116 for the proclamation of the miracle to the people. The public announcement of the miracle of healing is also seen, for example, in the many inscriptions from Epidaurus (cf. R. Herzog, Die Wunderheilungen von Epidauros, Leipzig, 1931) and in thankofferings to the miraculous healing god, as instanced, for example, by O. Weinreich (op. cit., pp. 4 ff.): the speeches of Aelius Aristides, the epigram of the rhetorician Aeschines and the play Asclepius by Aristarchus.

[2] Cf. J. Schniewind and E. Lohmeyer, ad loc.

The first thing that calls for notice is the way in which the conversation of Jesus with his disciples which comprises the first part of the pericope, is formed (Mark 6.35–38; Matt. 14.15–18). Here it should be observed that the disciples not only appear as partners with Jesus in the discussion but that Jesus gives them a considerable share in the miraculous feeding. The command of Jesus δότε αὐτοῖς ὑμεῖς φαγεῖν (Mark 6.37; Matt. 14.16) with its emphatic 'ye' is surprising for the very reason that 'one would rather have expected an ἐγὼ δώσω'.[1] When it is borne in mind that in the further course of the narrative the disciples are also portrayed, not as partakers of the meal but as distributors of it to the multitude, it is beyond all doubt that they figure prominently in the whole action.[2] The Gospel of Luke also shows that this matter firmly belongs to the story of the feeding (cf. Luke 9.13, 16, etc.). Of course this cannot lead to any illusion that it is not Jesus who is the real actor in the occurrence. He shows himself to be the host not only by giving the command to make the multitude sit down in groups, but above all it is he also who first gives the bread to the disciples to distribute (Mark 6.41 and par.). Quite obviously the miracle takes place not through the disciples but through Jesus.[3] Thus it is without doubt a matter of an epiphany of Jesus before his disciples—that it takes place before the multitude is nowhere so much as hinted[4]—but it takes place through an act in which the disciples share.

But we must now return to the introductory conversation between Jesus and his disciples! Precisely here in comparison with Mark, Matthew shows not only abbreviations but also alterations. In the first place the 'bold counter-question' (E. Klostermann) with which the disciples meet the commission of Jesus to them to give to the multitude to eat is omitted: ἀπελθόντες ἀγοράσωμεν δηναρίων διακοσίων ἄρτους, καὶ δώσομεν αὐτοῖς φαγεῖν; (Mark 6.37). It is very possible that Matthew (as indeed Luke also) felt that such an answer by a disciple to his master was not becoming. But the actual reason for this

[1] T. Zahn, *Matthäus*, p. 512.

[2] This applies 'from the first instigation which they give to the gathering up of the fragments left after the meal' (T. Zahn, *ad loc.*). Cf. also E. Lohmeyer, *Markus*, pp. 126 f.

[3] The role of the disciples may thus not be interpreted on the lines suggested by R. Gutzwiller (*Jesus der Messias*, p. 200): 'Under their hands the miracle of the increase of the bread takes place.'

[4] Because the story is reported as an epiphany before the disciples the stylistic amazement of the multitude about the miracle is omitted at the end of the narrative.

abbreviation is not contained in that explanation. The counter-question of the disciples in Mark 6.37 takes up again the words of Jesus by the catchwords καὶ δώσομεν αὐτοῖς φαγεῖν. If it is true that what at first sight seems a meaningless and impossible command of Jesus to the disciples is nevertheless meaningful, in the sense that in the mind of the narrator it points the way to the event that is to follow in which the disciples actually do give to the multitude to eat,[1] then the answer of the disciples is given its actual importance. It shows the complete lack of understanding by the disciples not only of the person and mission of their master but also of the commission given to them by him. As Mark expressly states in other places (Mark 6.52; 8.17 ff.) they remain outside the reach of the event of revelation. What is there said as a reference back with regard to the stories of the feedings is found as a peculiarity of Mark in his account of the feeding of the five thousand itself.

If Matthew does not mention that bold counter-question the reason for this lies in the fact that he interprets the role of the disciples differently. There is no trace of a lack of understanding of the commission of Jesus (Matt. 14.16 δότε αὐτοῖς ὑμεῖς φαγεῖν) in the reply of the disciples. Such a misunderstanding as that in Mark is excluded by the fact that Matthew precedes it with the small sentence οὐ χρείαν ἔχουσιν ἀπελθεῖν. This at once makes clear that Jesus is not thinking of the food which one has to buy in the townships. It is obvious that he means nourishment which the disciples have with them. Hence they immediately announce the amount of food which is available (Matt. 14.17: ὧδε). Thus the disciples understand what Jesus means, though they do not obediently carry out his commission but point out—obviously as an expression of their limited faith[2]—how meagre are their provisions: 'We have here but five loaves and two fishes.'

Thus whereas Mark portrays the disciples as lacking in understanding, in the dialogue according to Matthew they understand but are defective in the matter of faith. It is in the wake of this interpretation that the unbecoming counter-question of the disciples falls.

In the account of the miraculous feeding itself (Mark 6.39–41;

[1] Thus E. Lohmeyer, p. 126.
[2] J. Schniewind, *Markus*, p. 98, discusses the possibility of this interpretation in commenting on Mark 6.35 ff. It is suggested not only by the formulation in Matt. 14.17 but also in Matt. 16.8 ff. It corresponds besides with the new interpretation by Matthew of the role of the disciples, who are presented by Mark as not understanding; cf. below, pp. 291 ff.

Matt. 14.19) also the role of the disciples is accentuated. They assist by giving the food of the meal to the people and thus carry out the orders given them by Jesus. At the same time the theme of the narrative touched on in the words δότε αὐτοῖς ὑμεῖς φαγεῖν is now put into execution. That holds for all three Synoptics in the same way, except that Matthew has brought out the theme more clearly and more exclusively than the other two. According to the presentation in Mark (6.39–40)and Luke (9.14–15) the disciples receive the commission to arrange the multitude in groups and to make them sit down. Further the carrying out of this commission is expressly observed. It is true that Matthew also reports a 'command' (Matt. 14.19 κελεύσας) that the multitude should sit down on the grass, but neither is the carrying out of the command reported nor is it directed to the disciples. Obviously Matthew's wish is only to present the disciples in their mediating role in connexion with the meal. They receive the commission to bring the food (Matt. 14.18 φέρετέ μοι ὧδε αὐτούς). As these words occur only in the first Gospel it is not impossible that by them the evangelist also wishes to present the disciples in bringing the food as only concerned with the feeding itself. What happens to the crowd thus slips still more into the background.

Finally it is striking that in his portrayal of the miraculous feeding itself Matthew chooses a formulation of his own for the activity of the disciples. Mark writes (Mark 6.41): Jesus ἐδίδου τοῖς μαθηταῖς ἵνα παρατιθῶσιν αὐτοῖς, namely the multitude. Luke's description is similar (Luke 9.16): . . . καὶ ἐδίδου τοῖς μαθηταῖς παραθεῖναι τῷ ὄχλῳ. Matthew on the other hand reads (Matt. 14.19): . . . ἔδωκεν τοῖς μαθηταῖς τοὺς ἄρτους, οἱ δὲ μαθηταὶ τοῖς ὄχλοις. The difference is not great, but it is significant. Whereas the other two evangelists speak only of a giving by Jesus, though the disciples 'distribute' (παρατιθέναι), in Matthew the giving, from ἔδωκεν on, applies to the activity of the disciples as well. There thus arises, however, a clear allusion to the command of Jesus to his disciples about giving (δότε αὐτοῖς ὑμεῖς φαγεῖν). To express the matter differently: Matthew brings to expression in linguistic form, too, the theme of the role of the disciples in his portrayal of the miraculous feeding.

The new relating of this story of the feeding by Matthew is thus seen to be a carefully executed piece of work. The abbreviations and alterations concern the role of the disciples, who at the commission of Jesus feed the multitude.

Matt. 15.32–38

The second story of feeding in Matthew's Gospel discloses similar differences from Mark's account (8.1–9), as are seen with regard to the feeding of the five thousand. In the first place here again it is the role of the disciples which is involved.

When Jesus (Mark 8.1–3; Matt. 15.32) calls the disciples to him, lays before them the needy situation of the multitude and explains that he does not want to send them away hungry his words contain an indirect summons to them to provide the multitude with food. The reply of the disciples understands the words of Jesus in this sense. By a small idiosyncrasy Matthew also shows that the disciples regard the feeding as impossible, but nevertheless in principle as their task (Matt. 15.33: πόθεν ἡμῖν ἐν ἐρημίᾳ ἄρτοι τοσοῦτοι ὥστε χορτάσαι ὄχλον τοσοῦτον;). In Mark on the other hand the disciples do not refer to themselves in their counter-question but say quite generally: πόθεν τούτους δυνήσεταί τις ὧδε χορτάσαι ἄρτων ἐπ' ἐρημίας; (Mark 8.4). In his portrayal of the feeding itself the first evangelist uses the same formula for the role of the disciples as in his report of the first feeding: . . . καὶ ἐδίδου τοῖς μαθηταῖς, οἱ δὲ μαθηταὶ τοῖς ὄχλοις (Matt. 15.36; cf. Matt. 14.19).[1] Thus in this feeding of the four thousand also Matthew has developed more clearly the thought of Matt. 14.16 δότε αὐτοῖς ὑμεῖς φαγεῖν.

It is noticeable besides that the two stories of the feedings are also accommodated to each other in Matthew's Gospel in another respect. Thus their conclusion is told in almost the same words, except for the giving of the numbers and the designation of the baskets.[2] The announcement of the provisions by the disciples in the second story of the feeding contains not only the number of loaves as in Mark (8.5), but also the number of the fishes (Matt. 15.34; cf. Mark 6.38; Matt. 14.17) as in the first. Finally the distribution of the fishes to the multitude, which is portrayed in Mark in a special scene, is omitted by Matthew (likewise, moreover, by Luke, 9.12–17). Granted the fishes are still mentioned at the feeding itself, but only in a preliminary way; they are then entirely forgotten. Thus according to Matt. 14.19 Jesus takes both the loaves and the fishes and gives thanks over them, but he only breaks the loaves in order to pass them to the disciples for

[1] In Mark 8.6 the formulation is similar to that in Mark 6.41.

[2] Matt. 14.20; 15.37: καὶ ἔφαγον πάντες καὶ ἐχορτάσθησαν and (in 15.37 only with a different word order) καὶ ἦραν τὸ περισσεῦον τῶν κλασμάτων and also the little word πλήρεις. In Matt. 14.21; 15.38 the same contents occur in the following expressions: οἱ δὲ ἐσθίοντες ἦσαν . . . and χωρὶς γυναικῶν καὶ παιδίων.

them to hand them on (. . . κλάσας ἔδωκεν τοῖς μαθηταῖς τοὺς ἄρτους
. . .). The express wording that Jesus only breaks the loaves and
gives them to the disciples Matthew has in common with Mark
(Mark 6.41 . . . κατέκλασεν τοὺς ἄρτους καὶ ἐδίδου τοῖς μαθηταῖς . . .).
Mark, however, goes on to report the distribution of the fishes
(6.41b). The result of this omission by Matthew is that he only deals
unmistakably with a feeding upon the loaves. There is not even a
hint of a reference to a distribution of the fishes.[1]

In this connexion a comparison of the feeding of the four thousand
in the two evangelists is quite revealing. In Mark a scene which refers
only to a meal of bread (Mark 8.6) is followed by a quite new meal
scene with fishes only, with its own introduction (Mark 8.7 καὶ εἶχον
ἰχθύδια ὀλίγα) and in which the prayer of thanks is repeated (Mark
8.7 καὶ εὐλογήσας αὐτά . . .). However this remarkable fact in Mark
is to be interpreted Matthew betrays that it already occurred in the
text before him. Jesus asks the disciples only about the loaves as in
Mark, but is immediately also given information about the fishes
(Matt. 15.34): καὶ ὀλίγα ἰχθύδια. Precisely these three words in
Matthew give the impression of an insertion and point back to the
ἰχθύδια ὀλίγα of Mark 8.7. Matthew has indeed omitted the fish meal
but wanted nevertheless to refer to it. Accordingly the fish are taken
over into the account of the meal of loaves. That the mention of them
is not original can be seen from the fact that in the present context of
Matt. 15.36 obviously the fish are broken, too, which sounds quite
peculiar. One can only explain this by assuming that the fishes have
been introduced into the text of the meal of the loaves only, found in
Mark 8.6. The question why Matthew mentions the fishes at all,
although he says nothing about the distribution of them, may be
answered by saying that he does it in faithfulness to the tradition he
received.

The alteration, or rather, abbreviation of this pericope has
produced three results: in the first place the second feeding is made
more closely parallel to the first; secondly the two feeding scenes
which stand quite unconnected alongside each other are formed into
a compact story in which there is no longer any reference to two
meals, but only the one; and finally, the meal of the loaves is placed
right in the centre and has attracted to itself the feeding with the
fishes. The meaning of this alteration is unmistakable: the miraculous

---

[1] In Luke (9.16b) τοὺς ἄρτους is omitted so that his account *can* be understood
of the distribution of loaves and fishes.

feeding is now more exclusively reported in words which give it a clear accord with the celebration of the Lord's Supper. That Matthew understood the two feedings in this way is self-evident, not only from the fact that every Christian would inevitably understand the picture given in Mark 6.41 and 8.6 in the light of the words at the Last Supper, even if they were originally meant to do no more than describe the Jewish custom at meals; and yet further, in his new relating of the first of these passages he shows by using κλάσας instead of κατέκλασεν that the account of the Last Supper was in his mind.[1]

If the two instances of the feedings in Matthew's Gospel are taken together, as indeed they are assimilated to each other by the evangelist himself, two things can be perceived in the retelling of them. The omission of the scene with the fishes gives the miraculous occurrence more clearly the marks of the Lord's Supper, though it must be granted that Matthew is not alone in this, as the Lukan account of the feeding of the five thousand shows. The other thought, however, that the disciples exercise a mediating role is markedly developed only by the first evangelist.

Matt. 17.14–20

The story of the healing of the epileptic boy in Mark's Gospel (Mark 9.14–29) is remarkable in several respects. In the first place it is a combination of two miracle stories. The first concerns the inability of the disciples to heal the sick boy and contains the lament of Jesus about the unbelieving generation. The second no longer speaks of the disciples, but devotes more attention to the person of the father whose exclamation expresses the paradox of unbelieving belief.[2] Thus both accounts contain a saying about faith (Mark 9.19 and 9.23), and it may well be that their fusion should be understood in the light of that and that the new narrative which arose as a result gains its unity through the theme of the power of faith.[3]

In the second place, this is the only Synoptic miracle story to which a conversation containing instruction is attached referring directly to the matter reported, namely the inability of the disciples to heal. It is significant that in this pericope there is no reference to the effect of the miraculous deed of Jesus on those present,[4] especially

---

[1] Cf. E. Lohmeyer, p. 237.
[2] Cf. R. Bultmann, *SynT*, p. 211.
[3] Cf. the expositions of E. Lohmeyer (pp. 184 ff.) and of J. Schniewind (p. 125).
[4] Vincent Taylor points this out, *The Gospel according to St Mark*, p. 401.

in such an extraordinarily difficult case of sickness. Instead of referring to the people present the story ends with the question of the disciples about the reason for their failure. This makes it clear that the miracle is not reported here for its own sake but for the sake of the instruction of the disciples which is attached to it.

Finally the setting of this miraculous healing in the context of the whole Gospel strikes one at first as quite remarkable. One would prefer rather to see it among the earlier collections of miracle stories (Mark 1.21–45 or Mark 4.35–5.43), but not on the way of Jesus and his disciples from Caesarea Philippi to Jerusalem (Mark 8.27–10.52).[1] It is not difficult, however, to recognise why this story is placed in this context. The conversation with the disciples draws from the miracle story instruction for the disciples and thus directs attention to the role of the disciples as workers of miracles. It is this circumstance which doubtless caused Mark or his authorities to place the healing of the epileptic boy in the period of the instruction of the disciples about discipleship and the life of the congregation (Mark 8.27–10.52).[2]

That this miracle story is comprised under the theme of discipleship is shown in three ways: by the content of the narrative itself, by the instructive conversation which is attached to it and by its place in the outline of Mark's Gospel. The sharply abbreviated form of the story in Matthew's Gospel is best understood in the light of the theme of discipleship (Matt. 17.14–20).

The most striking mark of the retelling of the story by the first evangelist lies in the omission by him of the scene with the father (Mark 9.21–24). There is no question that by this abbreviation a thoroughly transparent story, the sole theme of which is the failure of the disciples, has taken the place of Mark's complicated picture. This theme of the disciples' failure is expressed shortly and clearly by the father of the sick boy (Matt 17.16): οὐκ ἠδυνήθησαν αὐτὸν θεραπεῦσαι—this is taken up again by the disciples as a kind of catchword in their question to Jesus (Matt. 17.19): διὰ τί ἡμεῖς οὐκ ἠδυνήθημεν ἐκβαλεῖν αὐτό—and finally it is clarified by Jesus in conclusion (Matt. 17.20): καὶ οὐδὲν ἀδυνατήσει ὑμῖν. This link-up by

[1] This is the opinion of J. Wellhausen, *Das Evangelium Marci*, Berlin, 1903, p. 65: '. . . the two miracles of healing interspersed here provide a formal disturbance', when the section Mark 8.27–10.52 is reviewed. B. W. Bacon also finds Mark 9.14–29 'clearly misplaced' (*Matthew*, p. 238).

[2] Cf. H. Riesenfeld, 'Tradition und Redaktion im Markusevangelium', *NT Studien für R. Bultmann*, Berlin, 1954, p. 163.

the catchword is the work of the evangelist himself (in Matt. 17.16, 20). And further it has not a merely formal meaning in the sense of linking more closely the miracle story and the closing conversation; it indicates the actual theme. This is clear from the passages in Mark's narrative on which Matthew dwells and those in which he abbreviates. Of the three descriptions of the sickness he omits the two most impressive ones (Mark 9.18, 20) and adopts the third only (Mark 9.22a; Matt. 17.15b). On the other hand he preserves the father's statement about the incapacity of the disciples and the lament of Jesus about the unbelieving generation, in their totality (Matt. 17.16–17). The healing of the boy by Jesus is retained briefly, conventionally and formally (Matt. 17.18) in glaring contrast to the vivid description in Mark (Mark 9.25–27). Here no special interest is recognisable; one has rather the impression that the evangelist 'is hurrying with long strides to the final point',[1] so to speak. The goal is the conversation of Jesus with his disciples about this case—not of particularly severe sickness (τοῦτο τὸ γένος Mark 9.29!), but of the disciples' failure. It is this conversation which is fashioned by the evangelist in a special way. The catchwords about faith form a second bridge back into the pericope itself (Matt. 17.20 ὀλιγοπιστία, πίστις and 17.17 ὦ γενεὰ ἄπιστος—alongside the catchword ἀδυνατεῖν or δύνασθαι). The last sentence shows absolutely the aim of the whole narrative (Matt. 17.20): . . . καὶ οὐδὲν ἀδυνατήσει ὑμῖν.[2] It is the instruction how the disciples are to overcome their failure. Thus Matthew's retelling of this healing story has created a unified whole in which the concluding conversation is no longer an appendage but expresses the real goal of the pericope.[3]

As the Lukan reproduction of the story shows (Luke 9.37–43), the scene of the believing-unbelieving father is missing there, too. That is the more remarkable because in all other miracle narratives the third evangelist preserves the longer Markan text over against the Matthaean abbreviations. Hence it has been supposed that Mark has here expanded a shorter text and thus it is he and not Matthew who

---

[1] Thus H. Greeven ('Die Heilung des Gelähmten nach Matthäus', *Wort und Dienst*, 1955, p. 74) on Matt. 17.14–20.

[2] Matt. 17.21, which occurs in many manuscripts, most of all in the Byzantine group of texts, has no claim to originality, as it is missing from the best witnesses (B, ℵ, Θ) and from some Latin (e, ff¹) as well as the oldest Syriac versions (sin., cur.) and is best explained as an addition from the parallel passage in Mark 9.29.

[3] Cf. E. Lohmeyer, p. 271.

has done the altering.[1] But even under these assumptions the evidence given above of a careful shaping of the narrative by the first evangelist remains. Nevertheless the new riddle, why Mark breaks up this clear narrative of instruction on the theme of discipleship, must be solved, especially as he, too, is concerned about the instruction of the disciples (Mark 9.28–29). The alleged addition by Mark of the conversation between the father and Jesus itself introduces a measure of obscurity into the narrative.

To the subject of the impotence of the disciples there is added in Mark's account in the request of the father (Mark 9.22: . . . ἀλλ᾽ εἴ τι δύνῃ, βοήθησον ἡμῖν) the further question whether Jesus is able to heal in this difficult case of sickness. Jesus expressly takes up this question about his power in his answer (Mark 9.23): τὸ εἰ δύνῃ, πάντα δυνατὰ τῷ πιστεύοντι. The meaning of these words, however, is not altogether clear in the present context. Is Jesus here giving direct information about his wonder-working power, about which the father doubted, and does he point to himself as the believer to whom all things are possible?[2] That would be unique in the Gospels! Or does he intend this answer as a summons to the beseeching father to believe so that the healing may take place? This is how according to Mark the father understood the words of Jesus (cf. Mark 9.24). That also agrees with the position in the Synoptics according to which Jesus helps him who believes but his power fails in the presence of unbelief.[3] This interpretation, however, is not satisfactory in view of the wording of the saying, however much it is supported by the evangelist Mark himself. The saying obviously refers to the efficacy of the faith of the miracle-worker.[4] Hence the third explanation of the saying according to which Jesus is here giving instruction to his disciples about the source of miracle-working power is the one originally intended. That would entirely suit the context of the Markan pericope in question, for it is directed towards that kind of instruction (Mark 9.28–29). Certainly this meaning is obscured in

[1] Thus J. Weiss, *Das älteste Evangelium*, pp. 249–50; W. Bussmann, *Synoptische Studien*, I, *Zur Geschichtsquelle*, 1925, pp. 81–83.

[2] Thus J. Schniewind, p. 125; cf. also E. Lohmeyer, pp. 189–91.

[3] Thus A. Schlatter, *Markus*, pp. 170–1. The majority of manuscripts firmly support this interpretation by inserting πιστεῦσαι after εἰ δύνῃ with the resultant meaning: If you could believe! This reading is clearly a correction of the difficult original text, but it agrees entirely with the sense of the evangelist Mark.

[4] Cf. E. Lohmeyer (p. 188) on Mark 9.23: 'This saying has frequently been understood as meaning that faith sets no limits to the divine action; here, however, the reference is to what faith can achieve not what it can allow to happen.'

THE RETELLING OF MIRACLE STORIES 191

the present text because the evangelist understands the saying of Jesus to refer to the faith of the petitioner.[1] There is, of course, something to be said for and against all three interpretations in view of the narrative as we now have it in Mark, and therefore all of them fail to satisfy.

Matthew got rid of this lack of clarity by taking the instruction about the faith which can achieve all things out of the story itself and placing it in the conversation of Jesus with his disciples (Matt. 17.19–20). He shows thereby, on the one hand, a knowledge that the theme of the faith which works miracles belongs to this story. The saying about the faith which removes mountains and above all the concluding sentence which he has added: καὶ οὐδὲν ἀδυνατήσαι ὑμῖν (Matt. 17.20) state exactly the same as the saying that all things are possible to him that believeth (Mark 9.23). On the other hand, however, Matthew has succeeded in showing that there is no longer any question about whether and how Jesus can heal, but whether and how the disciples can. We are here concerned unequivocally with the faith of the wonder-worker, with exclusive reference, of course, to the disciples.

Granted, then, that Matthew is not concerned with the father's doubt about the power of Jesus and thus with the paradox of unbelieving belief, the father is also depicted from the beginning as a believing petitioner (Matt. 17.14b, 15). For this reason it is not really possible to refer the lament of Jesus about the faithless generation to him. The people also can scarcely be in mind, as they play no part in Matthew's picture except in the transitional notice (Matt. 17.14a). Thus the only reference left is to the disciples in spite of the fact that at first sight this looks doubtful.[2] This difficulty is avoided, however, if the words of Jesus are understood solely as an expression of the situation of the Son of God in his activity among men as a whole.[3]

[1] Cf. A. Fridrichsen (Le problème du Miracle, Paris, 1925, p. 54) on Mark 9.23: 'This saying is, in fact, addressed to the disciples. When the father cries: "I believe, Lord; help me in my unbelief!"—we have there without doubt the sigh of a Christian exorcist who feels that he is powerless; this saying, in the mouth of the father, is emptied of meaning through being placed in a setting in which his faith in Jesus is not in question.'

[2] The word γενεά is never used by Mark and Matthew for the disciples, but usually for the (unbelieving) contemporaries of Jesus and then it always has 'a condemnatory overtone' (F. Büchsel, TWNT, I, p. 661). Besides, the designation of the disciples as 'faithless and perverse' contradicts the picture of the disciples in Matthew's Gospel, where the disciples are shown at worst as having little faith.

[3] Thus E. Lohmeyer, Markus, pp. 186 f., and V. Taylor, The Gospel according to St Mark, p. 398.

Yet the question remains open what meaning Matthew attached to them in the framework of his retelling of the healing of the epileptic boy in which he has left them. If we disregard the meagre report about the healing of the sick boy (Matt. 17.18) it is plain to see how this lament of Jesus about the faithless generation is enclosed by the two references to the failure of the disciples (Matt. 17.16 and 19), which is traced back by Jesus to their little faith (Matt. 17.20). There is no other possibility than that Matthew refers these words of Jesus to the disciples, especially as they are uttered immediately after the beseeching father had spoken of their impotence and thereby indirectly of the little faith of the disciples. The saying about the faithless generation must therefore be interpreted in the sense of little faith and be understood as a prior hint at the conversation with the disciples. Only in this way does it make sense in Matthew and fit in with the theme of discipleship which determines the Matthaean account.

In his reproduction of the same case of healing, Luke (Luke 9.37–43) has obviously pursued another thought. It is true that in his case too a compact narrative results from the omission of the scene with the father, but it is presented entirely as a typical miracle story. He also adopts the second description of the sickness from Mark (Mark 9.20; Luke 9.42), so that in the encounter of the demon with his master the whole frightfulness of the sickness—contributing to the enhancing of the miraculous deed which follows—is once more revealed. He enriches the first description of the sickness with new information (Luke 9.39 καὶ μόλις ἀποχωρεῖ ἀπ᾽ αὐτοῦ συντρῖβον αὐτόν) and refers to the sick one as the only son, whom Jesus returns to his father after the cure (Luke 9.38 and 42). The beseeching father does mention the impotence of the disciples, but this theme is not separately pursued. It only serves to show the exceeding greatness of the master in contrast to the impotent disciples.[1] In agreement with this the conversation of Jesus with his disciples is entirely omitted from the conclusion. In place of it there is a stylistic ending of a miracle story (Luke 9.43): ἐξεπλήσσοντο δὲ πάντες ἐπὶ τῇ μεγαλειότητι τοῦ θεοῦ. The third evangelist understands the narrative as a miracle story which—in conjunction with the Transfiguration—sets forth the epiphany of the power of God in Jesus.

---

[1] Perhaps this is a stylistic characteristic; cf. R. Bultmann, *SynT*, p. 221, and M. Dibelius, *Formgesch.*, p. 79 [ET², p. 82].

B. *Expansion as a means of interpretation*

The investigation so far has shown that the abbreviations in the miracle stories in Matthew's Gospel must be understood as the means of a careful interpretation, which is also recognisable at the same time in the wording of the text and in the setting of the narrative concerned in the outline of the whole Gospel. The next task is to show that this conclusion also applies to the expansion of individual miracle stories by Matthew. The leading thoughts of Matthew's retelling of the stories are again the themes of faith and discipleship.

1. *The theme of faith*

The narratives of the centurion of Capernaum (Matt. 8.5–13) and of the Canaanite woman (Matt. 15.21–28) are very similar to each other.[1] In both cases the help of Jesus is given to Gentiles, the healing takes place from a distance and only follows after a somewhat lengthy conversation. Indeed, to be precise, there are no real narratives here, but conversations at the end of which, in each case, the notion of faith is introduced by Matthew (Matt. 8.13 and 15.28). Precisely herein is a clear sign that in both pericopes it is the theme of faith with which he is concerned.

Matt. 8.5–13

As this story is absent from Mark's Gospel the parallels in Luke must be drawn upon for purposes of comparison (Luke 7.1–10).

Whatever may have been the original form of this pericope it is certain, on the basis of the agreement between Matt. 8.8–10 and Luke 7.6b–9, that the conversation between the centurion and Jesus, with the saying about the unique faith of this Gentile man, is the kernel of it. In this way the theme of faith is given to the pericope from the beginning.

The situation in which this conversation occurred is differently depicted by Matthew and Luke. Whether the words of the centurion and Jesus were transmitted from the beginning in the context of a narrative,[2] or whether it was the evangelists who, each in his own way, 'created'[3] the narrative beginning and the narrative conclusion, for what was in the beginning a dialogue without any setting, must remain open. The following observations point to the fact that they, at least in part, helped to determine the framework. The

---

[1] Cf. R. Bultmann, *SynT*, pp. 38 f.
[2] Thus E. Lohmeyer, *Matthäus*, p. 156.
[3] Thus M. Dibelius, *Formgesch.*, p. 245 [ET², p. 244].

concluding verse in Matthew undoubtedly bears Matthaean traits. This is shown by the comparison of Matt. 8.13 with other statements peculiar to the first evangelist (Matt. 9.22b; 9.29; 15.28; 17.18b). Luke, from another source, has given the conversation a detailed and unique introduction (Luke 7.2–6a)[1] which he has skilfully linked with the dialogue[2] by means of the insertion of a sentence (Luke 7.7a). The framework as fashioned by the evangelists indicates how they used and understood the saying about faith in the middle.

At the close of his pericope Matthew again takes up the catchword of faith (Matt. 8.13 ὡς ἐπίστευσας γενηθήτω σοι) .Here Jesus brings the conversation with the centurion to an end in so far as he gives him an answer and concludes the course of the conversation;—in Luke there is no proper conversation at all, since the saying about the faith of the centurion is not directed to the man himself but to those who were accompanying Jesus. Moreover the centurion's request is met in Matthew by the expected help in that Jesus speaks the desired word which heals the sick man (Matt. 8.13). In this way the narrative conclusion of the evangelist depicts the logical expansion of the conversation and is derived, so to speak, from the conversation itself. In other words: the conclusion is fashioned in the light of the theme of faith.

But the same also applies to the introduction which Matthew places before the sayings of the centurion and Jesus. The request itself (Matt. 8.6), which is not actually expressed, though it is mentioned (Matt. 8.5 παρακαλῶν), is an evidence of faith. Above all this is shown by the context into which the saying of the believing centurion is inserted (Matt. 8.8–9). Here the meaning which is to be found in the answer of Jesus to the first words of the centurion is decisive (Matt. 8.7): ἐγὼ ἐλθὼν θεραπεύσω αὐτόν. This sentence can be understood as a promise or as a question. In the context of the whole the better understanding undoubtedly results from regarding it as the astonished or indignant question of Jesus, whether he as a Jew would be expected to enter into a Gentile house and so transgress the precepts of the law which forbids intercourse with Gentiles.[3] Only in this way does the strongly emphasised ἐγώ gain significance, for this would be unnecessary in the promise that Jesus would come

[1] Luke's source can be recognised according to W. Bussmann (Synopt. Studien, II, Zur Redenquelle, 1929, p. 57) by the difference in the words he uses. Q (along with Matthew): παῖς, ἱκανός; Luke's special source: δοῦλος, ἄξιος.

[2] Cf. the combination of the catchwords: (7.4) ἄξιος (7.7) ἠξίωσα.

[3] Cf. T. Zahn, p. 338, and E. Lohmeyer, p. 157.

and heal the servant. The ἐγώ would gain more importance still if in the mind of the evangelist, in the light of Matt. 8.4, it could be understood as the statement of the Christ who is the fulfiller of the law.[1] If in this way the words of Jesus are understood as a rejection of an improper demand the new saying of the centurion which amazed Jesus receives its full meaning. Otherwise the question arises why this extraordinary request which contains such a strong expression of faith was not uttered right at the beginning (T. Zahn). Now, however, the centurion not only seizes the words of Jesus as catchwords (Matt. 8.7 ἐλθών/8.8 εἰσέλθῃς); he assents to the hesitation of Jesus to come into his house and recognises thereby the barrier that separates him from the people of God (Matt. 8.8 οὐκ εἰμὶ ἱκανός . . .). On the other hand, however, his faith finds the way in which Jesus can give him unlimited help (Matt. 8.8 μόνον εἰπὲ λόγῳ). There thus arises here an exact parallel to the Matthaean narrative of the Canaanite woman (Matt. 15.21–28), where Jesus likewise refuses to help a Gentile woman, but is then similarly conquered by her faith. As in her case the faith of the woman is called great by Jesus (Matt. 15.28), so here it is reported that Jesus was amazed at the faith of the centurion (Matt. 8.10). Within the Gospel of Matthew there is thus nothing strange about this interpretation of the conversation between the centurion and Jesus. It rather agrees with the position described in Matt. 15.21–28 concerning the faith of a heathen person. Then, however, it is clear that the introduction to the saying of the centurion in Matthew's Gospel is also fashioned in the light of the theme of faith.

As the Lukan narrative no longer resumes the theme of faith in its conclusion (Luke 7.10), neither does it in its introduction (Luke 7.1–7). There the thought of worthiness and/or unworthiness, rather, is operative, obviously because of the words of the centurion (Luke, 7.6b): οὐ γὰρ ἱκανός εἰμι ἵνα ὑπὸ τὴν στέγην μου εἰσέλθῃς. Thus the Gentile man does not himself come to Jesus, since, according to his own words, he regards himself as unworthy (Luke 7.7a, inserted by Luke). He sends rather a deputation of Jewish elders, who, however, make a point of emphasising his worthiness (Luke 7.4). In the light of this recommendation Jesus is ready to help and goes to the house of the centurion (Luke 7.6). In actual fact this coming of Jesus provides a further opportunity to show the worthiness of the man in

---

[1] For the interpretation of Matt. 8.4 in the sense of the fulfilling of the law by Christ see below, pp. 255. ff.

terms of his humility. By means of a second deputation of friends he explains that he is not worthy that Jesus should come to him. It is clear that in his introduction Luke is more interested in the person of the centurion than in his faith, which is expressed in his words (Luke 7.7b and 8). Thus the healing saying of Jesus which Matthew logically supplies at the conclusion is absent in his case.

That Matthew is interested in the matter of faith as such can be seen finally in the two sayings which he inserts into the discourse of Jesus (Matt. 8.11 and 12). They occur in Luke in another context (Luke 13.28–29). In Matthew they clearly serve to interpret the saying of Jesus about the faith of the centurion.

By the addition of these two sayings the word of Jesus about faith becomes a normal discourse to those accompanying him. In the first place it is clear that the faith intended here is not to be understood simply as faith in a worker of miracles, for this faith not only brings about the desired miracle (Matt. 8.13) but gains entrance into the kingdom of God. The refusal of this faith, on the other hand, means exclusion from salvation.[1] In the second place by means of this two-fold statement (Matt. 8.11 and 12) the saying of Jesus (Matt. 8.10) is developed. It speaks on the one hand of the extraordinary faith of the Gentile man and on the other of the fact that it has not been found in Israel. In this way Matthew interprets the saying of Jesus about the faith of the centurion as a promise to the Gentiles to whom faith opens up admission to the Messianic Meal, and as a word of judgment over Israel who by her unbelief, in spite of her privileges (οἱ υἱοὶ τῆς βασιλείας), has shut herself out. In the last resort this discourse of Jesus is not directed towards the believing centurion but to 'those who were following' (τοῖς ἀκολουθοῦσιν Matt. 8.10). It is quite certain that this means the Jews, and in the first place those who were following Jesus. It would be strange, however, if in the mind of the evangelist Jesus were not also referring here to the Church 'that was following', to which Matthew belonged. It should be noticed that the evangelist does not denote the people addressed by Jesus as a 'multitude' as Luke does (Luke 7.9), although in the light of Matt. 8.1 (. . . ἠκολούθησαν αὐτῷ ὄχλοι πολλοί) that would have been understandable. As Matt. 13.38 shows, the peculiar expression οἱ υἱοὶ τῆς βασιλείας could be used by the members of the Church in reference to themselves. Further, the judgment over Israel is portrayed in Matt. 8.12 in words which elsewhere in Matthew's Gospel speak of

[1] Cf. G. Bornkamm above, pp. 28 f., and A. Schlatter, *Der Glaube im NT*, p. 113.

the judgment in the congregation of Jesus (Matt. 13.42, 50; 22.13; 24.51; 25.30). Although, then, unbelieving Israel was intended in the first place in Matt. 8.12, nevertheless the reference to those 'recipients of grace who received their calling in vain'[1] also contained admonitory meaning for the Church of Matthew, for that her Lord is also her severe judge and that the disciples of Jesus can fail to reach the goal was impressively testified to her throughout the whole Gospel.[2]

In this way, by his expansion of the discourse of Jesus, Matthew secures not only a material interpretation of faith but also an address to those 'who were following'.

Matt. 15.21–28

As the comparison of this story of the Canaanite woman with the Markan parallel (Mark 7.24–30) shows, there stands in the middle of the received account the dialogue between the beseeching woman and Jesus, which in both cases ends with a healing saying of Jesus (Mark 7.29; Matt. 15.28). As there is no proper miracle story here this Synoptic pericope is reckoned with a measure of correctness by form-critical enquiry among the tradition of the sayings of Jesus.[3] Certainly with regard to Mark's composition at least one must speak with a measure of correctness of a miracle story, so far as that is possible in the present case of a healing at a distance. For the second evangelist gives the conversation a narrative setting which shows the marks of a miracle story. Thus he reports in the introduction how the miracle worker does not wish to be recognised by anyone, but he cannot be hid. Immediately (εὐθύς) he is approached by a woman (Mark 7.24b, 25). We hear at the end how this woman in response to the promise of Jesus goes home and finds her child healed (Mark 7.30). Twice the sickness is spoken of: in the introduction of the woman (Mark 7.25) and in connexion with her plea for help (Mark 7.26). In Matthew these characteristics are absent and only brief reference is made to the sickness (Matt. 15.22). In his case the dialogue not only stands in the middle of the pericope but rather the pericope itself consists exclusively of a dialogue, to the end of which the healing is quite formally attached. There can be no question of a narrative setting in the usual sense, since the expansion in Matt.

---

[1] A. Schlatter, *Matthäus*, p. 280.
[2] Cf. above G. Bornkamm, pp. 15 ff., and G. Barth, pp. 58 ff.
[3] Cf. R. Bultmann, *SynT*, p. 38; M. Dibelius, *Formgesch.*, p. 261 [ET², p. 261], and V. Taylor, *The Gospel according to St Mark*, p. 347.

15.22–24 presents two new points of conversation before the traditional conversation.[1]

The difficult question arises concerning the relationship of Mark
and Matthew in this pericope. One may, in fact, ask whether
Matthew is not using an older form of the story than the composition
in Mark's Gospel.[2] One may point to the fact that here Matthew has
quite strikingly departed from his custom of abbreviating the Markan narrative. It is further notable that the Matthaean version
shows harder traits, whereas Mark introduces the milder πρῶτον-
clause in Mark 7.27.[3] But against all these arguments counter-
arguments can be brought. Against the first objection it must be
remembered that here as elsewhere Matthew abbreviates the novelistic peculiarities of the Markan text, above all at the beginning and
the end (cf. Mark 7.24b, 25a, 30). On the other hand, he also inserts
sayings in other places in conversation scenes.[4] It is, then, correct
that the Matthaean version shows harder and more Jewish traits, but
that is no argument for a literary priority. We are here transplanted
to the Jewish-Christian world and its theological tradition. It is
significant that the strict Jewish-Christian standpoint is acknowledged by the Matthaean narrative and yet is overcome by the great
faith of the Gentile woman, and in the presence of Jesus himself. In
other words: Matthew's retelling of the story also presupposes assent
to the mission to the Gentiles, but bears in mind the theological
thoughts of the Jewish-Christian congregation. The enigma, why the
first evangelist in that case does not make use of the sentence in Mark
which stresses the precedence of the mission to the Jews (Mark
7.27)[5] is best resolved by accepting the view that it is a later insertion
into the Markan narrative.[6]

This whole question may remain open, however, for we are
concerned here only with the form of the Matthaean narrative as

[1] Although the second piece of conversation takes place between the disciples
and Jesus (Matt. 15.23b, 24) it is clear that Jesus does not respond to 'the demand
of the disciples: "Send her away", but to the supplicating of the woman: "Lord,
have mercy on me!" ' (E. Lohmeyer, p. 253).

[2] Cf. R. Bultmann, *SynT*, p. 38.

[3] Thus B. C. Butler, *The Originality of St Matthew*, Cambridge, 1951, pp. 130 f.;
cf. A. Schlatter, *Matthäus*, p. 491.

[4] Thus V. Taylor, *The Gospel according to St Mark*, p. 347, with reference to Matt.
9.13; 12.5–7, 11–12. Cf. also R. Bultmann, *SynT*, p. 61.

[5] A. Schlatter sees in the πρῶτον (Mark 7.27) the πρῶτον of Rom. 1.16 (*Matthäus*, p. 491).

[6] Thus R. Bultmann, *SynT*, p. 38.

such, and not with how it arose. Our task is rather to discover its goal.

Although there can be no doubt that Mark and Matthew report an actual healing miracle by Jesus, the form of the narrative makes clear that it is not the miracle as such that was important but the conversation which the healing brought forth. Hence this 'miracle story' is not handed on among the typical miracle reports (such as Mark 4.35 ff., or Matt. 8-9), but in the context of sections which concern the disciples,[1] or to be more exact, in immediate connexion with the instruction about the question of what is pure and what impure (Mark 7.1-23; Matt. 15.1-20). The position of the pericope in the outline of the Gospel makes clear that in it we are concerned with teaching. It contains, so to speak, the attitude of Jesus to a disputed question, namely the mission to the Gentiles.

This teaching must be derived indirectly from the story and the conversation in it; it is not expressly formulated in a saying as in the case of the preceding section (Mark 7.15, 20-23; Matt. 15.20b). It is contained in the fact that the story shows how Jesus, in spite of objecting in the beginning and in spite of the priority which the Jews enjoy, nevertheless gives his help to a Gentile woman. At the same time, in the Markan narrative it is made to appear as though Jesus was outwitted by the adroit and nimble-tongued woman.

Matthew clarified this situation by saying that Jesus could not withhold his help in view of the woman's faith (Matt. 15.28): ὦ γύναι, μεγάλη σου ἡ πίστις· γενηθήτω σοι ὡς θέλεις. In Matthew the whole narrative is directed towards this last sentence which has a majestic note about it. It is expressed in a much more striking and decisive way than the corresponding passage in Mark 7.29. At the same time it forms the crowning conclusion of the conversation, followed only by the full stop in the form of the confirmation of the healing expressed in a very formal way (Matt. 15.28b). Ultimately, however, this last answer of Jesus brings out the theme of the pericope. Mark had shown that it is the fact of the healing that is important for him here (Mark 7.29: διὰ τοῦτον τὸν λόγον ὕπαγε, ἐξελήλυθεν ἐκ τῆς θυγατρός σου τὸ δαιμόνιον), and he therefore reports how the woman returns home and finds her child well. In Matthew only the fact and power of faith are expressed.

The Matthaean expansion fits significantly into this context. At the same time it strengthens the resistance with which Jesus meets

[1] Cf. Mark 6.7 ff.; 6.30 ff.; 6.45 ff.; 7.17 ff.; 8.1 ff.; 8.14 ff.!

the request of the woman and provides the formula concerning the great faith with its factual justification. Finally light is also shed on the problem at issue inasmuch as the (religious) opposition between Israel and the Gentile world is echoed in the terms Israel (15.24) and Canaan (15.22).[1]

In this way the goal of the Matthaean presentation is clearly recognisable. In the treatment of the question concerning the mission to the Gentiles it takes into account the strict Jewish-Christian point of view, which Jesus himself here represents. At the same time, however, it is shown that in spite of that Jesus recognised faith as the way of the Gentiles to salvation.[2] Consequently Matthew has done nothing other than interpret the thought expressed by Mark in his narrative. The two of them, however, obviously have different addressees in mind. Mark shows the Gentile Christians that precedence must be acknowledged to belong to the Jewish nation (Mark 7.27: πρῶτον). Matthew makes clear to the strict Jewish-Christians that faith opens the way for the Gentiles to Jesus.

2. *The theme of discipleship*

Here belong the narratives of the storm at sea and the walking on the sea. It is peculiar to both that they take place exclusively between Jesus and his disciples, while other people—with the exception of Matt. 8.27 οἱ ἄνθρωποι—are not mentioned. An indication is thus already given that they have to do with the theme of discipleship.

Matt. 8.18–27

The Markan parallel to this story of the stilling of the storm occurs as the first in a cycle of three miracle stories (Mark 4.35–41 as part of Mark 4.35–5.43). After portraying Jesus as a teacher (Mark 4.1–34; cf. Mark 4.2 καὶ ἔλεγεν αὐτοῖς ἐν τῇ διδαχῇ αὐτοῦ) Mark depicts him by means of typical examples as a miracle worker (nature miracle, exorcism of demons, healing and awakening of the dead). At the conclusion of these two collections of pericopes he places the rejection

---

[1] Cf. E. Lohmeyer, p. 252.

[2] A. Schlatter, *Matthäus*, pp. 489 f., has very aptly formulated this paradox: 'In the dealings of Jesus with the Gentile woman the two rules which govern his relationship with the Gentile world find expression. The separation ordained by God between the Gentiles and Israel remains sacrosanct. . . . At the same time, however, it is made plain that there is a power which overcomes this restriction because with regard to the Gentile woman the rule is also sustained that confidence that kindly help will be given evokes help and no faith is put to shame and annihilated. The union of the two points of view is achieved by the complete submission of the suppliant to the saying of Jesus.'

of Jesus in Nazareth (Mark 6.1–6) in which there is clearly a reference
back to the activity portrayed in them (Mark 6.2). Mark thus chose
and related the story of the stilling of the storm as an example of the
mighty works (δυνάμεις Mark 6.2). In line with this the typical
marks of a miracle story come to the fore in it. The greatness of the
need is vividly outlined (4.37); in the middle of the narrative stands
Jesus' word of command to the elements (4.39: σιώπα, πεφίμωσο),
and as a result of this the stilling of the storm is reported in a twofold
statement (καὶ ἐκόπασεν ὁ ἄνεμος, καὶ ἐγένετο γαλήνη μεγάλη). It is
noteworthy that the designation 'disciples' is completely absent,
although they are doubtless in the back of Mark's mind (cf. Mark
4.34). Furthermore the accusing question addressed to Jesus (Mark
4.38: διδάσκαλε, οὐ μέλει σοι ὅτι ἀπολλύμεθα;) does not sound at all
disciple-like. It expresses graphically the extreme peril which
existed. In brief, the Markan narrative is a primitive miracle story in
the authentic style.

The Matthaean reproduction of this story provides an insertion in
Matt. 8.19–22. It contains two scenes which depict Jesus in conversation with men who wish to become his disciples or ought to do so.
Luke presents them in another context (Luke 9.57–60). They have
no recognisable relationship with a journey by sea and were first
linked with the stilling of the storm by the evangelist Matthew.

It is clear that these two scenes precisely interrupt the context of
Mark's Gospel in Matthew. After the connecting verse of Matt. 8.18,
which corresponds to Mark 4.35 and introduces the sea journey, one
expects immediately the beginning of the journey as in Mark 4.36 ff.
Instead of that this natural context is disturbed by the conversations
about discipleship. It is true that they are not inserted into the actual
narrative, but they are linked with it as closely as possible. That is
clear not only through their position between the transitional notice
and the beginning of the pericope but above all through a clear
catchword link.[1] In order to achieve this the evangelist has to substitute the more appropriate ἀπελθεῖν for the διελθεῖν of Mark (4.35)
and Luke (8.22) so as to gain a link with the expression ὅπου ἐὰν
ἀπέρχῃ (Matt. 8.19 = Luke 9.57). At the end of the insertion the
catchword ἀκολουθεῖν forms the link. Hence Mark 4.36 is completely
refashioned. Mark sketches the departure on the crossing in a most

---

[1] Matt. 8.18 ἀπελθεῖν—8.19 (Luke 9.57) ἀπέρχεσθαι, 8.21 (Luke 9.59) ἀπελθεῖν.
Matt. 8.21 ἕτερος δὲ τῶν μαθητῶν—8.23 οἱ μαθηταὶ αὐτοῦ.
Matt. 8.22 ἀκολούθει μοι—8.23. . . ἠκολούθησαν αὐτῷ.

graphic way: how 'they' took Jesus with them (ὡς ἦν ἐν τῷ πλοίῳ) and how there were other ships about. Matthew, on the other hand, reports very formally that Jesus went first into the boat and his disciples followed him (Matt. 8.23): καὶ ἐμβάντι αὐτῷ εἰς τὸ πλοῖον, ἠκολούθησαν αὐτῷ οἱ μαθηταὶ αὐτοῦ. This selection of the words ἀκολουθεῖν and οἱ μαθηταὶ αὐτοῦ has not only formal meaning, of course, for the linking by catchword. Rather it makes plain the fact that Matthew interprets the story of the storm at sea as a story of discipleship.[1] The insertion of the scenes of discipleship in Matt. 8.19–22 thus serves this interpretation and this can also be perceived in the pericope itself.

The introductory connecting note itself is significant. According to Mark (4.35; and also Luke 8.22) Jesus unites himself with his disciples in the summons: διέλθωμεν εἰς τὸ πέραν. According to Matthew the sea journey is set in motion by a command of Jesus (Matt. 8.18): . . . ὁ Ἰησοῦς . . . ἐκέλευσεν ἀπελθεῖν εἰς τὸ πέραν. In connexion with Matt. 8.23 this command must be understood as a call to discipleship. Then, however, the inserted conversation scenes in Matt. 8.19–22 portray the answer, so to speak, to this call to discipleship. In both scenes there ensues first of all the speech of one who was ready to follow and then in the second place the reply of Jesus in which the conditions are made clear. Matthew has achieved this order by a rearrangement as far as the Lukan material is concerned in the second conversation scene. The removal of the call to discipleship from the beginning of the scene (Luke 9.59) into the second half (Matt. 8.22) can only be because the call to discipleship in the Matthaean context has already taken place (Matt. 8.18) and would be superfluous at this point. On the other hand, the renewed call to discipleship in its present place in Matthew has a special meaning. It is no longer intended to be a first call to discipleship but to overcome reservations which stand in the way of an undivided discipleship. If the observation is accepted that it is not just any man to whom the call is given here (cf. Luke 9.59 εἶπεν δὲ πρὸς ἕτερον) but one of the disciples (Matt. 8.21 ἕτερος δὲ τῶν μαθητῶν) we are faced with the remarkable position that this command to discipleship is directed to one who as a μαθητής is obviously engaged in discipleship already.[2] Whether the γραμματεύς in Matt. 8.19 should be regarded

---

[1] G. Bornkamm points this interpretation out, above, pp. 54 ff.
[2] The use of the term κύριε (Matt. 8.21) to address Jesus, which then recurs in the mouth of the disciples of Jesus (Matt. 8.25) also points in the same direction.

as a disciple must remain open. The term διδάσκαλε used in reference to Jesus, which elsewhere in Matthew's Gospel occurs only in the mouth of those who are not disciples, suggests a negative answer.[1] On the other hand, one may be justified in concluding from the formulation in Matt. 8.21 ἕτερος δὲ τῶν μαθητῶν that the partner of Jesus in the first conversation was also a disciple.[2] Be that as it may, in any case the point in the second scene is no longer concerned with the first decision *in favour of* discipleship but with the repeated demand for a new decision in terms of complete obedience *within* discipleship.[3] In this way, however, the interpretation of Matthew brings out the situation of the Church practising discipleship. If it is borne in mind that the story of the stilling of the storm portrays for Matthew a possible occurrence in the course of discipleship, it becomes entirely clear that the insertion of the scenes concerned with discipleship into the context of this narrative is both formally and materially a means of interpretation. In the first place they set out the reply to the summons of Jesus to discipleship; in the second they make clear what this discipleship means;[4] and in the third they present the occurrence that follows as an example for disciples.

In the narrative of the stilling of the storm itself the hand of the interpreter can also be seen. The description of the external circumstances is restricted to the barest necessities. Above all there is no mention of the pictorial description of Jesus asleep on a cushion in the stern (Mark 4.38a). The transposition of the scene which Matthew undertakes in his narrative is important. Whereas in Mark (4.38–40, cf. Luke 8.24–25) the stilling of the storm takes place first and the words of censure addressed to the disciples follow, in Matthew the words of reproach occur first and the miracle follows (8.25, 26). In short, Mark places the nature miracle of the stilling of the storm in the centre and the words addressed to the disciples are

[1] Matt. 12.38; 19.16; 22.16, 24, 36.
[2] The designation γραμματεύς does not contradict this, since according to Matt. 13.52 and 23.34 there were obviously also Christian scribes. That this term is intended 'to awaken a prejudice and prepare the way for the refusal' (J. Wellhausen, *Das Evangelium Matthaei*, Berlin, 1904, p. 38; similarly E. Klostermann, *ad loc.*) is not based on the text, which makes no reference to a refusal.
[3] For this reason it cannot be agreed that in τῶν μαθητῶν (Matt. 8.21) there is to be found a 'careless addition' by Matthew (E. Klostermann, *ad loc.*).
[4] E. Klostermann, p. 77, judges that the first scene 'has to do with the deprivations of discipleship and the second with the precedence of the duty of discipleship over everything else'. Cf. also G. Bornkamm above, p. 54.

an appendage. By transposing the scene Matthew has created a conversation between the disciples and Jesus and placed this in the centre, so that now the stilling of the storm looks like an appendage. In this way it is no longer Jesus and the elements that constitute the theme of the narrative but Jesus and his disciples who are in peril. The miracle story becomes a story about the disciples, so to speak.[1] The evangelist works into the story of the stilling of the storm the picture of the Church in her discipleship.

Matt. 14.22–33

This narrative of Jesus walking on the sea also concerns an event which has to do solely with the disciples. The separation from the crowd is firmly retained by both Mark (6.45) and Matthew (14.22). In their presentation of the disciples, however, the two evangelists differ. That comes out most clearly at the end of their narratives.

Mark interprets the behaviour of the disciples in face of the epiphany of their Lord as a sign of their lack of understanding. This is indicated by his verse of interpretation (Mark 6.52): οὐ γὰρ συνῆκαν ἐπὶ τοῖς ἄρτοις, ἀλλ' ἦν αὐτῶν ἡ καρδία πεπωρωμένη. If the feeding of the five thousand requires a special understanding, which the disciples obviously do not display, their attitude to Jesus when he appears on the sea confirms their failure to understand. The story in Mark is told from this point of view. The horror of the disciples at the epiphany of Jesus is described in two ways (Mark 6.49, 50a).[2] Even the revealing and comforting words of Jesus (Mark 6.50b) cannot dispel the paralysing horror which seems to be heightened in the extreme at the end of the pericope (Mark 6.51b).

The reproduction of the story in Matthew also portrays the horror of the disciples, though only at the beginning (Matt. 14.26).[3] At the end, on the other hand, stands their confession of their Lord who has

[1] Individual formulations by Matthew confirm this interpretation; cf. G. Bornkamm above, pp. 55 f.

[2] It is entirely probable that this duplication is due to the fusion of two stories: of the walking on the sea and the stilling of the storm, which have not been completely interwoven into a new unity, as E. Lohmeyer, *Markus*, pp. 131 f., shows by means of several observations (cf. also R. Bultmann, *SynT*, p. 216). The literary roughness as such, however, in the form of the twofold statement in Mark 6.49–50 brings out impressively the lack of understanding on the part of the disciples.

[3] In this verse Matthew has drawn together into one single sentence Mark's twofold statement about the disciples seeing Jesus and their fright. By this means he has not only got rid of the literary roughness of the Markan text but also his strong emphasis on the disciples' lack of understanding.

wonderfully revealed himself to them (Matt. 14.33) : οἱ δὲ ἐν τῷ πλοίῳ
προσεκύνησαν αὐτῷ λέγοντες· ἀληθῶς θεοῦ υἱὸς εἶ.

The most important thing in Matthew's retelling is the scene
which he has inserted into the Markan context (Matt. 14.28–31).
That this is an insertion is made clear by several observations. In the
first place it is framed by verses which in Mark follow immediately
upon each other (Matt. 14.27 = Mark 6.50 and Matt. 14.32 =
Mark 6.51a). In addition there are linguistic characteristics. Whereas
in the material of the pericope which they have in common the
expression περιπατεῖν ἐπὶ τῆς θαλάσσης (Mark 6.48 f.; Matt. 14.26)
or ἐπὶ τὴν θάλασσαν (Matt. 14.25) is used, in the insertion ἐλθεῖν or
περιπατεῖν ἐπὶ τὰ ὕδατα (Matt. 14.28, 29) occurs. It is significant that
in Matt. 8.32 Matthew also uses the expression τὰ ὕδατα for the
Galilean 'sea'. The rest of the vocabulary also similarly points to
the evangelist. The word κύριε (14.28, 30) occurs repeatedly as a term
of address to Jesus in the Matthaean narratives (8.2, 6, 8, 21, etc.).
Matthew also shows a liking for using the notion of little faith (8.26;
14.31; 16.8; 17.20). The words καταποντίζειν and διστάζειν are found
in him alone in the New Testament (14.30; 18.6 and 14.31; 28.17).
Peter's cry for help (14.30 κύριε, σῶσόν με) corresponds to the
prayer in the cry of the disciples during the storm on the sea (8.25).
The concept κελεύειν, which is completely absent from the second
Gospel, is inserted by Matthew in four places into the Markan text
(8.18; 14.9, 19; 27.58) and is used in two further passages in material
peculiar to himself (18.25; 27.64). This all points to the fact that the
insertion really does stem from the hand of Matthew.[1]

Furthermore, it is easy to recognise how the evangelist has firmly
bound his insertion to the rest of the pericope. As in the case of
Matt. 8.19–22, he also uses here the catchword technique. In this
way a bridge is made from 14.27 (ἐγώ εἰμι) to 14.28 (εἰ σὺ εἶ) and
still further to the end of the story in 14.33 (ἀληθῶς θεοῦ υἱὸς εἶ). The
word ἄνεμος (14.24, 30, 32) and the idea of fear (14.26, 27, 30) link
the pericope in the closest way with the inserted portion. By means of
the transformation of the Markan conclusion into an adoring confession the scene of the saving of Peter and of the whole ship from the
peril at sea attains its meaningful and adoring conclusion. It is
thus clear that the inserted scene is fused with the traditional

[1] Cf. G. D. Kilpatrick, *Origins*, pp. 38–44: the first evangelist is employing here
as in other passages (Matt. 15.15 ff.; 16.17 ff.; 17.24 ff. and 18.15 ff.) a special oral
Petrine tradition, which he was the first to write down.

narrative into a whole and must be understood accordingly.

In the middle of the new narrative there does not now stand an epiphany of Jesus before the uncomprehending disciples. Rather this epiphany sets them free to exercise a fearless faith, as Peter shows (Matt. 14.28, 29). With his words κύριε, εἰ σὺ εἶ he clasps the revealing saying of Jesus θαρσεῖτε, ἐγώ εἰμι. His request is precisely the believing answer of the disciple to the appearing of his Lord. It is true that the horror of the disciples at the sight of their Master walking on the sea is described in similar words to those found in Mark, but it is understood as an expression of fear (Matt. 14.26 καὶ ἀπὸ τοῦ φόβου ἔκραξαν). At the call of Jesus: μὴ φοβεῖσθε (Matt. 14.27) Peter, one of those who were afraid, overcomes his anxiety and is ready for the highest faith. That he is able to walk on the water like Jesus proves that he had this faith.

The whole scene of Peter walking on the sea, however, presents a disciple on the way of discipleship. As in Matt. 8.18, it is set in motion by a command of Jesus (Matt. 14.28 κέλευσόν με). But then, in face of the danger Peter is seized by fear and cries out for help as the disciples did in the storm at sea (Matt. 14.30 κύριε, σῶσόν με, cf. 8.25). Both narratives are also linked together in Matthew by referring to the disciples as of little faith (Matt. 8.26; 14.31) and by Jesus rescuing these men of little faith from danger. The first evangelist has also approximated the two narratives to each other by speaking in both cases not so much about the peril of the disciples from the sea as of that of the boat (Matt. 8.24; 14.24). Of course, the scene of Peter walking on the sea contains something entirely unique: it shows the greatness of the promise made to faith within discipleship (Matt. 14.28, 29), but does not remain silent about the inability of the disciple to hold firmly to this promise during a time of testing (Matt. 14.30).

Thus here also it is the theme of discipleship[1] which has been determinative in the way Matthew has shaped his narrative and he has done this by adhering closely to the pericope as he received it, with its report of Jesus walking on the sea and the unbounded horror of his disciples. He shows Jesus as the Lord who gives to his disciples the power to follow him, and interprets the motive of the uncomprehending horror of the disciples from the point of view of fear and their little faith.

[1] Matthew expressly designates the disciples as such in the story (Matt. 14.26 as against Mark 6.49).

C. *The omission of Mark 7.31–37 and 8.22–26 by Matthew*

In view of the many means which Matthew employs in retelling the miracle stories, whether abbreviation or expansion or various transpositions, it is surprising that he has completely passed over two healing miracles of Jesus contained in Mark's Gospel without attempting any similar interpretation in his revised account. Without doubt both miracle stories are closely related in that they speak quite unedifyingly of Jesus as they would of a profane miracle-worker. Hence Wellhausen is of the opinion that Matthew was 'put off by the magical procedure'.[1] But then the question immediately arises why he has not done the same here as in the case of the healing of the woman with the haemorrhage, which he stripped of all its magical traits. Vincent Taylor thinks that the reason for the omission is the extraordinarily realistic nature of the description.[2] This explanation is not really satisfactory, however, since the first evangelist retains other novelistic narratives of Mark's, though he strips them of their vivid imagery.

It must be acknowledged that both miracle stories were not exclusively of importance to the evangelist Mark because of their realistic nature. Both narratives stand in Mark's Gospel at the end of a series of pericopes the structure of which, despite deviations in matters of detail, is built along parallel lines.[3] Both cycles fill the period which stretches from the return of the apostles to Jesus following their mission (Mark 6.30 ff.), to the confession of Peter at Caesarea Philippi (Mark 8.27 ff.). Here the disciples, who previously in the pericopes have as good as played no part, come more markedly into the field of interest. The change occurs in the stories of the feedings (Mark 6.35–44; 8.1–9) and the narrative of Jesus' walking on the sea (Mark 6.45–52), and in the giving of instruction on the question of purity (Mark 7.1–23) and the leaven of the Pharisees (Mark 8.14–21). In these two cycles (Mark 6.35–7.37 and 8.1–26) Mark shows that the disciples show no understanding before the secret of the person of Jesus. The evangelist's conclusion in the first cycle about the hardened hearts of the disciples (Mark 6.52) corresponds to the formulation of the question addressed to them by Jesus in the second cycle (Mark 8.17)—a statement which equates the inner state of the

---

[1] J. Wellhausen, *Marci*, p. 64.
[2] V. Taylor, *The Gospel according to St Mark*, p. 369, on Matt. 8.22 ff. and similarly p. 352 on Mark 7.31 ff.
[3] Cf. E. Klostermann, pp. 74 f., on Mark 8.1–26.

disciples with that of the opponents of Jesus (cf. Mark 3.5). Thus they also fail to understand the teaching of Jesus both in Mark 7.17 ff. and in Mark 8.15 ff. Furthermore, towards the end of the second cycle Jesus designates his disciples—granted it is in a question, but it is nevertheless clear—as blind and deaf (Mark 8.18): ὀφθαλμοὺς ἔχοντες οὐ βλέπετε, καὶ ὦτα ἔχοντες οὐκ ἀκούετε;—an expression reminiscent of the characterisation of those 'outside' in Mark 4.12. Here Mark alludes expressly to the healing of the blind man of Bethsaida (Mark 8.22–26) and the healing of the deaf man (Mark 7.31–37). Since the sayings about the blindness and deafness of the disciples are peculiar to the second evangelist, the meaning of the passage will be intelligible in the light of them. The two cycles of pericopes between the return of the disciples to Jesus and their confession of him as the Christ through the mouth of Peter mark the way of the disciples from failure to understand to the opening of their eyes and ears for the secret of Jesus. We are dealing with a clear theological construction by Mark in which a symbolic meaning is given to the two healing miracles. They must be understood in the light of the removal of the disciples' lack of understanding which is presupposed in Peter's confession. Here in particular the disturbing profane traits gain their meaning. The fact that Jesus puts his fingers into the ears of the deaf man (Mark 7.33), and that he spits on the eyes of the blind man (Mark 8.23) and lays his hands upon them (Mark 8.25)—these all draw their meaning from the fact that they provide an image for the opening of the eyes and ears of the disciples. This symbolic interpretation is also suggested by the position of the healings, not among the actual δυνάμεις of Jesus such as are collected in Mark 4.35–5.43, for example, but here before Peter's confession of Christ. Thus the indications are that Mark understood these indelicate healings of Jesus figuratively and that is why they are placed and preserved in their present position.[1]

Whether Matthew was familiar with these two miracle stories cannot, of course, be known with certainty. It is nevertheless very probable. He follows Mark's order of the pericopes in both cycles very carefully, without, of course, including the two healings. They must have been less important for him, since according to his Gospel

[1] A symbolic interpretation of the two healings is advocated by E. Klostermann, pp. 73, 77; J. Sundwall, *Die Zusammensetzung des Markusevang.*, p. 48; A. Richardson, *The Miracle-Stories of the Gospels*, London, 1941, pp. 82 ff., and V. Taylor, *The Gospel according to St Mark*, pp. 97 f.

the opening of the eyes and ears of the disciples did not first take place at Caesarea Philippi (cf., for example, Matt. 14.33). Hence, furthermore, the two parallel series of pericopes had not the same theological meaning for him as for Mark. In short, he would not have created them; they were provided for him. In Mark, however, they only possess a recognisable meaning if the two healing miracles are included. Hence Matthew must have known them in the context of Mark's composition and omitted them. That he had the second evangelist's arrangement, with its theological character, before him is shown by his adoption of two passages about lack of understanding on the part of the disciples (Matt. 15.16, 17 from Mark 7.18 and Matt. 16.9 ff. from Mark 8.17 ff.). It is true that he does not interpret them as evidence of a failure to understand the person of Jesus, but as a failure to understand his teaching.[1]

The question about the reason for the omission of the two miracle stories by the evangelist Matthew is not adequately answered by referring to their irreverent character. But neither is it a sufficient explanation to say that for Matthew the symbolical meaning does not hold because the disciples are depicted as understanding from the beginning. There is no reason why he could not have interpreted the narratives differently and so have told them differently from the second evangelist.

At this point it is important to remember that in retelling the strongly novelistic miracle stories of Mark, Matthew deletes the stylistic traits and illustrative details, but builds his theological treatment on significant points in the narrative before him. Thus, for example, the exorcism of the demons at Gadara is concentrated on the Christological statement which has arisen in Matt. 8.29, by altering Mark 5.7. The healing of the woman with the haemorrhage is completely subordinated to the saying about saving faith, which Matthew found in the Markan text already (Mark 5.34 = Matt. 9.22). The decisive thing for his new account is obviously that the tradition puts into his hand a point of departure for his interpretation, whether for the theme of Christology or of faith or of discipleship.

[1] Cf. also the 'traces' of the two healings in Matthew's Gospel: Mark 7.31 ff. in the summary account in Matt. 15.29–31 (on this V. Taylor, *The Gospel . . . Mark*, p. 354) and Mark 8.22–26 in the healing of the blind man in Matt. 20.29–34, where Matthew, against the Synoptic parallels, reports a case of healing through the touching of the eyes and suddenly uses the word ὄμμα (20.34; cf. Mark 8.23), although he had just used the word ὀφθαλμός (20.33); on this J. Wellhausen, *Matthaei*, pp. 102–3!

Such points of departure for a theological interpretation cannot be found, however, in the two miracle stories with which we are concerned. There is no statement about faith or about the dignity of Jesus. The sick are not presented in any sense as people who might have been capable of exercising faith. They are utterly and entirely objects of the acts of Jesus: they are brought to him, requests are made on their behalf and he carries out the techniques of healing upon them. They have no share in what is going on, they are simply mute and blind.[1]

Jesus appears solely as a wonder-worker. He is neither addressed by the sick as Lord nor is either of the sick addressed by him as the Lord.[2] Nor is any doctrinal theological expression of Jesus transmitted. Above all, the healing of the blind man of Bethsaida depicts Jesus in conversation with the blind man as a physician with his patient.

Consequently it follows that neither the theme of Christology nor that of faith nor that of discipleship is contained in these two miracle stories of Mark's Gospel.[3] As they do not have for Matthew the symbolic meaning of the opening of the eyes and ears of the disciples, they obviously no longer conceal any kerygmatic statement which could have been of interest to him and have justified him in retelling them.

If one surveys from this point of view the evangelist Matthew's retelling of the miracle stories, it is plain that the miracles are not important for their own sakes but by reason of the message they contain. The abbreviations, such as occur, above all, in the healing miracles proper, show that no importance is attached to the details and the pictorial nature of what happened. The expansions of the miracle stories confirm this negative result in so far as, on the one hand, they occur in scenes with conversations about doctrine and have no narrative function (Matt. 8.5 ff.; 15.21 ff.), and on the other they occur in specific stories of the disciples, and there depict Jesus vis-à-vis the disciples (Matt. 8.18 ff.; 14.22 ff.). The positive result of

[1] For these reasons both cases of healing fit in with the symbolical meaning attributed to them by Mark, for in his view the disciples are incapable of exercising faith, but being blind and dumb have no share in what is actually going on.

[2] The word ἐφφαθά (Mark 7.34) is not an address to the sick man, but belongs, especially as it is transmitted in a foreign language, as an effective word of command, to the technique of healing. Cf. R. Bultmann, *Syn T*, p. 222.

[3] Cf. M. Dibelius, 'Evangelienkritik und Christologie', *Botschaft und Geschichte*, I, p. 341, on Mark 8.22 ff.: in the middle point stands the cure. 'We can find no kind of reference to faith or salvation as a theme for preaching.'

these things is to show a doctrinal concern on the part of the evangelist. He relates these stories as examples of the nature of faith and/or
discipleship. In addition, in other miracle narratives interest in a
Christological statement can be seen. In the retelling of the Synoptic
miracle stories which fall under the heading of these three themes
Matthew has exercised great concern to bring to the fore the essential
theological content of the statements. In a sentence, the re-narrating
of the miracles of Jesus is undertaken for the instruction of the Church.

II. THE FORM OF THE MIRACLE STORIES IN MATTHEW

Form-critical investigation reached its findings for the Synoptic
tradition above all through the study of Mark's Gospel. M. Dibelius
himself says expressly that in fixing the paradigm: 'It is Mark
essentially who provides the material.'[1] The stylistic traits, as
Bultmann sets them out for the miracle stories,[2] are found by far
the most frequently in the narratives of Mark, to a smaller extent
in Luke, but least of all in Matthew.[3] The last observation already
indicates the inadequacy of the form-critical category of miracle
stories if one is to be just to the facts of Matthew's Gospel.

Further, the distinction between paradigm and tale can only be
sustained with considerable effort in the first Gospel. According to
Dibelius the chief characteristic of the tale is that it shows 'a certain
joy in invention',[4] as, for example, the 'interest in somehow describing the miracle'.[5] The retelling of the miracles by Matthew, however,
shows no trace of a desire to invent; and there is very little trace of a
desire to describe the miracle.

One essential mark of the paradigm is the 'brevity and simplicity
of the narrative'.[6] Now this characteristic does apply to a considerable extent to the miracle stories of Matthew's Gospel.[7] The other

[1] *Formgesch.*, pp. 39 f.; cf. p. 67 on the tale (*Novellen*) [ET[2], pp. 42 f., 71].
[2] *SynT*, pp. 221 ff.
[3] Cf. O. Perels, *Die Wunderüberlieferung der Synoptiker in ihrem Verhältnis zur
Wortüberlieferung*, Stuttgart, 1934, pp. 82–84.
[4] M. Dibelius, *Formgesch.*, p. 67 [ET[2], p. 70].
[5] *Ibid.*, p. 117 [p. 120].
[6] *Ibid.*, p. 46 [p. 48].
[7] One cannot help thinking immediately of certain Matthaean miracle stories
when Dibelius says: 'The concentrated brevity of the Paradigms rests upon a
concern which makes the material subject to the purpose of the preacher, hinders
wandering, and silences the unessential. Further, what is only vivid or only arresting
cannot be regarded as essential from the standpoint of a sermon' (*Formgesch.*, p. 51
[ET[2], p. 53]).

characteristic of the paradigm is similarly found in the miracle stories of the first Gospel, namely the 'culmination of the narrative in a thought that is useful for the sermon'.[1] Thus in Matt. 8.13; 9.22; 15.28 and 17.20 Matthew has worked in a saying of Jesus which has a general reference to faith as the climax or the final point of a miracle story; and the story of Jesus walking on the sea issues, in an impressive 'choral ending' (Matt. 14.33), to which the sermon can be linked.

The question arises whether the miracle stories of Matthew's Gospel are not paradigms rather than tales. Dibelius himself has hinted at the possibility of an approximation of the tales to the form of the paradigm and thinks: 'We see a development of this kind in the Christianising treatment of many Markan tales by Matthew before our eyes.' The first evangelist has 'often altered the style of the tales in the interests of edification and has thus made them ripe for preaching'.[2] One must, of course, remember that the 'worldly' tales in Mark's Gospel also contain edifying elements, as, for example, in Mark 4.40; 5.34, 36; 6.50 (E. Fascher).[3] It is significant that in his re-styling of the tales it is precisely these passages to which Matthew devotes his attention.[4]

Our concern now is to discover the characteristics of the miracle stories in Matthew's Gospel and from these to determine their form more exactly. The results of form-critical work as carried out by M. Dibelius and R. Bultmann are taken for granted. A number of observations on this subject have already been made in the previous chapter, such as the 'anti-novelistic' attitude of Matthew which is recognisable everywhere and his interest in the conversation, or rather, sayings of Jesus within the miracle story. This must all now be taken up systematically, put together and assessed.

[1] *Ibid.*, p. 55 [p. 58].

[2] M. Dibelius, pp. 202 f. [pp. 201 f.].

[3] E. Fascher, *Die formgeschichtliche Methode*, Giessen, 1924, p. 75. Cf. also C. Bouma, *De literarische vorm der Evangelien*, Rotterdam, 1921, p. 106.

[4] He puts the saying of Jesus to the disciples during the storm at sea (Mark 4.40) in the middle of the story and introduces the concept of little faith. He makes the saying about saving faith (Mark 5.34) the sole theme in the healing of the woman with the haemorrhage. The admonition to Jairus to have faith without fear (Mark 5.36) does not appear in Matthew; but from the beginning the father of the deceased child shows an unshakeable faith. With the revealing saying of Jesus at his epiphany on the sea (Mark 6.50) Matthew immediately links the scene of Peter walking on the sea and his faith, or rather, little faith. The first evangelist 'develops' the edifying content of the tales of Mark in the course of his retelling of them.

The characteristics of the form of the miracle story in Matthew can be observed above all in the healing miracles. Some typical examples of them will first of all be considered in order to discover what these characteristics are (A). It is seen that these characteristics also occur in other miracle stories. By means of further examples from the first Gospel these particular characteristics can be designated as peculiarly Matthaean (B). As form-critical investigation cannot prove that its forms occur everywhere in a pure state, so also with regard to the Matthaean miracle stories one can only reach a conception of 'the' form as a result of observations resulting from the overall picture.[1] If the assumption must be made with regard to the pre-literary development that the various historical material at the back of the Synoptic narratives could not be moulded into pure forms so that the pattern can be perceived more in one place and less in another,[2] the same is true of the writing-up of the miracles by Matthew. In one case it is carried out clearly, in another less clearly, according as the material received in the tradition allowed. It is only within limits so designated that a judgment about the form of the miracle stories in Matthew can be pronounced (C).

A. *Definition of formal characteristics in Matthew's miracle stories*

For the sake of simplicity we shall start from three healing miracles of Jesus which at the same time present different possibilities for re-telling by Matthew. The first concerns a pericope in which the first evangelist agrees very closely with the other two (Matt. 8.2–4: the healing of the leper). The second concerns a narrative in which he has considerably abbreviated in comparison with Mark and Luke (Matt. 9.20–22: the healing of the woman with the haemorrhage). The last concerns the healing of the two blind men (Matt. 9.27–31), for which there is no recognisable direct synoptic parallel, but which is obviously a special form of the healing of the blind man of Jericho (Mark 10.46–52 and par.). These three pericopes will now be examined with reference to their formal peculiarities.

1. *The healing of the leper*

As the Synoptic comparison of this pericope shows, the same basic material of the narrative is found in all three evangelists. The request

[1] One must 'take from the mass of witnesses that which is typical, without overrating particular deviations' (M. Dibelius, *Formgesch.*, p. 39 [p. 42]).
[2] Cf. E. Fascher, *Die formgesch. Methode*, p. 227, and L. Köhler, *Das formgeschichtliche Problem des NT*, Tübingen, 1927, pp. 27, 34.

for healing in direct speech, the answer of Jesus to this request (accompanied by the touching of the sick man) likewise in direct speech, the acknowledgment that the healing has taken place and finally the direction of Jesus to the healed man to go and show himself to the priests. The close relationship is seen above all in the section containing the words that were uttered. Here to a large extent they are verbally the same, above all in the request and the healing saying. We must be all the more careful then in studying the deviations of the three Synoptic accounts from each other.

In Mark the descriptive clothing of the conversation stands out. It gives a certain pictorial element to the occurrence and the people. That applies to the beginning (Mark 1.40): καὶ ἔρχεται πρὸς αὐτὸν λεπρὸς παρακαλῶν αὐτὸν καὶ γονυπετῶν λέγων αὐτῷ, to the recognition that the healing has taken place (Mark 1.42): καὶ εὐθὺς ἀπῆλθεν ἀπ᾽ αὐτοῦ ἡ λέπρα, καὶ ἐκαθαρίσθη, to the angry attitude of Jesus to the man who had been healed (Mark 1.43): καὶ ἐμβριμησάμενος αὐτῷ εὐθὺς ἐξέβαλεν αὐτόν and to the final verse (Mark 1.45). The deviations of Matthew and Luke from Mark are found above all in these descriptive sections. The two evangelists differ from each other, however, in their reproduction of the narrative in important points.

Luke is at pains to retain as far as possible all the descriptive details of Mark. Indeed, he adds still more details to Mark's account. He relates, for example, that the leper was a 'man full of leprosy' (Luke 5.12)[1] and that he saw Jesus (Luke 5.12). If one may designate these details of the Lukan account as clarifications it is still important to remember that they are brought about in Luke by the expansion of the descriptive wording.

Matthew, who presents the shortest of all the three Synoptic accounts, abbreviates the descriptive part almost completely. Generally he substitutes formal expressions for it which are not illustrative at all but typical.[2] Thus in Matt. 8.2a there is no longer any narrative but only the introduction of the request, and likewise Matt. 8.3b is simply an echo of Jesus' word of authority, firmly attached by means of the catchword καθαρίζειν. In this way Matthew has put the conversation of Jesus with the sick man more decidedly in the middle than is the case even in Mark. In his case there comes clearly to expression, what is somewhat concealed in Mark by the

[1] Doubtless a heightening of the disease; cf. E. Klostermann, ad loc., and T. Zahn, p. 334.
[2] Cf. Matt. 8.2 with 9.18.!

many descriptive details, that this miracle story consists of speech and counter-speech: of the request for healing and the word of authority through which the healing takes place.[1]

This clarification is not reached, however, by the abbreviation of the descriptive element alone and its standardisation but also by means of the repetitions of the word καθαρίζειν within so small a space. This catchword links the separate parts of the pericope with each other and by the similarity of sound gives it as a whole something of a formal nature. Matthew could have avoided this if, like Luke, he had chosen the other formulation from Mark 1.42.[2] He did not do this, but constructed the remarkable statement that the leprosy became clean. Herein he differs from that elegant stylist Luke, who as far as possible avoids such repetitions. Matthew, like Luke, finds the threefold occurrence of καθαρίζειν in Mark, but works out this repetition more strongly, by using brevity in the descriptive part of the pericope on the one hand and by retaining καθαρίζειν in the third place on the other.

Hence for the Matthaean reproduction of the Markan narrative the following characteristics must be set out:

(a) Matthew abbreviates the descriptive element or displaces it by his own formal linguistic usage at the beginning and the end of the miracle story.

(b) The threefold use of the word καθαρίζειν is retained and the similarity of its sound is brought out.

(c) The conversational character of this healing miracle stands out clearly in that the descriptive moment is entirely subordinated to the conversation: it forms the introduction and the conclusion.

2. The healing of the woman with the haemorrhage

The considerable abbreviation by Matthew (Matt. 9.20–22) in comparison with the Markan narrative (Mark 5.25–34) poses first of all the question whether Matthew is really dependent on Mark here or is not rather following another tradition of his own. The following considerations make it very improbable, however, that Matthew is independent of Mark. The placing of the miracle story within the

---

[1] The saying of Jesus to the man who had been healed (Mark 1.44 and par.) does not belong to the actual miracle story and is not considered in this context.

[2] Mark 1.42 καὶ εὐθὺς ἀπῆλθεν ἀπ' αὐτοῦ ἡ λέπρα, καὶ ἐκαθαρίσθη.

Luke 5.13 καὶ εὐθέως ἡ λέπρα ἀπῆλθεν ἀπ' αὐτοῦ.

Matt. 8.3 καὶ εὐθέως ἐκαθαρίσθη αὐτοῦ ἡ λέπρα.

narrative of the raising of Jairus' daughter is only intelligible in connexion with Mark's account of this story since it there brings out the
halt in the journey, during which the child which is sick unto death
does, in fact, die. The behaviour of the woman, who comes to Jesus
'from behind' and desires to touch 'only' his garment, is only intelligible in the situation which Mark depicts, namely that Jesus is
hemmed in by a great crowd. The same applies to the remark that
Jesus turns round and sees the woman.[1] Finally Matthew follows the
Markan account both with regard to order and the choice of words.
Dependence on Mark is seen in the following passages:

Matt. 9.20a αἱμορροοῦσα.   Mark 5.25 ἐν ῥύσει αἵματος.
Matt. 9.20b προσελθοῦσα.   Mark 5.27 ἐλθοῦσα.
Matt. 9.22 στραφείς.   Mark 5.30 ἐπιστραφείς.
Matt. 9.22 ἰδὼν αὐτήν.   Mark 5.32 ἰδεῖν τὴν τοῦτο ποιήσασαν.

Thus here also one must firmly retain the dependence of Matthew
upon Mark and also at the same time ascribe the formal arrangement of this miracle story to Matthew's conscious fashioning.

It is noticeable that two or three of the Matthaean verses contain
a direct speech which, through the absence of all the intervening
scenes in Mark (Mark 5.29–33) have been brought together to form
a kind of conversation. Granted the 'speech' of the woman only
reproduces her own thoughts, as Matthew expressly emphasises
(Matt. 9.21 ἐν ἑαυτῇ). The structure of the conversation is not
affected by that, however, since the speech of Jesus in reply, as it
were, deals with the behaviour and thinking of the woman, as is
made clear above all by the connecting catchword (Matt. 9.21
σωθήσομαι/Matt. 9.22 σέσωκέν σε). In the middle of the Matthaean
arrangement there thus stands the 'conversation' of Jesus with the
sick woman. And further still: this conversation is the real content
of the miracle story. This is brought about by altering the order of
the events as they are reported by Mark and Luke. There the healing
is already mentioned before the utterance of Jesus, immediately after
the touching of his garment (Mark 5.29; Luke 8.44). Here, however,
the healing itself is removed from the centre to the circumference so
that the answer of Jesus immediately follows the woman's speech.
That is why the saying about saving faith no longer limps along

[1] The multitude is mentioned in Mark 5.24 already. In Mark 5.27 with reference to the coming of the woman and in Mark 5.30 with reference to where Jesus
stood it is expressly stated: ἐν τῷ ὄχλῳ.

behind as it does in Mark and Luke (Mark 5.34; Luke 8.48). There it must be understood as a confirmation and interpretation of the miracle which has already taken place and it only gains meaning through additional items after the healing has taken place.[1] In Matthew's arrangement it is the saying which brings the healing about, as is shown by the registering of the miracle which follows— and this is done not only by positioning but again by the express linking of catchwords (Matt. 9.22 ἡ πίστις σου σέσωκέν σε. καὶ ἐσώθη ἡ γυνή . . .).

As with the healing of the leper, this threefold linkage by means of a catchword in Matthew is brought out all the more through the deletion of Mark's intervening verses and is underlined by the use of σῴζειν in the concluding verse.[2] In this way not only is the external coherence of the story established but there is also expressed a clear link between the woman's faith, which is expressed in Matt. 9.20–21 by action and 'speech', and her healing.

This passage provides confirmation of the conclusion already reached above that the extraordinarily marked abbreviation of the Markan narrative is undertaken for positive reasons.[3] The catch-word linkage between the faith of the woman and her cure indicates that Matthew's retelling of the story is, in fact, intended to be an illustration of the saying about saving faith. Because Matthew's concern is to instruct not to narrate, his descriptive parts remain very bare. His formalistic use of language is again seen for instance in προσελθοῦσα (Matt. 9.20) for ἐλθοῦσα (Mark 5.27) or in the formation of the concluding sentence (Matt. 9.22b; cf. 8.13; 15.28; 17.18).

If the characteristics of the Matthaean version of this story are brought together the following points emerge:

(a) The descriptive part is radically abbreviated down to a few more or less formal intimations at the beginning and the end of the pericope.

---

[1] By Mark 5.34; Luke 8.48 the healing which has taken place is interpreted as a result of faith, which was expressed in the touching of the garment. Moreover, the addition, 'Go in peace' (Mark and Luke) makes the saying about saving faith a word of comfort for the anxious woman (Mark 5.33; Luke 8.47). The second addition in Mark (5.34: καὶ ἴσθι ὑγιὴς ἀπὸ τῆς μάστιγός σου) confirms, by means of the saying of Jesus, the healing which has already taken place through contact and shows that this surreptitious healing through mere contact was felt to be unusual.

[2] It is significant that for the sake of his catchword connexion Matthew uses ἐσώθη and not ἰάθη as in 8.13 and 15.28.

[3] Cf. above, pp. 178 f.

(*b*) All intervening scenes and all subordinate persons have dis-appeared (the multitude and the disciples) so that only the encounter of Jesus and the sick woman remains.

(*c*) Through the abbreviation of the Markan narrative a clear bridge of catchwords has arisen and been developed.

(*d*) In the middle there now stands the 'conversation' which reaches its climax in the saying about saving faith.

It is very instructive to compare this Matthaean version of the story with that of Luke. The third evangelist shows himself, like Mark, to be a narrator, though, of course, his narrative is clearer and simpler than Mark's (Luke 8.43–48). Thus he impressively abridges the story of the sick woman (8.43 for Mark 5.25 f.) and produces a 'more considered arrangement'[1] in Luke 8.45–46 for Mark 5.30–31. He leaves out some details of the Markan account, doubtless to improve the clarity and easy flow of the narrative.[2] Nevertheless he retains all the stylistic elements of the miracle story present in Mark: the detailed description of the sickness, the healing through contact, its sudden inception as well as the peculiar sequel between Jesus and the sick woman. The observation that a δύναμις has gone out of the miracle-worker is not made by the narrator but by Jesus himself (Luke 8.46). Jesus thus designates himself as the bearer of a mysteri-ous 'power'. The futile attempt of the restored woman to hide from Jesus (Luke 8.47) corresponds to this heightening of the miraculous traits in the person of Jesus. Her anxiety in the presence of the person of the miracle-worker is the more understandable: 'She is conscious of guilt because she has taken advantage of the miraculous power of Jesus without his consent.'[3]

It has already been pointed out[4] that Luke has further heightened the miraculous character of the narrative by emphasising the futility of the physicians' art and, by way of contrast, the immediacy of the healing, which is expressly announced to the multitude. The 'form' of the Lukan version is quite consciously that of a miracle story, a 'tale' in Dibelius' sense.

In this context the circumstance is seen to be of importance that Luke passes over the 'speech' of the woman (Mark 5.28 = Matt.

[1] Cf. E. Klostermann, *Lukas.*, p. 103.
[2] E.g., Mark 5.26 καὶ πολλὰ παθοῦσα ὑπὸ πολλῶν ἰατρῶν and Mark 5.27 ἀκούσασα τὰ περὶ τοῦ Ἰησοῦ and also Mark 5.29 . . . καὶ ἔγνω τῷ σώματι ὅτι ἴαται ἀπὸ τῆς μάστιγος.
[3] E. Klostermann, *Markus.*, p. 52.
[4] Cf. above, pp. 180 f.

9.21), possibly for reasons of style, since in Mark and Matthew it depicts a basis, brought in after the event, for the extraordinary behaviour of the woman and it interrupts the natural connexion between the contact and the cure. This very verse was indispensable for Matthew, however, since it expresses the faith of the sick woman and makes the saying of Jesus about saving faith intelligible. But Luke obviously lays no emphasis on this matter. The concluding sentence about saving faith (Luke 8.48) sounds like an afterthought in his case and Mark's and is not firmly wrought into the story as it is in Matthew.

In this passage the difference between the two evangelists can be seen: to Matthew the miracle story is the bearer of a doctrine and he works this clearly out by giving scant attention to matters of description and actuality. Luke sees in the narrative a miracle story and lays obvious stress on the corresponding features, having in mind a simple and easy-flowing account of what happened.

3. *The Healing of the Two Blind Men*

This healing story is reported twice by Matthew, once as with the other Synoptic writers on the journey of Jesus to Jerusalem (Matt. 20.29–34; cf. Mark 10.46–52 and Luke 18.35–43) and the other time in a cycle of the miracles by Jesus (Matt. 9.27–31). The relationship between the two narratives in Matthew's Gospel is made clear by a number of observations.

In the first place there are actual agreements: In both two blind men are healed by Jesus, and both by contact, details which are peculiar to Matthew in comparison with Mark 10 and Luke 18. In both cases the healing does not take place immediately, but only after a renewed request by the blind men.[1] Finally, before both the healings Jesus engages in an unusual conversation with his petitioners. In addition there are linguistic agreements: the use of παράγειν in Matt. 9.27 and 20.30, of ἀκολουθεῖν in Matt. 9.27 and 20.29 and of ἅπτεσθαι in Matt. 9.29 and 20.34.

These agreements in matters of fact and language support the conclusion that the healing of the blind men in Matt. 9.27 ff. is a retelling of the Matthaean version of the Synoptic healing of the blind men at Jericho in Matt. 20.29–34. This conclusion can be expressed in the following way: the evangelist Matthew has twice retold the incident of the healing of the blind men in Mark 10.46–52,

---

[1] That is how the expression ἐλθόντι δὲ εἰς τὴν οἰκίαν προσῆλθον αὐτῷ οἱ τυφλοί (Matt. 9.28) must be interpreted in the context.

once in close dependence on Mark's example (Matt. 20) and the
second time in greater independence of this original (Matt. 9). The
second retelling has fallen out much more Matthaean than the first,
in which the connexion with the Markan original has been more
carefully preserved.

In the linguistic dress in Matt. 9.27 ff. one can already recognise
the evangelist: the remarkable constructions at the beginning of
verses 27 and 28 correspond to the Matthaean reconstruction at the
beginning of the story of the stilling of the storm:

9.27: καὶ παράγοντι ἐκεῖθεν τῷ Ἰησοῦ ἠκολούθησαν αὐτῷ[1] δύο τυφλοί . . .

9.28: ἐλθόντι δὲ εἰς τὴν οἰκίαν — προσῆλθον — αὐτῷ οἱ τυφλοί . . .

8.23: καὶ ἐμβάντι αὐτῷ εἰς τὸ πλοῖον ἠκολούθησαν αὐτῷ οἱ μαθηταὶ
αὐτοῦ . . .[2]

The placing of the title 'son of David' after the cry for mercy is a
peculiarity of Matthew (cf. Matt. 9.27; 15.22; 20.30, 31 with Mark
10.47, 48 and Luke 18.38, 39).

Finally the healing word of Jesus to the two blind men in Matt.
9.29 is seen to be a typical formulation of Matthew's which he also
uses in a similar way in two other places:

Matt. 9.29 κατὰ τὴν πίστιν   γενηθήτω ὑμῖν
Matt. 8.13 ὡς ἐπίστευσας   γενηθήτω σοι
Matt. 15.28   γενηθήτω σοι ὡς θέλεις

These linguistic observations confirm the conclusion that Matt.
9.27 ff. presents a Matthaean retelling of the Synoptic healing of the
blind men in Matt. 20.29–34. On the basis of this conclusion this free
Matthaean reproduction is particularly revealing for his treatment
of the miracle story and its form. One can observe Matthew's handi-
work, as it were, in two stages, on the way from Mark 10 to Matthew
20 and from Matthew 20 to Matthew 9. It is to be expected that the
uniqueness of the first evangelist will come out most clearly in the
second stage, of course.

Matt. 20.29–34

In the first place we again come across the omission of descriptive

---

[1] The omission of αὐτῷ by the manuscripts B, D and k can best be understood
as the removal of the double and stylistically clumsy second dative. Later insertion
is more difficult to understand.

[2] Cf. also the Matthaean transitional sentences:

Matt. 5.1b   καὶ καθίσαντος αὐτοῦ   προσῆλθαν αὐτῷ οἱ μαθηταὶ αὐτοῦ . . .
Matt. 8.1   καταβάντος δὲ αὐτοῦ   ἠκολούθησαν αὐτῷ ὄχλοι πολλοί . . .
    ἀπὸ τοῦ ὄρους
Matt. 20.29   καὶ ἐκπορευομένων αὐτῶν   ἠκολούθησεν αὐτῷ ὄχλος πολύς.
    ἀπὸ Ἰεριχὼ

details. That the blind man was a beggar (Mark 10.46 = Luke 18.35) is left out as a decorative non-essential. The extremely lively scene of the coming of the blind man to Jesus (Mark 10.49 f.) has disappeared, or been altered (Matt. 20.32a). The concluding remark that the cured man followed Jesus towards Jerusalem has been abbreviated by the omission of the place name so that the act of following carries a general meaning. Thus in the Matthaean version all concrete details have been expunged in so far as they do not belong essentially to the narrative, as the command to the multitude to keep silence and the second cry for help do (Matt. 20.31).

Why Matthew leaves out the saying about saving faith (Mark 10.52 = Luke 18.42) and adds the new traits of the mercy of Jesus and the healing through contact (Matt. 20.34) can only be conjectured.[1] At all events the meaning cannot be that Matthew does not look on the attitude of the two blind men as evidencing saving faith, for the parallel passage (Matt. 9.29) contradicts this. The new Matthaean data can scarcely be regarded as an increase of concrete details, however, since the exercise of mercy by Jesus is a typical Matthaean trait[2] and the touching of the eyes must be understood as a stylistic healing technique.

The consequence of the abbreviation of the descriptive part is that all unimportant circumstances (Mark 10.46, begging), all secondary people (Mark 10.46, the disciples and Mark 10.49, the multitude), and all subordinate scenes (Mark 10.50, the running of the blind man to Jesus) are omitted. The blind men are no longer called to Jesus by the mediation of the multitude, but Jesus addresses himself directly to them.[3] In this way he replies directly to the second request of the blind men. By doing this, however, Matthew has developed the conversation in this miracle story, too, and placed it in the centre. The main section of the story in Matthew consists basically of three pieces of conversation: the cry of the blind men—the multitude's command to them to keep quiet (20.30b, 31a); the second cry of the blind men—the call of Jesus (20.31b, 32a); the question of Jesus—

[1] The theme of the Matthaean narrative is manifestly not saving faith but the mercy of Jesus towards the blind men, whose eyes he opens for his way and the following of it (cf. its being placed after Matt.'20.20–28).

[2] Cf. below, pp. 258 f.

[3] Although Luke likewise markedly abbreviates the Markan scene of Mark 10.49–50 in his case the multitude nevertheless retains its mediating role: Luke 18.40 σταθεὶς δὲ ὁ Ἰησοῦς ἐκέλευσεν αὐτὸν ἀχθῆναι πρὸς αὐτόν. Thus it is only Matthew who attaches importance to the immediacy between Jesus and the sick men.

the reply of the sick men (20.32b, 33). The introduction of this conversation (Matt. 20.30a) remains, through the omission of the name
and the detail about begging (Mark 10.46), still more schematic than
the original, and the same holds for the concluding sentence in
Matt. 20.34b through the omission of 'on the way' (Mark 10.52).

By this formulation Matthew still preserves the structure of the
Markan narrative which offered him these three pieces of conversation and likewise consists almost exclusively of conversational scenes.
In the light of the Markan narrative it is already difficult to speak of
a typical miracle story.[1] Though Matthew brings out the conversational situation more strongly, it must be recognised that he introduces nothing really new into the traditional material in his version,
but interprets it appropriately.

As characteristics of the Matthaean version here again the following
points must be mentioned:

(a) The abbreviation of the descriptive portions, so far as they are
not essential for the pericope.

(b) The removal of all incidental people, subordinate scenes and
non-essential actions with the result that the encounter of Jesus with
the blind men stands out clearly and directly.

(c) By the omission of the scene of Mark 10.50 all description of
the blind men has vanished and they are simply presented as blind
and suppliant.

(d) The conversation between Jesus and the blind men has the
sole place in the story.

The procedure of Luke in reproducing this healing story of Jericho is
characteristic again for him. He, too, almost exclusively presents pieces
of conversation, and even adds a new one between the blind man and
the multitude (Luke 18.36 f.). The very insertion of this scene,
however, shows that Luke was interested in the way in which the
blind man 'heard that it was Jesus of Nazareth' (Mark 10.47). Thus
we learn that he enquired with determination (ἐπυνθάνετο,
imperfect) and was given an answer. In a similar way it is made
clear how the blind man came to Jesus. In view of his complete
blindness it is somewhat improbable that he came to Jesus (Mark
10.50).[2] Hence Luke reports more suitably that Jesus commanded

---

[1] Cf. R. Bultmann, *SynT*, p. 213; M. Dibelius, *Formgesch.*, p. 49; and O. Perels,
Die Wunderüberlieferung der Synoptiker, p. 42.

[2] Cf. V. Taylor, *The Gospel . . . Mark*, p. 449: 'The fact that he is able to
approach Jesus unaided suggests that his blindness is not total. . . .'

that the man should be brought to him (Luke 18.40). Thus Luke regards the incident, like a picture, as a completed event and, like a good reporter, gives a clear presentation of it—an interest which is not present in Matthew at all. For precisely the question how the sick man came to Jesus, from whom the multitude separated him, Matthew leaves completely open, although he mentions that the multitude surrounded the blind men and later that Jesus healed them by contact.

Most characteristic, however, is the conclusion of the pericope in Luke. He reports a word of command by Jesus at the healing, ἀνάβλεψον (Luke 18.42) and tells how both the sick man and the crowd, whom he expressly understands as witnesses of the miracle, and to that extent needs in his presentation (Luke 18.43), praise God. As in the story of the woman with the haemorrhage, here, too, he follows the literary form of the ancient healing miracle in which the praise of God and the publication of the miracle before all the people have their firm place.[1] Since Luke has introduced these additions, the healing saying and the twofold praise of God, into the Markan text they must have been important for him. As typical traits of a current miracle narrative they reveal his intention: he interprets the healing of the blind men as a typical miracle, an interest absent from Mark and on which no traceable emphasis is laid in Matthew in spite of his addition of Matt. 20.34a.

Matt. 9.27–31

It has been said that this case of the healing of a blind man, which is peculiar to Matthew is not 'told . . . with any love'.[2] In view of the fact, however, that the evangelist has found it necessary to report the healing of the blind man here once again, one would expect, on the contrary, that special care would be taken in the presentation of it. It must be granted that the evangelist shows no particular love for this narrative as such. Rather here, too, all illustrative narration is left on one side. There is no longer anything to point to a concrete and unique event. The descriptive details are very colourless:

Matt. 9.27 . . . παράγοντι ἐκεῖθεν, ἠκολούθησαν

Matt. 9.28 ἐλθόντι δὲ εἰς τὴν οἰκίαν, προσῆλθον αὐτῷ . . .

---

[1] Cf. O. Weinreich, *Antike Heilswunder*, p. 116, who, among the typical points in the miracle inscriptions of the shrine of Asclepius on the island in the Tiber at Rome, cites the following: The person healed comes and praises God before all the people; all the people rejoice with him. Cf. also above, p. 181, note 1.

[2] J. Wellhausen, *Matthaei*, p. 43; similarly E. Klostermann, p. 83.

Matt. 9.29 τότε ἥψατο τῶν ὀφθαλμῶν αὐτῶν . . .

Matt. 9.30 καὶ ἠνεῴχθησαν αὐτῶν οἱ ὀφθαλμοί.

All unimportant people are omitted. Although the multitude played some sort of a role in the healing of the blind men in Matthew 20, since their attempt to silence them was the necessary presupposition for the second request, nevertheless Jesus and the blind face each other here alone.

In the centre stands the conversation of Jesus with the blind men which accompanied the healing and that has to do with faith. The healing saying of Jesus in Matt. 9.29 κατὰ τὴν πίστιν ὑμῶν γενηθήτω ὑμῖν is new in comparison with the healing of the blind men in Matthew 20 and is doubtless the climax of the whole pericope. The introduction of this saying about faith, which in its formulation and content is Matthaean (cf. Matt. 8.13; 15.28; 17.20), must be due to a special interest of the evangelist. For the whole pericope is planned around this saying, as the preceding conversation shows, for in it is unfolded wherein faith consists (Matt. 9.28b, 29). The catchword bridge in 9.28 πιστεύετε/9.29 πίστιν which encloses the conversation of Jesus with the blind men, also points to this connexion. In comparison with Matt. 20.32, 33 this conversation has been shaped completely afresh—from the angle of saving faith.[1]

If one desires to pronounce a judgment on the form of this account of the healing of the blind men one must say that Matthew is not here presenting a miracle story, but a kind of ideal scene in which he wishes to illustrate the essence of that faith which belongs to the miracle.[2] He carefully omits all dispensable details in order to produce a really typical story. It is thus, in fact, correct that he does not *tell* the story with love, but it is inappropriate to see here solely a variant of Matt. 20.29–34.[3] For Matthew has fashioned this variant

[1] The thought of saving faith is not mentioned in Matt. 20.29 ff., but it is anchored in the parallel traditions (Mark 10.46 ff. and Luke 18.35 ff.) and is to this extent not entirely new in Matt. 9, but only in comparison with Matt. 20.

[2] The notion of 'ideal scenes' is used by R. Bultmann in connexion with the form of the controversy and scholastic dialogues in the Synoptic tradition (*SynT*, pp. 39 ff.). According to his definition a scene which can be 'designated' ideal is one 'which has its origin not in a historical situation but in an idea which it is intended to illustrate by means of a picture' (p. 47, note 1; cf. pp. 39 f.). In our context no historical judgment is given by the use of the concept. For it may well be that an historical event may be at the basis of the healing of the blind men. The concept is used strictly in the form-critical sense, meaning that in an ideal scene a principle is illustrated by means of an occurrence.

[3] Thus E. Klostermann, p. 83.

with great care, not indeed as a narrator but as a teacher who gives instruction about faith.

Consequently a noteworthy process can be observed in the development of the healing of the blind men from Mark 10 via Matthew 20 to Matthew 9. This occurrence must be described in the following way. The story is divested of its narrative character, at first partially and then completely. The secondary people retire at first half-way and then completely. The conversation between Jesus and the blind men occupies more and more room; the problem of how they come to Jesus becomes to the same degree unimportant. Finally the conversation accompanying the healing alone comes to occupy the centre. The theme of saving faith, suggested from the beginning, at last enters the arena in a new form and then alone dominates the conversation. Out of a descriptive miracle narrative with highly individualistic traits there comes an ideal scene, a paradigm, which illustrates the faith to which a miracle is granted.

This process can serve, like a model, to show the peculiarity of Matthew in his reproduction of the miracle stories. And one can recognise the form towards which the miracle stories in Matthew are pressing. Even if the development of this form is not everywhere so far advanced as it is in the case of the healing of the blind men in Matthew 9, similar phenomena can nevertheless be observed everywhere. This can be seen first of all in a comparison of the three examples so far considered. The following characteristics are common to them:

(a) The recession of the descriptive element and the predominance of formal expressions, particularly at the beginning and the end.

(b) The leaving out of all secondary people and secondary actions.

(c) The increasing meaning of the conversation between the suppliant and Jesus.

(d) The appearance of catchword connexions within the pericope.

(e) The role of faith, which is developed in conversation.

B. *Formal characteristics in the Matthaean miracle stories*

The five characteristics discovered in the previous section must now also be sought in the other miracle stories of Matthew's Gospel and objectively assessed.

1. *The formal mode of narration*

It has been shown that Matthew not only greatly abbreviates the descriptive parts of the healing miracles but that in his reproduction he also makes use of formula-like expressions, especially at the beginning and the end.

First of all the *introductions* of the Matthaean healing miracles must be compared with each other:

8.2 καὶ ἰδοὺ λεπρὸς προσελθὼν προσεκύνει αὐτῷ λέγων . . .

8.5b . . . προσῆλθεν αὐτῷ ἑκατόνταρχος παρακαλῶν αὐτὸν καὶ λέγων . . .

9.18b . . . ἰδοὺ ἄρχων εἷς προσελθὼν προσεκύνει αὐτῷ λέγων . . .

9.20 καὶ ἰδοὺ γυνὴ αἱμορροοῦσα δώδεκα ἔτη προσελθοῦσα ὄπισθεν ἥψατο τοῦ κρασπέδου τοῦ ἱματίου αὐτοῦ

9.28 . . . ἐλθόντι δὲ εἰς τὴν οἰκίαν προσῆλθον αὐτῷ οἱ τυφλοί

15.22 καὶ ἰδοὺ γυνὴ Χαναναία ἀπὸ τῶν ὁρίων ἐκείνων ἐξελθοῦσα ἔκραζεν λέγουσα . . .

17.14b . . . προσῆλθον αὐτῷ ἄνθρωπος γονυπετ ῶναὐτὸν καὶ λέγων . . .

The placing of these together makes it clear that all the beginnings are more or less stereotyped. They are as a rule introductions to the annexed request for help[1] and contain simply the name of the suppliant (when the sick person himself makes the request also the indication of the sickness) and his petitioning approach.[2] In this connexion the following words are often used: προσέρχεσθαι and προσκυνεῖν.

Above all the regular use of forms of προσέρχεσθαι catches the attention (exception Matt. 15.22). This word is typical for Matthew's Gospel.[3] The question arises what is meant by the frequent use of it in the introductions to the miracle stories.

One characteristic can be established in this connexion from the very beginning. The word προσέρχεσθαι nearly always denotes the approach of others to Jesus.[4] Of course, the word is also occasionally used by Matthew when it is a matter of the approach of one man to another. This is shown by the account of Peter's denial (Matt. 26.69–75). In this very place a comparison with the Synoptic parallels is revealing. To take first of all the first scene of the denial:

---

[1] Matt. 9.20 is an exception; in Matt. 9.28 the approach must without doubt be understood as a renewed request, cf. above, p. 219, note 1.

[2] The healing of the blind men in Matt. 20.29 ff. is not considered here because in view of its special content there is no mention of an approach in the introduction to it.

[3] According to Bauer, *s.* προσέρχομαι, Matthew uses it about fifty times.

[4] Cf. J. Schneider, *TWNT*, II, pp. 681, 29 ff.

Matt. 26.69 καὶ προσῆλθεν αὐτῷ μία παιδίσκη λέγουσα . . .

Mark 14.66, 67 . . . ἔρχεται μία τῶν παιδισκῶν τοῦ ἀρχιερέως, καὶ ἰδοῦσα τὸν Πέτρον θερμαινόμενον ἐμβλέψασα αὐτῷ λέγει . . .

Luke 22.56 . . . ἰδοῦσα δὲ αὐτὸν παιδίσκη τις καθήμενον πρὸς τὸ φῶς καὶ ἀτενίσασα αὐτῷ εἶπεν . . .

From the contrast between the detailed and vivid presentation in Mark and Luke and the sparsity of Matthew, the tame and formal mode of expression of the first evangelist contained in the words προσῆλθεν αὐτῷ λέγουσα, stands out clearly. Obviously he is only concerned about the spoken words that follow.

Looking, then, at the third scene of the denial:

Matt. 26.73 μετὰ μικρὸν δὲ προσελθόντες οἱ ἑστῶτες εἶπον τῷ Πέτρῳ . . .

Mark 14.75 . . . καὶ μετὰ μικρὸν πάλιν οἱ παρεστῶτες ἔλεγον τῷ Πέτρῳ . . .

Luke 22.59 καὶ διαστάσης ὡσεὶ ὥρας μιᾶς ἄλλος τις διϊσχυρίζετο λέγων . . .

It is noteworthy here that Matthew does not abbreviate in comparison with Mark's Gospel, but inserts into the likewise brief Markan sentence the word προσελθόντες, which is really superfluous. For the bystanders have no need first to approach Peter if they wish to speak with him. In other words: the combination of the forms of προσέρχεσθαι and λέγειν is manifestly a fixed formula of Matthew's in introducing conversations.

The whole of Matthew's Gospel supports this conclusion, especially when compared with the other Synoptic parallels. As in Matt. 26.73, Matthew loves to insert forms of προσέρχεσθαι in the introduction fully-reported speech; for example:

Matt. 4.3 καὶ προσελθὼν ὁ πειράζων εἶπεν αὐτῷ . . .

Luke 4.3 εἶπεν δὲ αὐτῷ ὁ διάβολος . . .

Matt. 8.19 καὶ προσελθὼν εἷς γραμματεὺς εἶπεν αὐτῷ . . .

Luke 9.57 . . . εἶπέν τις πρὸς αὐτόν . . .

Matt. 24.3 . . . προσῆλθον αὐτῷ οἱ μαθηταὶ κατ' ἰδίαν λέγοντες

Mark 13.3 . . . ἐπηρώτα αὐτὸν κατ' ἰδίαν Πέτρος . . .

Luke 21.7 ἐπηρώτησαν δὲ αὐτὸν λέγοντες . . .

Matt. 26.17 . . . προσῆλθον οἱ μαθηταὶ τῷ Ἰησοῦ λέγοντες . . .

Mark 14.12 . . . λέγουσιν αὐτῷ οἱ μαθηταὶ αὐτοῦ . . .

Luke 22.9 οἱ δὲ εἶπαν αὐτῷ . . .

Where Matthew formulates introductions to conversations which belong to his special material, the same formula-like connexion again appears, as, for example, in Matt. 15.12 and Matt. 18.21. The same applies where he reformulates introductions to conversations in Mark, in a shorter form:

Matt. 13.10 καὶ προσελθόντες οἱ μαθηταὶ εἶπαν αὐτῷ . . .

    Mark 4.10 καὶ ὅτε ἐγένετο κατὰ μόνας ἠρώτων αὐτὸν οἱ περὶ αὐτὸν σὺν τοῖς δώδεκα τὰς παραβολάς . . .

Matt. 17.19 τότε προσελθόντες οἱ μαθηταὶ τῷ Ἰησοῦ κατ᾽ ἰδίαν εἶπον . . .

    Mark 9.28 καὶ εἰσελθόντος αὐτοῦ εἰς οἶκον οἱ μαθηταὶ αὐτοῦ κατ᾽ ἰδίαν ἐπηρώτων αὐτόν . . .

And finally the controversy and scholastic conversations in Matthew's Gospel are throughout introduced by the same formula-like expression, in so far as they begin with a question, for example, Matt. 9.14 (cf. Mark 2.18; Luke 5.33); Matt. 15.1 (cf. Mark 7.1 ff.) and Matt. 18.1 (Mark 9.33 ff.; Luke 9.46); further Matt. 19.16 (cf. Mark 10.17; Luke 18.18) and Matt. 21.23 (cf. Mark 11.27 f.; Luke 20.1.2).

    This chain of examples clearly shows that the combination of προσέρχεσθαι and λέγειν is, in fact, a stereotyped formula of Matthew's for the introduction of speeches and conversations. Our glimpse at the parallel passages in the Synoptics shows that, on the one hand, he inserts them into brief introductions to conversations, but on the other he refashions existing sentences by means of them or displaces by them a richer more vivid Markan introduction. The latter observation in particular is very revealing, for it corresponds to the findings in the introductions to the healing stories, in which the formalistic expression has likewise largely superseded more detailed information, as, for example, in Matt. 8.2; 9.18, 20; 17.14.

    Thus there issues in Matthew's Gospel a certain parallelism between the introductions of the healing stories on the one hand and the controversy and scholastic conversations on the other, especially as the word προσέρχεσθαι is frequently followed in the miracle stories by a quotation (Matt. 8.2; 9.18) or by a normal conversation (Matt. 8.5; 9.20; 17.14). In both the combination of προσέρχεσθαι and λέγειν has become a formula for introducing a conversation and has no descriptive function, but rather gives the impression of conformity to a type.[1] The intention is obviously to direct attention from the individual unique event to the general doctrine, or rather, proclamation contained in what follows.

    [1] Thus in the cases discussed here it is questionable whether the participle of προσέρχομαι serves 'to enliven the narrative', as Bauer, s.v., thinks.

Alongside προσέρχεσθαι there is to be found three times in the introductions to the healing miracles the quite formalistic word προσκυνεῖν:

Matt. 8.2   καὶ ἰδοὺ λεπρὸς προσελθὼν προσεκύνει αὐτῷ λέγων ...

Matt. 9.18 ἰδοὺ ἄρχων εἷς προσελθὼν προσεκύνει αὐτῷ λέγων ...

Matt. 15.25   ἡ δὲ ἐλθοῦσα προσεκύνει αὐτῷ λέγουσα ...

In these cases too it is not so much a matter of narrating as of bringing into conformity to a type. For προσκυνεῖν denotes worship of the Lord. The use of the word in Matthew makes that clear. It is plain that προσκυνεῖν is one of his favourite words. Luke has it, apart from the passage Matt. 4.9, 10 = Luke 4.7, 8, only once (Luke 24.52), in reference to the worship of the risen Lord in heaven.[1] Mark uses it twice, in Mark 5.6 in reference to the subjection of the demon and in Mark 15.19 at the mocking of Jesus. In Matthew's Gospel it is never used by enemies or mockers, but only in the sense of genuine worship of Jesus: Matt. 2.2, 8, 11 in the story of the wise men, Matt. 14.33; 28.9, 17 with reference to the circle of the disciples and similarly in Matt. 18.26[2] and then in Matt. 8.2; 9.18; 15.25 and 20.20 by suppliants. In all these places the evangelist has inserted the word into the tradition. When that has also happened in the introductions to the miracle stories it is obviously intended that, of the incident recorded there in the life of Jesus, only the situation of adoring petition shall be kept in mind, and that is still accessible to the believing congregation in the presence of her Lord.[3]

That such a conforming to type has not been equally effected in all the miracle stories is no doubt due to the fact that Matthew felt bound to the tradition. He has only used the word προσκυνεῖν where

[1] If the reading of the Egyptian and Byzantine group of texts is original.

[2] In line with the whole address to the disciples (Matt. 18) the servant in the parable is certainly a member of the congregation.

[3] J. Horst, Proskynein, Gütersloh, 1932, pp. 217 ff., distinguishes between the petitioning worship of Matt. 8.2; 9.18; 15.25 as a kind of non-religious act of homage, such as was also customary in the presence of Rabbis (pp. 64 f.), and the adoring worship of Matt. 14.33; 28.9, 17, which denotes confession of the Son of God or the Risen Lord (p. 186) and which does not precede but follows the epiphany. That προσκυνεῖν in Matt. 8.2; 9.18; 15.25; 18.26 is a gesture of supplication is shown not only by the imperfect form (Blass-Debrunner, §328), but also by the relevant passages in Mark, which expressly understand a request, and further by the parallel verses in Matt. 18.26 and 18.29:

18.26 πεσὼν οὖν ὁ δοῦλος   προσεκύνει αὐτῷ λέγων ...
18.29 πεσὼν οὖν ὁ σύνδουλος αὐτοῦ   παρεκάλει αὐτὸν λέγων ...

But this passage in particular shows that Matthew reserves the word προσκυνεῖν for a request to the Lord and does not use it for a request to men. One can therefore not deny the character of adoration to the petitioning worship offered to

Mark had written a similar word.[1] Matthew again shows himself in his interpretation at this point to be altogether a hander-on of tradition.

In other healing miracles, too, formal introductions can be recognised:

Matt. 9.2 καὶ ἰδοὺ προσέφερον αὐτῷ παραλυτικὸν ἐπὶ κλίνης βεβλημένον . . .

Matt. 9.32 ἰδοὺ προσήνεγκαν αὐτῷ κωφὸν δαιμονιζόμενον . . .

Matt. 12.22 τότε προσηνέχθη αὐτῷ δαιμονιζόμενος τυφλὸς καὶ κωφός . . .

In summary reports the same construction occurs:

Matt. 8.16 . . . προσήνεγκαν αὐτῷ δαιμονιζομένους πολλούς . . .

Matt. 14.35 καὶ προσήνεγκαν αὐτῷ πάντας τοὺς κακῶς ἔχοντας . . .

Comparison with the Synoptic parallels shows that the word προσφέρειν is a stereotyped usage of Matthew's for the bringing of the sick to Jesus.

The *conclusion* of the healing miracles likewise exhibits formal language. That can be immediately seen by the following examples:

Matt. 8.13b καὶ ἰάθη ὁ παῖς ἐν τῇ ὥρᾳ ἐκείνῃ

Matt. 9.22b καὶ ἐσώθη ἡ γυνὴ ἀπὸ τῆς ὥρας ἐκείνης

Matt. 15.28b καὶ ἰάθη ἡ θυγάτηρ αὐτῆς ἀπὸ τῆς ὥρας ἐκείνης

Matt. 17.18b καὶ ἐθεραπεύθη ὁ παῖς ἀπὸ τῆς ὥρας ἐκείνης

A look at the corresponding parallel passages in Mark and Luke shows that these, for Matthew typical concluding formulae at the same time supplant detailed narration (cf. Luke 7.10; Mark 5.29–33; Mark 7.30, and Mark 9.26–27). In Matt. 17.18b one can also recognise the formula-like nature of the expression because the sentence after the acknowledgment that the demon has been driven out (Matt. 17.18a) is no longer really necessary. Yet the second formalistic statement here has positive meaning as the express use of the catchword θεραπεύειν in Matt. 17.16 (Mark and Luke ἐκβάλλειν) and Matt. 17.18 shows. It is significant that a similar use of a catchword in two other instances also links the concluding formula with the pericope itself: Matt. 8.8, 13 (ἰᾶσθαι) and Matt. 9.21, 22 (σῴζειν). Thus this concluding formula obviously not only serves as a substitute for purely descriptive matter but it also expresses a positive relationship.

Jesus. On the contrary, Matthew obviously desires to give the requests the character of adoration by his special choice of words.

[1] Cf. the mention of prostration in Mark 1.40; 5.22; 7.25.

The same conclusion is reached with regard to the healing of the leper (Matt. 8.2–4), although there the concluding formula is absent. The brevity of the statement, however, καὶ εὐθέως ἐκαθαρίσθη αὐτοῦ ἡ λέπρα (Matt. 8.3) and the connecting link through the verb καθαρίζειν correspond, essentially, wholly to the position presented above.

Finally, the formula-like recording of the healing in four of the five miracle stories mentioned here follows immediately on the conversation of Jesus with the suppliants, or to be more exact, on the concluding healing saying of Jesus (exception Matt. 17.14 ff.). A similar observation, though not so clear, can be made in the case of the two instances of the healing of the blind men in Matthew 9 and 20, in which Matthew brings out the situation of the conversation especially clearly. A more or less brief introduction and a conclusion as short as it is formal, enclose the conversation, which at least in Matthew 9 ends with the healing saying of Jesus.

Consequently it follows that to the formal beginning of the healing story there corresponds, as a rule, a formal conclusion and both serve as a frame for the conversation of Jesus with the suppliant.[1]

Matthew's formal manner of narrating is to be seen similarly in the miracle stories not yet considered. Thus there are parallel formulations in the two miracle stories in Matthew's Gospel which still bear descriptive traits rather firmly and do not contain any conversation, in the healing of Peter's mother-in-law and in the raising of Jairus' daughter. In the first place this applies at the beginning, or new beginning of both pericopes:

Matt. 8.14 καὶ ἐλθὼν ὁ Ἰησοῦς εἰς τὴν οἰκίαν Πέτρου εἶδεν τὴν πενθερὰν αὐτοῦ . . .

Matt. 9.23 καὶ ἐλθὼν ὁ Ἰησοῦς εἰς τὴν οἰκίαν τοῦ ἄρχοντος καὶ ἰδὼν τοὺς αὐλητάς . . .

The comparison with the parallel passages of Mark shows here, too, that Matthew, by linking on to the material in the tradition, has formed his stereotyped beginning by combining Jesus' coming and the seeing.[2]

Formula-like verbal similarities are found in the two stories of the sea journey in which the danger to the ship is stressed:

[1] A real exception to this rule is only found in Matt. 8.14–15. The exorcisms of the demons (Matt. 8.28–34; 9.32–34) are not healings in the strict sense, and the healing of the paralytic (Matt. 9.2–8) is more a controversy conversation than a healing story.

[2] Cf. Mark 1.29 and Mark 5.38.

Matt. 8.24 ὥστε τὸ πλοῖον καλύπτεσθαι ὑπὸ τῶν κυμάτων

Matt. 14.24 τὸ δὲ πλοῖον . . . βασανιζόμενον ὑπὸ τῶν κυμάτων

Reference should also be made again to the similarity of the cry for help of the disciples in Matt. 8.25 and of Peter in Matt. 14.30.[1]

The command of Jesus in the first feeding story and that at the healing of the epileptic boy are formulated in almost the same words:

Matt. 14.18 φέρετέ μοι ὧδε αὐτούς

Matt. 17.17 φέρετέ μοι αὐτὸν ὧδε

a formulation which is not found at all in the story of the feeding in the other Synoptic writers and which at the healing of the boy is expressed in other terms.[2] Attention has already been drawn to other similar sounding formulations in the two feeding stories in Matthew.[3]

All the observations collected here on the narratives of Matthew's Gospel fit in with what E. von Dobschütz demonstrated as the peculiarity of the evangelist by a study of the tradition of the sayings in the first Gospel: Matthew loves assonances, likes repetition and delights in what is stereotyped.[4] The principle must also be recognised as valid in our context: 'when in Matthew we find the same words in two passages we have to recognise here his work and not tradition.'[5] That in this inclination of the first evangelist towards the stereotyped we are confronted with a catechetical motive[6] would entirely fit in with the perception that behind the retelling of the miracle stories in his Gospel there is his interest in providing instruction.[7]

[1] Cf. above, p. 206.
[2] Cf. Mark 9.19; Luke 9.41.
[3] Cf. above, pp. 183 f.
[4] 'Matthäus als Rabbi und Katechet', *ZNW* 27, 1928, pp. 338 ff.
[5] *Ibid.*, p. 340.
[6] *Ibid.*, pp. 344 f.
[7] This didactic and catechetical interest in the employment of formulae instead of vivid narration can also be seen in other passages of the first evangelist, for example in the story of the finding of the ass (Matt. 21.1b–6) or the room (Matt. 26.17–19). Strictly speaking only the other two evangelists tell of a finding (Mark 11.4; 14.16; Luke 19.32; 22.13: . . . εὖρον . . .) and thus lay emphasis on the confirmation of the wonderful prescience of Jesus. Matthew puts in place of the narration of the finding the formula about the obedience of the disciples:

Matt. 21.6 πορευθέντες δὲ οἱ μαθηταὶ καὶ ποιήσαντες καθὼς συνέταξεν αὐτοῖς
ὁ ᾿Ιησοῦς . . .

Matt. 26.19 καὶ ἐποίησαν οἱ μαθηταὶ   ὡς συνέταξεν αὐτοῖς
ὁ ᾿Ιησοῦς . . .

an expression which he also uses elsewhere (1.24). He is not concerned with the miraculous element, but with the obedience of the disciples to the command of Jesus, and in precisely this way he directs the attention of his Church towards her obedience (cf. Matt. 28.20).

2. *The omission of non-essential people and actions*

This characteristic has already been considered in connexion with the investigation of the abbreviations in the Matthaean miracle stories. It was seen there that the omission of non-essential people and actions is a means of interpretation.[1]

At this point the observation is important that in this way Matthew brings out in striking fashion the law of scenic twofoldness.[2] Only two partners appear in the narratives, or rather, occupy the foreground: Jesus and Peter's mother-in-law (8.14–15), Jesus and the demons (8.28–34, there is no longer any reference to the man healed), Jesus and the scribes (9.2–8, the bearers of the sick man and the multitude appear only at the circumference), Jesus and the disciples (8.18–27, the other ships are no longer mentioned; 14.15–21, the multitude steps into the background).

Whereas in the story of the centurion of Capernaum according to Luke two deputations appear, in Matthew the centurion appears before Jesus alone, and then only as a suppliant.[3] The same applies to the meeting of Jesus with the blind men (Matt. 9.27 ff.; 20.29 ff.), to the woman with the haemorrhage and Jairus (Matt. 9.18–26) and to the father of the epileptic boy (Matt. 17.14–20). The leper (Matt. 8.2–4) and the Canaanite woman (Matt. 15.21–28), also face Jesus alone[4] and are described simply as suppliants. Further, Jairus is no longer worried (cf. Mark 5.36), the woman with the haemorrhage is no longer filled with anxiety (cf. Mark 5.33), the father of the boy is no longer the doubter (cf. Mark 9.22–24) and the blind man no longer comes up to him (cf. Mark 10.50). The people who appear before Jesus are characterised only as suppliants and seeking help.

In this we have an explanation for the conversation between the suppliant and Jesus receiving major emphasis, as also on the other hand for the conversational character of the healing story being strengthened, or only properly established, through the omission of non-essential people and actions.

3. *Conversation as the centre of the miracle stories*

Many of the observations so far made on the form of the Mat-

---

[1] Cf. above, pp. 168 ff.

[2] Cf. R. Bultmann, *SynT*, pp. 307 f.

[3] In Luke the centurion is also described as 'worthy'; cf. above, pp. 195 f.

[4] The mention of the disciples in Matt. 15.23 does not alter this at all, as their speech is only intended as setting for the saying of Jesus in 15.24, which is really directed to the woman, cf. above, p. 198, note 1.

thaean miracle stories point to the fact that for the evangelist the words spoken in them carry decisive meaning as distinct from the descriptive portions. Obviously speech and counter-speech is the thing that matters most for him in the miracle stories.

Of course, there are also in the tradition as it came to him narratives in which the miracle itself does not occupy the centre, but the conversation that precedes it. That is the case, for example, with the healing of the blind man of Jericho (Mark 10.46 ff.), with the centurion of Capernaum (Matt. 8.8–10 = Luke 7.7b–9) and with the Canaanite woman (Mark 7.24–30). The conversation of Jesus with the suppliant has here pushed the miracle to the side. It is Matthew, however, who in all three cases brings out the conversational character of these stories most clearly. This can be shown most effectively by means of the story of the centurion.

Whereas Luke sets the conversation between Jesus and the centurion in the framework of a normal story and gives it a purely descriptive beginning (Luke 7.2–3) and a similarly descriptive ending (Luke 7.10) and arranges it in a novelistic fashion,[1] Matthew reports in all only one dialogue consisting of two pieces of conversation, the introduction and conclusion of which are formal, that is, are not intended as descriptive. What matters to the first evangelist is obviously the conversation between the suppliant and Jesus. In the story of the Canaanite woman and the healing of the blind men in Matthew 9 and 20 as well he has placed the conversation completely in the centre. The elements of the miracle story, such as are found in Mark 7.24b and in the clearly typical conclusion[2] of the case of healing from a distance, he has removed, or rather replaced by his stereotyped formulae in Matt. 8.13 and 15.28. But these very formulae, in association with the preceding, similarly stereotyped formula about faith, set the notice of a miraculous event in relationship with the conversation, which in both cases in Matthew Jesus denotes as an expression of faith.

In the other healing stories, too, Matthew lays emphasis on the sections containing speeches. Nearly all his healing miracles begin, after a brief formal introduction, with direct speech: Matt. 8.2;

---

[1] Cf. the heightening of the need (Luke 7.2 ἤμελλεν τελευτᾶν) and the underlining of the personal relationship between the centurion and his servant (Luke 7.2 ὃς ἦν αὐτῷ ἔντιμος).

[2] Note the formalistic nature and the similarity of the two sentences in Mark 7.30 and Luke 7.10.

8.6; 9.18; 9.21; 9.27; 15.22; 17.15; 20.30. The fact of the direct speech gains in importance when it is remembered that Mark and Luke frequently present such a request for healing in indirect speech (Mark 7.26.32; 8.22; Luke 7.3; 8.41), and in one case Luke even omits (Luke 8.44) the speech (thought) of the woman with the haemorrhage which is given in Mark (5.28) and Matthew (9.21). Hence one may conclude, in the first place, that the request addressed to Jesus in direct speech is an essential component in the construction of the healing miracle in Matthew's Gospel.

This request for healing frequently exhibits the same traits. Thus Matthew often uses the form of address κύριε (Matt. 8.2; 8.6; 15.22; 17.15; 20.30, 31), which Mark never uses in a request and Luke only once (Luke 5.12). Further, Matthew shows a liking for the formula ἐλέησον in a request. Besides using it in passages which he has in common with the other Synoptic writers (Matt. 20.30, 31 and then Matt. 9.27) he puts it in two other places on his own responsibility (Matt. 15.22 and 17.15).[1]

Where no proper conversation follows a request as in Matt. 8.5–13; 15.21–28 and 20.29–34 or 9.27–31, there still arises through the healing saying of Jesus which presents his answer to the request, a kind of conversation which forms the chief content of the miracle story. The notice of the miraculous happening itself then sounds like an afterthought (Matt. 8.2–3 and Matt. 9.20–22).

In the story of the raising of Jairus's daughter (Matt. 9.18–26) no actual healing saying of Jesus occurs, yet the action of Jesus in Matt. 9.23–25 is a response to the request expressed by the father in Matt. 9.18 and must to that extent be regarded as an answer to this request.[2] Hence it can be said that there is an element of dialogue here at least in the broader sense.[3]

It is not in the healing miracles alone, however, that Matthew has given conversation a central place. Through the transposition of scenes in the stilling of the storm the evangelist has created a conversation in which Jesus replies to the disciples' cry for help with his reproach on account of their little faith (Matt. 8.25, 26a). By his

---

[1] On this see below, p. 265.

[2] Cf. above, p. 180.

[3] Cf. the use of the notion 'pertaining to a dialogue' in O. Perels 'as an expansion of the usual linguistic usage . . . to denote interchange of persons in conversation *and action* in a narrative . . . for dialogue offers the best image for the pregnant kind of "business" interspersed with conversation' (*Die Wunderüberlieferung der Synoptiker*, p. 59, note 30).

insertion into the story of Jesus's walking on the sea Matthew has given this pericope a conversation at the centre (Matt. 14.28–31). Peter replies to the saying of the Lord and receives a further answer to his request (Matt. 14.27–29a). His cry for help is followed not only by his rescue but again by a reproach for his little faith (Matt. 14.30b–31).

Other passages also show Matthew's predilection for forming or enlarging conversations. Thus in Matt. 18.1 ff. he makes out of Mark 9.33 ff. a regular didactic conversation in which, in reply to a particular question, Jesus gives the relevant answer.[1] In the Sabbath healing of the man with the withered hand (Matt. 12.9–14) he similarly makes out of the Markan text a scholastic conversation in which his opponents appear as questioners and Jesus gives them a professional's answer.[2] In the healing of the paralytic, by omitting the scene of the removal of the roof (Mark 2.4), Matthew places the controversy about power to forgive sins more firmly in the centre. In the controversy about divorce in Matt. 19.3–9 in place of the somewhat disordered Markan version (Mark 10.2–9) he forms two clear exchanges of conversation each with a question and answer (Matt. 19.3/4–6; 7/8–9). The conversation with the rich young man embraces three exchanges, again each with a question and an answer (Matt. 19.16/17; 18a/18b,19; 20/21), whereas Mark and Luke have only two exchanges and only in the first a genuine question. In the second conversation appended to the pericope of the rich young man (Matt. 19.27–30) Matthew lets Peter pose a particular question which is not found in Mark and Luke.[3] At the end of the parable of the wicked husbandmen a conversation follows in Matthew inasmuch as in reply to the final question put by Jesus, it is not the workers who reply but Jesus' opponents (Matt. 21.40–41). Finally, in the controversy about the son of David, instead of the one piece of conversation in Mark and Luke, Matthew has two (Matt. 22.42a/42b; 43–45/46).[4]

This survey shows how very much the evangelist Matthew thinks and writes in the form of conversations. It is not surprising that he

---

[1] Cf. 18.1 (question) τίς ἄρα μείζων ἐστὶν ἐν τῇ βασιλείᾳ τῶν οὐρανῶν;
    18.4 (answer) οὗτός ἐστιν ὁ μείζων ἐν τῇ βασιλείᾳ τῶν οὐρανῶν.
[2] Cf. 12.10 (question) εἰ ἔξεστιν τοῖς σάββασιν θεραπεῦσαι;
    12.12 (answer) ὥστε ἔξεστιν τοῖς σάββασιν καλῶς ποιεῖν.
[3] Matt. 19.27: τί ἄρα ἔσται ἡμῖν;
[4] Of course, there is no reply to the question of Jesus in the second piece of conversation as none was intended (Matt. 22.46: no one was able to answer him a word). But here no answer is nevertheless an answer.

also uses, or rather develops this form in his reproduction of the miracle stories. It should, however, be underlined here also that he only does this where the Markan text has reported a conversation with the suppliant (cf. Matt. 8.2–4; 9.20–22; 15.21–28). He fails to do it where that was not the case (for example, Matt. 9.18 ff.).

4. *Linkage by catchwords within the miracle story*

In the story of the healing of the leper, Matthew has brought out most impressively, by means of his short presentation, the firm connexion through catchwords present in the Markan text, between the request of the sick man, the healing saying of Jesus and the actual healing:

Matt. 8.2 ἐὰν   θέλῃς, δύνασαί με   καθαρίσαι
Matt. 8.3a   θέλω,   καθαρίσθητι
Matt. 8.3b   καὶ εὐθέως   ἐκαθαρίσθη αὐτοῦ ἡ λέπρα

The same findings occur in the healing of the woman with the haemorrhage (Matt. 9.20–22): request, healing saying and actual healing are here linked together by the catchword σῴζειν. Matthew has achieved this again by means of strict abbreviation of the Markan narrative and also his reformulation (Matt. 9.22b). In both cases there arises in this way, on the one hand a close connexion between request and healing saying and on the other between these two and the healing itself. A similar threefold linking by means of catchwords is also found in the scene of Peter walking on the sea. The request of Peter, Jesus' word of command and the actual miracle are joined together by the keyword ἐλθεῖν:

Matt. 14.28   ... κέλευσόν με   ἐλθεῖν πρός σε ἐπὶ τὰ ὕδατα
Matt. 14.29a   ... ἐλθέ ...
Matt. 14.29b   ... καὶ   ἦλθεν πρὸς τὸν Ἰησοῦν

The request of the centurion of Capernaum is answered by the action of Jesus as it is depicted in the last verse:

Matt. 8.8b ... μόνον εἰπὲ λόγῳ   καὶ ἰαθήσεται ὁ παῖς μου
Matt. 8.13 ... καὶ εἶπεν ὁ Ἰησοῦς ... καὶ ἰάθη ὁ παῖς ...

There does not occur here a threefold linkage by catchword but the actual connexion remains the same. The healing word of Jesus takes up the catchword of faith with which in 8.10 Jesus has characterised the centurion's request. The miracle itself follows in accordance with the centurion's plea: a word and the servant is cured. Furthermore the healing word gives the occurrence of the catchword linkage its justification: things happen according to the suppliant's faith. A less clear catchword linkage occurs in the healing of the two blind men in Matt. 9.27 ff. The catchword πιστεύετε (9.28) really links the request of the blind men with the healing word of Jesus (9.29: κατὰ τὴν πίστιν . . .). But here again the express assurance that the healing takes place according to faith gives the use of the catchword material justification.

Something like a catchword correspondence at least is found in the raising of Jairus's daughter, where the action of Jesus corresponds to the desire expressed to him in the request:

Matt. 9.18b . . . ἐλθὼν ἐπίθες τὴν χεῖρά σου ἐπ᾽ αὐτήν, καὶ ζήσεται

Matt. 9.23 καὶ ἐλθὼν ὁ ᾽Ιησοῦς . . .

Matt. 9.25 . . . εἰσελθὼν ἐκράτησεν τῆς χειρὸς αὐτῆς, καὶ ἠγέρθη . . .

Even if the formal and literal correspondence is not completely carried out it is clearly present in actual fact. Although the catchword of faith does not occur in this narrative it is perfectly clear that this miracle, too, takes place in response to suppliant faith.

Probably in the healing of the blind men of Jericho also one must understand the insertion of σπλαγχνισθεὶς δὲ ὁ ᾽Ιησοῦς ἥψατο τῶν ὀμμάτων αὐτῶν (Matt. 20.34) as a kind of corresponding answer to the repeated cry for help (Matt. 20.30–31): the cry for mercy is followed by the mercy of Jesus.

In the healing of the epileptic boy (Matt. 17.14–20) the speech of the father is linked with the actual healing by the catchword θεραπεύειν (Matt. 17.16, 18): confidence in the Lord in face of the impotence of his disciples is justified.

By the notion of linkage by catchwords is generally meant the technique of putting together different units of the tradition which are independent of each other, above all of sayings, on the basis of a common catchword.[1] In our context this notion is used to denote a technique of narrating, through which actual relationships *within* a pericope are to find expression.[2] In the miracle stories of Matthew's Gospel the following parts of the pericope are linked by means of catchwords: request, healing saying and actual healing.

In other places, too, the first evangelist links different parts of a pericope by catchwords. In the description of the birth of Jesus (Matt. 1.18–25) no doubt composed by the evangelist himself, a

[1] Cf. R. Bultmann, *Syn T*, pp. 325 f.

[2] J. Sundwall has shown in his investigation *Die Zusammensetzung des Markus evangeliums* ('The arrangement of Mark's Gospel') that the catchword principle ('word-response') is used not only within the narrative material to link individual pericopes but also in the actual making of them.

heaping up of catchwords can be perceived, some used three times, linking up the single parts: the command of the angel (1.20, 21), the word of Scripture (1.23) and the event or human action (1.24, 25):

Matt. 1.20/24 παραλαβεῖν τὴν γυναῖκα

Matt. 1.21/23/25 τίκτειν υἱόν

Matt. 1.21/23/25 καλεῖν τὸ ὄνομα αὐτοῦ

In the healing of the paralytic the catchword ἐξουσία links the controversial conversation and the miraculous healing (Matt. 9.6, 8). In the doctrinal conversations in 12.10 ff. and 18.1 ff. question and answer are linked together by catchwords.[1] In the controversy about pure and impure (Matt. 15.1–20) at the end the question raised at the beginning is taken up again in catchword fashion.[2] A comparison with Mark shows that Matthew has first created this catchword setting of the whole passage by importing the word νίπτεσθαι in Matt. 15.2 and by adding Matt. 15.20b. In the conversation with the rich young man the formulation εἰς ζωὴν εἰσελθεῖν in the reply of Jesus (Matt. 19.17) corresponds to the expression ἵνα σχῶ ζωὴν αἰώνιον in the question (Matt. 19.16). In the parable of the wicked husbandmen the interpretative verse added by Matthew in Matt. 21.43 corresponds to the last verse of the parable (Matt. 21.41).

These examples of catchword linkages and correspondences of verses and parts of verses show that we have before us an instrument frequently used by the evangelist to link together matters that belong together and to set forth actual relationships.

5. The role of faith in the miracle stories

If the presence of a catchword connexion in many of the miracle stories shows that a firm connexion exists between request, healing word and actual healing, this connexion in the peculiarly Matthaean healing word about faith is conveyed in an express formula (Matt. 8.13; 9.29; 15.28). It is necessary to assess the significance of this fact for the understanding of the form of the miracle story.

Where the formula about faith appears in Matthew's miracle stories it always points towards what the suppliant person has spoken (Matt. 8.5 ff.; 9.22 ff., 27 ff.; 15.21 ff.). The faith is expressed in the request; and Jesus acts in a way that corresponds to the suppliant

---

[1] Cf. above, p. 236, notes 1 and 2.

[2] Matt. 15.2: οὐ γὰρ νίπτονται τὰς χεῖρας, ὅταν ἄρτον ἐσθίωσιν.

Matt. 15.20b τὸ δὲ ἀνίπτοις χερσὶν φαγεῖν οὐ κοινοῖ τὸν ἄνθρωπον.

faith. Even where the formula about faith is absent the correspondence of the catchword indicates the same material relationship (Matt. 8.2 ff.; 9.18 ff.; 14.28 ff.; 20.29 ff.). The conversational form, the catchword linkage and the Matthaean formula of faith combine in all these miracle stories to express that what faith desires is granted to it.

As the investigations of the abbreviations in the double story of the raising of Jairus's daughter and the healing of the woman with the haemorrhage show, these measures serve to bring out the essential connexion between faith and the miracle in the mere course of the story, in that everything superfluous, not directly pointing to the matter in hand, is omitted. The story of the centurion of Capernaum in Matthew likewise shows, precisely by comparison with its Lukan form, by contrast, how only that which is essential to the matter in hand is reported. The same applies to the healing of the leper, to the healing of the blind men in Matt. 9.27 ff. and to the story of the Canaanite woman.

This all leads to the result that the Matthaean formula ὡς ἐπίστευσας γενηθήτω σοι not only has theologically relevant significance for the understanding of the miracle stories but also contains the formal principle which shapes them.

The conversational form of request and reply brings to expression the relation between faith and the answer to it; the catchword linkage between request, reply and miracle unites faith and the answer to it very closely together; and the saying about faith not only formally, as the answer to the request, depicts the climax of the miracle stories but it also formulates the very point intended by the whole story in a pregnant sentence.

This point is not new, of course. For the formula about saving faith ἡ πίστις σου σέσωκέν σε is found in all three evangelists.[1] The fashioning of a miracle story as a conversation and with the aid of linking catchwords is also found already in the tradition as Matthew received it (for example, Mark 1.40 ff.; 10.46 ff.).[2] Yet the first evangelist, in his reproduction of the miracle stories, has brought out the matter contained in this formula about saving faith incomparably more powerfully. He has brought his understanding of this formula

---

[1] Matt. 9.22 = Mark 5.34 = Luke 8.48; Mark 10.52 = Luke 18.42; Luke 7.50; 17.19.

[2] According to M. Dibelius the healing of the blind man of Jericho (Mark 10.46 ff.) is a 'healing reported in the style of a paradigm' (*Formgesch.*, p. 84 [ET[2], p. 87]).

to more exact expression (Matt. 8.13; 9.29; 15.28). He has called a series of miracle stories to serve, so to speak, this formula with the result that they are now clear paradigms of the point expressed in it.

C. *The form of the miracle stories in Matthew*

The characteristics of the miracle stories in Matthew's Gospel enumerated in the preceding section point to the conclusion that one cannot really speak of miracle 'narratives'. Neither the notion of the miracle story (R. Bultmann) nor that of the 'tale' (M. Dibelius) applies to them. Rather, it has been shown that they exhibit the form of a conversation. That applies above all to the healing miracles, in which from the very beginning through the expression of a request for healing and the healing word of Jesus, the marks of a conversation are imparted.

In the healing miracles the following form of construction can be recognised:

1. Formal introduction in which the suppliant is quite briefly introduced and an attitude of supplication is expressed (for example, προσκυνεῖν, παρακαλεῖν).

2. The request in direct speech in which faith is expressed and which can be carried on in a twofold exchange of conversation.

3. The reply of Jesus corresponding to the request, generally in the form of a healing saying, sometimes only in the form of a corresponding action, but occasionally both.

4. A brief formalistic notice that the miracle has taken place, without a lengthy stay over it.

In the light of this scheme the comparison with the conversations in Matthew's Gospel calls for attention, as it occurs, for example, in the didactic conversation about the question who is the greatest in the kingdom of heaven (Matt. 18.1–4) and about the question of divorce (Matt. 19.3–9). The first example is particularly illuminating, since it is a fresh Matthaean creation from Markan material (cf. Mark 9.33–36), and hence it presents the Matthaean structure best of all:

1. Formalistic introduction in which the questioner is quite briefly introduced (Matt. 18.1a).

2. The question in direct speech for which an answer is sought (Matt. 18.1b).

3. The answer of Jesus in clear correspondence to the question, together with an instructive action (Matt. 18.2–4).

The conversation about the question of divorce shows the same form, except that there it is a matter of two exchanges of conversation, each embracing a question and the answer. At the end of the twofold conversation, however, stands a saying of Jesus which clearly replies to the main question raised at the beginning, on what grounds a marriage may be dissolved (cf. Matt. 19.9 and 19.3).

There can be no question that Matthew has standardised his healing miracles as conversations and has approximated their form to that of the controversy and scholastic dialogues. It is not surprising in view of the special content of a miracle story that there is in the healing miracles a report of a suppliant attitude and, in a formal way, of the actual miracle. What is important, however, is the following: as in a didactic conversation the climax lies in the saying of Jesus, the healing miracle correspondingly reaches its goal in the miracle-working saying of Jesus. This saying of Jesus, however, is in almost all cases a saying about faith (Matt. 8.13; 9.22, 29 and 15.28), and never a healing saying in the stylistic sense.[1] The observation that the emphasis in these healing stories actually lies on this saying of Jesus about faith confirms that the point is to be found in it and not in the healing itself. In short: the healing story presented by Matthew in the form of a conversation reaches its formal and material climax in the saying of Jesus about faith and is, as a whole, nothing other than an illustration of this saying. The form of the healing miracle in Matthew's Gospel corresponds most closely therefore to the paradigm in Dibelius' sense.[2]

[1] Cf. Mark 5.41 and 7.34, where the healing saying is preserved in the foreign language; or the other healing sayings in Luke 7.14; 8.54; 18.42; or the sayings containing a command in Mark 1.25 (= Luke 4.35), Mark 4.39; 5.8; 9.25.

[2] Cf. the characteristics of the paradigm (according to *Formgesch.*):

(1) 'The action reaches its climax, which cannot be surpassed, either in a saying or deed of Jesus' (p. 42) [p. 44].

(2) The 'simple description which is confined to the most necessary matters'; 'on the more intimate circumstances, the time of the day, the occasion, other people, and generally on the place practically nothing is reported' (p. 46) [p. 48]. With regard to the suppliants we learn 'nothing except that they wish to come into contact with Jesus. What we do learn, however, and what alone we are supposed to learn is this: how Jesus responds to this contact' (p. 47) [p. 50]. In the paradigmatic healing stories the topic of the miraculous is missing (p. 51): 'the only important thing is that Jesus healed and how he revealed in a short saying the meaning and object of his action to the person healed and the witnesses' (p. 53) [p. 55].

(3) At the end there often stands a saying of Jesus 'which has a general meaning and which, as a rule for faith or life, gives the whole story an immediate reference to the hearers' (p. 54) [p. 56].

The fact that the healing saying in Matthew is no miracle-working word of power but is concerned with faith already shows that his healing miracles are not intended primarily as miracle narratives. The absence, to a considerable extent, of so-called stylistic traits points in the same direction. The saying-character of these healing miracles, the meaning of which is not so much the relating of a miracle as the developing of a saying about miracle-working faith, does not really allow them to be reckoned among the group of what Bultmann calls miracle stories. Admittedly, as far as content is concerned they report miracles, yet their form, and this is what matters, is in no way in the style of a miracle story.[1] The conversational form and the dominant place of a striking saying of Jesus leads to the conclusion that some of the healing miracles in Matthew's Gospel should rather be classified as apothegms.[2]

The transition from the one form to the other is, of course, neither deliberate nor arbitrary. In the Synoptic Gospels there occur many examples of mixed forms. Among the paradigms of Dibelius miracle healings are numbered, as they are among the apothegms of Bultmann.[3] Then a stylistic relationship is also observed between the two

---

The 'tales', on the other hand, are distinguished by the extent of the descriptive element (pp. 73 ff.) [pp. 76 ff.]; they give 'insight into the technique of the miracle . . . a point on which the paradigms are almost completely silent' (p. 78) [p. 81], and they reveal no 'attempt to draw instruction or edification from the material' (p. 74) [p. 78].

[1] It is not surprising that stylistic traits are not entirely absent from the Matthaean miracle stories in view of their content. M. Dibelius ('Zur Formgeschichte der Evangelien', TR N.F. 1 (1929), p. 201) rightly says it is not a question of whether in a pericope 'the self-evident traits of the topic, the saying of Jesus and the description of the impression made occur, but whether these interests in the actuality of the miracle dominate the text'. Such an interest in the actuality of the miracle, however, does not dominate the Matthaean healing miracles.

[2] According to R. Bultmann (SynT) apothegms are 'items the point of which consists of a saying of Jesus contained in a brief framework' (p. 11). 'In an apothegm interest rests entirely on the saying of Jesus', which, 'for stylistic reasons' occurs 'at the end' (pp. 62 f.). The interest is 'completely exhausted with the saying of Jesus' and does not attach to the sick person whose healing is reported (p. 63). Information given about the situation is sparse (pp. 63 f.) and 'in the matter of action it is sufficient that the people come to Jesus and ask him, or that a characteristic behaviour is briefly described which . . . provokes the saying of Jesus' (p. 66). One can perceive these characteristics of the apothegm with appropriate modifications in the healing stories of Matthew, and one must judge with regard to them as Bultmann does with regard to Mark 3.1–6; 7.24–30; Matt. 8.5–13: 'The healings are not related here as "miracle stories" but in the style of the apothegm' (p. 66).

[3] Cf. Formgeschichte des Evangeliums, p. 40 [p. 43] and SynT, for example p. 66.

forms. R. Bultmann sees this in the objectivity of the account: 'Here as there all that matters is the point, there the saying of Jesus, here the miracle.'[1] Of course, in Matthew's Gospel the relationship of the miracle stories to the conversations is much more far-reaching in that they also have been given a conversational form and their point is often in a saying of Jesus, not in the miracle itself. This special stylisation is certainly due to the first evangelist.[2]

This process of an approximation of the miracle stories to the style of a paradigm or an apothegm can also be observed in other miracle stories.

The healing of the paralytic, it is true, is already in Mark a paradigm for the saying about the power of the Son of Man to forgive sins (cf. Mark 2.10 ἵνα δὲ εἰδῆτε . . .). Matthew has made the dominating position of this saying still clearer, however, by the abbreviation at the beginning and the alteration of the conclusion. In a similar way the story of the centurion of Capernaum is, not only in its setting but also in its expansion, completely subordinated to the saying of Jesus about faith.

Into the healing of the withered hand on the Sabbath (Matt. 12.9–14) the evangelist has worked a scholastic conversation in which the question is posed (12.10) and answered (12.12) whether it is permissible to heal on the Sabbath. Whereas Mark (Mark 3.1–6) transmits a scholastic conversation in which Jesus justifies his attitude before his opponents, Matthew derives from the scholastic conversation a decision about teaching on behaviour on the Sabbath, and does so obviously for his Church. In this way the miracle performed by Jesus in accordance with this decision regarding teaching appears as an illustration for this decision. If Mark has already derived instruction for the disciples from the healing of the epileptic boy, by means of the attached conversation (Mark 9.28–29), Matthew by

---

[1] *SynT*, p. 220.

[2] The thesis of a marked formal parallelism between the miracle- and saying-story in the old tradition is the result of an investigation by O. Perels on *Die Wunderüberlieferung der Synoptiker in ihrem Verhältnis zur Wortüberlieferung* (pp. 107 f.). However valuable many of his observations are, the theory of the pregnant dialogue as the original form of the Synoptic miracle story out of which there then developed, by alteration and expansion, the different types of miracle narrative which we now possess (pp. 89 ff.), remains, of course, doubtful. It is striking that the 'old' form is frequently found precisely in Matthew's Gospel. Whether indeed the first evangelist has in each case preserved this old form, cannot be shown. Be that as it may one must conclude that it is he especially who was interested in the parallelism between apothegm and healing story.

the more general form of the instruction (on the miraculous power of faith in general, Matt. 17.20) and the abbreviation of the miracle story has created 'a kind of apothegm'.[1] The immediate connexion between the cursing of the fig tree and the instruction to the disciples based on it must be judged in a similar way (Matt. 21.18–22 as against Mark 11.12–14, 20 ff.).[2]

The exorcism of the demons at Gadara Matthew has placed completely in the service of the Christological statement (Matt. 8.29) in that only the destruction of the demons is reported and nothing about the person of the healed man. He thereby makes it known that the story as such is a paradigm for this Christological statement first inserted by him. The healing of Peter's mother-in-law is obviously conceived as an immediate example of the quotation from Scripture about the vocation of the Christ (Matt. 8.17) and is correspondingly given Christological emphasis by Matthew.

The stories of the sea journeys of the disciples do not, it is true, bear the form of a paradigm, but they nevertheless exhibit characteristics which show that in them statements are made about the nature and the trials of discipleship. Finally in the stories of the feedings, pointers can be found to the fact that Matthew, starting from the command of Jesus to the disciples (Matt. 14.16), especially emphasises their role.

In view of these varied findings it is not easy to reach a general judgment on the form of the miracle stories in Matthew's Gospel as a whole. Nevertheless a tendency on the part of the evangelist in the direction of the form of the paradigm as against the tale, or rather, to the form of the conversation as against that of a miracle 'narrative', is perceptible everywhere. The miracles of Jesus are given an illustrative meaning, with different themes, of course, and with the help of different methods:

(a) The form of the paradigm occurs most clearly in the healing miracles, which are standardised as conversations and often have as their point an utterance of Jesus 'of general meaning'. Their theme is the faith involved in miracles. As regards its content the scene of Peter walking on the sea also belongs here. In this group Matthew employs the sometimes threefold catchword linkage.

(b) The subordination of a pericope to a central statement found in it occurs in the healing of the paralytic and in the exorcism of the

[1] R. Bultmann, *SynT*, pp. 61 f.
[2] Cf. below, pp. 285 f.

demons at Gadara. In the latter story Matthew has himself created the paradigm character, in the former he has considerably strengthened it. The theme is Christology. The healing of Peter's mother-in-law also properly belongs to this group, for it serves as an example of the Christological quotation from Scripture which follows it.

(c) The theme of discipleship determines the stories of the sea journey, the walking on the sea, the feedings and the healing of the epileptic boy. It would not be correct to speak of a paradigmatic form in the normal sense here, but the shortening of novelistic traits on the one hand and alterations within the narrative on the other, together with the placing of scenes at the beginning (Matt. 8.19–22), their insertion (Matt. 14.28–31) and addition at the end (Matt. 17.19–20), point in the direction of a pattern which derives abiding illustrative instruction from the reported events of the past.

III. THE MIRACLE STORIES AS WITNESSES FOR MATTHEW'S CHRISTOLOGY

Whereas Mark twice reports a group of miracle stories (Mark 1.21–45 and 4.35–5.43) and Luke even three times (Luke 4.31–5.26; 7.1–17 and 8.22–56), Matthew has collected the miracle narratives of Jesus in only one passage (Matt. 8–9). In the light of the evangelist's composition it is easy to see why he has proceeded in this way. The similarly-worded verses in Matt. 4.23 and Matt. 9.35 show by their contents (summary account of the activity of Jesus in word and deed) and their position (in the one case before the Sermon on the Mount and in the other immediately after the chapters containing the miracles), that Matthew's purpose in the chapters enclosed by these verses is to portray the double office of Christ: his teaching and his healing activity. His collection of the miraculous deeds of Jesus thus has a Christological function. The evangelist presents Jesus at the beginning of his Gospel not only as the Messiah of the word (in the Sermon on the Mount) but also as the Messiah of deed (by his miraculous deeds).[1]

This systematic nature of Matthew's Gospel is shown not only by the framework, however, but also by the two miracle chapters themselves. Just as the 'Sermon on the Mount' in Matthew is a collection

[1] Cf. J. Schniewind, pp. 37 and 106, and A. Schlatter, *Matthäus*, p. 120.

of Jesus' sayings about the new righteousness which exhibits nevertheless a meaningful arrangement,[1] Matthew has also arranged
Jesus' miracles in a well-ordered cycle. It is revealing to make clear
to oneself this order of the two Matthaean miracle chapters. As they
go back to the evangelist they can give pointers on his Christological
understanding of the miracles of Jesus which he reports.

The last pericope of the collection reports the healing of a dumb
demoniac (Matt. 9.32–34). It certainly does not portray a miracle
story in the strict sense. It is true that it concerns the exorcism of a
demon, but it is nevertheless quite clear that the chief weight does
not lie on this but on the twofold reaction of the multitude and the
Pharisees, which in both cases is brought to expression in a quotation.[2] It is thus not intended to provide still another example of the
exorcisms of Jesus. They were already described much more impressively in Matt. 8.28–34. Rather this miracle report draws the concluding line under the whole collection in that it shows—in a certain
sense even stylistically—how people behave in the presence of the
miraculous activity of Jesus. For this purpose the short pericope
which serves as an introduction to the Beelzebub controversy was
most appropriate (Luke 11.14–15).[3] This is how it comes about that
Matthew has twice worked it into his Gospel (9.32–34; 12.22–24).

In both reproductions the first evangelist, in contrast to Luke,
who only speaks quite generally about the amazement of the multitude (Luke 11.14), has expressed the reaction of the multitude in
words. Even if in the accusation by the enemies of Jesus that he is in
league with the devil (Luke 11.15; Matt. 12.24) and in the speech
of Jesus in his defence, what is at issue already, even though not
mentioned, is the question of Christology, it is precisely Matthew
who puts this Christological question openly in the mouth of the
multitude (Matt. 12.23 καὶ ἔλεγον· μήτι οὗτός ἐστιν ὁ υἱὸς Δαυίδ;).
In a similar way he has also made clear by means of direct speech in
Matt. 9.32–34 that the multitude replies with appreciation to the
miracles of Jesus (Matt. 9.33 καὶ ἐθαύμασαν οἱ ὄχλοι λέγοντες·
οὐδέποτε ἐφάνη οὕτως ἐν τῷ Ἰσραήλ). But it can thus be seen again that
in this last pericope what the evangelist is concerned about is the
twofold echo of the miraculous deeds of Jesus which he has set forth

---

[1] E.g. Matt. 5.3–12, 13–16, 17–20, 21–48; 6.1–18, etc.

[2] Cf. E. Lohmeyer, p. 180, on Matt. 9.32–34.

[3] The marked literal agreement between Luke 11.14–15 and Matt. 9.32–34 is
doubtless traceable to a common source (Q), which Matthew has modified to a
greater extent in 12.22–24.

by way of example in what has gone before.[1] We shall not be astray in seeing in the speech of the multitude a hidden reference to the Christological meaning of all the miracles reported.[2] The conclusion of the collection of miracles also shows that the evangelist has arranged them under the theme of Christology.

The first clear section in this collection of miracles comprises Matt. 8.2–17. Here healings are exclusively reported which not only have their clear conclusion in the quotation from Scripture in Matt. 8.17 but also receive their interpretation as the fulfilment of the prophecy of the servant of God.

The grouping of the following material is not so clearly recognisable, but nonetheless it is present. Thus the three miracle stories in Matt. 9.18–31 form a section of their own. Their position itself indicates this. The three pericopes in Matt. 9.2–17 as controversy dialogues are clearly distinguishable from them. In the first of these controversy conversations there is a reference to a miraculous deed of Jesus, but not in the second and third. The exorcism of the demon in Matt. 9.32–34 does not belong to the group, since it forms the conclusion to the whole composition. In the matter of content the three miracle stories belong together, since the theme of faith is treated in them, as is seen by the sayings of Jesus in Matt. 9.22 and 9.29.[3]

There remains as a third section the group in Matt. 8.18–9.17. Here it is the most difficult to discover an ordering principle. Nevertheless observations do accrue which justify us in taking them together as a group. With 8.18 it is clear that a new section is introduced which is characterised by separation from the multitude. Whereas the multitude first appears again in Matt. 9.33, the disciples play a role in the pericopes of Matt. 8.18–9.17, though previously (in Matt. 8.2–17) and afterwards (in Matt. 9.18–31) they are as good as not mentioned. The stilling of the storm is interpreted by Matthew

---

[1] In the frame of this composition it is easy to see why at the end of the two preceding miracle stories Matthew reports the spreading of the knowledge about Jesus (Matt. 9.26, 31).

[2] It is worthy of notice that in three places Matthew reports on this double reaction to the miraculous deeds of Jesus: Matt. 9.33–34; 12.22–24 and 21.14–16. In all three places he gives the positive reaction in quotations and in such a way that in the course of the presentation in his Gospel the Christological acclamation becomes increasingly more unveiled. It is clearest in Matt. 21.15 (Hosanna to the son of David), less clear in the question in Matt. 12.23 and quite hidden in the multitude's cry of amazement in Matt. 9.33.

[3] Cf. above, p. 180.

as a story of discipleship. In the controversy conversations, moreover, we have to do with questions of the congregation which find their model solution through the Lord of the congregation. Thus there, too, the concern is not only with Jesus but likewise with his disciples.[1] One can explain the quite remarkable appearance of controversy dialogues in a cycle of miracles by recognising that Matthew was really only concerned with the healing of the paralytic, but he had to take over the other two pericopes because they firmly belonged together in the tradition. But all the more would the evangelist have attached importance to a miracle narrative the meaning of which lay not in the miraculous deed itself but in the evidence furnished by it that Jesus and his congregation have authority on earth to forgive sins. Thus Matthew's concern was not only to present the Jesus of the miracle stories as a worker of miracles but also as the Lord of his congregation. In this background the other two controversy conversations (Matt. 9.9–17) in the miracle chapter do not appear strange any more. Even if their occurrence at this place is based on the demand of tradition the fact remains that Matthew also works out the congregation's problem of discipleship in 8.18–27 and that he makes known in 9.2–8 that the authority of the Lord is present also in his congregation (Matt. 9.8). In a sentence: one may understand the pericopes collected in the section Matt. 8.18–9.17 under the heading, 'The Christ of the miracle stories is the Lord of his congregation'.

That the two groups of chapters, 5–7 and 8–9, belong together can easily be seen in the light of the framework-verses, Matt. 4.23 and 9.35. There is, however, no question that beyond them the tenth chapter also belongs to this context. It cannot be by chance that in the beginning of the mission speech in 10.1 there arises through the formulation καὶ θεραπεύειν πᾶσαν νόσον καὶ πᾶσαν μαλακίαν a clear reminder of verses 4.23 and 9.35 (Jesus as θεραπεύων πᾶσαν νόσον καὶ πᾶσαν μαλακίαν). The comparison of Matt. 10.1 with the parallel passage in Mark 6.7 shows that Matthew has inserted this expression into the Markan text. It has already been clearly shown in another connexion that verbal agreement in formulation not only represents a favourite medium of the evangelist's style but also denotes important material connexions.[2] From this it already follows that the

[1] The remarkable τοῖς ἀνθρώποις in Matt. 9.8 is to be understood in this sense; cf. below, pp. 273 f.
[2] Cf. above, pp. 237 ff.

mission chapter of Matthew 10 should be closely linked with those that have preceded it.[1]

This connexion is also underlined by the verses in between, Matt. 9.36–38: in the work described in Matt. 4.23–9.35 Jesus needs fellow workers. According to Matt. 10.1, however, these fellow workers of Jesus are his disciples whom he inducts into his work by the mission speech.[2]

It is quite obviously Matthew's opinion that the disciples should do the work of Jesus. The content of their proclamation is the same as that of the preaching of Jesus (Matt. 10.7; 4.17). Their healing activity comprises according to Matt. 10.8 all the miracles reported in Matt. 8–9 (with the exception of the healing of the blind).[3] These clear allusions must be considered in so far as Matthew has created them through insertions into the Markan text (Mark 6.7–12). These insertions into the mission speech of Jesus to his disciples in Matt. 10.1, 7, 8 are intended to say, in connexion with the preceding chapters, nothing else than that Jesus gives his disciples a share in his authority, as it is set out in Matt. 5–9. That applies above all to the authority to work miracles. Hence Matthew takes over Mark's formulation which only speaks of power over unclean spirits (Mark 6.7), but he interprets this authority through the addition of καὶ θεραπεύειν πᾶσαν νόσον καὶ πᾶσαν μαλακίαν (Matt. 10.1) as also an authority to heal every kind of sickness, as the list in Matt. 10.8 shows, where exorcism is only one task among others. Such a detailed list of the miraculous healings the disciples are commissioned to perform is found only in the mission speech of Matthew's Gospel.[4] It can scarcely be doubted that this measure of detail is occasioned by the collection of the miraculous deeds of Jesus which immediately precedes the mission speech.

All these observations confirm that Matthew intended a close material connexion of the mission of the disciples in chapter 10 with the activity of Jesus depicted in the preceding chapters. Such a con-

[1] K. Thieme, 'Matthäus der schriftgelehrte Evangelist', *Judaica*, 5, 1949, pp. 137 f., and T. Zahn, p. 389, draw attention to the bracketing of the activity of Jesus in Matt. 5–9 with the mission of the disciples in Matt. 10.

[2] Cf. A. Schlatter, *Matthäus*, p. 321: The mission speech describes 'the sharing of the disciples in the activity of Jesus'. T. Zahn, p. 387, speaks of a 'participation (of the disciples) in the vocational work of the Master'.

[3] The omission of the healing of the blind may be a matter of chance; that it was not committed to the disciples is according to Matt. 10.1 not probable, since the power to heal covers all sicknesses and infirmities.

[4] Cf. on the contrary Mark 6.12–13; Luke 9.1–2, 6 and 10.9.

nexion is likewise suggested by the narrative of the Baptist's question (Matt. 11.2–6). There, too, occurs a description of the work of Jesus which goes into detail (Matt. 11.5). This has long been acknowledged as a reference back to the deeds of Jesus in Matthew 8–9 and the deviation from the thread of Mark demanded by the collection of miracles explained with reference to this verse.[1] In actual fact the evangelist's presentation has here reached a kind of conclusion. After he has shown the Christ in his work in word and deed he now allows the Baptist to put the decisive Christological question (Matt. 11.3 σὺ εἶ ὁ ἐρχόμενος, ἢ ἕτερον προσδοκῶμεν;). That the real decision falls on this Christological question Matthew shows in his further presentation. Hence there follow the demarcation from John the Baptist (Matt. 11.7–19), the woes on the unrepentant Galilaean cities (Matt. 11.20–24), as well as the discussion of Jesus with the Pharisees (Matt. 12.1–45). The pericope that follows (Matt. 12.46–50) designates the disciples[2] as the true relations of Jesus and they are obviously the company of those from whom things are not concealed but to whom they are revealed (Matt. 11.25 ff.). The two kinds of hearer of the parables of Jesus in Matthew 13 correspond to the separation of the spirits thus displayed, on the one hand the disciples (Matt. 13.10),[3] to whom understanding is given so that they see and hear, and on the other 'those' (Matt. 13.11) to whom it is not given and who have eyes but do not see and ears but do not hear.

This short outline of the composition of Matthew's Gospel makes clear that the question of the Baptist has a double function: on the one hand it clearly expresses the decisive question which comes out of what has gone before and so forms a conclusion which once again illuminates the Christological theme of the preceding chapters. On the other hand, the chapters which follow must be understood even more in the light of this question and the negative or positive answers to it.

Granted, then, that the evangelist by means of the Baptist's question thus underlines the Christological meaning of the account up to

---

[1] Thus for example J. Wellhausen, *Matthaei*, pp. 42, 53. Certainly this reference back must apply on account of καὶ πτωχοὶ εὐαγγελίζονται not only to the miracles of Jesus but also to his preaching (Matt. 4.17; 5–7).

[2] According to Matthew the true relations of Jesus are not 'those who sit about him' (Mark 3.34) but 'his disciples', to whom Jesus points with his outstretched hand (Matt. 12.49.)

[3] They are again expressly designated as such, cf. Mark 4.10.

this point, the question then arises how the chapter on the mission of the disciples (Matt. 10) is to be understood in this connexion. Everything points to the fact that it, too, has a Christological meaning. It has already been seen that Matthew links the mission of the disciples very closely with his presentation of the activity of Jesus. Now we must assess the circumstance that the Baptist's question does not follow immediately after chapter 9. At first sight that would seem the most sensible, for the mission speech breaks the natural connexion between, say, Matt. 9.35 and 11.2.[1] According to the present structure of Matthew's Gospel the expression formulated by Matthew himself in Matt. 11.2—τὰ ἔργα τοῦ Χριστοῦ (= 'the Christ'—works of Jesus)[2]—refers not only to the activity of Jesus but obviously also back to the activity of the disciples prescribed in the mission speech, and this, according to Matt. 10.7, 8 corresponds exactly to that of Jesus. But then the reference of Jesus to 'what you see and hear' (Matt. 11.4, 5) also refers not only to his own proclamation in word and deed but also that of his disciples.

It follows therefore that Matthew presents Jesus at the beginning of his Gospel not only as the 'Messiah of the word' and the 'Messiah of deed' but also as the one who commissions, who gives his disciples authority to do the same Messianic work. Or, in other words: Jesus is not only the Messiah in word and deed whose authority was given by God but he is also the Lord who makes his disciples sharers in his authority. To this extent the deeds of the disciples, given authority by Jesus (Matt. 10.1), rightly belong to the ἔργα τοῦ Χριστοῦ.[3]

If we summarise the investigation of the miracle cycle (Matt. 8–9) and its framework (Matt. 4.17–11.6) the following Christological

---

[1] Luke has very understandably put the Baptist's question (Luke 7.18–23) immediately after two detailed accounts of miracles (Luke 7.1–10; 7.11–17) and expressly mentioned that knowledge of Jesus had reached the Baptist (Luke 7.17, 18a).

[2] J. Schniewind, p. 139.

[3] In this connexion reference must be made to the late-Jewish legal institution of the שָׁלִיחַ, according to which 'he that is sent by a man is as the man himself'; cf. K. H. Rengstorf, TWNT I, pp. 414 ff. [BKW Apostleship, pp. 13 ff.]. The world of ideas to which this view belongs certainly plays a part in Matt. 10. Thus in Matt. 10.2–4 the names of the twelve 'apostles' are mentioned and according to Matt. 10.1, 5 it is these very twelve whom Jesus sends on the mission. The saying about receiving a messenger (Matt. 10.40) similarly points to the thought world of the שָׁלִיחַ-institution, as does the fact that according to Matt. 10.15 the rejection of the preaching of the disciples whom he has sent incurs the same hard judgment as the rejection of that of Jesus (Matt. 11.22, 24; observe the similarity with Matt. 10.15!).

aspects, under which the miracle stories in Matthew must apparently be understood, result: they show Jesus:

(a) as the fulfiller of Old Testament prophecy, and therein
(b) as the servant of God acting with authority,
(c) as the Lord and helper of his congregation and
(d) as the one who makes his disciples sharers in his authority.

These four Christological themes in the miracle stories of Matthew's Gospel call for investigation.[1]

A. *The miracles of Jesus as the fulfilment of Scripture*

One may conjecture that the miraculous deeds of Jesus were already understood in the sayings source (Q) as the fulfilment of prophetic foretelling. For the reply of Jesus to the Christological question of the Baptist (Matt. 11.5 = Luke 7.22) clearly uses expressions from the book of the prophet Isaiah (35.5, 6; 61.1).[2] Of course in this saying of Jesus as in his sermon in the synagogue at Nazareth (Luke 4.18, 19) his whole activity in the form of preaching and miraculous deeds is conceived as the fulfilment of Scripture, but Matthew is the first to devote a complete section in the structure of his Gospel to the miraculous deeds of Jesus as the fulfilment of Scripture (Matt. 8.2–17), which he crowns with his typical formula quotation. In this way he makes the miracles of Jesus also, exactly as he does many other events of his life, serve the thought which runs through his whole Gospel: that Jesus is the fulfiller of the Old Testament.

Matt. 8.2–17

This section has a programmatic meaning for all the miraculous healings of Jesus. On the one hand it occurs within the systematic development of the activity of Jesus (Matt. 5–9). On the other, it shows, above all by the summary report in Matt. 8.16 which is understood not biographically but systematically, and which introduces the quotation, that this quotation applies not only to the three healing

---

[1] The theme of faith, which determines the section in Matt. 9.18–31, does not belong directly to Christology and will be developed later in ch. IV.

[2] Cf. E. Klostermann, *Matthäusev.*, p. 95, and J. Schniewind, pp. 139 f. Of course, in the saying of Jesus not only is the Old Testament quoted but the activity of Jesus is written up with Old Testament words. For the healing of lepers and the raising of the dead are not mentioned in the prophetic saying, but they form according to Matthew (8.2–4; 9.18–26) and Luke (5.12–16; 7.11–17) a considerable part of the activity of Jesus. Thus the saying is coined in the light of Old Testament prophecy and the events in the story of Jesus himself.

actions of Jesus which are reported in detail but to his whole activity as a miracle-working Saviour in general.[1]

In the composition of Matt. 8.2–17 Matthew proves himself to be an outstanding systematiser. It presents itself as a well-thought-out whole. After three individual examples there follows a generalising summary of the miraculous activity of Jesus, the theological interpretation of which is stated at the close.

It should further be observed that Jesus appears thematically as the miracle-working Saviour only in Matt. 8.2–17. In the section Matt. 8.18–9.17 no healing stories in the strict sense are reported and those in Matt. 9.18–31 deal with the theme of faith. The Christological theme in Matt. 8.2–17 can be seen not only from the context and the quotation from Scripture, but in the text of the pericope itself. The retelling of the healing story of Peter's mother-in-law is clearly Christologically determined.[2] But the two other narratives provided as examples also show a special interest in the person of Jesus. The centurion of Capernaum, in his speech (86–9), sketches an impressive picture of the complete authority of Jesus which has nothing to compare with it in the miracle stories of the rest of the Synoptic tradition.[3] In a similar way the request of the leper speaks of the wonderful power of Jesus, who only needs to will it and the miracle happens (Matt. 8.2). The answer of Jesus (Matt. 8.3 θέλω, καθαρίσθητι) specifically takes up this thought and shows Jesus himself in a royal majesty, which does not occur with the same pregnancy in any other miracle story. In other words: all three miracle stories in their Matthaean form bring out particularly forcefully the person of Jesus,[4] his power to do things and his will to do them. Hence one may say that the miracle stories in Matt. 8.2–17, Christologically, are primarily interested in the person of Jesus as the miracle-working Saviour.

When Matthew closes precisely this systematic section about

---

[1] Cf. above, pp. 171 f.

[2] Cf. above, pp. 169 f.

[3] For Matt. 8.5–13, it is true, faith was recognised as the determining theme of the Matthaean retelling of the passage (cf. above, pp. 193 ff.), but this faith nevertheless is directed towards the mighty Lord, as must be concluded from the analogy in Matt. 8.9. It should also be noticed that the summary report in Matt. 8.16 takes over precisely this trait of the complete authority of Jesus from Matt. 8.8 (λόγῳ), so that this detail in the story of the centurion gains general and fundamental meaning for all the miraculous healings.

[4] The judgment of J. Schniewind on Matt. 8.2–4 applies to the whole section: 'In Matthew only the majesty of Jesus is shown' (Das Ev. nach Matth., p. 107).

Jesus as the miracle-working Saviour with a statement about the fulfilling of the Old Testament, he makes it clear that he does not look upon Jesus in his miraculous deeds after the fashion of a Hellenistic θεῖος ἄνθρωπος. Whereas the so-called θεῖοι ἄνθρωποι desire and are expected to accredit themselves and their teaching by means of miraculous deeds and supernatural capacities as being divine,[1] the miraculous deeds obviously in the opinion of the evangelist are not in themselves sufficient proof of the Messianic dignity of Jesus. Only the evidence that through them Scripture, and so the will of God expressed in it, is fulfilled gives them Christological meaning. It is not the miracles that attest, rather they themselves must first be attested. Matthew shows that the miracles of Jesus are expressions of his obedience. To be precise: on the one hand they are regarded as acts of Jesus' obedience to the will of God and on the other they are understood as a legitimate part of his Messianic work, which in Matthew is depicted above all as the carrying out of the will of God and the victorious carrying through of his righteousness.[2]

In this connexion the following observation is very revealing. As the Messiah of the word (Matt. 5–7) programmatically explains at the beginning of his teaching on the new righteousness, that he has not come to destroy the law and the prophets but to fulfil them, and in view of this attaches importance to the smallest commandment (Matt. 5.17 ff.), the evangelist shows the 'Messiah of deed' at the beginning of his miraculous activity as the one who fulfils the Scripture (Matt. 8.2–17). This parallelism is not fortuitous, but is basic in the composition of Matthew 5–9, in which the activity of Jesus in teaching and miraculous deeds is systematically developed. Accordingly both sides of Jesus' activity are specifically characterised as the fulfilling of Scripture and thereby Christologically legitimised.

Matt. 8.2–4

The thought that Jesus in his miraculous healings is the fulfiller of Scripture finds expression not only in Matthew's arrangement but, furthermore, it is also found within the first of the stories presented in Matt. 8.2–17. At the end of it stands the command of Jesus to the healed leper to show himself to the priests and there offer the gift commanded (Matt. 8.4). It is somewhat unsatisfying to see this only

---

[1] Cf. R. Reitzenstein, *Die hellenistische Mysterienreligionen*, Leipzig, 1927³, pp. 25 f., and H. Windisch, *Paulus und Christus*, Leipzig, 1934, pp. 62, 67.

[2] On this Matthaean Christology of the obedience of Jesus and the carrying through of God's will, cf. G. Barth above, pp. 137 ff.

as the demonstration of the effected healing and thus as a stylistic trait.[1] This kind of command is too unusual for that. Above all, Matthew certainly did not understand it in this sense, especially as he elsewhere attaches no kind of importance to the demonstration of the miracle, and in fact often passes over the corresponding references in Mark (for example, Mark 5.15, 29 ff., 42b, 43b). It may be granted that the command of Jesus can be understood as a stylistic demonstration of the accomplished healing, but it is very questionable whether this interpretation is necessary or even merely probable. For obviously the miracle story is meant to be understood in the light of the statement of Jesus which follows it and not simply the statement in the light of the miracle story.[2] In short, the command of Jesus to the healed leper adds a new point to the story beyond the miraculous healing.

The fact that Jesus specifically enjoins obedience to the Mosaic law presupposes that he recognises this law. Consequently the healing story of the leper gains by this saying of Jesus a definite Christological sharpening in so far as the Christ who is acting with authority 'in contrast to the fanatical view that the law is to be abolished, directly affirms the law and therein sees his own Messianic dignity'.[3] In this way there is in Mark already, not a mere miracle story but a kind of paradigm which ends with a saying of Jesus and expresses the nature of his Messiahship.[4]

When Matthew places this healing of the leper in the section in which he shows the miracle-working Jesus as the fulfiller of Scripture, and when he puts it at the beginning of this section, this is entirely in line with the special witness of this pericope. Granted, he develops this special witness to a greater degree than is the case with the other Synoptic writers: on the one hand his more austere reproduction shows Jesus impressively as the miracle-working Saviour; on the other, however, he does not report as Mark (1.45) and Luke (5.15) do what the healed man does in reply to Jesus' command. In this way it becomes clear that this command of Jesus is the entire goal of this

---

[1] Thus R. Bultmann, *Syn T*, p. 212, and M. Dibelius, *Formgesch.*, p. 76.

[2] Cf. E. Lohmeyer, p. 154: 'The closing saying of Jesus cannot confirm the miracle but only interpret it.'

[3] K. L. Schmidt, 'Das Christuszeugnis der synoptischen Evangelien', *Jesus Christus im Zeugnis der Heiligen Schrift und der Kirche*, Beiheft zur Ev. Theol., 2. Munich, 1936, p. 21.

[4] Cf. V. Taylor, *The Gospel . . . Mark*, p. 185, on the form of Mark 1.40–44, and E. Lohmeyer, *Markus*, p. 48, on Mark 1.44.

story. But because the further behaviour of the man is not mentioned any more the command of Jesus must be understood less as a command than in the sense of an attestation of himself.[1] In this way the first evangelist emphatically underlines the Christological direction of the pericope and brings it still nearer to the form of a paradigm.

When Matthew reports this particular healing miracle with its self-attestation of Jesus as the first of all the miraculous deeds of Jesus the meaning of this is clear, not only in view of the context of Matt. 8.2–17 but also in view of the fact that in the Sermon on the Mount as well Jesus bears witness to himself (5.17) at the beginning of the introductory programmatic section on the meaning of the law (Matt. 5.17–20). Thus analogous to the external correspondence of Sermon on the Mount and collection of miracles there is a clear material identity in the presentation of Christology. In his first healing miracle Jesus confirms what he has explained in the Sermon on the Mount by way of introduction.[2]

Matt. 9.13a

In connexion with his presentation of the Messiah of deed Matthew quotes a further passage of Scripture. It occurs in the controversial conversation about Jesus mixing with tax-collectors and sinners (Matt. 9.9–13). This quotation from Hosea in Matt. 9.13a ἔλεος θέλω καὶ οὐ θυσίαν is obviously a favourite quotation of the evangelist, for he has also inserted it into the Markan context in Matt. 12.7. Furthermore, the thought that God demands mercy occurs repeatedly in the first Gospel.[3] In our context the only question to raise is what is the meaning of this quotation from Hosea in the framework of Matt. 9.9–13 on the one hand, and of Matthew 8–9 as a whole, and consequently for the interpretation of the miraculous deeds of Jesus, on the other.

The quotation is inserted by Matthew into the saying of Jesus at which the pericope (Matt. 9.9–13) is aimed and which contains a self-attestation of Jesus about his mission: οὐ γὰρ ἦλθον καλέσαι δικαίους ἀλλὰ ἁμαρτωλούς (Matt. 9.13b). This saying not only replies

---

[1] The omission of Mark 1.45 by Matthew is more clearly explained in this sense than by the tendency of Matthew to suppress 'the cases of an incapacity, of a non-attained intention of Jesus' (thus E. Klostermann, *Matthäus.*, p. 20), especially as in Matt. 9.30b, 31 such a case is also reported by Matthew.

[2] It is confirmed in this passage that reception of the law and Matthaean Christology go together (G. Bornkamm, above, pp. 37 f.

[3] Cf. G. Bornkamm above, p. 26. It is significant that all the passages cited there belong to the special material of the first evangelist.

to the question of the Pharisees (Matt. 9.11); it also points by means of the words καλέσαι . . . ἁμαρτωλούς to the action of Jesus in which he calls the tax-collector Matthew and invites tax-collectors and sinners to the feast. If one considers that in Matt. 9.9 and 9.10 there are two different and independent events, it is clear that the pronouncement of Jesus holds the originally disunited pericope together and makes it into a new whole. It is intended to make a Christological statement and that is why it stands, not fortuitously, in the section dealing with the 'Messiah of deed'.

When Matthew inserts the quotation from Hosea into Jesus' answer to the question of the Pharisees it is obviously intended as an interpretation of this reply. If it is true that the answer of Jesus is designed to illuminate his action, this will also apply to the quotation which is inserted into the answer. But then the sentence πορευθέντες δὲ μάθετε τί ἐστιν· ἔλεος θέλω καὶ οὐ θυσίαν (Matt. 9.13a), taking its reference strictly, cannot mean that the opponents of Jesus should learn that God demands mercy and not sacrifice and that they should behave accordingly; it must rather be understood as summoning them to comprehend that he, in the deeds to which they are objecting, is doing the will of God as stated in Hos. 6.6. There thus occurs in this passage, less a command regarding ethical behaviour, although that may also be present, than, in the mind of the evangelist, the summons to the Christological knowledge[1] that Jesus acts in accordance with Scripture. Thus what is found in Matt. 9.9–13 corresponds with Matthew's concern to show Jesus in his actions as the Christ on the basis of his fulfilling of Scripture. It is characteristic for the evangelist that he is not satisfied to justify the action of Jesus on grounds of natural insight (those who are well do not need a physician, but those who are sick). It is the evidence of the fulfilling of Scripture that first gives Jesus' statement about himself its Christological relevance.

If Matthew by means of the quotation from Hosea designates Jesus as the one who is merciful in accordance with the divine will, that applies not only to his connexion with tax-collectors and sinners. In Matthew's Gospel mercy is repeatedly exalted as an essential moment of his action. To this extent the quotation from Hosea in

[1] In the formula πορευθέντες δὲ μάθετε there is thus no disavowal (so rightly E. Klostermann, p. 81), but it is in line with the 'scholastic expression' צא לְמֵד of the Rabbis, which calls for the appropriation of knowledge but does not lead in the direction of conduct, as the examples supplied by Billerbeck, I, p. 499, show. Cf. also E. Lohmeyer, p. 174: Matt. 9.13a is 'a Christological quotation'.

Matt. 9.13 has a meaning for the interpretation of the acts of Jesus that exceeds the narrower context. In this sense Matthew's beloved expression ἐλέησον in the requests of the miracle stories must be called to mind[1] as well as the mention of the mercy of Jesus in the healings before the feeding of the five thousand (Matt. 14.14; on the other hand, Mark 6.34 speaks of Jesus teaching), in the feeding of the four thousand (Matt. 15.32 = Mark 8.2) and in the healing of the blind men at Jericho (Matt. 20.34). The sending out of the disciples by Jesus to share in his work is also grounded in his mercy (Matt. 9.36) and in Matt. 8.2–15 his mercy is seen in the fact that he turns his help to those who are rejected and despised.[2]

B. *The miracles as mighty works of the Servant of God*

In his investigation of the quotations from the Old Testament in Matthew's Gospel K. Stendahl comments on the passage in Matt. 8.17: 'It is closely linked up with the context and the phraseology of the Gospel.'[3] Matthew appears to give here his own translation of the Hebrew text of Isa. 53.4. His formulation corresponds neither with the translation style of the LXX nor with the actual translation of the passage in the LXX.[4] In the third place, however, it fits in entirely with the linguistic usage of the evangelist elsewhere.[5] But beyond all this yet further revealing observations can be made. It is striking that the concept νόσος occurs in the whole Gospel only in the closer environs of Matt. 8.17 and here it is concentrated: Matt. 4.23, 24; 9.35 and 10.1. All these passages are clearly summary reports which Matthew himself has formulated or (in 10.1) expanded by an expression of his own.[6] It is precisely these passages which form the framework in which the evangelist has enclosed his composition on the activity of the Christ. From this it not only follows that the translation νόσος in Matt. 8.17 agrees with the linguistic usage of the evangelist, but it can also be seen that this translation fits in with

---

[1] Cf. above, p. 220.

[2] Cf. A. Schlatter, *Matthäus*, p. 269: 'The reason why Matthew begins with the healing of the leper is clear from the fact that the Gentile follows the leper. Both stand outside the holy congregation . . .' and E. Lohmeyer, p. 153, who points out that the woman 'in this (Jewish) society has only limited rights and duties'.

[3] *The School of St Matthew*, p. 107.

[4] Cf. K. Stendahl, pp. 106 f.

[5] Cf. the evidence in A. Schlatter, *Matthäus*, pp. 282 f.

[6] The Matthaean character of Matt. 4.23; 9.35; 10.1b is crystal clear. A look at the concordance immediately shows the linguistic usage of Matthew in Matt. 4.24.

his editorial and theological intentions. Matthew translates the passage from the Old Testament according to the context, so to speak: according to the material context which he intends. The catchword linkage so attained by the concept νόσος makes a bridge from the passages which form the framework, with their summary account of Jesus' healing, to the presentation of this healing activity in detail (Matt. 8.2–17). This confirms, as other observations have already suggested, that the quotation in Matt. 8.17 applies to the whole activity of Jesus as miracle-working Saviour.[1]

It remains to ask in what sense Matthew quotes the passage from Isa. 53.4 in Matt. 8.17. In the first place there can be no doubt that he speaks of real physical sicknesses. This is shown not only by his translation in contrast to the spiritualising understanding of the LXX and the Targum,[2] but also above all by the nearer (Matt. 8.2–17) and the remoter (Matt. 4.23–9.35) context in which he puts the quotation, which deals with instances of the healing of the sick. How, then, is the 'bearing of sicknesses' understood by Matthew?

According to the original Hebrew text of Isaiah 53 the servant of God is 'a man of sorrows, and acquainted with sickness' (Isa. 53.3a),[3] he appears to his fellow-men as 'smitten of God, and afflicted' (Isa. 53.4b)[3]—statements which immediately surround the Matthaean quotation about the bearing of sicknesses. From this it is clear that the bearing of sicknesses in Isaiah 53 means that the bearer himself is a sick person.[4] Furthermore, his suffering is substitutionary, as, for example, is shown by the sentence: 'and the Lord has laid on him the iniquity of us all' (Isa. 53.6b).[5] The third thought which calls for acknowledgment is that this substitutionary suffering does away with the sicknesses and guilt of others. For 'upon him was the chastisement that made us whole, and with his stripes we are healed'

---

[1] Cf. above, pp. 171 f., 253 ff.

[2] LXX Isa. 53.4: οὗτος τὰς ἁμαρτίας ἡμῶν φέρει καὶ περὶ ἡμῶν ὀδυνᾶται. The text of the Targum reads (according to Billerbeck, I, pp. 482 f.): 'Therefore he will intercede for our guilt and our sins will be forgiven for his sake.' The other passages about bearing the guilt of sin are also interpreted in this sense as intercession and forgiveness for his sake (Isa. 53.11b, 12b).

[3] [RV text or margin.]

[4] Cf. the word 'pierced' (Isa. 53.5a). Above all נָגוּעַ (Isa. 53.4) denotes, if not 'one smitten with leprosy (נֶגַע) nevertheless a sickness with which God smites a man in a special way' (H. W. Wolff, *Jesaja 53 im Urchristentum*, Berlin, 1952³, p. 23, n. 25). It is significant that on the basis of this passage one section of the Rabbinic tradition expected that the Messiah would be a leper; cf. Billerbeck, I, p. 481, and T. Zahn, p. 345.

[5] [RSV.]

(Isa. 53.5b).[1] In its Old Testament position, and in the light of the meaning of the context there, the statement 'he has borne our griefs and carried our sorrows' (Isa. 53.4a)[1] means that a sick person substitutionarily takes upon himself (= bears) the sicknesses of others and abolishes them (= carries them away).

When Matthew in Matt. 8.17, however, speaks of bearing sicknesses he cannot mean the substitutionary suffering of a sick person. For his context shows nothing of the thought that Jesus became a sick person in the place of others.[2] Rather he is presented as the mighty Lord who frees the sick from their sicknesses. Hence the first evangelist can only have understood his quotation from Isa. 53.4 in the sense of doing sicknesses away, not in the sense of suffering them. There is no mention whatever of any kind of suffering. And it does not really seem thinkable that Matthew wished to designate the miracle-working Jesus as the suffering servant of God.[3]

Admittedly it cannot be disputed that the thought of the servant of God plays a part in Matthew's presentation of Christ. This is shown above all by the detailed quotation from Isa. 42.1–4 in Matt. 12.18–21. But there, too, it is not the suffering of the servant of God that is mentioned; rather, that he does not wrangle, does not break a bruised reed and brings justice to victory. This quotation takes its meaning entirely from its Matthaean context which reports that Jesus withdrew from his opponents and healed sick people (Matt. 12.15). Furthermore, the linguistic form of the quotation shows that Matthew formed it in the light of the actual relationship in which he wished to place it.[4] This example of a quotation from the Old Testa-

---

[1] [RSV.]

[2] It is to be noted that Matthew does not quote the very statements about the sickness of the servant.

[3] The interpretation attempted by T. Zahn (*Das Ev.d.Matth.*, p. 345) according to which 'the sympathy of a friend of men with his sick brothers and the tiring work of the doctor continued into the night to relieve their pains is also a taking upon oneself of their sicknesses and a bearing of their pains' not only feels artificial but seeks to understand the quotation less from its present Matthaean setting than from its original Old Testament one. The explanation of J. Schniewind, too (*Das Ev. nach Matth.*, p. 112), that the miracles of Jesus are here 'described as a part of the suffering of the servant of God', remains questionable. K. Bornhäuser (*Das Wirken des Christus*) rightly establishes that Matt. 8.17 'does not' suggest 'so much an inner bearing of suffering as the removal through miraculous power'.

[4] Cf. the illuminating investigation of G. Barth, above, pp. 125 ff. K. Stendahl (*The School of St Matthew*, pp. 97 ff.) shows precisely in the Matthaean quotations from the Old Testament that many of the unusual verbal details present an 'ad hoc interpretation' of the Massoretic text such as was required by the meaning of the context as intended by the evangelist.

ment is a parallel to the way in which the first evangelist completely inserts the quotation from Isa. 53.4 in Matt. 8.17 into the desired context of the healings of the sick by Jesus, and also shapes it linguistically from that point of view. Obviously his intention of interpreting the healing miracles of Jesus caused him to take from among the manifold statements about the suffering servant of God only that thought which is appropriate here, about the bearing of sicknesses, which appears only in Isa. 53.4a, and to interpret this thought not in the sense of suffering but in the sense of the doing away of sicknesses.[1] The selection of the words λαμβάνειν and βαστάζειν corresponds with this understanding. The words denote here nothing other than the taking away and doing away of sicknesses.[2] There is no indication that the evangelist had any intention by this quotation to interpret the miraculous deeds of Jesus in any other sense than that of mighty works. It is precisely as such that they are intended, by the evidence of the fulfilling of the Old Testament word of God, to be identified.[3]

Thus our findings must be formulated as follows: on the one hand, in the healing stories Matthew works out the concept of the Lord (*Kyrios*) and understands them entirely as manifestations of his might; but on the other, with Matt. 8.17 he interprets them as the work of the servant of God of Isaiah 53. He presents the Christ as the Lord in the majestic sense of the word and yet precisely in doing so he designates him as the one who reproduces the will of God. The thought of the lowliness of the Christ therefore brings only one side of the available material to expression: namely the obedience of the

---

[1] This evidence of a quotation bound up with the context may not be taken as proof that Matthew deals 'atomistically' with Isa. 53. There is indeed a mention of the doing away of sicknesses there, too (cf. H. W. Wolff, *Jes. 53 im Urchristentum*, p. 73). Besides, the referring of Isa. 53.4 to the healings of Jesus cannot be taken to mean that Matthew did not read something else in Isa. 53 as well (cf. A. Schlatter, *Matthäus*, p. 283).

[2] Cf. A. Schlatter, *Matthäus*, pp. 282 f., and J. A. Bengel, who interprets ἔλαβεν with 'abstulit a nobis' (*Gnomon, ad loc.*)!

[3] If the lowliness or the suffering had been an important trait for Matthew in the Christological interpretation of the miracle stories there would certainly have been some trace of this in the text of the pericopes, in accordance with the rule discovered above that Matthew expresses his interpretation of the received narratives not only by means of setting and arrangement but also by the form of the text, whether it be by omission, addition or change of wording (cf. ch. I on the retelling of the miracle stories by Matthew, above, pp. 165 ff.). But even in Matt. 8.2–16, all measures of that kind point to the opposite of humility. And what is more, no such traces of the humility of Jesus can be shown in any of the first evangelist's miracle stories.

Christ to the will of God. More exactly one must speak of the obedient humiliation[1] of the mighty one, who in his humiliation does not lose his might but uses it, not for himself, of course, but in the service of the rejected, despised and sick. This is the thought which Matthew has taken as the basis of the collection of healings gathered round the quotation in Matt. 8.17: Jesus directs his helping power to the leper, the Gentile and the sick woman.

One could thus also formulate the interpretation of Jesus' miraculous deeds as the mighty work of the servant of God under the concept of showing mercy. This is possible because the concept ἔλεος in the sphere of Old Testament thought no longer denotes, as in Greek circles, a feeling but in the first place a deed and, as the translation of חֶסֶד in religious terminology, has increasingly acquired the meaning of God's faithful merciful aid.[2] Matthew himself has shown in Matt. 9.13a that the 'Messiah of deed' is the merciful one who is in line with the will of God and this Hos. 6.6 comprehensively denotes by the word ἔλεος. Furthermore there are many hints in the miracle stories that Matthew understands them as works of mercy.[3] The brief sentence σπλαγχνισθεὶς δὲ ὁ Ἰησοῦς ἥψατο τῶν ὀμμάτων αὐτῶν, which Matthew (20.34) introduces into the story of the healing of the two blind men, can only be understood in this sense. This is scarcely intended to express a stirring of the feelings of Jesus but his merciful reply to the sick men's twofold cry for help, for mercy (Matt. 20.30, 31). The very form of this cry for help, which Matthew uses particularly frequently shows, by its linking of ἐλέησον with the term of address κύριε that merciful help is expected and received from a mighty one, from the Lord.[4]

In this connexion attention must yet again be directed to the fact that the work of Christ as the servant of God in the miracle stories takes place in the fulness of the divine power and is triumphant. The

[1] A. Schlatter, Matthäus, p. 283: 'With his healing activity what Jesus called ταπεινοῦν ἑαυτόν took place.'

[2] Cf. R. Bultmann, TWNT, II, pp. 474–7.

[3] Cf. above, pp. 258 f.

[4] In this way the interpretation of the miracle stories by Matthew falls in with his Christological line, according to which 'the proclamation and fulfilling of the δικαιοσύνη required by God . . .' is 'the predominant function of the Messiah here on earth' (G. Bornkamm, above, p. 36). To the proclamation of the will of God in the law by the Christ in Matthew (Matt. 9.13; 12.7) corresponds his fulfilling of this will of God not only in mixing with tax-collectors and sinners but also in his miraculous deeds in which Matthew likes to use the ideas of mercy. Thus the miraculous deeds of Jesus, too, are an objective fulfilling of the Old Testament, or rather, of its law.

sick are healed, demons are driven out and the powers of nature are subdued. The thought of the triumphant activity is not only attested by means of Isaiah 53, however,[1] but is also based on the fact that the evangelist sees in Jesus the risen and exalted Lord to whom all power in heaven and on earth is given (Matt. 28.18). Finally Matthew himself shows that this thought was important for him. In the other quotation the servant of God in Matt. 12.18–21, from Isa. 42.1–4 the goal of his activity is designated as the triumphant establishing of justice: ἕως ἂν ἐκβάλῃ εἰς νῖκος τὴν κρίσιν (Matt. 12.20). This sentence in this form is traceable neither in the Massoretic text nor in the Targum, LXX or Peshitta and has therefore been framed by Matthew independently.[2] Above all the insertion of εἰς νῖκος which has no foundation in any known possible previous text must be reckoned to his account. If this Matthaean form of the quotation is no accident but the result of a careful and learned theological interpretation,[3] then the purpose of the triumphant activity of the servant of God must have been of great importance to the evangelist.

It is thus seen that the evangelist Matthew is also interested in showing Jesus in the miracle stories in his whole triumphant power. In this way without doubt the earthly Jesus acquires the traits of the risen Lord of the congregation. Hence the miracle stories in Matthew's Gospel do not show the thaumaturge who seeks to gain recognition and admiration through his deeds, but the servant of God as he works on behalf of the helpless. The congregation may still perceive, however, how her Lord still proves himself mightily as the one who shows mercy.[4]

---

[1] Isa. 52.13 'Behold, my servant shall prosper, he shall be exalted and lifted up', and Isa. 53.10b '. . . the will of the Lord shall prosper in his hand' [RSV].

[2] Cf. K. Stendahl, The School of St Matthew, pp. 107 ff., and G. Barth, above, p. 127.

[3] This is shown by K. Stendahl, op. cit., pp. 107 ff., and G. Barth, pp. 125 ff.

[4] The fundamental difference between the Synoptic miracles of Jesus and those of the θεῖοι ἄνθρωποι appears to lie not in the mighty deed itself but in the thought of the new creation, which is absent from the latter but decisive for the former. Jesus heals the disrupted life or abolishes that which jeopardises it (cf. A. Schlatter, Matthäus, p. 267). The divine men of antiquity also brought about miracles for the well-being of men, it is true, but they were to some extent of quite a different kind. Cf. the examples in L. Bieler, Theios Aner, I (Wien, 1935): Empedocles 'caught . . . once the trade-wind in a tube, which he had prepared on the mountains . . . Proclus in a wonderful way brought rain to Attica which was suffering from drought. . .' (p. 103).

C. *The Lord and his congregation in the miracle stories*

Many individual observations point to the fact that in the Jesus of
the Matthaean miracle stories the risen Lord of the Church is
intended. That is seen already in the term of address κύριε which the
evangelist uses in numerous places.[1] The frequent occurrence of
προσκυνεῖν must be understood in the same sense.[2] In addition there
is the fact, perceivable everywhere, that the Jesus of the first Gospel
in the miracle stories lacks earthly human traits.[3] By the use of one
small example it can be illustrated that it is above all the way of
Matthew to present Jesus in the miracle stories as the Lord. In the
narrative of the raising of Jairus's daughter according to Mark,
Jesus puts to the company of mourners a half-surprised, half-
reproachful question (Mark 5.39 τί θορυβεῖσθε καὶ κλαίετε;), according to Luke he expresses an admonition meant in a comforting sense
(Luke 8.52 μὴ κλαίετε), but in Matthew with a sharp command he
turns the mourners out of the house (Matt. 9.24 ἀναχωρεῖτε). It could
be shown that these differences are characteristic for the Christ-
picture of the Gospels concerned;[4] but what matters here is the fact
that in the first Gospel Jesus is presented as the commanding Lord.

It should further be pointed out that the form of the miracle
stories in Matthew's Gospel is often that of a conversation whereby
the request very often takes the form of a prayer. One may think of
κύριε, σῶσον (Matt. 8.25; 14.30) and the use of the formula ἐλέησον
(Matt. 9.27; 15.22; 17.15; 20.30, 31). Above all nearly all the healing miracles have the form of a conversation consisting of a request
and Jesus' reply giving help. There can be no doubt that Matthew
in this way portrays the situation of a prayer and the hearing of it,
and thus in the place of a narrative about a past miraculous act he
lays before the eyes of the congregation her present possibility of
meeting with the miracle-working Lord. It is the role of the believing

---

[1] Mark uses this term of address only in 7.28 and (weakly attested) in 10.51.
In Matthew it occurs frequently in the narrative material: 8.2, 6, 8, 25; 14.28, 30;
15.22; 17.15; 20.30, 31, 33.

[2] Cf. above, p. 229.

[3] Cf. E. Klostermann, in the additional note on Matt. 3.1 on the biased alterations of Matthew on the text of Mark's Gospel, pp. 20 f.

[4] In Mark's Gospel questions by Jesus frequently occur: for example Mark
5.9, 30; 6.38; 8.5, 23; 9.16, 21, 33, etc., passages in which Matthew has, as a rule,
erased the questions (exception Mark 8.5 = Matt. 15.34). For Luke the comforting admonition in the mouth of Jesus is characteristic; cf. Luke 7.13 (μή κλαῖε),
7.50 and 17.19. Commands of Jesus are often found in Matthew's Gospel, for
example Matt. 8.32; 8.18 and 14.19 (κελεύειν); 21.6; 26.19.

suppliant which he commends to the congregation, even though this suppliant in the miracle story is not expressly characterised as a disciple.

Finally the insertion of θάρσει in the greeting of Jesus to the sick (Matt. 9.2, 22) also points to the sphere of the congregation in which these words are understood as a comforting of the needy by their Lord (cf. the comforting word of Jesus to his disciples in Mark 6.50 = Matt. 14.27 θαρσεῖτε, ἐγώ εἰμι· μὴ φοβεῖσθε).[1]

Matthew tells other miracle stories in the light of discipleship. He does so clearly in the story of the stilling of the storm (Matt. 8.18–27) and of the walking on the sea (Matt. 14.22–33).[2] At this point attention should be directed to the peculiar role acquired by the ship in the Matthaean version of the two miracle narratives. On both occasions it is not the people in the boat who are mentioned when reference is made to the danger, but it is the ship itself that is in peril because of the waves (Matt. 8.24; 14.24).[3] The similarity of the statements even to the very words[4] shows that here conscious fashioning is at work. It is revealing that Matthew designates the people on board the ship in 14.33 not simply as 'the disciples', which after 14.22, 26 would have been readily understood, but as οἱ ἐν τῷ πλοίῳ. The continuation of this verse: they worshipped him saying, 'Truly you are the Son of God' gives away the fact that here the disciples of the earthly life of Jesus are an image of the congregation of the risen Lord. In accordance with this, Matthew also places in the centre of both stories the presentation of the relation between Jesus and his congregation, which comes to expression in the conversation, that is, the prayer and Jesus' answer. One may therefore surmise that the prominence given to the ship in both stories is due to the fact that the evangelist understood it as an image of the congregation.

By the choice of the idea of little faith in several places in, and in connexion with, the miracle stories (Matt. 8.26; 14.31; 16.8; 17.20)

---

[1] It is not a matter of chance that Matthew omits the greeting θάρσει by the multitude to the blind man of Jericho (Mark 10.49). Patently the comforting word is reserved for Jesus; cf. H. Greeven, 'Die Heilung des Gelähmten nach Matth.', *Wort u. Dienst*, 1955, pp. 76 f.

[2] Cf. above, pp. 200 ff.

[3] Mark describes in Mark 4.37 first of all the storm at sea which imperils the ship, whereas Luke does not mention the ship in this connexion at all, but only speaks of the storm and the danger to the people (Luke 8.23). Mark reports in the story of the walking on the sea on the need of the disciples as they row (Mark 6.48).

[4] Cf. above, p. 232.

Matthew also inserts the situation of the Church into the pericopes. For little faith denotes precisely the situation of unbelief among the disciples, but not the absence of faith altogether,[1] for that would not be compatible with being a disciple.

It is quite on the line of this 'ecclesiastical' interest in the life of Jesus when Matthew depicts the 'Messiah of deed' in chapters 8–9 not only as the miracle worker, but also as the one who authoritatively decides the questions of the congregation as over against their opponents (Matt. 9.2–17). Thus the story of the Canaanite woman (Matt. 15.21–28) has acquired its special Matthaean profile from a problem facing the congregation, namely the question of the mission to the Gentiles. It traces back the admission of Gentile Christians to the Church on the ground of their faith, to Jesus himself.

If the influence of the situation of the Church on the miracle stories is shown in many observations (on the form, the omissions and insertions, the fashioning of the text, the choice of words and even on the position of the pericopes in the Gospel), the further question arises—what does the picture of the Church look like, which is mirrored in the miracle stories of Matthew?

She appears homeless in following her Lord (Matt. 8.20), like a small ship in extremest need and danger (Matt. 8.24; 14.24). She lives in a world which disputes in a hostile way her manner of life and action (9.2–17). She stands in danger of little faith and she lacks authority (17.14 ff.). In a word: she is the Church in her lowliness, on earth, in this aeon.

This situation of the Church in the time before the 'coming of the Son of man in his kingdom' (Matt. 16.28) is mirrored in the whole of Matthew's Gospel. Thus in the specifically Matthaean parables of the kingdom of heaven, for example (Matt. 13.24–30; 13.47–50), the Church is seen to be living not yet in the consummation, but in the time between as a mixed body.[2] In this connexion Matthew speaks (incidentally as the only one of the Synoptic writers) of the end of the world (Matt. 13.39, 40, 49); and it is significant that the whole Gospel in accordance with its last words is, as it were, open to the end of the world (Matt. 28.20 ἕως τῆς συντελείας τοῦ αἰῶνος). In the light of this very conclusion one may assume that the evangelist understands his Gospel as a Gospel for the time of the Church

---

[1] An instance of the loss of faith altogether is found in Mark 4.40, whichever reading is original, and in Luke 8.25.

[2] Cf. G. Bornkamm above, p. 19.

between Easter and the parousia of her Lord. For with the words 'teaching them to observe all that I have commanded you' (Matt. 28.20) Jesus points his disciples for their teaching activity between Easter and the end of the world to what his discourses in Matthew's Gospel contain by way of example.[1] If, however, the discourses in the first Gospel are principally directed to the Church it is not surprising if the miracle stories, too, are cut to fit the situation of the Church.

The way in which the first evangelist understands the situation of the Church in her lowliness is seen most clearly in the Matthaean retelling of the story of the stilling of the storm. Obviously the danger into which the ship falls corresponds to the position previously described by Jesus in the warning given to one who was ready to follow him: the Son of man has nowhere to lay his head (Matt. 8.20). Here it is clearly stated that the Church shares the lowliness of her Lord during his earthly life.[2] With this also agrees the saying of Jesus which he directs to his disciples in the mission speech apropos the announcement of persecution: the disciple is not above his teacher, nor the servant above his master (Matt. 10.24 f.).

The further question now arises what the miracle stories have to say about the relationship in which Jesus stands to this his congregation in her lowliness. As the two stories of the storm at sea and the walking on the sea show, Jesus proves himself to be the helper of his disciples in their trouble: he stills the storm (Matt. 8.26; 14.32), he saves Peter from sinking (Matt. 14.31). In both cases he answers the disciples' anxious cry in prayer (Matt. 8.25; 14.30). In a similar way Jesus replies helpfully to the believing request of the sufferers in the healing miracles. As he scolds the little faith of his disciples (Matt. 8.26; 14.31) he calls them to faith in that he expressly bestows his help on believing prayer (Matt. 8.13; 9.22, 29; 15.28).

In this connexion the story of the exorcism of the demons at Gadara calls above all for consideration (Matt. 8.28–34). It not only contains an important Christological statement but is itself the direct illustration of it: ἦλθες ὧδε πρὸ καιροῦ βασανίσαι ἡμᾶς (Matt. 8.29).[3]

---

[1] Cf. E. Lohmeyer, 'Mir ist gegeben alle Gewalt', *In Memoriam E. Lohmeyer*, p. 41, and N. A. Dahl, 'Die Passionsgesch.bei Matth.', *NT Studies* II, p. 29.

[2] This thought, as is well known, lies at the back of the instruction given to the disciples by Jesus on his way to the cross, in Mark 8.34–38; 10.42–45, and in the corresponding Synoptic parallels, precisely in connexion with his way of suffering (cf. the mention of suffering in Mark 8.31 and 10.45).

[3] Cf. above, pp. 172 ff.

It turns on the understanding of the two words πρὸ καιροῦ, which obviously contain the peculiarly Matthaean element in this new version of the saying in the mouth of the demons about the coming of Jesus (cf. Mark 1.24) and so in the retelling of the exorcism of the demons of Gerasa (Mark 5.1–20). In Mark's Gospel this statement right at the beginning of Jesus' appearance lifts for the reader the veil of the secret which surrounds his activity. The mission of Jesus is described as that of driving out demons (Mark 1.24), a thought which is particularly important for Mark's Gospel.[1] The destruction of the demons, however, as Jesus argues in his discussion with his opponents (Mark 3.22 ff.) is the end of Satan's rule,[2] or in other words, the irruption of the reign of God. To this extent the exorcism of the demons in the synagogue at Capernaum is a confirmation of a programmatic kind for the summary of the sermon in Mark 1.14: πεπλήρωται ὁ καιρὸς καὶ ἤγγικεν ἡ βασιλεία τοῦ θεοῦ.[3] The exorcism of the demons is the token of the turn of the ages.

Matthew cannot use this statement about the mission of Jesus to destroy the demons in the same sense as Mark. His understanding of the still future βασιλεία and of the Church as a community still living before the end of the 'aeon' speaks against it. Hence he interprets the statement about the authority of Jesus over the demons by means of the addition πρὸ καιροῦ. That can then only mean: it applies already 'before the final damnation',[4] that is, before the turn of the ages, before the end of the world, towards which Jesus is still looking in his saying in Matt. 28.20. But then πρὸ καιροῦ means the same as 'in the time of the Church'. According to this Matthew sees in the exorcism of the demons of Gadara the evidence of the authority of Jesus, now already, before the end, in the time of the Church, to deliver up the demons to their eschatological judgment. He exercises his eschatological position of Lordship already now, prematurely as it were, on the earth, too.[5] This very πρὸ καιροῦ must have been important to a church, which, it is true still awaited the end of the world, but which in spite of that still already confessed the rule of her exalted Lord, whose active

---

[1] Cf. J. M. Robinson, *The Problem of History in Mark*, pp. 33 ff.

[2] Cf. Mark 3.26 . . . ἀλλὰ τέλος ἔχει (it is Satan who is meant). Only Mark has this small clause. Thus we know that he attaches particular importance to it.

[3] Cf. R. H. Lightfoot, *The Gospel Message of St Mark*, pp. 20 f.

[4] Thus J. Wellhausen, *Matthaei*, p. 39. Cf. E. Klostermann, *ad loc.*

[5] Obviously the expression καὶ ἐπὶ τῆς γῆς (Matt. 28.18) corresponds to the word ὧδε (Matt. 8.29) in substance.

presence was promised to her till the end of the world (Matt. 28.20).[1]

It should be clear that the expression ἐπὶ τῆς γῆς (Matt. 9.6) in the story of the healing of the paralytic in the mind of Matthew also means not only the earth as the place of the earthly activity of Jesus but also the place in which the congregation lives under the rule of her exalted Lord. This is supported by the peculiar conclusion of the pericope which points in the direction of the authority of the Church to forgive sins (Matt. 9.8).[2] The same words ἐπὶ τῆς γῆς, which occur in Matt. 16.19 and 18.18 in the context of government in the congregation in immediate proximity to the concept ἐκκλησία (Matt. 16.18; 18.17) and likewise denote the sphere of the Church as she acts with authority, also point to the same thing.

In this way a new peculiarity of the Matthaean Christology in the miracle stories has come into view. Jesus is not merely the helper of his Church on earth, he also grants her participation in his authority.

D. *The participation of the congregation in the authority of her Lord*

Analysis of the composition of Matthew 5–10 has shown that Matthew not only presents Jesus as the one who teaches with authority and as the wonderful Saviour, but also as the Lord who gives his disciples a share in his authority. This thought is no novelty of the first evangelist in the Synoptic tradition.[3] Mark and Luke also present the sending forth of the disciples by Jesus in such a way that he transfers his authority to them (Mark 6.7; Luke 9.1).[4] That comes to expression in their case too through their composition, in so far as in both the sending forth is preceded by a cycle of miracle stories the meaning of which is to show the authority of Jesus through his miraculous deeds (Mark 4.35–5.43; Luke 8.22–56).[5] The sayings-

---

[1] As A. Resch (*Ausserkanonische Paralleltexte zu den Evangelien*, Heft III, pp. 136 ff. on Luke 8.28) shows, the writers of the ancient Church attached importance precisely to these words πρὸ καιροῦ, *ante tempus*.

[2] Cf. below, pp. 273 f.

[3] That those who believe in Christ are empowered to do mighty works is, of course, attested outside the Synoptic tradition (for example, Rom. 15.19; Gal. 3.5; Heb. 2.4; Acts 3.1–10).

[4] In Mark it is above all authority òver demons (6.7). The double commission: preaching and exorcising of demons (Mark 3.14 f.) corresponds to the work of Christ (Mark 1.39).

[5] In Mark and Luke the activity of the disciples consists of preaching and healings, as the report about the execution of their commission shows (Mark 6.12 f.; Luke 9.6). In Luke this is already clearly stated at the commissioning (9.2) and in the second commissioning speech it is also expressly laid down (10.9). The transfer of authority is reported by them as by Matthew (Matt. 10.1) only for miraculous

source also knows the fact that the person sent is the equivalent representative of him who sends him (Matt. 10.40; Luke 10.16). And in the miracle tradition the problem of the disciples' inability to heal the epileptic boy (Mark 9.14 ff.) presupposes that the disciples were empowered to perform miracles of healing.

Neither of the other two Synoptics, however, has worked out this thought, that Jesus gives his disciples a share in his authority, so clearly and impressively as Matthew. He alone has collected the miraculous deeds of Jesus into a single group (Matt. 8–9), has linked them so closely with the teaching of Jesus (Matt. 5–7) (with the help of the same words and the repetition of a verse, Matt. 4.23; 9.35) and so placed them in a programmatic Christological context. He alone places the sending forth of the disciples between this comprehensive presentation of the activity of the Christ and the enquiry of the Baptist (Matt. 11.3), so that the activity of the disciples has a direct Christological reference.[1]

On the other hand, however, Matthew is also the only evangelist who makes known the participation of the disciples in the authority of Jesus not only in the composition of his Gospel but also in the form of the miracle stories themselves.

Matt. 17.14–20

The healing of the epileptic boy in Matthew is not interested in the evidence of the superior miraculous power of Jesus nor in the paradox of unbelieving belief, but solely in the problem of the defective authority of the disciples.[2] This theme is also present, it is true, in Mark, but it is first in Matthew that it becomes absolutely determinative. As the concluding conversation shows (Matt. 17.20) what interests him, to express it positively, is how the disciple comes into active participation in the authority of Jesus to perform healing miracles. It is striking that the instruction of Jesus on this question no longer speaks of the individual case before us (cf. Mark 9.29), but of the authority to perform miracles generally. Since this whole miracle story is aimed by Matthew both formally and materially at

---

deeds, in Mark only for the exorcism of demons (Mark 6.7), in Luke (9.1) as in Matthew (10.1) also for healings. There can be no doubt that in the view of the second and third evangelists, too, the disciples enter into Jesus' own work, the example of which both in teaching and miraculous deeds they present in what has gone before (Mark 4.1–34; 4.35–5.43, and Luke 8.4–18; 8.22–56).

[1] Cf. above, pp. 249 ff.
[2] Cf. above, pp. 188 f.

the instruction of the disciples[1] it shows a transfer of the centre of gravity from the miraculous power and the miraculous deed of Jesus to the participation of the disciples in it.

Matt. 14.22–33

The shift of the Christological interest into the ecclesiastical can also be observed in the pericope of Jesus walking on the sea, into which Matthew has worked the scene of Peter walking on the sea (Matt. 14.28–31).[2] In Mark's Gospel this narrative is presented as an epiphany of Jesus before the disciples (Mark 6.45–52). As Matthew shows at the end of his new account (Matt. 14.33), he has not taken away this character from the narrative. He has rather underlined it in that there follows the self-revealing saying of Jesus (Matt. 14.27) the correspondingly appropriate confession of the disciples (Matt. 14.33). The essential difference from Mark's Gospel lies not only in the fact that the disciples here understand the revelation of the son of God. Matthew has inserted a new scene between the revealing saying of the Lord and the adoring confession of the disciples. The confession of the disciples obviously applies to the Lord as he is presented in the passage that lies between. In short: the scene of Peter walking on the sea not only has an ecclesiological meaning inasmuch as it uses the motive of discipleship,[3] it also has a Christological aim. Christ is not only the deliverer of his own from need and danger; rather, he gives his disciple a share in his power to walk on the water.[4] That is brought clearly to expression above all at the beginning of the scene (Matt. 14.28 f.). Jesus does not decline Peter's wish, but grants him by his command permission to do it. And in the question of Jesus to those of little faith (Matt. 14.31) there can be heard alongside the reproach an expression of surprise, not that Peter was able to walk on the water, but that he sank in the waves. 'All this does not go beyond the fact that Jesus transfers his authority to those whom he sends' (Matt. 10.1).[5]

---

[1] Cf. above, p. 190 f.   [2] Cf. above, pp. 204 ff.
[3] Cf. above, p. 206.

[4] T. Zahn (*Das Ev.d.Matth.*, pp. 513 f.) draws attention to this moment when he says that the power of Jesus 'momentarily' passes over 'to the disciple', and A. Schlatter (*Matthäus*, pp. 470 f.) says with particular emphasis: 'In that Peter too is empowered to leave the ship and to stand alongside Jesus, it . . . is stated that the disciple too participates in the power of Jesus. Jesus displays to the disciples the almighty presence of God, not in reference to himself only, and sees therein not a possession given to himself alone for him to guard it jealously. Rather the longing of the disciple is fulfilled and he is meant to stand where Jesus stands. . . .'

[5] A. Schlatter, *Matthäus*, p. 471.

Matt. 9.2–8

In the healing of the paralytic, Matthew has given the saying of Jesus about the authority of the Son of Man on earth to forgive sins the predominant place.[1] And this is seen above all in the alteration of the conclusion of this story. The praising of God by the crowd does not refer here any longer to the miracle as such but to the fact that God has given such power 'to men' (Matt. 9.8). This peculiar formulation is understood by most interpreters as meaning that 'to men' refers basically to Jesus, who in Matt. 9.6 calls himself the Son of Man. That would mean here in its original sense 'the man'.[2] However illuminating this may be at first sight it loses something of its credibility, of course, when it is remembered that in Matt. 9.8 there occurs a deliberate alteration of the Markan text by the first evangelist. What interest led him to do this? May Matthew, in a historicising fashion, have attached importance to the fact that people then present at the occurrence in question referred the saying about the Son of Man—and this is quite possible—to some man or other, or rather, to men in general?[3] Is it credible that the evangelist expresses himself so vaguely that he writes τοῖς ἀνθρώποις but means Jesus? And finally, is it probable that he understood the expression ὁ υἱὸς τοῦ ἀνθρώπου in the mouth of Jesus not as a Messianic title of dignity but as a general designation for 'man'? All these questions can only be answered in the negative—for in the first place no historicising interest is traceable in Matthew, but on the contrary, wherever possible the evangelist imports the situation of the Christian congregation into the account of the earthly Jesus; in the second place he seeks to clarify by his alterations but not to introduce obscure statements; and finally, the concept Son of Man, as is shown for example, by Matt. 16.13 in comparison with Mark 8.27, is understood by the evangelist as a self-designation of Jesus, and consequently Messianically. The interpretation of Matt. 9.8 which is in question is beyond comprehension if Matthew has modified the Markan text; it would only be intelligible if he had here 'retained a highly original trait of the original account'.[4] But that cannot be shown, nor is it probable if one considers the explanation of A. Schlatter: 'In the plural τοῖς ἀνθρώποις the conviction of Matthew

[1] Cf. above, pp. 175 ff.
[2] Thus J. Wellhausen, T. Zahn, J. Weiss, E. Klostermann, J. Schniewind and others.
[3] Cf. the interpretation in T. Zahn, pp. 372 f.
[4] Thus J. Weiss, *Das älteste Evangelium*, p. 156, note 1.

is manifest, that the authority of Jesus to forgive sins has become the possession of the congregation.'[1] This interpretation is illuminating because it agrees with what is also found in other passages, namely that Matthew emphasises the fact that Jesus grants his disciples participation in his authority. In this way the interpretation of Mark 2.12 in Matt. 9.8 is entirely understandable. The plural τοῖς ἀνθρώποις includes Jesus and his congregation and one can see once again that the Christology has acquired an ecclesiological accent. The evangelist Matthew gives the controversial conversation of Mark 2.1–12, which is concerned with Christ alone, but by which 'the Church wanted to trace back to Jesus *its* own right to forgive sins',[2] an application to the congregation, too, which is recognisable in the very wording of the text.

The healing word of faith

It is a striking thing that in the healing miracles of Matthew's Gospel there is never (apart from one exception, Matt. 8.3) an authoritative word of Jesus reported in connexion with the healing.[3] Instead of that Jesus speaks about the faith of the suppliant. The saying of Jesus about faith (Matt. 8.13; 9.22, 29; 15.28) actually takes the place of the miracle-working word of authority.[4] This state of things can only be understood as meaning that for Matthew less interest attaches to the actual deed of the miracle-worker than to the faith to which the miracle is granted. So, too, in the accounts of Jesus' own miraculous deeds for other people the question which is uppermost concerns the way in which the person receives a share in the miraculous power of Jesus, here, of course, not in the sense that the person is empowered to work miracles (as in Matt. 14.28 ff. and

---

[1] A. Schlatter, *Matthäus*, p. 301, with reference to Matt. 16.19 and 18.18; similarly R. Bultmann, *SynT*, pp. 15 f. B. W. Bacon, *Matthew*, pp. 189 f. on Matt. 9.8: 'The authority of Jesus Matthew takes for granted; his interest is to show that it is transmitted to "men" who still go forth in Jesus' name healing and preaching the (Messianic) forgiveness of sins.' Cf. also A. Fridrichsen, *Le problème du Miracle*, p. 92, and H. Greeven, *Wort u. Dienst*, 1955, pp. 70, 76.

[2] R. Bultmann, *SynT*, p. 16.

[3] It is true that Matt. 8.3 is no authoritative word in the usual style but is clearly Jesus' answer to the request of the leper. The healing sayings in Matt. 9.6 and 12.13 do not stand in proper miracle stories, but in debates of which faith is not the theme. It is, however, significant that Matthew never of himself supplies such an authoritative word in an instance of healing, as say Luke (18.42) does; rather in one place he wipes it out altogether (Mark 5.41 = Luke 8.54). Mark also provides such an authoritative word in Mark 4.39; 7.34; 9.25 and Luke in Luke 7.14, passages which have no parallel in the other evangelists.

[4] Cf. above, p. 242.

Matt. 17.14 ff), but so that he receives a miracle. The result is that for a number of miraculous healings in Matthew's Gospel the Christological theme is united with the question how the believer comes to share in Christ and his benefits.

It is well known that in connexion with the question how the congregation comes to participate in the authority of her Lord faith plays a decisive role. It is necessary in a new chapter to investigate what is the understanding of faith in the miracle stories of Matthew's Gospel.[1]

IV. THE INTERPRETATION OF FAITH BY MATTHEW IN THE MIRACLE STORIES

The concept of faith in the Synoptic tradition in most at home in the miracle stories. That can easily be seen at a glance from Mark's Gospel. If one removes the passages which betray the linguistic usage of the Christian Church (Mark 1.15; 9.42 and 16.11 ff.),[2] it can be seen that with few exceptions (Mark 11.31; 13.21; 15.32) the word family πίστις/πιστεύειν appears only within or (as in Mark 11.22 ff.) in closest connexion with a miracle story.[3] Matthew's Gospel shows a very similar state of things.[4] Here the use

[1] It should be pointed out here that in Matt. 19.28 as well, the thought occurs that the Christ gives his disciples a share in his authority. This saying is inserted by Matthew into the answer of Jesus to the question (expressly formulated in Matthew only) of Peter: What shall we have (who have left all and followed thee)? Jesus promises his disciples a share in his judging authority as Son of Man: ὁ δὲ Ἰησοῦς εἶπεν αὐτοῖς· ἀμὴν λέγω ὑμῖν ὅτι ὑμεῖς οἱ ἀκολουθήσαντές μοι, ἐν τῇ παλιγγενεσίᾳ ὅταν καθίσῃ ὁ υἱὸς τοῦ ἀνθρώπου ἐπὶ θρόνου δόξης αὐτοῦ, καθήσεσθε καὶ αὐτοὶ ἐπὶ δώδεκα θρόνους κρίνοντες τὰς δώδεκα φυλὰς τοῦ Ἰσραήλ.

Comparison with the related saying in Luke 22.28–30 shows, first, that Matthew expresses the thought of participation in the judging authority altogether more clearly, if not first clearly at all, and secondly, that this state of affairs can already be seen in the formal parallel structure.

Thus there is found in Matthew's Gospel a close link between Christology and ecclesiology not only inasmuch as the disciples share the lowliness of Jesus and his way of suffering (cf. say Mark 8.27–37 and par.) but even as they share in his glory, too.

[2] On the use of πίστις/πιστεύειν in the sense of accepting the Gospel, or rather, coming into faith and living in faith in the sphere of the Christian Church, cf. R. Bultmann, Theology of the NT, pp. 89 ff., and TWNT, VI, pp. 209 ff. [BKW Faith, pp. 68 ff.].

[3] πιστεύειν Mark 5.36; 9.23, 24; 11.23, 24.
πίστις Mark 2.5; 5.34; 10.52; 4.40; 11.22.
ἀπιστία Mark 6.6; 9.24; ἄπιστος Mark 9.19.

[4] The only specific Matthaean use of πίστις in a new sense compared with Mark occurs in Matt. 23.23; cf. G. Bornkamm above, pp. 26 ff, and G. Barth above, pp. 112 ff. The placing of πιστεύειν in Matt. 21.32 and 24.26 corresponds

of πιστεύειν in the proper Christian sense occurs in only one place, and there it is taken over from Mark (Matt. 18.6 = Mark 9, 42). It is Luke who has first given more space in his Gospel to this Christian usage of πιστεύειν,[1] and that applies not only to material that is peculiar to Luke but also within common Synoptic material (Luke 8.12, 13; 12.46; 22.67). In Mark on the contrary it is found, significantly, apart from one single passage (Mark 9.42), only outside the proper pericopes, in editorial constructions (Mark 1.15 and 16.11 ff.). This survey already shows how the notion of faith appears predominantly in the early tradition in connexion with the miracles. That applies in the first place to its occurrence in the narrative material. But this connexion between faith and miracles is also found in the sayings tradition. This is shown in the saying about the faith of the heathen centurion (Matt. 8.10 = Luke 7.9) and the saying about omnipotent faith which was handed down and employed in various forms (Mark 11.23; Matt. 21.21; 17.20 and Luke 17.6). Its utilisation in conjunction with a miracle story in the first two Gospels likewise points to a material relationship between faith and miracles. Finally the statement of Jesus found in all three Synoptic writers, 'Thy faith hath saved thee', which often accompanies a healing miracle, presupposes such a firm relationship.

A. *The material connexion between faith and miracle in the Synoptic tradition*

If one desires to understand the relationship between faith and miracle in the Synoptic miracle stories one must from the very outset keep one conception at a distance. A look at the miracle accounts shows that here faith does not follow the miracle but precedes it. The connexion between faith and the miracle is thus not that the latter calls forth the former and provides a basis for it. That means two

---

to the use in Matt. 21.25 = Mark 11.31 and Matt. 24.23 = Mark 13.21. The passages in Matt. 8.10, 13; 9.28, 29; 15.28 as well as the notion of little faith (Matt. 8.26; 14.31; 16.8; 17.20) are found only in miracle stories, apart from Matt. 6.30 (Luke 12.28, Q). The word πιστός (Matt. 24.45; 25.21, 23) must be left out of consideration here, since it does not mean believing, but faithful, reliable.

[1] The concept of faith in the sense of accepting the Christian Gospel is recognisable in Luke 22.67; 24.25 and 24.11. In Luke 8.12, 13 'believing' is equivalent to being a Christian and becoming one respectively and in Luke 12.46 ἄπιστος certainly bears the meaning of unbelieving, non-Christian (cf. R. Bultmann, *TWNT*, VI, p. 205, [*Faith*, p. 61]). In the word 'faith' in Luke 17.5; 18.8; 22.32 the meaning being a believer, a Christian, is at least an overtone.

things: with regard to the miracle, that it is not performed for the sake of propaganda and it is not intended as a means for converting the unbeliever, and with regard to faith that it does not here mean the recognition of the Messianic dignity of Jesus or the acceptance of the Christian proclamation.[1] Moreover, the Synoptic tradition has in many places brought out the rejection of miracles for purposes of propaganda and attestation, as in the repulsing of the demand for a sign (Mark 8.11–12 and par.) or the disregarding of it by Jesus (Mark 15.32 and par.) and also in the warning against the propaganda miracles of the false prophets and Messianic pretenders (Mark 13.21–22 and par.).[2]

At the end of the narrative of the rejection of Jesus in Nazareth Mark indicates that faith is a more or less indispensable presupposition for Jesus' miraculous healing (Mark 6.5.6): καὶ οὐκ ἐδύνατο ἐκεῖ ποιῆσαι οὐδεμίαν δύναμιν, εἰ μὴ ὀλίγοις ἀρρώστοις ἐπιθεὶς τὰς χεῖρας ἐθεράπευσεν. καὶ ἐθαύμασαν διὰ τὴν ἀπιστίαν αὐτῶν. One may not press the οὐκ ἐδύνατο but understand it as meaning that 'the indispensability of faith for Jesus' miraculous help' is thus strongly brought into prominence.[3] At the same time, however, by the limitation (εἰ μή . . . Mark 6.5b), obviously inserted, the misunderstanding is averted that Jesus was dependent in his working of miracles on the faith of men. But in any case there exists a material connexion between faith and

---

[1] It is not intended, of course, to dispute the possibility that the miracle stories were used in Christian missionary preaching to win unbelievers (cf. M. Dibelius, *Formgesch.*, pp. 90 ff. [pp. 92 ff.] on the meaning of the 'tales' in the context of the early Christian mission) and that the Christian preacher must also have understood by faith in the miracle stories the believing acknowledgment of the Lord Jesus. It is not intended, further, to dispute that the praise of the miracle-worker, understood historically and psychologically must have been the presupposition for people turning at all with their requests to Jesus for help. What matters here, however, in the first place is only the material connexion between faith and miracle in the miracle stories themselves.

[2] As Acts 2.22 ('Jesus . . . a man attested to you by God with mighty works and wonders and signs') shows, Luke understands the mighty deeds of Jesus as evidence of his divine mission. It is certainly not fortuitous that this propagandistic evaluation of the miraculous deeds occurs in a missionary sermon. It is always Luke who works out especially firmly in the miracle stories the acclamation of people as they express their praise (for example Luke 5.26; 7.16 and 18.43) and thereby emphasises their evidential character for the divine mission of Jesus. One must see in this a special peculiarity of the third evangelist, which is not yet so developed in Mark and in Matthew is almost totally untraceable.

[3] A. Schlatter, *Matthäus*, p. 457. Cf. A. Fridrichsen, p. 53: 'La grandeur de l'incrédulité se montre en ce que Jésus n'y "pouvait" faire que très peu de guérisons ce qui signifie qu'on ne recherchait pas son secours . . . Il aurait pu faire des miracles, si l'occasion lui en avait été donnée, c'est l'explication de: οὐκ ἐδύνατο.'

the miracle. Matthew shows by his brief and simple formulation at this point that he understood Mark in this sense: καὶ οὐκ ἐποίησεν ἐκεῖ δυνάμεις πολλὰς διὰ τὴν ἀπιστίαν αὐτῶν (Matt. 13.58). It is clear without more ado that by the deletion of ἐθαύμασεν (Mark 6.6) Matthew first really brings out clearly the connexion between the small number of healings and the unbelief of the Nazarenes. What is here negatively expressed Matthew has positively developed in his retelling and formal shaping of the Synoptic healing miracles, namely that the miracle takes place in accordance with the request of the suppliant.[1] There can be no question that the first evangelist in particular has a marked interest in this material connexion.

The psychological explanation of this connexion between faith and the miracle is excluded from the very beginning. For in several miracle stories it is not the faith of the sick person but that of his relatives (Mark 7.24 ff.; 9.14 ff.) or friends (Mark 2.3 ff. and Matt. 8.5 ff.) to which Jesus replies with his saving help. This fact and the two accounts of healing from a distance exclude the possibility of understanding the miracle in the sense of a suggestive influence of Jesus on the sick person by word or gesture, and along with this also the interpretation according to which in faith 'that is found which we today call "psychical disposition"', 'without which Jesus cannot heal'.[2]

A second possible interpretation for the relationship between faith and miracle similarly does not call for consideration. According to this the miracle takes place because the believer shows obedience to the word of Jesus. This understanding finds no support in the overwhelming majority of the Synoptic healing stories and finds in the healing of the ten lepers in Luke's Gospel (Luke 17.11–19) its sole example.[3] With this there also drops out the understanding of a

---

[1] Cf. above, pp. 239 f.

[2] Thus E. Fascher, *Die formgesch. Methode*, pp. 124 f. Cf. contrariwise A. Schlatter, *Der Glaube im NT*, p.119, and J. Schniewind, *Markus*, p. 57.

[3] Stories in which 'an order is given through the carrying out of which the miraculous event takes place' are found (according to O. Perels, *Die Wunderüberlieferung der Synoptiker*, p. 5) apart from in Luke 17.11 ff. also in Luke 5.1 ff. and Matt. 14.28 f. It is significant that this motive emerges in legendary passages. This makes it clear that we are here dealing with a later development. It should, however, also be pointed out in this connexion that in the miracle inscriptions of Epidaurus the following pattern frequently appears: The god gives the sick person or one seeking help in a dream a command and through obeying this the miracle happens on the following day. As examples there may be named miracle number 57 (according to R. Herzog, *Die Wunderheilungen von Epidauros*, p. 31) which refers

miracle as a reward for faith, as it can be found among the Rabbis. For there the dividing of the Red Sea, for example, is understood as a reward for the obedient faith of the Israelites, and it can actually be said 'that the Israelites were redeemed from Egypt only as a reward for their faith, as it says: and the people believed' (Exod. 4.31).[1]

The notion of faith in the Synoptic miracle stories is understood as a rule as 'trust in the miraculous power of Jesus'.[2] Yet this interpretation of the notion of πίστις seems somewhat unsatisfying, since the moment of activity does not come properly to expression in it, and this is peculiar to it in the healing miracles of the Synoptic tradition. It is very striking that in them 'faith' denotes the action of people and only to that extent their inner attitude to Jesus. The most impressive example of this kind occurs in the story of the healing of the paralytic, in which all three Synoptic writers report that Jesus 'saw' the faith of those who brought the sick man to Jesus (Mark 2.5 and par.). Mark (2.4) and Luke (5.18 f.) also make this faith visible for the hearer of the story by describing the pains which the friends of the sick man take to bring him to his helper. In the narrative of the healing of the woman with the haemorrhage the way the sick woman acts is designated by Jesus as faith (Mark 5.34 and par.). The same state of things is shown in the healing of the blind man at Jericho, in which Jesus similarly pronounces the action of the blind man, namely his unmistakable and indefatigable crying for help (Mark 10.47 f. and par.), and according to Mark (10.50) also his immediate and hasty advance, as saving faith.[3] The very saying used in these two last-named narratives: thy faith hath

---

to a paralytic: '. . . This man came into the shrine, slept in the healing room and saw a dream: he dreamed that the god stood before him, took him by the hand, took him to the holy hearth and commanded him to warm himself at the fire. When the sun rose he did what the god had commanded and became well.'

[1] Cf. Billerbeck, III, pp. 198 f.

[2] Thus E. Klostermann, on Mark 2.5 and on Matt. 8.10. M. Dibelius, *Formgesch.*, p. 75, defines as: 'confidence in the power of the miracle worker'. J. Schniewind, p. 51, translates with 'rely' and on Mark 2.5 says to reckon on God's assisting power present in Jesus. E. Lohmeyer, p. 103, interprets Mark 5.34: 'Faith in the healing power of the Master'. V. Taylor, *The Gospel . . . Mark*, on Mark 1.40b: confidence; and on Mark 2.5 confident trust in Jesus and his power to help. R. Bultmann, *TWNT*, VI, p. 206 [*Faith*, p. 64] speaks of 'belief in Jesus' miraculous power' and of 'confidence in miraculous divine help'.

[3] Cf. M. Dibelius, *Formgesch.*, p. 49 [52]: That the blind man 'throws his cloak aside and springs up only shows his readiness and his confidence, in short, his faith'.

saved thee (Mark 5.34; 10.52), gives faith an 'active' share in the miraculous deliverance.[1] What in all these cases is designated as faith is the actions by which the people create for themselves a meeting with Jesus. And when Mark in two places (2.4; 10.50) brings these actions with special love and care before our eyes this is not simply a case of descriptive decoration but, to be sure, it is also an illustration of this very faith.[2] When Matthew shows a preference for illustrating faith by means of a conversation (Matt. 8.5–13; 15.21–28) that does not mean any deviation from this line. In fact, these conversations must also be understood as actions through which Jesus is pressed to intervene with his help. When every time at the end of these conversations Jesus speaks of faith it is clear, precisely from these examples, that faith represents 'an activity of the believer, an energetic, importunate, grasping after the help of God . . .'[3]

It is significant that this 'active' believing has to develop and achieve its end in most cases in the face of special difficulties. Thus faith makes its own way to Jesus in spite of the outward obstacle of the crowd: in the story of the healing of the paralytic, the woman with the haemorrhage and the healing of the blind men at Jericho. It overcomes the religious barriers between Judaism and the Gentile world (Mark 7.24 ff. and above all Matt. 15.21 ff.; 8.5 ff.). Even when Jesus hesitates, as happens, for example in the healing of the blind men in Matt. 9.27 ff., or indeed when he keeps a declining silence, as Matthew reports in the narrative of the Canaanite woman (Matt. 15.23), faith wins for itself the granting of its demand. Even where death has already taken place (Matt. 9.18) and in what is from a human point of view a hopeless case (Mark 9.14 ff.), and still more, even in the face of a man's own unbelief (Mark 9.24) the longing which expects deliverance by Jesus does not give up. Hence it is no accident that in the miracle stories the concept of willing sometimes represents the concept of believing. In the story of the healing of the blind man at Jericho the behaviour of the blind man is first described as an act of willing (Mark 10.51 and par.) but then as

---

[1] Cf. T. Zahn, *Das Ev. d. Matth.*, p. 385: Jesus sees the healing according to Mark 9.22 'not as his own deed but as a deed of faith on the part of the woman'; and E. Lohmeyer, on Mark 5.34: This sentence 'attributes to faith what the Master at least indirectly brings about and directly confirms. . . .'

[2] Cf. A. Schlatter, *Der Glaube im NT*, p. 105, note.

[3] Thus formulated by C. E. B. Cranfield, 'St Mark 9.14–29', *Scottish Journal of Theology*, III, 1 (March, 1950), p. 66.

a saving faith (Mark 10.52 and par.). In Matthew the place of θέλετε in the question of Jesus to the blind men (Matt. 20.32) is taken in the other passage (Matt. 9.28) by πιστεύετε. It is in agreement with this conclusion when the first evangelist in his formula about saving faith can interchange the concepts of believing and willing (Matt. 8.13; 15.28). This recognisable parallelism or indeed interchangeability of believing and willing in particular passages confirms the observation that faith in the Synoptic miracle stories denotes not merely trust, but also a 'movement of the will, which presses in its desire towards Jesus'.[1]

A third characteristic of the use of the concept of faith in the Synoptic miracle stories, in addition to the moments of activity and willing, is that it always arises where a request has already been expressed or a desire become visible, to which it then refers back.[2] The miracle is always the fulfilling of a desire previously expressed whether expressly uttered as a request or only brought out in some action.[3] This state of things applies to all the healing miracles in the Synoptic Gospels, but also to a considerable number of the so-called nature miracles.[4] If, in the light of this, faith in the miracle stories is always expressed as a request one can rightly say that it 'is essentially praying faith'.[5]

If this definition of faith in the Synoptic miracle stories as praying faith is right it will necessarily follow that even where a request for help is made to Jesus, but the idea of faith does not appear, nevertheless the same content of supplicating faith is present. That applies to the healing of the leper, who turns to Jesus with the request: 'If thou wilt thou canst make me clean.'[6] The same applies to the request of the Canaanite woman in Mark's Gospel and this is then

---

[1] A. Schlatter, *Matthäus*, p. 277. Cf. J. A. Bengel, *Gnomon*, on Matt. 15.28: Fides est etiam in voluntate. (Faith is even in the will.) This understanding of faith in the sense of a movement of the will is already present in Judaism. Cf. A. Schlatter, *Der Glaube im NT*, pp. 80 f.

[2] Cf. Mark 2.5 and 2.3, 4; 5.34 and 5.25–28; 5.36 and 5.22–23; 10.52 and 10.47–48; 4.40 and 4.38; 9.23–24 and 9.17–18, 22b; Matt. 8.13 and 8.6–9; 9.29 and 9.27–28; 15.28 and 15.22–27.

[3] Cf. A. Fridrichsen, *Le problème du Miracle*, p. 52.

[4] Cf. the request of the father at the raising of his daughter (Mark 5.23 and par.), the 'request' of the disciples at the stilling of the storm (Mark 4.38 and par.) and at the feeding of the five thousand (Mark 6.36 and par.) and the request of Peter as he walks on the sea (Matt. 14.28).

[5] R. Bultmann, *TWNT*, VI, p. 206 [BKW *Faith*, p. 65].

[6] These words of the leper surely express his faith not his doubt; cf. J. A. Bengel, *Gnomon*, on Matt. 8.2, and V. Taylor, *The Gospel . . . Mark*, p. 187.

expressly designated as faith in Matthew's Gospel (Mark 7.26–28, cf. Matt. 15.28). The same applies again to the healing of the blind men at Jericho in Matthew's Gospel (Matt. 20.29–34), which does not contain the notion of faith, but must be understood in this sense as Mark 10.52 shows. Thus faith not only expresses itself as a request but the mere request is itself obviously a sign of faith, as, for example, with the healing of Peter's mother-in-law (Mark 1.30, Luke 4.38). In fact, the act of bringing the sick person is already evidence of faith according to Matt. 9.2. In the light of this the notices about the bringing of sick persons in the summary accounts (such as Mark 1.32 and par., and 6.54 f. and par.) or the coming of the sick to Jesus (such as Mark 3.7 ff. and Matt. 21.14) may be understood as signs of supplicating faith.

The knowledge that in the healing stories faith is set forth as praying faith and the miracle as the answer of Jesus to this supplicating faith opens up the understanding of the material connexion between faith and the miracle. Faith is related to the miracle as the request is to the answer to it. As the granting of the request can only follow when the request has previously been expressed, so the miracle happens in answer to the faith of those who desire it. There thus exists no kind of causal connexion between faith and the miracle, whether, say, of a magical or psychological kind. In short: 'La corrélation entre la foi et le miracle est donc tout à fait naturelle: qui veut trouver du secours auprès du thaumaturge, doit le lui demander, ce qui suppose de nouveau la "foi".'[1] In view of the fact that Jesus almost exclusively exercised his miraculous power in response to a believing request,[2] it is entirely in order to denote faith

[1] A. Fridrichsen, Le Problème du Miracle, p. 53. [The correlation between faith and miracle is thus quite plain: he who wishes to find help from the thaumaturge must ask it of him, which again implies 'faith'.]

[2] The absence of the request in the healing of Peter's mother-in-law in Matthew (8.14 f.) cannot be regarded as a serious exception to this rule in view of Mark 1.30 and Matthew's interpreting purposes (cf. above, pp. 169 ff.). The only genuine exception among the proper miracle stories is the raising of the young man at Nain (Luke 7.11–17), where Jesus steps in to help of his own accord. Here there is certainly a striking relationship with the raising from the dead outside the gates of Rome reported of Apollonius of Tyana (Philostratus, Vita Apollonii, IV, 45, in P. Fiebig, Antike Wundergeschichten, p. 26). According to H. J. Schütz (Beiträge zur Formgeschichte synoptischer Wundererzählungen, Diss., Jena, 1953, pp. 20 ff.) Luke and Philostratus have used a common anonymous formula 'of the merciful miracle man who awakens a dead person in the very last minute on the way to the grave' (p. 26), and made it serve their different interests. The stories of the feedings and the narrative of Jesus walking on the sea are not serious exceptions, since they contain epiphanies rather than miracles of assistance.

as the condition of the miracle.[1] Of course, that does not apply in the sense that faith necessarily brings the miracle to pass, but on the basis of the Old Testament thought that the Lord hears the prayer of his own, as is expressed in countless places. Above all one is led to think here of the Psalms, which bear witness to this connexion between prayer and the miraculous deliverance. Thus Psalm 107, for example, in ever-fresh strophes varies the sentence: 'they cried to the LORD in their trouble, and he delivered them from their distress . . . Let them thank the LORD for his steadfast love, for his wonderful works to the sons of men.' In Ps. 145.18 f. one finds, as it were, the sum of the devout man's experience of prayer: 'The LORD is near to all who call upon him, to all who call upon him in truth. He fulfils the desire of all who fear him, he also hears their cry, and saves them.'[2]

And yet there is a striking difference from the praying faith of the Old Testament, which remained largely a waiting and hoping faith.[3] For the faith that is directed to Jesus does not remain solely a waiting and hoping faith, but it finds the fulfilment of its desire in that it receives from Jesus what it asks, and that without delay. The 'rule' which is found in the Synoptic miracle stories that 'confidence in the helpful kindness brings help to pass and no faith is put to shame and destroyed'[4]—this rule, which is never broken, is the new and unique thing about the miracles of Jesus and the conception of faith used in connexion with it. Judaism also knew suppliants with miraculous results; there, too, miracles were desired and expected—but they were only granted for special merits. For 'the confidence of the Rabbinate keeps its ground always in human behaviour and arises from the value of one's own achievement.'[5] 'The particularly meritorious suppliant is called upon so that his prayer will effect in the presence of God what that of the person concerned in the need

---

[1] Cf. A. Schlatter, *Der Glaube im NT*, p. 107; A. Fridrichsen, *Le Problème du Miracle*, pp. 51 f.; L. Bieler, *Theios Aner*, I, p. 113, and A. M. Hunter, *The Work and Words of Jesus*, p. 56.

[2] Cf. also, for example, Pss. 33.18 ff.; 40.2 ff.; 42.6, 12; 43.5; 55.17; 91.14 ff. and Isa. 25.9; 30.19.

[3] This can clearly be seen purely on the basis of word statistics, which show that among the terms for relationship with God in the Old Testament words expressing hope and trust preponderate. The notion of faith by no means occupies the predominant position, but stands numerically only in the fourth place after the expressions of hoping and waiting. Cf. A. Weiser, *TWNT*, VI, p. 183 [BKW *Faith*, p. 2].

[4] A. Schlatter, *Matthäus*, p. 489, on Matt. 15.24.

[5] A. Schlatter, *Das Wunder in der Synagoge*, Gütersloh, 1912, p. 81.

cannot himself attain from God.'[1] According to the New Testament, however, even little faith and faithless fear are not made ashamed if they turn to Jesus for deliverance, as the help of Jesus in the storm at sea (Mark 4.35 ff. and par.) and the rescue of Peter as he sank (Matt. 14.30 f.) show, and these in each case follow as the answer to a cry for help.

If one surveys the use of the concept of faith in the Synoptic miracle stories, if one figures to oneself the meaning of the activity, of the willing and praying which it contains there, and if one considers the material connexion in which it stands with the miracle that follows, then the characterisation of it as praying faith appears quite comprehensive and right. That this praying faith in no case remains without fulfilment, whatever may be the form in which it is expressed, is one of its characteristics in the Synoptic miracle tradition. This characteristic is not grounded in the faith itself, however, but in the Lord to whom it is directed. The material connexion between faith and the miracle, between the request and the hearing of it is bound up in the last resort with the early Christian fundamental conviction that in the history of Jesus 'the acceptable year of the Lord' has begun.[2]

Only on the basis of this assumption is it comprehensible that Jesus gives to praying faith the unlimited assurance of the fulfilment of its desires: once through the saying about believing prayer (Mark 11.24 and par.), then through the rule that in the healing stories Jesus grants to faith the miracle that is sought, and finally through the fact that in answer to their cry for help Jesus also saves those of little faith and those who are afraid. This shows that the Synoptic miracle stories present to a large extent a collection of examples of the dependableness of this promise to believing prayer.[3]

B. *Faith as praying faith in Matthew*

As has already been seen through a number of observations Matthew understood faith in connexion with the healing miracles of Jesus, in the sense of tradition, as supplicating faith. It remains now to show

---

[1] A. Schlatter, *Das Wunder in der Synagoge*, p. 82. Cf. the healing of the son of R. Gamaliel, for which Hanina ben Dosa, who was famous as a man of prayer, was brought (P. Fiebig, *Der Erzählungsstil der Evangelien*, Leipzig, 1925, pp. 105 f.).

[2] A. Schlatter, *Der Glaube im NT*, p. 120, points in connexion with the hearing by Jesus of every believing request to the fact that in Jesus eschatology has become present.

[3] So A. Schlatter, *Der Glaube im NT*, p. 105.

that he does not simply adopt this understanding of faith, but brings it out impressively in a number of ways in his reproduction of the miracle stories.

In the first place the fact calls for mention that the form of the healing miracles in Matthew corresponds less to the form of the miracle narrative than to that of conversations.[1] Two observations seem here of material importance: first, the correspondence of request and answer emphasised with the aid of repeating a word and by the technique of the catchword; second, the circumstance that faith is always expressed in a request. These formal characteristics in particular bring the thought of praying faith in Matthew's healing stories into clear expression, even where the word faith is missing (as in Matt. 8.2–4; 9.18, 19, 23–26). The presentation of Jesus as Lord, to be worshipped, points to the fact that Matthew wants the conversation in which a request is expressed to be understood as a prayer directed to the risen Lord.

Secondly it should be recalled that in place of the miracle-working word of authority in the healing stories Matthew as a rule puts a saying about faith.[2] In the case of the healing of the leper, it is true, Matthew has preserved the saying of Jesus (Matt. 8.3). Nevertheless he does not understand it as a word of command for the carrying out of a healing miracle, as occurs, for example, in Mark 5.41 and 9.25. It is the majestic saying of the Lord, through which he answers the request of the sick man, as the catchword linkages clearly show.[3] Because Jesus' words of authority in Mark 5.41 and 9.25 cannot really be understood in this sense as the answer to a believing request, but belong to the technique of healing, they are removed by Matthew as superfluous.

How important to the first evangelist was the fact of supplicating faith can be made clear especially well from the story of the centurion of Capernaum. Here there is a clear correspondence between the request of the centurion (Matt. 8.8) and the answer to it by Jesus (Matt. 8.13).[4] When the centurion explains that Jesus needs only to speak a word and his servant will be made well one thinks involuntarily of a miracle-commanding word of authority, as the centurion also thought, in analogy with his own power of command (Matt.

[1] Cf. above, pp. 241 ff.
[2] Cf. above, p. 242.
[3] Cf. above, pp. 237 f.
[4] Cf. above, p. 228.

8.9). Instead of that, however, we do not hear later from the mouth of Jesus any word of authority, but the saying about faith (Matt. 8.13) after which, to be sure, the miracle takes place. As regards its effect it is thus a word of authority, but as regards its content it expresses the granting of the request 'in correspondence with the faith'. As Luke 7.7 shows, the request for a word of authority lay before Matthew. He has then established the clear correspondence between the request and its answer, which is absent from Luke, but he has done it in such a way that the saying about faith has taken the place of the expected word of authority.

Thirdly, the investigation of the form of the healing miracles in Matthew has shown that the saying about faith not only indicates the climax, behind which the healing has been pushed completely to the side, but that it also substantially formulates the statement-content of the whole pericope.[1] This normative saying about faith has been freshly coined by the evangelist Matthew, however. He has retained the traditional formula about saving faith in only one passage (Matt. 9.22), obviously because he found it there. Where he independently puts the saying about faith in an instance of healing (Matt. 8.13; 9.29; 15.28) he has given it his own form. It is clear, however, that he also understands the saying about saving faith in his own sense. The fact that Matt. 9.22 and 29 lie alongside each other in one group of pericopes which has faith as its actual theme[2] shows that the two sayings are meant to interpret each other. That can also be seen by the fact that the one saying (Matt. 9.29) can take the place of the other (Mark 10.52). And finally, Matthew also makes it clear in the healing of the woman with the haemorrhage that it is not really faith that saves, but that Jesus grants to the believer deliverance in accordance with his faith. In this way Matthew, in his reformulation of the saying about faith in the healing stories, has brought the connexion observed between faith and miracle in the Synoptic tradition into a pregnant formula. In it there is reference to the correspondence between faith and the miracle, through which the fitting together of request and answer comes to expression. In brief: the place of the formula about saving faith is taken, as it were, by the formula about praying faith. This interpretation of saving faith as praying faith can be brought to mind in detail in several instances in the healing stories in Matthew.

[1] Cf. above, pp. 231 f.
[2] Cf. above, p. 248.

(*a*) It is significant that Matthew uses his new formula about faith at the end of two stories which have an entirely conversational form (Matt. 8.13; 15.28). In them the believer is solely a suppliant, or more exactly, he is an intercessor who does not turn to Jesus for his own sake but for the sake of another. Precisely here the connexion between faith and the miracle, which is expressed in the formula at the end, is unequivocally no other than that between the request and the granting of it. The use of the expression 'Be it done for you as you have believed' or 'as you desire' especially in connexion with these explicit request conversations, confirms that it is meant in the sense of praying faith.

(*b*) The saying 'your faith has made you well' has been given a new place in Matthew's retelling of the healing of the woman with the haemorrhage (Matt. 9.22). Whereas in Mark (5.34) it occurs in the supplemental confirmation that the healing has taken place, in Matthew it precedes the healing and vouchsafes it. The possible misunderstanding that on the part of the woman it is a case of 'a faithful sneaking of healing'[1] is in this way removed. It is this very problem to which the scene in Mark's Gospel after the healing is devoted, in which Jesus afterwards grants, so to speak, what has already happened (Mark 5.30–34). In the first evangelist, however, the connexion between faith and the miracle is made clear from the very beginning. The touching of the garment by the woman is now solely an expression of her request, which cannot of itself, because of some magical causal connexion, bring about the miraculous healing. It is the answer of Jesus to the request and that alone that brings about the desired result. In this way Matthew brings out more clearly in this place, too, the position of supplicating faith than the tradition which lay before him. Hence the activistic-sounding formula ἡ πίστις σου σέσωκέν σε, which occurs only here in Matthew, can only be interpreted in the sense of praying faith.[2]

(*c*) In line with this Matthew, in his second retelling of the healing of the blind men of Jericho (Matt. 9.27 ff.) displaces the

---

[1] So J. Weiss, *Das älteste Evangelium*, p. 195.

[2] Cf. A. Schlatter, *Der Glaube im NT*, p. 127: 'Request and command are separated from each other by clear division by Jesus and he has not allowed that the former could transform itself into the latter. In the case of the leper ('if you will'), the centurion, the woman with the haemorrhage, the Canaanite woman . . . everywhere it is brought out that believing does not imperil the freedom and majesty of him to whom it is directed, but recognises them and remains faith by submitting itself to his will. . . .'

saying about saving faith (Mark 10.52) by his formula on praying faith: κατὰ τὴν πίστιν ὑμῶν γενηθήτω ὑμῖν (Matt. 9.29). What is special in this new narration is that Matthew, in the conversation between Jesus and the blind men, unfolds what kind of faith it is to which the miracle is granted (Matt. 9.28): καὶ λέγει αὐτοῖς ὁ Ἰησοῦς· πιστεύετε ὅτι δύναμαι τοῦτο ποιῆσαι; λέγουσιν αὐτῷ· ναί, κύριε. According to this the faith is directed solely to the power of Jesus to do the miracle. It does not bring it about itself, but gains it only through 'joining itself to Jesus'.[1] That means however: faith can of itself achieve nothing. So then the saying about faith in Matt. 9.29 says, on the one hand, that the miracle is granted to the believer (γενηθήτω ὑμῖν). On the other hand, the connexion between faith and the miracle is firmly held—as a relationship of correspondence (κατὰ τὴν πίστιν ὑμῶν). In short: the opposition of faith and its answer is firmly held, and also their close connexion.

It is confirmed, then, that Matthew interprets the role of faith in the healing stories in the sense of praying faith. It will not be a mistake to recognise in this interpretation a didactic, hortatory interest. It has already been seen, on the basis of the Synoptics' general connexion between faith and miracle, that the healing stories are an illustration of the promise which Jesus has given to believing prayer. Matthew brings this understanding, by means of his work on the healing miracles, still more clearly into currency. To this extent they contain, precisely in his case, an exhortation and a promise to the Church between the resurrection and the parousia of her Lord who no longer sojourns with her in bodily, earthly form. Yet, on that account, the experience of his aid is no less possible than in the miraculous healings during his days on earth. In that the evangelist Matthew portrays in the miracle stories the situation of believing prayer he makes these narratives accessible to his Church; he shows that Jesus responded to praying faith, and on the basis of his promise will still respond today. In this way the miracle stories in Matthew are placed more firmly in the service of the exhortation of the congregation than in the Synoptic tradition before him.

C. *Faith as participation in the miraculous power of Jesus*

The thought that faith can work miracles is expressed in the saying about the faith that can remove mountains or uproot trees, which is

---

[1] So A. Schlatter's definition of faith, for example, in his commentary on Matthew, pp. 268, 277.

handed on in all three Synoptics. Matthew has employed it in two places (Matt. 17.20; 21.21), whereas Mark and Luke only report it once (Mark 11.23; Luke 17.6). This already shows that the first evangelist is more interested in this thought of miracle-working faith. This is obviously linked with the fact that he emphasises that Christological trait by which the Christ, precisely through faith, gives his disciples a share in his miraculous power.[1]

Mark and Matthew place the saying about miracle-working faith in the context of the pericope about the cursing of the fig tree (Mark 11.12–14; Matt. 21.18–19). Whatever may have been originally at the basis of this narrative—an actual cursing or a parable which has been altered into a narrative—both evangelists understood it as a miraculous deed which really happened. Only thus could they use it as a starting-point for the instruction of the disciples about the miraculous power of faith. Most of all, the evangelist Matthew shows that he was thinking of a normal miracle story. In accordance with the style of such stories he reports the immediate occurrence of the miracle after the curse of Jesus (Matt. 21.19): καὶ ἐξηράνθη παραχρῆμα ἡ συκῆ, and similarly in accordance with that style he speaks of the astonishment of the disciples (Matt. 21.20): καὶ ἰδόντες οἱ μαθηταί ἐθαύμασαν . . . Furthermore he has made a direct link between the narrative and the conversation, whereas Mark has separated them by the report of the cleansing of the Temple by Jesus. In typical Matthaean fashion the didactic conversation is introduced by a clear question,[2] which concerns the connexion between the curse and the sudden occurrence of the miracle (Matt. 21.20 πῶς παραχρῆμα ἐξηράνθη ἡ συκῆ;). In that the question takes up the conclusion of the miraculous deed of Jesus by means of the catchwords ἐξηράνθη, παραχρῆμα, ἡ συκῆ the present Matthaean context makes completely clear that the cursing of the fig tree was regarded as a genuine miracle story, which along with the added conversation yields a 'paradigm for the power of faith'.[3] That it is the power of faith which is the theme Matthew also makes clear by his formulation of the instruction to the disciples[4] in which Jesus promises his disciples that they will do the same and in fact more than that (Matt. 21.21): . . . οὐ μόνον τὸ τῆς συκῆς ποιήσετε, ἀλλὰ κἂν τῷ ὄρει τούτῳ εἴπητε·

[1] Cf. above, pp. 270 ff.
[2] Cf. above, pp. 235 f.
[3] E. Lohmeyer, p. 302.
[4] In distinction from Mark 11.23 the disciples are directly addressed in Matt. 21.21.

ἄρθητι καὶ βλήθητι εἰς τὴν θάλασσαν, γενήσεται. Finally, there is also the striking fact that in reply to the disciples' question about the reason for the immediate action of the curse Jesus does not answer with an explanation about his own miraculous power, but with instruction about that of the disciples. Matthew, who on his own account places the question in the mouth of the disciples, must therefore have understood it from the very beginning as a question about the miraculous power of the disciples of Jesus.

Also, in conjunction with the healing of the epileptic boy which the disciples were unable to perform, the saying about the faith which can remove mountains speaks about the miracle-working power of the disciples of Jesus. If they have faith nothing will be impossible to them, as Matthew expressly observes (Matt. 17.20b καὶ οὐδὲν ἀδυνατήσει ὑμῖν). A confirmation of this unlimited promise is found in the episode of Peter walking on the water (Matt. 14.28–31), in which the impossible is made possible to the believer himself.

This scene in particular makes clear in a unique way what kind of miracle-working faith the disciple's is. It is a request to Jesus and receives its miraculous power from him. His word of command empowers the disciple to perform the miracle (Matt. 14.28, 29). The continuation of the event, in which the one of little faith sinks in the waves (Matt. 14.30), shows absolutely 'that the disciple does not possess this power of himself but receives it through faith'.[1] Consequently the miracle-working faith of the disciple is also seen to be praying faith, which seeks and obtains its power from Jesus.

Thus it is entirely significant when in conjunction with the saying about miracle-working faith (Mark 11.23; Matt. 21.21) the unlimited promise of an answer is given by Jesus to believing prayer (Mark 11.24; Matt. 21.22). The faith of which the first saying speaks is thus to be regarded as a supplicating faith.[2] Whereas Mark in this place makes a transition to a collection of sayings about faith in general and probably already begins a new section[3] in Mark 11.24, which 'no longer has to do with working miracles but' is concerned 'with normal praying',[4] Matthew has placed this saying about the unlimited promise to prayer (Matt. 21.22) completely under the question about the possibility of miraculous actions (Matt. 21.20)

---

[1] A. Schlatter, *Markus*, p. 132.
[2] Cf. E. Lohmeyer, *Markus*, p. 239.
[3] Cf. the linking formula in Mark 11.24.
[4] E. Klostermann, *Markusevangelium*, p. 133.

and understood it as an answer to it in the sense of miracle-working prayer.[1]

D. *Little faith and doubt*

It is significant that the disciple is never shown in Matthew's Gospel in victorious possession of his miraculous power. Reference to the power of the disciples, in faith, to perform miracles occurs always only in connexion with a failure by them. Thus the scene of Peter walking on the sea tells not only of his power but also of his inability to preserve it. Thus Jesus speaks in Matt. 17.20 on the occasion of the inability of the disciples to heal the epileptic boy, about the miracle-working power of their faith. And similarly he instructs them on the same point after their unbelieving question of surprise (Matt. 21.20). On the other hand, it is a striking thing that the nature and the promise of faith are always actually placed before our eyes by people who are not disciples. The examples of faith are not the disciples but the leper, the Gentile centurion, the unknown bearers of the paralytic, the woman with the issue of blood, etc. On the contrary the disciples are again and again designated as of little faith (Matt. 8.26; 14.31; 16.8; cf. 17.20).

This conclusion, that the disciples in Matthew's Gospel expose their inability to believe, brings to mind the description of the disciples in Mark's Gospel. In this 'book of the secret epiphanies' they remain to the end unbelieving and devoid of understanding before the revelations of Jesus, whether by teaching or miracle.[2] Of course, the first evangelist does not regard the disciples as completely devoid of understanding. It is rather a characteristic of the disciples in Matthew's Gospel that understanding of the revelations is given to them (cf., e.g., Matt. 13.16 f.).[3] This portrayal of the disciples corresponds to the observation that Matthew sees, in principle, in the disciples of Jesus the congregation.[4] But yet the evangelist does not depict the disciples as in the full possession of understanding. He too shows, for example, their incapacity to understand without more ado the teaching of the Lord. It cannot be an oversight that he does not entirely abandon some passages about the lack of understanding on the part of the disciples in Mark's Gospel (for example, Mark 7.17 f.;

---

[1] From a purely external point of view this close connexion with what has gone before is clear from the omission of the linking formula of Mark 11.24.

[2] Cf. W. Wrede, *Das Messiasgeheimnis in den Evangelien*, pp. 93 ff.

[3] Cf. G. Barth, above, pp. 105 ff., on the word συνιέναι in Matthew.

[4] Cf. above, pp. 265 ff.

8.15 ff.) but retains them (Matt. 15.15 ff.; 16.6 ff.), or that besides
the traditional interpretation of the parable of the fourfold field by
Jesus (Mark 4.14 ff.; Matt. 13.19 ff.) he also includes the further
interpretation of the parable about the weeds (Matt. 13.36 ff.).
When the disciples, after the dismissal of the crowd, expressly ask
Jesus in the house for an explanation (Matt. 13.36 διασάφησον ἡμῖν
τὴν παραβολὴν τῶν ζιζανίων τοῦ ἀγροῦ), they at the same time designate themselves indirectly as lacking in understanding. In a similar
way Peter asks Jesus for an elucidation of his teaching about pure
and impure (Matt. 15.15). Finally the disciples are themselves
characterised by Jesus as lacking in understanding (Matt. 15.16 f.;
16.9, 11). Granted, these passages must be explained as belonging to
the tradition as Matthew received it; they were provided for him by
Mark's Gospel. But one may not trace them back to an inconsistency
by Matthew in his portrayal of the disciples of Jesus.[1] If he does not
everywhere erase the thought of the disciples' lack of understanding
it must have suited his conception of discipleship, that is, he must
have interpreted it differently from Mark. This, too, can actually be
seen. True the disciples are incapable of understanding the teaching
of Jesus of themselves, but they do not remain devoid of understanding. After instruction by Jesus it is stated that they reached
understanding (Matt. 13.51; 16.12; 17.13).[2] So Jesus does not
remain for his disciples the not-understood, mysteriously divine
Lord, but he is depicted as the teacher of his Church. The disciples
no longer fail in their understanding before, as it were, their confession of Christ but after it. Hence one cannot really speak of
Matthew's removal of the lack of understanding on the part of the
disciples but only of an interpretation. The lack of understanding is
a situation within the congregation of Jesus which is based upon the
confession of the risen one.

In a similar way Matthew's Gospel utilises the passages in Mark's
Gospel where there is reference to unbelief or lack of understanding
on the part of the disciples in the presence of the miracles of Jesus. In
his interpretation the first evangelist again and again uses the concept
of little faith. Thus the disciples in the storm at sea are no longer
understood as devoid of faith (Mark 4.40) but as of little faith (Matt.
8.26). At the epiphany of Jesus on the water Jesus is in fact recog-

---

[1] So Wrede, *Das Messiasgeheimnis*, p. 159.
[2] G. Barth, above, p. 108, rightly states that 'the lack of understanding on the
part of the disciples is limited to a merely temporary, provisional one'.

nised as the Lord and the Son of God (Matt. 14.28, 33), but the fear remains and is called little faith (Matt. 14.26, 30, 31). Their heart is no longer hardened at the feeding miracle (Mark 6.52; 8.17, 18), but their conduct is nevertheless designated by Jesus as little faith (Matt. 16.8). And finally Jesus names as the reason for the disciples' failure at the healing of the epileptic boy, according to Matthew, their little faith (Matt. 17.20).

It is true that Matthew already found this notion of little faith in the tradition he received. It appears in the saying of Jesus against anxiety, which Matthew (6.30) and Luke (12.28) found in the sayings source. The first evangelist took up this notion and inserted it at other places in his Gospel, a procedure which can also be observed elsewhere in his case.[1] And of course the notion of little faith in the saying of Jesus about anxiety is not really new, but rather its use there corresponds to the linguistic usage of the Rabbis.[2] Thus anxiety about food for the coming day is a sign of little faith according to the saying of R. Eliezer the Elder (c. 90): 'He who has bread in his basket and says: What shall I eat tomorrow? belongs to those of little faith.' Similarly the Israelites who, contrary to the command of Moses, kept some of the miraculous food in the wilderness for the following day, are reckoned as of little faith. Thus Jesus and the Rabbis used the concept of little faith to denote lack of trust in God in the presence of his kindness, which Jesus recognises in the lilies of the field, which count much less with him than people, and which the Rabbi perceives in the fact that a man has bread in his basket and finds food in the wilderness for the present day.

The designation 'men of little faith' (מְחוּסְרֵי אֲמָנָה‎ or קְטַנֵּי אֲמָנָה‎) is also found in other Rabbinic sayings. It expresses the contrast to the 'men of trust' (of faith אַנְשֵׁי אֲמָנָה‎) so that men of little faith means those who have no faith. Yet little faith, on the other hand, does not really mean unbelief; for those are called men of little faith who belong to the people of God, who are righteous, who have thus proved their faith at least earlier.[3] In this way, however, the notion

---

[1] E. von Dobschütz, 'Matth. als Rabbi und Katechet', ZNW 27, pp. 341 f., shows that Matthew inserts a verse or concept which he found in the tradition in other suitable places, e.g. the refrain about weeping and gnashing of teeth: Luke 13.28 = Matt. 8.12, then Matt. 13.42, 50; 22.13; 24.51; 25.30.

[2] Cf. on what follows, Billerbeck, I, pp. 438 f.

[3] Thus the Israelites in the wilderness, that is, after they had passed through the Red Sea and been delivered from the Egyptians, are called men of little faith by reason of their disobedience. R. Johanan (died 279) said: 'Noah was of little faith; if the water had not reached to his ankles he would not have entered the

of little faith denotes, so to speak, a situation of unbelief within the life of believers.[1]

This state of things corresponds exactly with what we recognise about the use of the concept of little faith in Matthew's Gospel. If the saying of Jesus in the Sermon on the Mount about anxiety is directed to the disciples, so, too, the saying about little faith in all further passages is used only in conversations between Jesus and his disciples (Matt. 8.26; 14.31; 16.8; 17.20). It always appears in a trying situation: whether it is anxiety about food (Matt. 6.30; 16.8), a threat to life (Matt. 8.26; 14.31) or whether it is an especially difficult case of healing the sick, which the disciples cannot master (Matt. 17.20). As Jesus in the Sermon on the Mount depicts the groundlessness of anxiety by pointing out God's provision for the birds under the heaven and the lilies of the field so he reminds his disciples in their little faith and anxiety about the bread in his two feeding miracles (Matt. 16.8 ff.). As the little faith of the disciples at the healing of the epileptic boy (Matt. 17.20) is only understandable as the designation of a situation within discipleship, after the power to perform healings has been given by Jesus, so also is the little faith of Peter (14.31).

When the evangelist Matthew uses the motive of little faith in those passages where Mark speaks of the disciples' unbelief and impotence in connexion with the miracle tradition, there lies in this a clear intention. It is his purpose to show that the disciples of Jesus in these passages have really failed as disciples. Far removed from a mitigation in favour of the disciples,[2] the choice of the notion 'men of little faith', or rather, 'little faith' depicts a depreciation of the disciples as disciples, in so far as their little faith holds fast to unbelief within discipleship. In this way a similar result is reached to that in the case of Matthew's adoption of Mark's thought of the lack of

---

ark.' And R. Eleazar (c. 270) said about the little faith of the righteous: 'What means: "For who has despised the day of small things?" Zech. 4.10? Who brings it about that the table of the righteous will appear in the future to have been robbed (i.e. that they do not receive a full reward)? Their little faith קַטְנוּת. because they did not trust in God.'

[1] A. Schlatter, Der Glaube im NT, denotes as ὀλιγόπιστος him 'who does not hold firmly to the faith he formerly practised, but discontinues it in the new situation because of its special difficulty' (p. 112). The word expresses 'a contrast to faith' (p. 593).

[2] So W. Wrede, Das Messiasgeheimnis, p. 159, on Matt. 16.8 and E. Klostermann on Matt. 8.26.

understanding on the part of the disciples: Matthew does not abolish the motive of the unbelief of the disciples in Mark's Gospel, he rather interprets it with the help of the notion of little faith.

This interpretation is shown not only by the choice of the word ὀλιγόπιστος, but also in the whole of the pericopes in which the notion occurs. It is precisely the situations depicted in them that are fitted to elucidate the notion of little faith. In the story of the storm at sea one can recognise that the little faith is nevertheless a kind of faith, a broken form of faith as it were.[1] For with that very request which is still the expression of their little faith (Matt. 8.25 κύριε, σῶσον, ἀπολλύμεθα), the distraught disciples turn to Jesus and are heard. Therein however, they show a certain trust in their Lord. The same applies to Peter's cry for help as he was sinking (Matt. 14.31).

On the other hand, it is made clear by the setting of little faith over against faith as a grain of mustard seed in Matt. 17.20 that it is not a matter of a small faith over against a great faith. The obviously conscious paradoxical formulation that faith as a grain of mustard seed can remove mountains means that the smallest thing brings about the greatest. Hence the little faith which cannot bring about the healing cannot be a little faith, a mustard-seed faith. Obviously it is the form of unbelief which occurs in a disciple of Jesus within discipleship, without carrying with it a fall from faith in Jesus or an abandoning of discipleship. Little faith thus obviously describes on the one hand a broken form of faith—in that it means a failure in discipleship—but on the other hand, a broken form of unbelief—in that it does not mean a fundamental rejection of Jesus.

This divided situation is also represented in Matthew's Gospel by the notion of doubt. It appears closely linked with that of little faith in Jesus' question to Peter ὀλιγόπιστε, εἰς τί ἐδίστασας; (Matt. 14.31). Whereas in Matt. 17.20 the faith that removes mountains has little faith as its opposite, in Matt. 21.21 it has doubt. Both concepts thus describe the same phenomenon. It is therefore not surprising that the first evangelist, alongside the concept of little faith, frequently uses that of doubt. He adopts it in Matt. 21.21 from Mark (11.23: διακρίνεσθαι), while in two other places he introduces it new, and does it with the help of another word (Matt. 14.31; 28.17: διστάζειν). The use of the word 'to doubt' shows the same traits in Matthew's Gospel as that of little faith. In all three cases doubt is not, for example, the attitude of an opponent but of a

[1] On this idea cf. A. Schlatter, Der Glaube im NT, p. 42.

disciple.[1] Doubt, too, is a broken form of faith, the 'inner division, not the refusal of faith but also not faith'.[2] Both, doubt and little faith, arise, as Matt. 14.30 f. teaches, in the believing disciple through looking at 'impressions deriving from experience which contradict what faith desires from God',[3] and destroy the undivided devotion of the believer to Jesus. Both notions are therefore fitted to denote the situation of the disciple who, on the one hand directs his faith to the risen Lord, but, on the other hand, in view of the facts of this world is again and again under pressure. From this position the interest of the evangelist Matthew in these two notions explains itself. They link the history of Jesus and his disciples in the time before Easter with the history of the Church and her experiences after Easter.

V. MATTHEW AS TRANSMITTER AND INTERPRETER

When Matthew introduces the concept of little faith into the miracle stories, or rather uses it in connexion with them, precisely in those passages where Mark had spoken of the unbelief, the lack of understanding or the inability of the disciples, this fact must be described in three ways. First, Matthew takes over the thought of the failure of the disciples; he is thus a transmitter. Second, he interprets it in a new sense; he is thus an interpreter. And third, this interpretation of the thought handed down is in the interest of its actualisation for the discipleship of the present time. These three moments obviously belong together, if one desires to characterise the essence of the tradition as it appears here.

One is led to a similar understanding of how the tradition is transmitted with the observation that the first evangelist, in his presentation of a series of Jesus' healing miracles, brings the thought of praying faith most clearly to expression, by abbreviation, stylisation and refashioning of the saying on which everything turns, even this thought of praying faith which is already intended in the tradition which lay before him. The interpreter is, at the same time, as it were, the transmitter. He does not really introduce a new thought into the tradition, but rather reveals himself as its exegete in the exact sense of the word; he elucidates what it contains. His interest in doing this

---

[1] That applies unequivocally for Matt. 14.31 and 28.17. In Matt. 21.21 the reference to the disciples is clarified by the fact that the whole saying is formulated as an address to them.

[2] A. Schlatter, Der Glaube im NT, p. 124, on Matt. 21.21.

[3] A. Schlatter, Matthäus, p. 620, on Matt. 21.21.

is certainly again directed to the congregation of disciples. If the miracle stories in Mark's Gospel, at least in the total view of the second evangelist, served the ruling thought of the secret manifestation of the Son of God, Matthew makes at least a part of them serve for instruction on the nature and the promise of suppliant faith, instruction which a Church in danger of little faith and doubt needed just as much as the testimony of the miraculous power of her Lord.

When Matthew arranges the miraculous deeds of Jesus under the systematic viewpoint of the fulfilment of Scripture that, it is true, is in accordance with his own theological angle as it is seen in the whole of the first Gospel with its quotations from Scripture. Nevertheless there is no arbitrary innovation about it. For the reply of Jesus to the question of the Baptist already interprets his deeds as the fulfilling of prophetic foretelling in that it echoes words of the prophet Isaiah. The first evangelist thus only carries out expressly what was programmatically indicated there. There can hardly be any mistake about the reason for this. Though the miracles of Jesus through being stylised as epiphanies would be effective of themselves in a Hellenistic environment, in the circles of Jewish thought they could only count and carry conviction as deeds of the Christ if they occurred in fulfilment of Scripture.

The process of transmitting is thus always at the same time one of interpretation. In the sphere of the preaching, teaching and admonishing Church it is not simply the handing on of reports about events of the past. Rather, 'the historical account becomes a means for the proclamation of the good news'.[1] That is why it is always fashioned with the hearer and his situation in mind. If the section of instruction for the disciples in Mark (8.27–10.52) presupposes the situation of the Church after Easter and Pentecost, as has been rightly shown,[2] there is no occasion for surprise that Matthew, too, gives the miracle stories a slant in the direction of this situation, albeit in a very different way. One may regret this process of the 'Christianisation' of the material because it conceals the original form of the tradition, but in the light of the nature of the early Christian tradition it is not only understandable but necessary. There is no tradition without interpretation.

---

[1] M. Dibelius, 'Evangelienkritik und Christologie', *Botschaft u. Gesch.*, I, p. 295.
[2] Cf., for example, J. Wellhausen, *Einleitung in die ersten drei Evangelien*, p. 71, and H. Riesenfeld, 'Tradition und Redaktion im Markusevangelium', *NT Studien für R. Bultmann*, p. 160.

Of course, it can be seen in Matthew's Gospel in particular that this interpretation is not arbitrary. The investigation of the retelling of the miracle stories by Matthew has shown that it is governed to a high degree by particular interests. The abbreviations of the evangelist fall upon what is unessential and work out all the more clearly what was intended not only by him but also by the tradition itself as he received it. Still more, the retelling is in many cases fashioned in the light of a saying of Jesus in the pericope and brings it more firmly into prominence. Thus the guiding thought in the interpretative retelling is already in the tradition itself.

In this connexion it is instructive to call to mind once again that Matthew omits entirely two miracle stories of Mark (Mark 7.31–37; 8.22–26). The reason for this, we conjectured, was that he found no points of connexion for his retelling, or rather, interpretation in the pericope as he received it.[1] If it is correct that the traditional connexion between faith and miracle represents a formative principle for Matthew's interpretation of the healing miracles, in the light of this one can also judge that it is a critical principle in the handing on of the healing stories. The two Markan narratives are obviously passed by because there is in them no indication of this connexion between faith and the miracle and it would therefore have had to be imported into them. If this opinion proves right it shows that in this place, too, the interpretation of Matthew is not arbitrary, that is, does not take place without regard for the tradition before him, or more exactly: retelling and interpretation do not take place if there is no justification in the tradition for it.

This can also be clearly seen from the form which the miracle stories have acquired in Matthew's Gospel. The standardisation, say, of the healing stories as conversations is not new, since the joining together of request and reply also occurs in many of the Markan pericopes. By the abbreviation of the narrative accompaniments, however, Matthew brings it into a position of more or less exclusive dominance.[2] Where it was not already present Matthew has not introduced it into a pericope.[3]

If one desires, then, to understand Matthew as the interpreter of the miracle stories one must understand him at the same time as their

[1] Cf. above, pp. 207 ff.

[2] In Matt. 8.2–4 the conversational form is taken over, in 20.29–34 and 9.27–30 it is carried out more firmly, in 8.5–13 and 15.21–28 it has become exclusive, and in 9.20–22 it is first really established.

[3] Cf., for example, Matt. 8.14–15; 9.18, 19, 23–26.

transmitter. If there is no tradition without interpretation the inter-pretation remains bound nevertheless to the tradition.

If miracle stories are passed over because they do not admit of any devotional interpretation, this shows that the miracle stories for Matthew are the bearers of a message, of teaching or admonition. Their handing on and interpretation take place for the sake of the material statement they contain. They are intended to show the Church by means of the picture of the earthly Jesus who her Lord is and what provision she may expect from him.[1] The interpretation of the miracle stories by Matthew is thus borne by the conviction: 'What Jesus once did on earth he does still.' This conviction, as J. Schniewind emphasises, is only understandable on the basis of the Church's 'basic confession' that her risen Lord is none other than the man Jesus of Nazareth, who lived in Palestine and was crucified under Pontius Pilate.[2] Or, to express it with the words of Matthew's Gospel: that this Jesus of Nazareth is now he to whom all authority in heaven and on earth is given and who is present in his Church to the end of the world (Matt. 28.18, 20).

[1] Cf. A. Schlatter, *Theologie der Apostel*, p. 66: the works of Jesus are related to the congregation in order 'that she may know how he is disposed towards her and how she should conduct herself towards him'; and A. Richardson, *The Miracle-Stories of the Gospels*, p. 137: the miracles are 'parables of the dealings of the living Christ with those who trust Him and obey His Word'.

[2] Cf. J. Schniewind, 'Zur Synoptikerexegese', *TR* N.F., 2 (1930), p. 159.

INDEX OF NAMES

INDEX OF SUBJECTS

(cf. also Contents)

INDEX OF PERICOPES

(in the order of Matthew's Gospel)